Melanie Mallet

STATUTORY INTERPRETATION

SECOND EDITION

D0899717

Other books in the *Essentials of Canadian Law Series*
Intellectual Property Law
Income Tax Law
Immigration Law
International Trade Law
Family Law
Copyright Law
Remedies: The Law of Damages
Individual Employment Law
The Law of Equitable Remedies
Administrative Law
Ethics and Canadian Criminal Law
Public International Law
Environmental Law 2/e
Securities Law
Youth Criminal Justice Law
Computer Law 2/e
The Law of Partnerships and Corporations 2/e
The Law of Torts 2/e
Media Law 2/e
Maritime Law
Criminal Law 3/e
Insurance Law
International Human Rights Law
Legal Research and Writing 2/e
The Law of Evidence 4/e
The Law of Trusts 2/e
Franchise Law
The Charter of Rights and Freedoms 3/e
Personal Property Security Law
The Law of Contracts
Pension Law
Constitutional Law 3/e
Legal Ethics and Professional Responsibility 2/e
Refugee Law
Mergers, Acquisitions, and Other Changes of Corporate Control
Bank and Customer Law in Canada

ESSENTIALS OF
CANADIAN LAW

STATUTORY
INTERPRETATION

SECOND EDITION

RUTH SULLIVAN

Faculty of Law, University of Ottawa

Statutory Interpretation, second edition
© Irwin Law Inc., 2007

Published in 2007 by

Irwin Law Inc.
14 Duncan Street
Suite 206
Toronto, ON
M5H 3G8

www.irwinlaw.com

ISBN-13: 978-1-55221-138-0

Library and Archives Canada Cataloguing in Publication

Sullivan, Ruth, 1946–
    Statutory interpretation / Ruth Sullivan. — 2nd ed.

(Essentials of Canadian law)
Includes bibliographical references and index.
ISBN 978-1-55221-138-0

1. Law—Canada—Interpretation and construction—Textbooks. I. Title.
II. Series.

KE482.S84S94 2007   349.71   C2007-902911-6
KF425.S94 2007

The publisher acknowledges the financial support of the Government of Canada through the Book Publishing Industry Development Program (BPIDP) for its publishing activities.

We acknowledge the assistance of the OMDC Book Fund, an initiative of Ontario Media Development Corporation.

Printed and bound in Canada.

1 2 3 4 5   11 10 09 08 07

SUMMARY
TABLE OF CONTENTS

DETAILED TABLE OF CONTENTS

CHAPTER 2:

INTRODUCTION TO STATUTORY INTERPRETATION 29

CHAPTER 3:

ORDINARY MEANING 49

FOREWORD
to the First Edition

In this book, Professor Ruth Sullivan has undertaken the task of explaining the process of statutory interpretation. She does so in a clear and readable style, not only with her extensive knowledge of the cases, but with the sophistication one would expect of one of Canada's best known writers in the field.

The author approaches the subject as an art rather than a science. Rules do not really govern, though they undoubtedly shape how one goes about attaching meaning to legislation. The weight given to rules and other factors that come into play in the interpretation of statutes varies with the situation. Among other things, one must take account of both the broad and specific contexts in which the legislation was enacted, its intended purpose, and the ordinary meaning of the words used. And one must also have an eye to the specialized setting in which it originated, including Parliamentary practice and drafting conventions. Moreover, the process is informed by general social values and the specific demands of the particular matter thought to be regulated—both at the time of enactment and the time the legislation comes up for interpretation. Central to this amalgam is a strong component of common sense.

These and other influences that go into the task of statutory interpretation are clearly brought out in the book. But Professor Sullivan is far from leaving us at this level of generality. Her identification of these factors is merely a prelude to a detailed examination and assessment of the various rules and other components that go into statutory interpretation in light of the latest and most authoritative cases, to which she devotes special attention.

Professor Sullivan's book should prove to be a very helpful guide to all those seeking enlightenment on the subject. I am pleased to commend it.

The Honourable Gerald V. La Forest
Supreme Court of Canada

To my sister, Anne McInerney

STATUTORY INTERPRETATION

Anyone who has practised law for even a short while soon realizes the central role of interpretation in law. Whether one is putting together a deal for a client, applying for a benefit, or attempting to avoid a penalty, words are sure to be involved and to require interpretation. In fact, it is impossible to do anything in law without interpreting the words of others and anticipating how others will interpret (or misinterpret) one's own. Legislation consists of words; so do judgments, contracts, trusts and wills, corporate by-laws, and rules of court. The law is extracted from these texts through interpretation.

Although this book focuses on statutory interpretation, much of it is relevant to the interpretation of legal documents like contracts and wills and to legal texts generally. It is meant to do a number of things:

- give basic information about the operation of legislation and the different types of legislation;
- establish a coherent framework for the disparate array of statutory interpretation rules;
- offer clear and concise explanations of each rule, with commentary and illustration;
- introduce readers to the constitutional framework in which interpretation occurs and the doctrinal issues that currently concern judges and other interpreters; and,
- above all, indicate how the rules are used in analysis of legislative texts and the construction of arguments to justify particular outcomes.

The book attempts to demystify interpretation by showing how solutions to interpretative problems are arrived at. In forming an initial impression of the meaning of a legal text, interpreters draw on their ordinary linguistic intuition and their common sense. In other words, they rely on the resources that ordinary readers bring to any piece of writing. But because the text being interpreted is legal, ordinary intuitions and common sense must be informed by legal values and principles. These legal materials are introduced into interpretation through the so-called rules — the principles, policies, presumptions, doctrines, and directives that make up the subject of this book.

The rules of statutory interpretation are important for several reasons. They tell interpreters what values and factors to take into account when dealing with a legislative text. They supply the vocabulary in which such texts are analyzed and explained. And they shape the arguments used by interpreters in defending their preferred interpretation and by judges in justifying their decisions.

Chapter 1 is an introduction to statute law and the various forms it may take. It explains the format of legislation and analyzes the components of the legislative sentence. It illustrates how paragraphing works and explains why it is useful for interpreters as well as drafters. Understanding this material is essential in analyzing legislative texts. Chapter 1 also explains the operation of legislation: when a statute becomes and ceases to be law, how amendments and revisions work, the effect of re-enactment, and the like.

Chapter 2 gives an overview of statutory interpretation. It sets out a number of basic concepts that inform interpretation and looks at the role assigned to judges when they resolve interpretation problems. It then surveys the range of rules relied on by interpreters to carry out their work. The most important of these, known as "Driedger's modern principle," indicates that judges are to interpret the words of a provision having regard to the entire context of that provision. The courts are still struggling to work out the full implications of this principle.

In addition to the formal rules and principles, common sense, shared values and assumptions, and community practices are the staples of statutory interpretation. What is important about them is not their truth so much as their commonality—the fact (or the hope) that they are shared by all the parties to the communication, starting with the legislature and ending with the courts. Commonality is a major theme of the book, and it leads to an important question: What happens when commonality is an illusion, when the parties to a communication do not share the same assumptions and values or even the same linguistic intuitions? This question is raised in Chapter 2, and recurs in various guises throughout the book.

Chapters 3 through 7 set out rules about meaning — ordinary meaning, technical and legal meaning, bilingual and bijral meaning, original meaning, and plausible meaning. In principle, under the plausible meaning rule, a court must not adopt an interpretation unless it is one the language of the text can reasonably bear. In practice, however, this rule is sometimes disregarded. Chapter 7 looks at the court's jurisdiction to correct mistakes in a legislative text and its more limited jurisdiction to fill gaps in legislative schemes.

Chapter 8 gives an overview of what is included in the concept of the "entire context" of a provision. Clearly it includes the Act in which the language to be interpreted is found, related legislation, and ultimately the entire body of law enacted by the relevant jurisdiction. It also includes the so-called "external context" — the conditions existing when the legislation was first enacted and the circumstances in which it operates from time to time. Finally, and more controversially, it includes the legal context, consisting of constitutional law, international law, common law and the law of other jurisdictions. Sometimes the so-called "extrinsic aids" are considered part of context, but these are dealt with separately in Chapter 14.

Chapters 9 through 12 explain and illustrate four types of analysis that are relied on in interpretation: textual, purposive, consequential, and policy analysis. These are relied on both in attempting to determine the intended meaning of a legislative text and in constructing arguments to justify a preference for a given interpretation. In textual analysis, the interpreter reads the text in light of the conventions of legislative drafting, such as uniform expression and the no tautology rule, and the presumptions based on those conventions, such as *ejusdem generis* (limited class) and *expressio unius est exclusio alterius* (implied exclusion). In purposive analysis, the interpreter determines how the provision to be interpreted relates to the legislature's purposes and fits into the scheme designed to achieve those purposes. Sometimes the legislature itself declares its purposes; at other times the interpreter must infer them from reading the text in context. In consequential analysis, the interpreter considers the consequences that will flow from adopting one or another proposed interpretation. If possible, interpretations that would defeat the purpose of legislation or otherwise lead to irrational results are rejected as absurd. Finally, in policy analysis, the interpreter considers which of the possible interpretations available would best promote the political values which the legislature is presumed to respect.

Although courts like to focus on textual meaning and legislative intent and to leave policy to the legislature, in fact statutory interpretation is permeated by political values. These enter interpretation formally through the so-called presumptions of legislative intent: the legislature is presumed to respect the *Charter*, to comply with international law, to wish to preserve individual liberty, to abhor discrimination, and so on. In the course of interpretation, courts may also invoke common law or equitable norms, or appeal directly to evolving community values such as multiculturalism or protection of the environment.

Chapter 13 deals with a special category of presumptions, namely those that govern the temporal, territorial, and personal application of legislation. In a sense these operate as non-application rules. In the absence of some indication of a contrary intention, legislation is presumed to not apply to facts occurring before it came into force. Equally, it is presumed to not interfere with rights acquired by persons before that time. Legislation is presumed to not apply to matters outside the territorial limits of the enacting jurisdiction. And finally legislation is presumed to not apply to the Crown or agents of the Crown.

Chapter 14 provides a survey of the so-called extrinsic aids to interpretation. It explains what is meant by legislative history and the evolving rules on the use of this material. It also explains what is meant by legislative evolution and lays out four steps involved in tracing the evolution of a particular enactment or provision. It also looks at the use of judicial, administrative, and scholarly opinion in statutory interpretation.

Finally, Chapter 15 explores the problem of overlap, which may occur between statutory provisions or between a statutory provision and the common law. Sometimes overlap is allowed and sometimes it is not. When overlap is impermissible, the interpreter has to figure out which law is paramount. The rules and techniques for making this determination are set out in the chapter.

Statutory interpretation is at once the most practical and the most theorectical of subjects. As a result of what has been called the "interpretive turn" in the recent theory of many disciplines, there is a vast body of literature that tackles legal interpretation from multiple perspectives.[1] While this book touches on a number of current theoretical concerns, it is more concerned with practice. Its primary focus is on the techniques and reasoning used by lawyers and judges on a daily basis to resolve interpretation problems. It is hoped that the many examples relied on in the book, drawn primarily from judgments of the Supreme Court of Canada, will offer the reader a helpful introduction to the complex art of statutory interpretation.

---

1   For an overview, see Dennis Patterson, *Law & Truth* (Oxford: Oxford University Press, 1999).

CHAPTER 1

INTRODUCTION TO STATUTE LAW

A. TYPES OF LEGISLATION

In law, a document that is capable of producing legal effects is called an "instrument." Instruments having the status of legislation may be made by a legislature or by a person or body to which the legislature has delegated a law-making authority. Instruments made by a legislature are called "statutes," "Acts," or "enactments." Instruments made by persons or bodies acting under delegated authority have a variety of labels, including "statutory instruments"; "delegated," "subordinate," or "executive legislation"; "regulations"; "orders in council"; "rules"; and sometimes "guidelines."[1] Legislative instruments produced by municipalities are called "ordinances" or "by-laws."

1) Statutes

Statutes are appropriately called "Acts" or "enactments" because they really are "acts" of the legislature; they are the means by which the legislature adds to, changes, or declares the law. Statutes state what the

---

1   More often guidelines are considered a form of "quasi-legislation," which has no binding legal effect.

legislature has decided the law should be within its "jurisdiction" or area of competence.[2]

The statements or provisions set out in legislation are law in the sense that they have the power to bind or empower the "subjects" of the legislature—that is, the persons over whom the legislature has authority. Although historically in Europe legislative authority was exercised by monarchs by virtue of divine right, in modern Western democracies it is conferred on legislatures by a constitution. The Constitution of Canada confers sovereign law-making power on both the federal and the provincial legislatures, subject to certain limitations.[3]

The federal legislature, consisting of the House of Commons, the Senate, and the Governor General representing the Queen, is called the "Parliament of Canada." It enacts statutes applicable throughout the whole of Canada with respect to federal "matters."[4] The provincial legislatures, consisting of a representative assembly and the Lieutenant Governor representing the Queen, enact statutes applicable within the provinces with respect to provincial matters.[5] The jurisdiction of territorial legislatures, which is more or less analogous to provincial jurisdiction, is conferred by federal statute rather than the *Constitution Act, 1867*. The enactments of all legislatures are subject to the *Canadian Charter of Rights and Freedoms*. Any attempt to curtail a *Charter*-protected right or freedom may be struck down by the courts unless it can be justified as reasonable in a free and democratic society.[6]

Acting within the limits imposed by the Constitution of Canada, Parliament and the provincial legislatures may exercise their powers in whatever way they see fit. That is what it means to be sovereign. The political decision-making engaged in by elected members of the legislature involves formulating the goals and norms of the community, an

---

2   For an interesting analysis of legislation in terms of the speech act theory developed by Austin, Searle, and others, see Frederick Bowers, *Linguistic Aspects of Legislative Expression* (Vancouver: University of British Columbia Press, 1989).

3   The Constitution of Canada is defined in s. 52 of the *Constitution Act, 1982*, being Schedule B to the *Canada Act 1982* (U.K.), 1982, c. 11.

4   These are the matters or subjects over which the Parliament of Canada is given law-making authority by ss. 91–106 of the *Constitution Act, 1867* (U.K.), 30 & 31 Vict., c. 3 [*Constitution Act, 1867*].

5   These are matters over which the legislatures of the provinces are assigned law-making authority by ss. 92–105 of the *Constitution Act, 1867*.

6   Section 1 of the *Charter* reads: "The *Canadian Charter of Rights and Freedoms* guarantees the rights and freedoms set out in it subject only to such reasonable limits prescribed by law as can be demonstrably justified in a free and democratic society." *Canadian Charter of Rights and Freedoms*, Part I of the *Constitution Act, 1982*, being Schedule B to the *Canada Act 1982* (U.K.), 1982, c. 11.

activity that often favours one group in society over another. It also involves selecting appropriate implementation strategies and enforcement mechanisms. The resources allocated to a legislative initiative may be great or small, and may be deployed in a number of ways. Compliance with legislative rules may be secured at high cost through close surveillance backed by force, or at low cost through self-monitoring and voluntary cooperation. So long as no constitutional limitation is violated, legislatures are answerable for these decisions to the electorate alone.

When it comes to communicating its decisions through enactments, legislatures may adopt any form of expression that seems appropriate. Drafters generally work with existing models and structures, thereby bringing a measure of consistency and predictability to the statute book.[7] Nonetheless, the range of legislation is vast and resists easy description. An Act may be one sentence long, or go on for a thousand pages. It may set out every detail of a legislative scheme, or delegate authority to others to come up with a workable scheme. It may be addressed to the public at large or to a specialized audience — to pharmacists, for example, or to recreational cyclists. Much modern legislation is addressed to the executive branch of government, to ministers and their departments, to boards and agencies and the like. Some of the standard ways of classifying Acts and other legislation are briefly reviewed in sections 2 through 6 that follow.

2) Public, Local, and Private Acts

Most enactments of Parliament and the provincial legislatures are public Acts. The distinguishing feature of a public Act is that it is impersonal. This means its application is defined in terms of general classes rather than particular identified persons, things, or events. The impersonal character of public legislation is well illustrated by federal offence provisions, which usually take the following form: "Every one who [engages in certain described conduct] is guilty of an offence." The provision is addressed to the public at large and applies to all persons who bring themselves within the description of conduct set out in the provision.

Most public Acts are addressed to the public throughout the enacting jurisdiction; these are called general Acts. However, it is possible for a public Act to be confined to the public within a particular locality; such Acts are called local Acts. Legislation governing working condi-

---

7   The expression "statute book" refers to the entire body of legislation that forms part of the law of a jurisdiction from time to time.

tions within a limited region of a province, for example, would be considered a local Act.

In practice, public Acts may apply to only a few persons, or even to no one at all. The point is that, legally, they are applicable to any person or any circumstances that may come within their general scope from time to time. Private Acts, in contrast, are directed at identified persons or situations present in the mind of the legislature at the time of enactment. The provisions of a private Act are applicable only to the persons mentioned by name or otherwise identified in the legislation, and to the particular facts described. Statutes declaring the divorce of a particular couple or winding up the affairs of a named corporation are classic examples of private Acts.

Private Acts may be initiated by government, but most often they are solicited by the individuals who have need of a legislative directive concerning their personal or commercial affairs. In some cases, a private Act is the least costly or even the only way out of an intractable problem.

Although private legislation is less common than it used to be, it remains a significant part of the business of all Canadian legislatures.

3) Permanent and Amending Acts

Permanent Acts, sometimes known as "parent Acts," are public Acts that stand alone as distinct and self-contained contributions to the statute book. Permanent Acts are generally meant to operate for an indefinite period of time. For convenient reference they are given convenient short titles (in addition to any long title)[8] and are eligible for inclusion in the multi-volume collections called Revised Statutes that are prepared for each jurisdiction.[9]

The key feature of a permanent Act is that it may be amended from time to time without losing its identity. Through the operation of amending legislation, new provisions may be added, existing provisions may be repealed, or the Act may be re-enacted in whole or in part.[10] Despite these events, the permanent Act continues to operate and retains its identity as an Act until it is formally repealed. The *Criminal Code*, for example, was first enacted in 1892. Although it has since been amended and re-enacted on numerous occasions, so that the current version bears little resemblance to the version of 1892, it remains

---

8   The components of statutes such as titles and headings are discussed later in this chapter and in Chapter 8.

9   The consolidation and revision of statutes are discussed later in this chapter.

10   Amendment, repeal, and re-enactment are discussed later in this chapter.

the *Criminal Code*. The public is bound by its provisions as formulated from time to time.

Amending Acts are statutes that operate on permanent Acts. The sections of an amending Act may add new provisions to a permanent Act, repeal existing ones, or replace existing provisions with new ones. For example, the first three sections of *An Act to amend the* Criminal Code *(Sentencing) and Other Acts in Consequence Thereof*[11] provide:

1. **Section 149 of the *Criminal Code* is replaced by the following:**

149.(1) Notwithstanding section 743.1, a court that convicts a person for an escape committed while undergoing imprisonment may order that the term of imprisonment be served in a penitentiary, even if the time to be served is less than two years.

(2) In this section, "escape" means breaking prison, escaping from lawful custody or ... being at large before the expiration of a term of imprisonment... .

2. **Paragraph 553(c) of the Act is amended by ... adding the word "or" at the end of subparagraph (viii) and by adding the following after subparagraph (viii):**

(ix) subsection 733.1(1) (failure to comply with probation order).

3. **Section 665 of the Act is repealed.**

As in all federal legislation, the amending provisions are set out in bold typeface, while the "new" provisions, intended either to replace existing provisions (as in section 1) or to be added to existing provisions (as in section 2), are set out in ordinary typeface. When the amending legislation comes into force, the new provisions "merge" with and become part of the permanent *Criminal Code*, while the amending provisions are "spent"; having done their work, they cease to have further legal effect.

A permanent Act may include amending provisions, called "consequential amendments" because they have become necessary as a consequence of the new permanent Act. What distinguishes an amending Act from permanent Acts that include amendments is that the former consists entirely of amendments, affecting either a single or several Acts. Once an entire amending Act comes into force it effectively disappears; the changes introduced by the Act operate, these changes are merged with the permanent Acts to which they relate, and the force of the amending Act is spent.

---

11   S.C. 1995, c. 22.

4) Enabling and Delegated Legislation

Legislation consists not only of statutes but also of regulations, rules, orders, by-laws, and other forms of subordinate or delegated legislation. These are all forms of law made pursuant to a delegation of law-making authority from the legislature to a subordinate office or body. In practice, delegations most often are made to the Governor or Lieutenant Governor in Council, to ministers, to government boards or agencies, to professional associations, to municipalities, or to courts. But, in principle, delegations can be made to anyone, for the power to delegate law-making authority to a person or body of one's choice is an incident of legislative sovereignty.[12]

Delegation is effected by enacting a provision that confers a power on a named delegate to make law with respect to the matters specified in the provision. Such provisions are usually referred to as "enabling" legislation. The scope of the authority conferred on the delegate is determined by interpreting the enabling provisions. So long as the delegated legislation comes within the scope of the enabling provision, it is valid. If the delegate exceeds its authority, the result is "*ultra vires*" or invalid.

An example of delegation is found in section 90 of Ontario's *Substitute Decisions Act:*

90. The Lieutenant Governor in Council may make regulations,

(a) prescribing forms;

(b) prescribing facilities for the purpose of the definition of "facility" in subsection 1(1);

(c) prescribing a fee scale for the compensation of guardians of property ... ;

...

(e) prescribing courses of training for assessors; ...

This enabling provision authorizes the executive branch of government to fill in some of the details of the scheme established by the *Substitute Decisions Act.* Few would object to such a delegation in that the authority conferred is narrow in scope and well defined and it authorizes the Lieutenanct Governor in Council to deal with administrative details as opposed to legislative policy. However, the powers delegated to the executive are often much broader in scope. Section 43 of the *Fisheries Act,* for example, provides:

---

12   The doctrine of legislative sovereignty is discussed in Chapter 2.

43. The Governor in Council may make regulations for carrying out the purposes and provisions of this Act and in particular, but without restricting the generality of the forgoing, may make regulations

(*a*) for the proper management and control of the sea-coast and in-land fisheries;

(*b*) respecting the conservation and protection of fish; ...

There follow another sixteen enumerated powers, including the power to regulate fishing, fishing vessels and gear, and the import and export of fish. All this amounts to a vast delegation of law-making power to the federal Cabinet. Such delegations are considered by many to be anti-democratic in that important policies decisions are implemented without the benefit of legislative debate.

Because it is made under authority conferred by a sovereign legislature, delegated legislation has the same legal force as statutes and for the most part is interpreted using the same rules and techniques. Generally, the enabling and delegated legislation are read together as comprising a single scheme. However, the enabling legislation is the dominant partner in this scheme and, unless the legislature expressly provides otherwise, inconsistencies between the two are resolved in favour of the enabling legislation.[13]

5) Reform and Program Legislation

Statutes are also classified as reform legislation, which is designed to reform some aspect of the common law, or as program legislation, which is designed to establish an institution, a department of government, or a regulatory program or scheme.

Reform legislation is enacted to clarify or to change the common law by codifying, modifying, or supplementing its rules.[14] The reform may be narrowly focused on a particular issue or it may be systematic and comprehensive, covering an area of law in a methodical way. In either case the resulting legislation consists of rules that are designed to operate within the framework of the common law and to be administered by the ordinary courts. Examples include Sale of Goods Acts, Insurance Acts, and Trustee Acts. In interpreting reform legislation, the emphasis is on understanding the shortcomings at which the reform is

---

13 The legislature sometimes enacts a so-called "Henry VIII clause," which provides that delegated legislation may override the legislature's own enactments.

14 Codification is explained in Chapter 15.

targeted, the mischief or problem for which the law did not adequately provide, and integrating the new rules into the existing body of law.[15]

Program legislation, by contrast, is generally enacted in response to broad political, social, or economic needs. It is enacted to deal with a problem that the legislature believes cannot be solved by tinkering with existing legal rules, but requires a program of government regulation or benefit distribution.[16] Such programs are established through a statute that sets out the program goals; creates the offices and structures necessary for the program to operate; confers appropriate administrative, legislative, and judicial powers on these offices; indicates how members of the public come in contact with the program; provides for any needed fees or offences; and establishes mechanisms for supervision and review.

The key feature of program legislation is the delegation of powers to the executive branch — not only administrative power to supervise the operation of the program, but also legislative power to create rules and standards and judicial or quasi-judicial power to resolve disputes. The exercise of these powers is supervised by the courts through appeal and judicial review.

The emergence of a significant body of program legislation in the nineteenth and twentieth centuries led to the development of the branch of law known as administrative law. Acting pursuant to this law, the superior courts of each jurisdiction review the work of the executive branch to ensure that it has been carried out in accordance with the rule of law.[17] Judicial review is based primarily on the principles of legality, natural justice, and fairness. The principle of legality, also known as the *vires* doctrine, ensures that every exercise of power is authorized by law; any attempt by the executive to exceed its powers by making an unauthorized decision, order, or regulation may be declared "*ultra vires*," or invalid and without legal effect.The principles of

---

15 This approach to law is famously set out in *Heydon's Case* (1584), 3 Co. Rep. 7a, 76 E.R. 637.

16 This type of legislation is often called "public law," because it involves the intervention of government in the lives of individuals in order to achieve political goals; on this basis, it is distinguished from the "private law" of property, contract, and tort that is said to govern relations among individuals without government intervention. These terms are not used in this text for two reasons. First, they are misleading in that they suggest that "private" law is less political and less public than "public" law. Second, there is no necessary correspondence between public and private law and the type of legislation used to declare that law. In fact, many aspects of private law are dealt with by legislatures in program legislation. See, for example, provincial workers compensation legislation, which deals with workplace accidents through a government-run program rather than common law contract and tort.

17 The rule of law is explained in Chapter 2.

natural justice and fairness ensure that individuals are given fair treatment, including notice and a chance to be heard, when their interests are affected by the exercise of executive power.

In interpreting program legislation, the focus is normally not on the common law but on the goals sought by the legislature and on the design of the implementing scheme. The meaning of each provision is best understood in light of its contribution to the goals and its function in the scheme.

6) Guidelines and Other Forms of Quasi-Legislation

In addition to the statutory instruments described above, the executive branch of government also produces a wide range of non-statutory instruments that set out norms, procedures, and directives designed to facilitate the orderly exercise of governmental functions. Quasi-legislation is often written for government employees, to tell them how to carry out their jobs. Some quasi-legislation sets out guidelines which government officials are to consult in making discretionary decisions, such as whether to issue a licence or grant an exemption. Other quasi-legislation explains how government officials interpret the legislation they administer. The tax interpretation bulletins produced by the Canada Revenue Agency are probably the best-known example of this type. They set out the position the government has taken in interpreting various provisions of the *Income Tax Act*. They are relied on not only by Canada Revenue Agency staff in administering the Act, but also by taxpayers in arranging their affairs and preparing tax returns.

While some quasi-legislation is explicitly authorized by statute, much is produced under the prerogative powers of government. What distinguishes all quasi-legislation from legislation is the fact that quasi-legislation is not legally binding. A prison guard who fails to comply with a directive may be disciplined by the employer but he or she has not broken the law. An applicant for a benefit who meets the criteria set out in a guideline may nonetheless be denied the benefit, provided the denial is within the statutory discretion conferred on the decision-maker. It is the Act, not the non-statutory guideline, that declares the law.

It is sometimes difficult to determine whether a given instrument is legislative or quasi-legislative. The title given to the instrument is not conclusive. For example, instruments entitled "Guidelines" are sometimes found to have statutory force when they are made under a statutory authority and rely on the conventions of legislative drafting.[18]

---

18   See, for example, *Friends of Oldman River Society v. Canada (Minister of Transport)*, [1992] 1 S.C.R. 3.

B. DRAFTING CONVENTIONS

Although the content of legislation is infinitely variable, its form and style are fixed to a large extent by the conventions of legislative drafting. These conventions vary in some respects from one jurisdiction to another, but the broad principles are the same throughout Canada. Conventions govern the style in which legislation is drafted, the form and structure of legislative provisions, the arrangement of provisions within an Act, the use of headings, notes, and other finders' aids, and the use of particular words. For example, to confer a power in legislation, the word "may" is normally used; to express the idea of obligation, "shall" or "must" is used.

One of the reasons legislation is considered dull and difficult reading is the style in which it is written. By convention, drafters use a utilitarian prose that shuns metaphor, irony, wit, embellishment, colloquialism, and rhetorical device of any sort. Another hallmark of legislative style is consistency and uniformity: once an idea is expressed in a particular way, the same language is used to express that idea each time the occasion arises. A variation in wording thus signals a significant variation in the idea. While these stylistic conventions facilitate clarity and certainty, they make for tedious prose. A third hallmark of legislative style is its unnatural concision. The drafter uses as few words as possible to state the law; repetition and redundancy are avoided; every word has a distinct function to perform in the legislative text. This convention makes for a shorter text, but one that is more difficult to read.

While some of the dullness and difficulty of legislative prose is due to its stylistic conventions, much of it is due to the complexity of the subject dealt with or to the need to be precise, especially in drafting legislation that is difficult to enforce. The best illustration of complexity combined with a high level of precision is the *Income Tax Act*. It becomes ever more complicated as Parliament relies on tax (or relief from tax) as an instrument of economic and social policy. It becomes more detailed and convoluted as Parliament attempts to plug the endless loopholes through which citizens attempt to pass.

Historically, legislation, like private law instruments, was written in "legalese." Legalese features extremely long and complicated sentences, use of "doublets" and "triplets" and long strings of near synonyms, use of Latin and archaic expressions and the triumph of precision over concision.[19] Instead of relying on general terms and common sense, the drafter

---

19   A doublet is a conventional expression in which two words that mean more or less the same thing are conjoined by "and"—as in "last will and testament."

tried to anticipate and expressly address every possibility. In recent years, the movement toward plain language drafting has greatly reduced legalese in the statute book, but it is still encountered in private law instruments.

C. ELEMENTS OF LEGISLATION

Legislation is composed of two elements: provisions and components.

1) Provisions

Provisions are statements that set out the law which the legislature intends to enact. Provisions may be substantive or interpretive. Substantive provisions regulate conduct, create obligations, offences, powers or entitlements, establish institutions or offices, set out procedures, confer privileges, impose taxes, and more. They are meant to add to or change, or in some cases reiterate, the substantive content of the law. Interpretive provisions are declarations or explanations that indicate the meaning or purpose of substantive provisions. Definitions, purpose statements, and sections stipulating the temporal or territorial application of legislation are examples of this type of provision. They offer direct descriptions of legislative intent.

2) Components

The components of legislation are words or phrases, or visual aids such as maps or charts, that provide information about the legislation and help structure it, making it easier to use and understand. The most common components are titles and subtitles, headings, tables of contents, marginal or sectional notes, historical notes, and preambles.[20]

3) The Legislative Sentence

A legislative sentence normally consists of three elements:

1) the subject: a description of the person or thing, or more often the class of persons or things, to which legal consequences are attached through the operation of the legislation;

Often one word has an Anglo-Saxon source while the other is derived from French. A triplet conjoins three similar words or phrases.

20   The use of components in interpreting legislation is discussed in Chapter 8.

2) the fact-situation (sometimes called the "case"): a description of the facts that must exist or the conditions that must be met for the legal consequences to attach; and

3) the legal consequences: a description of legally significant effects produced when the legislation operates.[21]

In the classic legislative sentence, the fact-situation is generally set out in a subordinate clause introduced by "where."[22] This clause is then followed by the main clause setting out the subject and the legal consequence. For example, a provision establishing an entitlement might take the following form:

> Where a person has reached the age of sixty-five and is unemployed, he or she may apply for a pension.

A provision imposing an obligation might read as follows:

> Where an applicant establishes that he or she has reached the age of sixty-five and is unemployed, the Commission shall determine the pension to which the applicant is entitled.

Sometimes the fact-situation appears in the middle of the sentence. It may be set out in a participial phrase or a clause introduced by a relative pronoun, or in a combination of clauses and phrases:

> A person may, upon reaching the age of sixty-five, if he or she is unemployed, apply for a pension.

> A person who reaches the age of sixty-five and is unemployed may apply for a pension.

The classic format is only a model and may be adapted or abandoned when appropriate. The important thing for the drafter is to use a structure that clearly identifies the legal subject, sets out the legal consequence, and indicates the prerequisites (if any) that must be met before the consequence can occur.

There are a number of standard variations on the classic format which drafters use for recurring situations. For example, many statutes contain offence provisions. In the *Criminal Code* these are drafted in the

---

21 This account is based on an analysis reviewed by E.A. Driedger, *The Composition of Legislation*, 2d ed. rev. (Ottawa: Minister of Supply and Services, 1976) at xxiv.

22 Plain language drafters consider the ubiquitous use of "where" in legislation to be a form of legalese and recommend that it be replaced by "when" or "if" when appropriate so as to reflect ordinary language usage.

following form: "every one who [engages in described undesired conduct] commits an offence and is liable to [a described punishment]."

> Every one who knowingly makes a false statement in an application for a pension is guilty of an offence and is liable to a fine of not more than five thousand dollars or to imprisonment for six months or to both.

The legislative subject "every one" comes at the beginning of the sentence followed by the fact-situation, which is set out in the subordinate clause introduced by "who." The subordinate clause limits the scope of "everyone" so that the consequence does not attach to all persons, but only to those who meet the description set out in the clause—those who have made a false statement in a pension application knowing it to be false. The legal consequence is then described in the predicate of the sentence; such persons commit a summary conviction offence and are liable to be tried and sentenced accordingly.

Another standard form of legislative sentence is found in provisions that confer powers on bodies or offices. These provisions often rely on the classic format, but add a description of the purposes for which the power may be exercised. To confer a search and seizure power, for example, a drafter might write: "where [described conditions exist] a peace officer may, for [a described purpose], enter [described premises], conduct [described search] and take away [described things]."

> Where an inspector believes on reasonable grounds that fishing gear used in contravention of this Act is present in a dwelling, the inspector may, for the purpose of securing evidence of any past contravention or preventing future contraventions, enter the dwelling and seize any fishing gear or any books, records, or other documents found therein.

The fact-situation is set out in a subordinate clause at the beginning of the sentence: an inspector must come to hold a certain belief on the basis of facts that justify that belief. If this prerequisite is met, the legal consequence automatically results, in this case an authority to do something that would otherwise be illegal. Entering the property of another without permission is normally a trespass; taking away property that belongs to another is normally theft and conversion. But if the person who does these things acts pursuant to a legal authority, he or she has a good defence. The recipient of this authority is the legal subject, described here as an inspector. In order to claim this authority, a person must be an inspector within the meaning of the section.[23]

---

23   The means by which a person becomes an inspector will normally be set out elsewhere in the Act or in other, related legislation.

Finally, all three elements must be interpreted in light of the purposes for which the authority is granted. An entry and seizure carried out by an inspector will not be authorized unless it is done for one of these purposes.

Some legislative sentences do not include a fact-situation. To confer regulation-making authority, for example, a drafter might write: "The Governor in Council may make regulations respecting [described matters]." The legal subject is the Governor in Council. The legal consequence is the authority to make valid, legally binding regulations. Because there is no limiting fact-situation, this consequence arises the moment the legislation comes into force and is exercisable when the Governor in Council thinks it advisable.

It would be possible to introduce a purpose statement into this legislative sentence. A drafter might write, for example:

> For the purpose of ensuring that any inquiries held under this Act are full, fair, and efficient, the Governor in Council may make regulations respecting ...

Although this purpose restricts the scope of the authority conferred on the Governor in Council, it does not remove the discretion to decide whether and when the power should be exercised. Compare the following example:

> Upon the recommendation of the Minister of Transport, the Governor in Council may, for the purpose of ensuring that any inquiries held under this Act are full, fair, and efficient, make regulations respecting ...

In this example the power conferred on the Governor in Council is exercisable only if the prerequisite comprising the fact-situation, a recommendation from the Minister of Transport, is met.

4) Sections, Subsections, and Paragraphing

Legislative provisions are set out in self-contained sections or subsections arranged in numerical order. Each section or subsection is meant to express a single complete idea that is normally expressed in the form of a single sentence, or occasionally two short sentences. When two or more ideas are closely related, they often are set out as subsections of a single section.

To avoid ambiguity and improve readability, legislative sentences are sometimes broken down into "paragraphs" and "subparagraphs" (in federal legislation) or "clauses" and "subclauses" (in provincial legislation). These subunits highlight the logical and grammatical structure of the sentence by setting out its analogous parts in parallel form. Consider the following, for example:

> 33. The Milk Licensing Board may refuse to grant a licence to conduct the proposed business where the Board believes the applicant is not qualified by experience, responsibility or resources or for any other reason that the Board considers sufficient.

This sentence can be read in two different ways:

> 33. The Milk Licensing Board may refuse to grant a licence to conduct the proposed business where the Board believes the applicant is not qualified
> (a) by experience, responsibility or resources, or
> (b) for any other reason that the Board considers sufficient.

> 33. The Milk Licensing Board may refuse to grant a licence to conduct the proposed business
> (a) where the Board believes the applicant is not qualified by experience, responsibility or resources, or
> (b) for any other reason that the Board considers sufficient.

Under the first reading, the Board is empowered to refuse a licence only where it believes the applicant to be unqualified. Under the second reading, the Board could refuse a licence for any reason it thinks appropriate (subject to administrative law constraints). The intended meaning is unclear in the unparagraphed version, but becomes immediately apparent when the sentence is paragraphed.

Paragraphing is useful not only in drafting legislation but also in understanding it and constructing arguments about its meaning. When faced with a difficult provision, an interpreter can try to break it down into its grammatical units and subunits to expose the elements of the sentence and the relationship among them. This type of textual analysis helps interpreters to understand the law and may reveal unsuspected ambiguity.[24]

5) Legislative Structure

Because the substantive content of legislation is infinitely variable, there is no one fixed structure or format for enactments. The organization of provisions within an Act or regulation follows the logic of the

---

24   For a detailed illustration of a textual analysis, see Chapter 9.

legislative scheme. To help communicate this logic, provisions may be grouped together in various ways. Closely related provisions are often presented as subsections forming part of a single section. Related sections are often grouped together under a heading that calls attention to the relationship among them—the shared theme or purpose. Complex or lengthy Acts are normally divided into divisions and parts, each with its own titles and headings and, when appropriate, its own interpretive provisions.

Even though the substantive content of legislation is variable, drafters try as much as possible to be consistent and to follow established models when arranging provisions within an Act. In federal enactments, for example, interpretive provisions appear at the beginning of the Act or the part or division to which they relate. These include definitions (set out in alphabetical order), application provisions, and statements of purpose or principle.[25] Other interpretive provisions—for example, transitional provisions—normally appear at the end.[26] It is also customary for consequential amendments to be placed at the end.[27]

D. TEMPORAL OPERATION OF LEGISLATION

Temporal operation is one of the more difficult topics in statutory interpretation. The temporal operation of a statute refers to its life span, beginning when it is first enacted and ending when it ceases to be law. Potentially there are four legally significant events in the temporal operation of a statute: enactment, commencement, re-enactment, and repeal. Everything that happens to a statute may be analyzed in terms of these four events. Delegated legislation experiences the same four

---

25   When a definition relates to a single section, it is usually set out in the final subsection of the section.

26   Transitional provisions tell interpreters which law should be applied to facts that are in progress when the new legislation comes into force. Since these provisions cease to be important once the transitional problems are dealt with, they are put at the end.

27   Consequential amendments are amendments that must be made to other legislation as a consequence of enacting a new Act. They are needed to avoid possible conflict between the new Act and existing legislation and to ensure the harmonious and effective operation of both new and existing legislative schemes. Because these amendments do not form part of the scheme of the Act in which they appear but rather "merge" with the legislation to which they relate, they are placed at the end. For an explanation of merger, see section A(3), above in this chapter.

events. However, as explained below, its temporal operation is complicated by its dependency on enabling legislation.

1) Enactment

A statute is enacted when it receives royal assent. In practice, a representative of Her Majesty approves a copy of the bill that has been passed by the legislature. At this moment, the legislation officially becomes part of existing law. However, even though it is law, it is not necessarily binding or capable of producing effects. Subject to certain exceptions, an Act does not become binding until it officially "commences" or "comes into force."[28] Prior to commencement, even though the legislation is law, it cannot be applied.

2) Commencement or Coming into Force

The impact of legislation is felt when it commences or comes into force. At this point it becomes binding on those to whom it applies, its powers become exercisable, and its rights and privileges can be claimed.

An act may provide for its own coming into force in a number of ways: by naming a day or a triggering event, or more often by providing that it is to come into force in whole or in part on a day to be fixed by Order in Council.[29] This latter approach allows the government to postpone implementation of the Act until appropriate preparations have been completed. On occasion an Act provides that it is deemed to have come into force at a time *prior* to enactment. Such provisions give the legislation a retroactive effect.[30] If an Act says nothing about its coming into force, a default rule applies. In most jurisdictions, the default rule says that the Act comes into force upon enactment.[31]

The distinction between law and enforceable law also applies to regulations and other forms of delegated legislation. Generally speaking, the steps necessary to make such legislation and the time at which it comes into force are set out in Interpretation Acts, Regulations Acts, and the like. At the federal level, for example, regulations as defined in the *Interpretation Act* are made when they are signed by the Governor

---

28   These exceptions are set out in the Interpretation Acts of Canadian jurisdictions. See, for example, ss. 5(3) and 7 of the *Interpretation Act*, R.S.C. 1985, c.I-21.

29   An Order in Council is an order made by the Governor or the Lieutenant Governor on the advice of Cabinet (the Privy Council at the federal level, the Executive Council in the provinces).

30   The retroactive application of legislation is explained and discussed in Chapter 13.

31   See, for example, s. 5(2) of the *Interpretation Act*, above note 28.

General, but under the *Statutory Instruments Act* they do not come into force until they are registered.[32]

3) Expiry or Repeal

Once enacted, legislation continues to form part of the law until it expires or is repealed. Expiry occurs when legislation provides for its own demise by designating a time at which it shall cease to be law. (Such a provision is often referred to as a "sunset" clause.) Repeal occurs when legislation is brought to an end through the operation of other legislation that declares it to be repealed. It is unusual for Acts to provide for their own expiry; the normal way of ending legislation is through repeal. In either case, the effects are the same. The legislation ceases to operate and ceases to form part of the law. In addition, any regulations made under repealed or expired enabling legislation become inoperative and cease to be part of the law.

It is possible for legislation to be amended before it comes into force. It is also possible for it to be repealed without ever having come into force.

4) Inoperability

Once in force, legislation continues in force until expiry or repeal. However, the operation of a provision may be interrupted by conflict with a paramount law. When two valid laws come into conflict and the conflict cannot be avoided through interpretation, it is resolved through hierarchy. The law with the higher status or ranking is said to be paramount, while the law with a lower status or ranking is rendered inoperative. Although the courts are inconsistent in analyzing the legal effect of inoperability,[33] the better view appears to be the following. When a provision is rendered inoperative, it does not cease to be law, but it ceases to have any force or effect. It is in the same position as a

---

32   See R.S.C. 1985, c. S-22, s. 9. The rule is subject to exceptions. Regulations may be exempted from this requirement or they may contain a provision that expressly provides for their early commencement.

33   The inconsistency arises because some Canadian courts adopt the British analysis of inoperability, which evolved through case law dealing with implied repeal. The British analysis appears to be codified in some Canadian Interpretation Acts that assimilate inoperability to repeal. However, because Canadian jurisdictions do not rely on implied repeal to actually repeal legislation, arguably the British analysis makes little sense in a Canadian context. Implied repeal and other sources of inoperability are discussed in Chapter 15.

provision that is enacted but has not commenced. It remains in this limbo until either it or the paramount law is repealed.

5) Re-enactment

Legislation is re-enacted when it is repealed and immediately enacted again without undergoing any substantive change. In some re-enactments the wording of the new legislation is identical to the old, while in others the wording is changed. But so long as the *substance* of the rule is not changed, the legislation is re-enacted rather than amended.

The chief significance of re-enactment is that it does not change the coming into force date of the re-enacted law. Ordinarily a repealed provision stops operating when the repealing legislation comes into force. And ordinarily a newly enacted provision first begins to operate when it comes into force. But in a re-enactment, because the repealed provision and the newly enacted one express the same rule, there is no interruption in temporal operation. The coming into force date of the re-enacted provision is considered to be the coming into force date of the old provision. This rule is called the "continuous operation of rules." It is codified in section 44(f) of the federal *Interpretation Act*:

> Where an enactment, in this section called the "former enactment", is repealed and another enactment, in this section called the "new enactment", is substituted therefore,
>
> ...
>
> (f) except to the extent that the provisions of the new enactment are not in substance the same as those of the former enactment, the new enactment shall not be held to operate as new law, but shall be construed and have effect as a consolidation and as declaratory of the law as contained in the former enactment.[34]

Legislation is re-enacted for a number of reasons: to consolidate or revise existing law, to declare the true meaning of existing law, or as part of the amending process. In a consolidation, legislation is updated, re-arranged, and re-enacted to make it available in a more convenient format.[35] In a revision, legislation is not only updated and re-arranged, but the style is adjusted and drafting errors are corrected.[36] In a declaration, legislation that has been a source of doubt or controversy is clarified through re-enactment in a new, clearer form. Finally, although

---

34 Most provincial and territorial Interpretation Acts lack a comparable provision. Those jurisdictions rely on the common law rule

35 The process of consolidation is described in more detail later in this chapter.

36 The process of statute revision is described in more detail later in this chapter.

the primary purpose of amendment is to change the law, many amendments include a partial re-enactment of existing law.

Partial re-enactment occurs when existing provisions are repealed and replaced by new ones that incorporate a desired change while retaining elements of the previous law. To the extent the new provision does not substantially differ from the repealed one, the legislation is re-enacted. Suppose, for example, that on 1 February 1950 the following provision was added by way of amendment to the *Criminal Code* and that it came into force immediately upon enactment:

> 250. Every one who fraudulently undertakes, for a consideration, to tell fortunes by reading palms or cards, by gazing into crystals or by any means whatsoever, is guilty of an offence punishable on summary conviction.

Suppose that on 1 February 1954 this provision was repealed and replaced by the following, which also came into force upon enactment:

> 250. Every one who fraudulently
> (a) undertakes, for a consideration, to tell fortunes by any means, or
> (b) pretends to use any kind of sorcery, enchantment, or conjuration,
>
> is guilty of an offence punishable on summary conviction.

Because the rule prohibiting the fraudulent use of sorcery embodied in paragraph (b) adds something substantially new, it operates as new law; its coming-into-force day is 1 February 1954. However, the rule prohibiting fraudulent fortune-telling is not new. It has only been reformulated in a less verbose style. Because the rule has been re-enacted rather than amended, its operation is not interrupted; its coming-into-force day remains 1 February 1950.

When enabling legislation is repealed, any regulations made under it cease to be law. However, if the enabling legislation is re-enacted, the regulations remain valid and operative.

6) Amendment

Amending legislation adds new provisions to the statute book or substitutes new provisions for existing ones. In so far as the new provisions make substantive changes to the law, they operate as amendments rather than re-enactments. Amendments operate and come into force on the day the amending legislation comes into force.

Suppose, for example, that the following provision, from a *Human Rights Code*, was first enacted on 1 February 1984 and came into force on 1 June 1984:

5.(1) Every person has a right to equal treatment with respect to employment, without discrimination on grounds of race, colour, ethnic origin, creed, age, family status or handicap.

Suppose that on 1 February 1995 the following amending Act received royal assent:

An Act to amend the *Human Rights Code*
Her Majesty, by and with the advice and consent of the Senate and the House of Commons of Canada, enacts as follows:

1. Subsection 5(1) of the *Human Rights Code* is replaced by the following:

5.(1) Every person has a right to equal treatment with respect to employment, without discrimination on grounds of race, colour, ethnic origin, creed, age, *gender, sexual orientation*, family status or handicap.

2. This Act shall come into force on 1 December 1996.

Upon coming into force on 1 December 1996, this amending Act would operate (a) by re-enacting the whole of subsection 5(1) of the 1984 *Code* without change and (b) by adding two new provisions to the subsection. The new provisions prohibit discrimination in employment on grounds of gender and on grounds of sexual orientation. The coming-into-force date of the re-enacted provisions would remain 1 June 1984, while the coming-into-force date of the new provisions would be 1 December 1996.

When enabling legislation is amended, it is necessary to consider the impact of the amendment on existing regulations. Most Interpretation Acts contain a provision like the following:

44. Where an enactment, in this section called the "former enactment," is repealed and another enactment, in this section called the "new enactment", is substituted therefor,
(a) all regulations made under the repealed enactment remain in force and are deemed to have been made under the new enactment, in so far as they are not inconsistent with the new enactment, until they are repealed or others made in their stead.[37]

It is not always clear whether existing regulations are consistent with the new enactment. Ideally, while preparing to amend the parent Act,

---

37 *Interpretation Act*, above note 28, s. 44(g).

the department responsible for administering the Act will review the relevant regulations and revoke or amend those that are inconsistent.

7) Codes and Codification

The term "codification" is used in common law in Canada in two distinct ways. First, it refers to the process of enacting common law rules in legislation, thus giving them the force and status of statute law. A codification of this sort does not change the law, but merely "codifies" it—that is, gives it a fixed statutory form. This type of codification is similar to re-enactment. The codified provision does not operate as new law.

The term "codification" also refers to the preparation of a statute or "code" that is meant to set out the entire body of rules on a subject in a coherent, systematic way. Codification in this sense affords an opportunity to bring together all existing statutory and common law rules, to reconcile inconsistencies, to fill gaps, and to make appropriate reforms. The finished product is meant to be a complete and definitive statement of the law on the subject, dispensing with the need to refer to previous law. Federal and provincial Labour Codes are examples of legislation that were enacted as codes in this sense.

It is possible for a statute to be a code for some purposes and not for others. The *Criminal Code*, for example, sets out an exhaustive list of criminal law offences precluding further resort to common law crimes; its list of defences, however, is not exhaustive and may be supplemented by the common law. It is also possible for legislation that was initially enacted as a code to lose its quality of exhaustiveness. If legislation is not amended, it may be overtaken by new events or by increasing complexity, so that provisions that once dealt adequately with a problem now require supplementation.

The decision to label something a code is generally a judgment call that depends on a number of factors, in particular on how comprehensive and systematic the legislation is and whether it is dealing adequately with the problem it was meant to address.[38]

8) Consolidation

In Canada, the term "consolidation" is used most often to refer to the purely mechanical process of updating legislation on a subject by in-

---

38   For the rules governing the recognition and interpretation of codification and codes, see Chapter 15.

corporating all relevant repeals, re-enactments, and amendments into the permanent Act. In a consolidation, the repealed language is taken out, the new language is added, and the resulting provisions are re-numbered. Apart from this tidying up, however, no change is made to either the substance or the form of the legislation. The purpose is simply to gather and present the legislation on a subject as it stands at the date of consolidation.

In Canada, most consolidations are unofficial, which means they are prepared by government departments or by private parties, without participation by the legislature. Unless a consolidation has been enacted, it does not constitute an authentic copy of the legislation and cannot be relied on in court. But if it has been properly and accurately done, it can be relied on for most other purposes. Canadian governments now provide an ongoing consolidation of the statute book in their jurisdiction, accessible on-line and in some cases through a loose-leaf service or through CD-ROM.

Although consolidations can be helpful, they also create pitfalls for the interpreter. They give a more or less accurate version of the law at the date of consolidation only, which may not be the version that applies to the facts with which the interpreter is concerned. It may be necessary to look behind the consolidation to recover the law as it stood in the past, or beyond the consolidation to subsequent repeals or amendments.

9) Statute Revision

In a statute revision, the legislative text is revised to ensure that its language is clear, consistent, readable, and error-free. Ideally, awkward or cumbersome constructions are rewritten, redundancies are eliminated, outdated terminology is modernized, and stylistic changes are made to bring the text in line with current drafting conventions. The one limit on revision is that the substance of the legislation must remain the same. When the work of revision is done, normally the old version of the legislation is repealed and replaced by the revised version. Since the substance of the Act has not been changed, this revision constitutes a re-enactment rather than an amendment. The revised text is strongly presumed, perhaps even conclusively presumed, to reproduce existing law.

10) General Statute Revision

It has been customary in Canadian jurisdictions to carry out a general statute revision every ten to fifteen years. In a general revision the entire body of statute law in existence on a certain day is consolidated and revised, then systematically arranged in a series of volumes and re-enacted in this new form. The idea is to produce a statute book that sets out the law as of a certain date in a single place, in an accessible format, and in a consistent and readable style.

Most general revisions are carried out pursuant to legislation. Typically, such legislation

- describes the tasks to be carried out by the revisors;
- establishes an office and the administrative machinery needed to do the work;
- provides for the re-enactment and coming into force of the finished product; and
- sets out rules for interpreting it.

A statute revision is meant to improve the form of legislation without in any way affecting the content or substance of the law. Thus, as explained above, in interpreting statute revisions, it is presumed that no change in meaning was intended. And since the revision is a re-enactment rather than an amendment of existing law, it does not affect the temporal operation of the legislation. Although technically the old legislation is "repealed" and the new legislation is enacted in its place, in substance the continuity of the law is preserved without interruption.

CHAPTER 2

INTRODUCTION TO STATUTORY INTERPRETATION

A. WHAT IS INVOLVED IN INTERPRETATION

When judges or other officials (for example, customs officers or labour relations boards) interpret legislation, they purport to discover its meaning by reading the language of the text in light of the rules of statutory interpretation. This standard description of the interpretive task is misleading in a number of respects. First, the term "discover" implies that interpreters are archaeologists rather than artists, that their goal is to locate meanings fixed in the past rather than create new meanings. This may be so in theory, but in practice interpretation involves *both* archaeology and art. Interpreters must work with a text whose wording was fixed in the past, but in reconstructing its meaning they must draw on current knowledge and their own understanding, experience, and skills.

The term "meaning" is also misleading in so far as it brings to mind thesaura, dictionaries, and formal definitions. What interests interpreters is not the abstract meaning of a text, but its meaning in relation to particular facts. Dictionary definitions are useful as a starting point, but lawyers and officials need to know how the legislation applies to the problem with which they are dealing. It is this concrete sense of meaning—the text as it applies to particular facts—that is sought in statutory interpretation.

Finally, the notion that statutory interpretation is a rule-governed activity is misleading. The "rules" are not really rules in the Dworkian sense and therefore they do not impose binding constraints on judges and other interpreters.[1] The failure to "follow" a rule of statutory interpretation is not an appealable or reviewable error. Although bad interpretations may be appealed or reviewed, the error lies in failing to interpret the statute correctly, not in failing to apply a particular statutory interpretation rule. As Lord Reid wrote in *Maunsell v. Olins*:

> They [the rules of statutory interpretation] are not rules in the ordinary sense of having some binding force. They are our servants, not our masters. They are aids to construction, presumptions or pointers. Not infrequently one "rule" points in one direction, another in a different direction. In each case we must look at all relevant circumstances and decide as a matter of judgment what weight to attach to any particular "rule."[2]

As Lord Reid indicates, the rules of statutory interpretation do not dictate outcomes in statutory interpretation cases. If the rules all point to the same interpretation, the interpreter is effectively bound. Any alternative interpretation would be set aside as incorrect or patently unreasonable. But if ordinary meaning supports one outcome, while purpose and presumed intent support another, the interpreter must rely on his or her own judgment to decide which outcome is better.

Although the rules of statutory interpretation do not determine outcomes, they are indispensable in formulating the arguments used by counsel to argue cases and by judges to justify outcomes once a conclusion has been reached. However impossible it may be to capture the actual process of decision making—a personal, complex, and often highly intuitive process—the resulting decision requires a legal justification. Statutory interpretation rules supply lawyers and judges with a vocabulary for describing interpretation problems and with legally acceptable reasons for preferring one solution over another. They permit a judge to say that the interpretation adopted is the most appropriate one in the circumstances, not because the judge personally prefers that interpretation, but because it takes into account considerations that are deemed relevant by the rules.

---

1   Ronald Dworkin writes that rules are binding; therefore, they cannot conflict with one another and they produce a single correct outcome. By contrast, principles are not binding but operate as pointers—reasons to prefer one solution over another. It is common for a set of facts to be subject to conflicting principles. See R.M. Dworkin, *A Matter of Principle* (Cambridge, MA: Harvard University Press, 1985).

2   [1975] A.C. 373 at 382 (H.L.).

B. SOURCES OF STATUTORY INTERPRETATION RULES

The so-called rules of statutory interpretation consist primarily of maxims, principles, presumptions, and directives introduced into the common law over the centuries.[3] However, there are other sources as well. Some interpretation rules are set out or based on provisions in the Constitution of Canada.[4] Rules for interpreting bilingual legislation, for example, are found in the *Constitution Act, 1867*, the *Manitoba Act, 1870*, and the *Constitution Act, 1982*. General interpretation rules are also found in statutes dealing generally with interpretation,[5] delegated legislation,[6] statute revisions,[7] and the like. Particular rules (such as definitions and purpose statements) are found in the particular statutes or statutory instruments to which they relate.

Even though the legislature is sovereign and can override common law rules,[8] both legislatures and courts tend to regard interpretation as the province of judges. Legislatures are concerned with the big picture—with the adoption of policy, the allocation of resources, the formulation of rules and workable schemes. Courts are concerned with the application of rules and principles in the context of particular facts. This is their special expertise. For this reason, legislatures are reluctant to tell judges how to do the work of interpretation. And when they do, their instructions are sometimes ignored. Interpretation is very much a common law subject, and for the most part the rules of statutory interpretation are found in case law.

---

3   Similar interpretation issues, and rules addressing them, are found in all text-based legal and religious traditions.

4   The Constitution of Canada is defined in s. 52 of the *Constitution Act, 1982*, being Schedule B to the *Canada Act 1982* (U.K.), 1982, c. 11.

5   See, for example, the *Interpretation Act*, R.S.C. 1985, c. I-21.

6   See, for example, the *Statutory Instruments Act*, R.S.C. 1985, c. S-22 and the *User Fees Act*, S.C. 2004, c. 6.

7   See, for example, the *Revised Statutes of Canada, 1985 Act*, R.S.C. 1985 (3d Supp.), c. 40.

8   The doctrine of parliamentary sovereignty and its significance is explained later in this chapter.

C. IMPORTANT CONCEPTS

1) Legislative Intent

The expression "legislative intention" or "legislative intent" is used by most interpreters to refer to the meaning or purpose that is taken to have been present in the "mind of the legislature" at the time a provision was enacted. It is the meaning the legislature wished to embody in the legislative text or the purpose it sought to accomplish by enacting the legislation.

The anthropomorphism of this usage is obviously troubling. A legislature does not have a mind, nor is it capable of formulating wishes or seeking goals. As a legal institution, a legislature may think and act through human agents. But which human agents represent the legislature for this purpose? All members of the legislature? All those who voted on the bill? Only those who voted in its favour? Only those who participated in its creation and formulation? What about the non-elected policy makers and drafters who actually formed intentions respecting the meaning and purpose of particular provisions? Should their intentions be considered? To avoid these difficult questions, legislative intention is sometimes attributed to the text itself, as in the expression "intent of the text."

Other aspects of the concept of legislative intent are equally troubling. Those who invoke it appear to assume that, first, at the time of enactment the legislature had views about the question now facing the court and, second, these views are discoverable by judges and other interpreters. While the first assumption is true in some cases, it is not true in all. Many issues come to court precisely because the legislature has failed to anticipate and provide for them. The second assumption seems dubious in light of modern theories of meaning that emphasize the role of the listener or reader in constructing the meaning of a communication. How can a court be sure that its understanding of a provision corresponds to what the proponents had in mind?

Despite these problems, references to legislative intent are ubiquitous in statutory interpretation and not likely to disappear, however weighty the theoretical objections. This is because statutes are obviously enacted for a reason, and the language in which they are drafted reflects deliberate and careful choices by some combination of people who legally speak for the legislature. Given the sovereign authority of the legislature under constitutional law, these choices cannot be ignored. Courts and other interpreters must at least try to understand the meanings and purposes that motivated the legislation in the first place. Such understanding is possible in so far as those meanings and purposes are constructed out of linguistic structures and conventions, cultural assumptions and a body of knowledge ("common" sense) that is more or less shared by the relevant players, namely, the participants in the legislative process, the persons to whom the legislation is addressed and the courts and other interpreters who determine its application.

2) Parliamentary Sovereignty

In the Canadian system of parliamentary democracy, the legislature is considered the primary source of law. In order to enact valid law, the legislature must respect the limitations on its power imposed by Canada's entrenched constitution. These limitations apply to both the subject matter that each legislature may deal with, as set out in sections 91 through 101 of the *Constitution Act, 1867,* and the permissible impact of legislation on rights protected under the *Canadian Charter of Rights and Freedoms* and the *Constitution Act, 1982.* Other provisions of the entrenched constitution impose manner and form requirements.[9] However, once these limitations and requirements are respected, the law enacted by the legislature is valid and paramount over other sources of law. If validly enacted legislation comes into conflict with either the common law or international law, the legislation prevails.

The doctrine of parliamentary sovereignty applies to both federal and provincial legislatures.[10] Each is sovereign within the sphere of its jurisdiction as set out under sections 91 and 92 of the *Constitution Act, 1867.* In the event of a conflict between validly enacted federal and provincial legislation, the federal legislation is paramount and prevails over provincial law.

The doctrine of parliamentary sovereignty has strongly influenced the attitude of judges towards legislation and the way they explain their role. Because the legislature is sovereign, courts are bound to give

---

9   For example, s. 133 the *Constitution Act, 1867* requires Acts of Parliament and of the Legislature of Quebec to be printed and published in English and French, and s. 53 requires federal appropriation and tax legislation to originate in the House of Commons. Section 133 illustrates a requirement of the form valid legislation must take while s. 53 illustrates a requirement of manner in which valid legislation must be enacted.

10 The position of territorial legislatures is somewhat anomalous. Technically, these legislatures exercise powers delegated by Parliament; however, in practice, for most purposes, territorial enactments function in the same way as provinical enactments.

effect to its instructions when they are expressed in valid legislation. This duty arises regardless of the court's own view of the legislation. In principle, Parliament's will must be heeded no matter how foolish or unfair its instructions may be. There are many cases in which judges give effect to the apparent meaning of a provision, despite their own feelings of disapproval, because they feel bound by the legislative will.

3) Rule of Law

The rule of law is highly prized in Canada's parliamentary democracy as a bulwark of a free and democratic society. It is mentioned in the preamble to the *Charter* and is implicit in many *Charter* provisions. It is the basis for a number of interpretive rules. Although highly revered, the concept of rule of law is difficult to define because it is used by different speakers to emphasize different things. Most would agree, however, that the rule of law consists of principles designed to constrain the exercise of governmental power and to ensure that power is exercised in a fair and efficacious way. The following rule of law principles are important in statutory interpretation:

a) No person can interfere with the freedom, security, or property of another person, except in accordance with the law. This principle applies to everyone, including government officials. For an act of a government official to be effective or binding, he or she must be able to point to a valid legal rule authorizing the act.

b) The law must be set out in advance and with sufficient clarity so that subjects can know what is expected of them and of others, can achieve a measure of security, and can plan for the future.

c) The law must be applied fairly, in a consistent and even-handed way, treating like cases alike.[11]

The courts are the primary guardians of the rule of law. They scrutinize the work of all persons purporting to exercise official power, from bureaucrats and police officers to administrative tribunals to Parliament itself. They ensure that these persons act pursuant to and within the limits of valid legal rules, whether statutory or common law. They also ensure that power is exercised for a proper purpose in a manner consistent with common law and *Charter* rights. Finally, they ensure that the exercise of power is not distorted by whim or prejudice

---

11   This is known as the principle of formal equality. It differs from substantive equality in that it assumes that the context in which law operates is the same for everyone.

or other abuse. The rule of law thus protects individuals from ill treatment and society as a whole benefits from the greatest possible measure of certainty, consistency, and equality in the interpretation and application of law.

4) Separation of Law and Politics

The separation of law and politics is generally regarded as an important aspect of both democracy and the rule of law. In a parliamentary democracy, the primary responsibility for making policy in the public interest is supposed to rest with Parliament, the elected branch of government, while implementing policy is the work of the executive branch. The responsibility for interpreting the law and ensuring legality rests with the courts.

This division of labour between legislature, executive branch, and courts depends on a number of beliefs. The first is that in a democracy political decisions should only be made by elected representatives of the people. Judges are not suited to make political decisions because they are not elected and they typically come from the small portion of the population that enjoys considerable wealth and power. They do not represent society as a whole.

A second belief is that judges lack the institutional resources of the legislature, resources on which it draws to make sound policy choices. Unlike the judiciary, the legislature controls its own agenda; it decides what issues or problems should receive public attention. Moreover, the legislature has large amounts of money and a government bureaucracy at its disposal. It can draw on the administrative experience and expertise of government departments, and it can also commission studies and surveys and seek out expert advice. Most important, perhaps, a legislature is not limited in the ways it can respond to the problems it addresses. It can raise or lower taxes, design new regulatory regimes or deregulate, fund new programs or cut existing ones, and delegate authority to anyone it thinks fit. Courts, in contrast, do not control their own agenda, and the flow of information they command is limited. They cannot create new programs or draft a complex set of regulations. Given their limited options and the limits on their time, money, information, and power, courts lack the resources that arguably are necessary for sound policy development.

A third belief is that judicial skills and professionalism enable courts to resolve disputes on the basis of law alone. Judges are assumed to be disinterested, impartial, and neutral participants in the resolution of disputes. They are presumed to be experts in establishing facts—what happened between the parties on a particular occasion, which witnesses are telling the truth and the like. They are also presumed to be experts at discovering the law as set out in statutes and cases. By applying this pre-existing law, created by others, to the facts of a case in a disinterested and impartial way, they insulate their judgments from their own personal views and preferences and ensure an outcome that depends entirely on legal rules.

Whether this idealized picture of judicial decision-making bears any relation to judicial practice is a matter of some controversy. Many would suggest that this picture is not only false but foolish, and that judicial decision-making would be greatly improved by an open acknowledgment of the role played by personal preference, unproven beliefs, and guesswork.

5) Common Sense

The expression "common sense" is used in this text broadly to refer to any fact, assumption, value, connection, or conclusion that a person takes to be obviously true and that he or she assumes is equally accepted by other members of the community—or at least by those of comparable intelligence and educational advantage. We all know that fire is hot, that babies cry when they're hungry, that being praised makes people feel good about themselves, that eradicating disease and hunger are desirable goals, that punishing a person for a crime that he or she did not commit is unjust. Many of us know, or think we know, that cigarettes cause cancer, that babies are better off being breast fed, that a university education is a good thing, that punishment deters crime.

The chief advantage of common sense for those who rely on it is that it does not require proof. Its truth is taken for granted. It can be relied on by judges and other interpreters without having to go through the trouble of sifting through evidence pro and con. Reliance on common sense is thus good in that it saves time and expense. It also permits interpreters to rely on truths that may not be susceptible of proof in the ordinary way. How does one go about "proving" the basic values of our society? How does one prove, for example, that everyone is entitled to fair treatment? And how does one prove that a particular practice is fair? These are things we know or recognize more or less automatically as matters of "common sense."

It is difficult to overstate the role of common sense in statutory interpretation. In most cases the courts do not receive evidence of the meaning of a legislative text. The ordinary meaning of legislation is a matter of first impression based on the interpreter's own reading of the text. This reading is informed by the interpreter's knowledge of language and knowledge of the world, both of which are assumed to consist largely of shared, obviously true understandings. The purpose of legislation most often is inferred from reading it in light of conditions existing at the time of enactment, while the consequences of legislation are identified by imaginatively constructing the chain of cause and effect that would follow from applying it to particular facts. In assessing both purpose and consequences, the court is called on to distinguish plausible from implausible impacts and desirable from undesirable ones. These evaluations are grounded in the assumptions and understandings that counsel and judges take to be obviously true and known to all.

While common sense is central to the practice of statutory interpretation, it has a worrisome side. First of all, what passes as common sense is not necessarily true or good. Secondly, what gets labelled common sense may not in fact be shared by others in the community. What is accepted as desirable and self-evident to some may be doubtful or hateful to others. What appears as common sense to most of us now may subsequently be revealed as nonsense, or even as evil. At one time, it was obvious to all that the world was flat, that burning was a good way to dispose of witches. Once a belief is labelled a "matter of common sense," it is taken for granted and little opportunity is afforded for challenge. Historically, in statutory interpretation cases, courts have been reluctant to receive evidence challenging the conventional wisdom on which outcomes may be based. This attitude is unfortunate and there are signs that it is changing. In the Supreme Court of Canada, Madame Justice L'Heureux-Dubé, in particular, emphasized during her tenure the value of receiving and sifting through evidence, pro and con, affecting the validity of the assumptions on which interpretations are based.[12] Even if these assumptions do not lend themselves to "proof" in the ordinary way, we nonetheless benefit from discussion and testing of their validity.

D. THE JUDICIAL TASK

There are at least two competing ways of understanding what a court is supposed to do when it interprets legislation. According to the traditional understanding, the primary task of the court is to discover and give effect to the intention of the legislature. That is, using the rules of lan-

---

12   See, for example, *Willick v. Willick*, [1994] 3 S.C.R. 670.

guage, supplemented by the rules of statutory interpretation, the court is to discover what law the legislature intended to enact and how that law was intended to apply to facts such as those facing the court. On this account, the task of interpretation is legal and technical rather than political. The content of the law is fixed by the legislature, and the court's only role is to ensure its efficacious implementation in particular cases.

This traditional understanding of the judicial role is appealing. At a theoretical level, it fits nicely with the doctrines of parliamentary sovereignty and rule of law, for it implies that outcomes are determined by rules fixed in advance by the legislature and are the same for everyone; they are not influenced by the preferences or prejudices of the judge who happens to be hearing the case.

The problem with this understanding of interpretation is that it rests on doubtful premises. It presumes that the legislature had a relevant intention with respect to the facts facing the court and that this intention is discoverable. Since these presumptions are false at least some of the time, a court that insists on the traditional view is likely to suffer a loss of credibility.

Most modern courts would prefer a more nuanced version of the traditional view, suggesting that the task is to give effect to the intention of the legislature in so far as that intention is discoverable from the language of the text. When the intention is not evident, resort must be had to the rules of statutory interpretation. And if the intention remains doubtful despite this further interpretive effort, the judge must then rely on his or her professional judgment to fashion an appropriate solution. This account of the judicial role acknowledges that creativity and choice in interpretation are sometimes unavoidable. If the language of the text is unclear and the interpretation rules don't all point in the same direction, a judge must draw on other sources in fixing the outcome. Judges assume this more active role, however, only when forced to do so by the ambiguity of the text and the indeterminacy of the rules. According to most judges, this combination of ambiguity and indeterminacy is exceptional rather than typical.

In sharp contrast to these more traditional explanations is what is usually called the "pragmatic" account of what occurs in statutory interpretation. The pragmatic account assumes that the intention of the legislature is not captured in the legislative text but must be constructed by the interpreter out of varied cultural, professional, and personal materials. These include linguistic conventions, legal principles, factual and cultural assumptions, as well as knowledge and experience that is more personal and idiosyncratic. Working with these materials, a court may construct a meaning or identify a purpose for a text and may further impute this meaning and purpose to the legislature, labelling it legislative intent. However, such labelling cannot change the fact that the meaning and purpose have been constructed by and are the responsibility of the interpreter.

In the pragmatic account of interpretation, the judicial goal is not to determine what the legislature intended, but to identify the outcome that is most appropriate in the circumstances, taking into account what the legislature enacted and anything else that is relevant. Identifying relevant considerations is the function of statutory interpretation rules. Assessing and weighing the relevant considerations, and choosing which outcome is best, is the function of the judge.

Although this account of interpretation clearly implicates the interpreter in the law-making process, and in doing so undermines the distinction between law and politics, it is not inconsistent with the doctrine of parliamentary sovereignty. Arguably, it describes a more appropriate division of powers between legislature and court, one in which the legislature initiates law making by enacting directives and allocating resources, while the court completes the process by elaborating those directives in the context of particular facts. Both activities are part of the law-making process and as such are necessarily and appropriately influenced by the beliefs, values, and preferences of the law makers as members of their respective institutions.

The primary drawback to the pragmatic account of interpretation is that it tends to undermine confidence in the rule of law. If the judicial task of interpretation is essentially creative, forcing judges to make choices that may be based in part on personal policy preference, then outcomes are not fully determined in advance by the legislature and they may not be the same for all. They depend to some extent on the identity of the interpreter. It is this threat to the cherished ideal of the rule of law that makes many judges and commentators resistant to the pragmatic view of interpretation.

The great strength and attraction of the pragmatic account is that it appears to describe what judges and other interpreters actually do when they interpret legislation. Unlike the traditional theory, it does not require a voluntary suspension of disbelief. It openly acknowledges that interpreting statutes is a complex and creative activity that is not reducible to the mechanical application of fixed legal rules.[13] And it raises an important question, namely, whether the persons who are

---

13   For a fuller discussion of the inadequacies of the traditional approach, see Ruth Sullivan, "Statutory Interpretation in the Supreme Court of Canada" (1998–99) 30 Ottawa L. Rev. 1–45.

given a power to interpret legislation—police officers and bureaucrats as well as members of administrative tribunals and courts—are appropriately chosen and adequately prepared for the task.

E. OVERVIEW OF INTERPRETATION RULES

1) Driedger's Modern Principle

The leading case on statutory interpretation is *Re Rizzo & Rizzo Shoes Ltd*.[14] In that case, the Ontario Court of Appeal held that an employer petitioned into bankruptcy in Ontario was not obliged to pay employee benefits under sections 40 and 40a of the province's *Employment Standards Act*:

> 40—(1) No employer shall terminate the employment of an employee who has been employed for three months or more unless the employee gives [notice in writing].
>
> ...
>
> (7) Where the employment of an employee is terminated contrary to this section,
> (a) the employer shall pay termination pay ...
>
> 40a ...
> (1a) Where,
> (a) fifty or more employees have their employment terminated by an employer in a period of six months or less and the terminations are caused by the permanent discontinuance of all or part of the business of the employer at an establishment;
>
> ...
>
> the employer shall pay severance pay ...

In the Supreme Court of Canada, Iacobucci J. (speaking for the court) wrote:

> The statutory obligation upon employers to provide both termination pay and severance pay is governed by ss. 40 and 40a of the *ESA*, respectively. The Court of Appeal noted that the plain language of those provisions suggests that termination pay and severance pay are payable only when the employer terminates the employment.

---

14   [1998] 1 S.C.R. 27. See also *Bell ExpressVu Limited Partnership v. Rex*, [2002] 2 S.C.R. 559.

For example, the opening words of s. 40(1) are: "No employer shall terminate the employment of an employee... ." Similarly, s. 40*a*(1a) begins with the words, "Where ... fifty or more employees have their employment terminated by an employer... ." Therefore, the question on which this appeal turns is whether, when bankruptcy occurs, the employment can be said to be terminated "by an employer."

The Court of Appeal answered this question in the negative, holding that, where an employer is petitioned into bankruptcy by a creditor, the employment of its employees is not terminated "by an employer," but rather by operation of law. ...

At the heart of this conflict is an issue of statutory interpretation. Consistent with the findings of the Court of Appeal, the plain meaning of the words of the provisions here in question appears to restrict the obligation to pay termination and severance pay to those employers who have actively terminated the employment of their employees. At first blush, bankruptcy does not fit comfortably into this interpretation. However, with respect, I believe this analysis is incomplete.

Although much has been written about the interpretation of legislation ..., Elmer Driedger in *Construction of Statutes* (2nd ed. 1983) best encapsulates the approach upon which I prefer to rely. He recognizes that statutory interpretation cannot be founded on the wording of the legislation alone. At p. 87 he states:

> Today there is only one principle or approach, namely, the words of an Act are to be read in their entire context and in their grammatical and ordinary sense harmoniously with the scheme of the Act, the object of the Act, and the intention of Parliament.
>
> ...
>
> I also rely upon s. 10 of the *Interpretation Act*, R.S.O. 1980, c. 219, which provides that every Act "shall be deemed to be remedial" and directs that every Act shall "receive such fair, large and liberal construction and interpretation as will best ensure the attainment of the object of the Act according to its true intent, meaning and spirit."

Although the Court of Appeal looked to the plain meaning of the specific provisions in question in the present case, with respect, I believe that the court did not pay sufficient attention to the scheme of the *ESA*, its object or the intention of the legislature; nor was the context of the words in issue appropriately recognized. I now turn to a discussion of these issues.[15]

---

15   *Ibid.* at paras. 18–23.

Since the *Rizzo* case, Driedger's modern principle has become the mantra of statutory interpretation in Canada. The key point of the principle is the point Iacobucci J. makes in introducing it—that statutory interpretation cannot be founded on the wording of the legislation alone. The words of the text must be read and analyzed in light of a purposive analysis, a scheme analysis, the larger context in which the legislation was written and operates and the intention of the legislature, which includes implied intention and the presumptions of legislative intent.[16] In the course of resolving an interpretation problem, an interpreter must also consider the relevance of a wide range of rules, principles and maxims.[17]

2) A Survey of the Rules

There is no standard way of classifying the rules of statutory interpretation.[18] Nor is there a standard way of ranking them—in order of importance, for example, or in order of application. At different periods, in different contexts, and in the minds of different judges, certain rules or approaches may dominate while others may be downplayed. The only constant in statutory interpretation is the text. In the survey that follows, the rules are presented under eight headings: a) rules about meaning; b) rules about application; c) types of analysis; d) rules based on drafting conventions; e) rules that introduce values into interpretation; f) rules that permit judges to change the text; g) rules governing the use of extrinsic aids; and h) rules dealing with overlap and conflict.

a) Rules About Meaning
i)   Under the *ordinary meaning rule*, it is presumed that the legislature intended to use language in its ordinary grammatical sense. In the absence of a reason to modify or reject it, the ordinary meaning of

---

16 See Elmer Driedger, *The Construction of Statutes*, 2d ed. (Toronto: Butterworths, 1983) at 106. For a pragmatic version of the modern principles, see R. Sullivan, *Sullivan and Driedger on the Construction of Statutes*, 4th ed. (Markham, ON: Butterworths, 2002) at 3.

17 For a complete and critical examination of Driedger's principle, see Stéphane Beaulac & Pierre-André Côté, "Driedger's 'Modern Principle' at the Supreme Court of Canada: Interpretation, Jusification, Legitimation" (2006) 40 Thémis 131–72.

18 As mentioned above, the "rules" of statutory interpretation operate as principles or guidelines rather than as binding rules.

a text should prevail.[19] It should prevail over strained or unnatural meanings. It should also prevail over technical meanings.

ii) When legislation deals with a technical subject and is addressed to a specialized audience familiar with that subject, ordinary meaning is likely to give way to any relevant *technical meaning* of words or expressions found in the text.[20]

iii) In reading bilingual legislation, interpreters must take both language versions into account and assign the same meaning to both. Under the *shared meaning rule*, it is presumed that the legislature intended the shared meaning, that is, the meaning that is found in both language versions, unless that meaning is unacceptable in light of other evidence of legislative intent.[21]

iv) In reading bijural legislation, interpreters must be aware of both legal systems—common law and civil law. Under the principle of complementarity, federal legislation is supplemented by civil law in Quebec and common law in the rest of Canada.[22]

v) Under the *original meaning rule*, interpreters should adopt the meaning the legislation had at the time it was first enacted. In practice, this rule permits a dynamic reading of a text in many circumstances.[23]

vi) In some circumstances the ordinary meaning of a text may be rejected in favour of an interpretation that better fits the context, or promotes the purpose, or avoids absurd consequences; it may be rejected in favour of an interpretation suggested by extrinsic evidence. However, under the *plausible meaning rule*, the interpretation adopted must be a (more or less) plausible reading of the legislative text. This rule imposes what is essentially a linguistic constraint: the interpretation adopted must be one that the language of the text can plausibly bear.[24]

b) Rules About Application

It is presumed that legislation does not apply extra-territorially; does not apply retroactively or interfere with vested rights; and (in most jurisdictions)[25] does not apply to the Crown or its agents.

---

19   For further discussion of this rule, see Chapter 3.
20   For further discussion, see Chapter 4.
21   For further discussion of bilingual interpretation, see Chapter 6.
22   For further discussion of bijural interpretation, see Chapter 5.
23   For further discussion of this rule, see Chapter 6.
24   For further discussion of plausibility, see Chapter 7..
25   British Columbia and Prince Edward Island are exceptions.

c) Types of Analysis

i) Legislation comes into being and is applied within a context. In *contextual analysis* interpreters read the text having regard to the Act as a whole, the larger legal context including international law, and the so-called external context, consisting of social, political, economic, and cultural conditions that are relevant to the conception or operation of the Act. An interpretation that is consistent with the context is preferred over one that is not.[26]

ii) Legislation is a distinct literary genre, like a poem or a play, with its own set of literary conventions. In *textual analysis* interpreters read the text in light of those conventions.[27]

iii) Legislation is enacted for a reason. In *purposive analysis* interpreters read the text in light of its purpose, including the purpose of the Act as a whole and of the particular provision to be interpreted. An interpretation that promotes the purpose is preferred over one that does not.[28]

iv) Legislation has no impact until it is applied. In *consequential analysis* interpreters consider the effects that are likely to flow from adopting a proposed interpretation. Interpretations that lead to beneficial consequences are presumed to be intended, while those that lead to irrational, unjust, or unacceptable consequences are rejected as absurd.[29]

d) Rules Based on Drafting Conventions

A number of the classic statutory interpretation rules are based on the linguistic and stylistic conventions used in drafting legislative texts. Conventions are practices used in communication among members of a linguistic community; they are ways of organizing and saying things that facilitate and enhance communication. To achieve successful communication, the conventions must be shared by both parties so that the meanings constructed by the speaker or writer when creating the text are similar to the meanings reconstructed by the listener or reader when interpreting the text.

First and foremost, of course, drafters observe the conventions of formal expository prose. They write grammatically correct sentences, using the lexicon and drawing on the common sense of the educated public. However, these standard features are qualified and supplement-

---

26 For further discussion of context, see Chapter 8.
27 For further discussion of textual analysis, see Chapter 9.
28 For further discussion of purposive analysis, see Chapter 10.
29 For further discussion of consequential analysis, see Chapter 11.

ed by special conventions associated with drafting. Anyone who reads legislation will soon be struck by its peculiarities—the presentation of sentences in numbered sections, for example, and the flat, repetitive style. Other examples include the prohibition on tautology and stylistic variation, and the repeated use of the same words or structures to signal particular meanings.[30] To express the idea of binding obligation, for example, the term "shall" is generally used.[31] To express the idea that something must be done in accordance with the regulations made under an Act, the word "prescribed" is used.

In principle, interpreters of legislation should make sure that the interpretation rules they rely on reflect the conventions that are actually used by drafters. However, in practice, this correspondence is simply assumed. The result is that drafters, to avoid miscommunication, are more or less forced to rely on the drafting conventions that are attributed to them by official interpreters like the courts.

Examples of rules based on drafting conventions, some of which have Latin names, include the following:

- the associated words rule (*noscitur a sociis*);
- the limited class rule (*ejusdem generis*);
- the no tautology rule;
- the consistent expression rule (same words, same meaning);
- the implied exclusion rule (*expressio unius est exclusio alterius*).[32]

e)   Rules That Introduce Values into Interpretation

Every act of interpretation is rooted in values, that is, assumptions about what is good, right, true, appropriate, desirable, and so on. Many values are shared by members of a community and operate at an intuitive, subliminal level. Although these values are crucial in communication, in drawing inferences about a speaker's intentions, they are normally taken for granted and are not acknowledged in the formal reasoning process.

However, some interpretation rules introduce values into interpretation in a formal and explicit way. The presumptions of legislative intent, for example, are designed to ensure that certain common law norms are appropriately respected in the drafting and interpretation of legislation. It is presumed that the legislature intends to comply with

---

30   In the context of statutory interpretation, tautology refers to any unnecessary or redundant language.

31   In some jurisdictions, as part of a movement encouraging the use of plainer language in legislation, "shall" is being supplanted by "must."

32   For further discussion of these rules, see Chapter 9.

constitutional and international law and with the values embodied in the *Charter*. It is presumed that the legislature does not intend to change the common law or to violate Aboriginal rights. It is presumed that the legislature intends to observe the principles of fairness and natural justice when dealing with the rights or interests of its subjects. Because the legislature is presumed to honour these norms, interpreters must take them into account and should be slow to attribute a meaning to legislation that would be inconsistent with them.[33]

The doctrine of strict and liberal construction offers another way for interpreters to introduce values into interpretation. Under this doctrine, legislation that interferes with individual rights and freedoms is strictly interpreted, while legislation that confers benefits on subjects or advances social welfare is interpreted liberally so as to advance the benevolent purpose of the legislation.[34]

f)   Rules That Permit Judges to Change the Text

Judges repeatedly assert that they have no jurisdiction to change or add words to a legislative text. That would amount to amending the text instead of interpreting it. On the other hand, legitimate interpretation often involves paraphrasing what the drafter has written or making explicit ideas left implicit in the text. The touchstone to distinguish interpretation from amendment is legislative intent. Interpretation uses different words to clarify what the legislature intended to say, while amendment changes what the legislature intended to say. Obviously the line between interpretation and amendment can be subtle and difficult to draw.[35]

There are no rules that permit judges to amend a text. However, to give effect to the true intent of the legislature, judges must sometimes adopt a strained interpretation or correct a legislative drafting error.

Courts distinguish between correcting a drafting error, which is permissible if the error is obvious and the intent is clear, and filling a gap in a legislative scheme, which (subject to some exceptions) is impermissible. Even if the gap is clearly inadvertant and failure to fill it will impair the effectiveness of the scheme, courts deny any jurisdiction to expand the scope of legislation so as to fill a gap.[36]

---

33   The presumptions of legislative intent are discussed in Chapter 12.
34   The doctrine of strict and liberal construction is discussed in Chapter 12.
35   This distinction is discussed in Chapter 7.
36   Drafting errors and gaps in the legislative scheme are discussed in Chapter 7.

g) Rules Governing the Use of Extrinsic Aids

Resolving interpretation issues can often be assisted by so-called extrinsic aids, including the following:

- Legislative source: consists of agreements that the legislation in question is intended to implement or of legislation (whether domestic or foreign) on which the legislation has been modeled in whole or in part.
- Legislative history: consists of material formally brought to the attention of the legislature during the legislative process, including Ministerial statements, committee reports, recorded debate and tabled background material.
- Legislative evolution: consists of the successive amendments and re-enactments a provision has undergone from its initial enactment to the time of application; note that subsequent evolution is not considered a legitimate aid.
- Expert opinion: consists of precedent, administrative opinion, scholarly legal publications as well as expert testimony.

The rules governing the admissibility and use of this material are complex and continue to evolve. In practice, the courts tend to accept whatever material is offered, provided it is relevant to the issue before the court and will not take the other party by surprise. However, courts sometimes treat such material as secondary, to be considered only if other aids to interpretation fail to resolve the ambiguity. And the weight accorded such material depends very much on the circumstances.[37]

h) Rules Dealing with Overlap and Conflict

A number of statutory interpretation rules are designed to deal with overlap between legislation and the common law or overlap between two or more legislative provisions. Under these rules, overlap is permitted in the absence of conflict, unless there is reason to believe that the legislature intended one or more of the provisions to be exhaustive.

In fact, it is common and perfectly acceptable for the same matter or set of facts to be governed by several different pieces of legislation and possibly by the common law as well. However, conflict between two or more applicable and legally binding rules is obviously unacceptable. To avoid such conflict, one or more of the rules may be "read down," that is, interpreted narrowly so as to avoid the problem. Otherwise, conflict is resolved through rules of paramountcy.

---

37   For further discussion of extrinsic aids, see Chapter 14.

Paramountcy rules establish hierarchies among different types of law based on their source, subject matter, or other criteria. Canadian paramountcy rules indicate that legislation is paramount over the common law, that federal legislation is paramount over provincial legislation, that human rights legislation is paramount over ordinary legislation, that statutes (usually) are paramount over regulations, and so on. When one law is paramount over the other, the paramount law applies to the exclusion of the other. In this way, the conflict is cured by ousting one of the overlapping laws.[38]

On occasion, the legislature wishes one of its enactments to displace the common law or to exclude the application of other legislation. It intends its enactment (which may be an entire Act or a single provision) to offer a complete and exclusive regulation of the matter dealt with. Such legislation is referred to as a "code."

---

38 Overlap, conflict, and the paramountcy rules are discussed in Chapter 15.

CHAPTER 3

ORDINARY MEANING

A. ORDINARY MEANING IS PRESUMED

The starting point of every interpretative exercise is determining the "ordinary meaning" of the text. This is what Driedger means when he says the words of an Act are to be read in their ordinary, grammatical sense. It is the meaning that spontaneously comes to the mind of a competent language user upon reading the text.

In practice, the ordinary meaning is presumed to be the meaning intended by the legislature and, in the absence of a reason to reject it, it should be adopted by the court. This presumption is the starting point of interpretation because it reflects the process by which readers respond to any text. As Frederick Bowers writes:

> Our first assumption in reading the words of any text is that the author is using them in their ordinary sense, and only if, after reading some way into the text, we have a growing suspicion that he is using words in a different from ordinary sense, with each succeeding word systematically tending in the same direction, do we retrace our steps and start to interpret those words anew.[1]

---

1 F. Bowers, *Linguistic Aspects of Legislative Expression* (Vancouver: University of British Columbia Press, 1989) at 116. See also s. 2 of the *Drafting Conventions of the Uniform Law Conference of Canada*, advising drafters that "[an] Act should be written simply, clearly and concisely, with the required degree of precision, and

In keeping with this basic principle, drafters normally rely on ordinary meaning when they draft legislation and readers are therefore entitled to do so as well.

The presumption in favour of ordinary meaning does not prevent interpreters from looking at the purpose of a provision or from invoking any of the so-called extrinsic aids to interpretation.[2] As emphasized by Driedger's modern principle, the ordinary meaning of a legislative text must be tested against the entire context, including the scheme and object of the Act and the intention of Parliament. Courts may and indeed should reject ordinary meaning when contextual factors suggest that some other meaning was intended. The point of the presumption is not to insist on literal interpretation, but rather to give weight to the ordinary meaning and to put the burden of justification on those who prefer an alternative interpretation.

B. WHAT IS MEANT BY ORDINARY MEANING

Many interpreters confuse the ordinary meaning of words with their dictionary meaning. The ordinary meaning of a word or a group of words is not their dictionary meaning, but the meaning that would be understood by a competent language user upon reading the words in their immediate context. Like any other text, a statute is read one sentence at a time. As each sentence is read, the reader forms an impression of its meaning based on the words and their arrangement within the sentence structure. This impression may be affected by the sentences coming immediately before or after. It may be affected as well by the reader's knowledge that he or she is reading a statute dealing with a particular subject and aimed at a particular purpose. These interactions of text, context, and purpose generally occur instantaneously and intuitively, without self-conscious analysis. They draw on the reader's knowledge of language and on the large body of facts, assumptions, values, and beliefs that are stored in the mind of individual

---

as much as possible in ordinary language," reproduced in R. Sullivan, *Sullivan and Driedger on the Construction of Statutes*, 4th ed. (Markham, ON: Butterworths, 2002) at 613–14.

2   Extrinsic aids consist of things outside the text to which a court may refer in attempting to determine legislative intent or the most appropriate interpretation. Examples are the legislative history of a provision, relevant international treaties, and published scholarly opinion. For further explanation and discussion, see Chapter 14.

readers and contribute to the "shared wisdom" or "common sense" of a community.[3]

The ordinary meaning of a word or group of words in a legislative text is thus the product of a complex interpretive process. It is the meaning that competent readers would attribute to the words, drawing on their personal knowledge and experience and taking into account as much of the surrounding text and situation as is needed to make sense of what is being said.

C. HOW ORDINARY MEANING IS ESTABLISHED

The ordinary meaning of a text is a fact and must be established as such, either through evidence or through judicial notice. Facts that are judicially noticed are taken as established without having to be proven through testimony or affidavit. To be judicially noticed, facts must be either (a) so well established that "everyone" knows them and takes them for granted or (b) non-controversial and readily established by reference to definitive sources.[4] The ordinary meaning of language is assumed to meet the first test, if not the second, and judicial notice is therefore the normal way of establishing it in statutory interpretation cases.

When judges take judicial notice of a fact, they are entitled to rely on their own knowledge of the fact in question. To establish ordinary meaning, they rely on their personal linguistic intuitions, which indicate (with more or less precision and clarity) what a given text says and implies. They may also seek assistance from other sources. Counsel arguing the case may make submissions based on their own intuitions and they may refer the court to reference works and other authorities such as dictionaries and encyclopedias. Finally, the judges themselves may carry out whatever private research they think is appropriate.

The reference tool relied on most often by judges and counsel is the dictionary. As noted above, dictionary meaning is not the same as ordinary meaning. Dictionary meaning is abstract; it indicates the range of meanings a word is capable of bearing having regard to many possible contexts in which it might be used. By contrast, ordinary meaning is rooted in the particular context in which the word appears. Because

---

3   For a discussion of common sense and the crucial role it plays in interpretation, see Chapter 2.

4   See *R. v. Find*, [2001] 1 S.C.R. 863 at para. 48. For a discussion of legislative facts, social facts, and judicial notice, see *R. v. Spence*, [2005] 3 S.C.R. 458.

each context is unique, it is impossible to "look up" the ordinary meaning of a word, still less a phrase or a sentence, in a dictionary or similar reference work. The only way to determine ordinary meaning is to read the text relying on the linguistic competence and knowledge that one brings to the text. This includes knowledge of shared linguistic conventions and of facts, assumptions, and values that contribute to the "common sense" of a community. It is this shared knowledge that makes "ordinary" meaning possible and justifies the courts' reliance on judicial notice.

Historically, courts have been unwilling to receive evidence concerning the ordinary meaning of a legislative text.[5] This unwillingness is open to criticism. When a court takes judicial notice of ordinary meaning, the assumptions and values on which its interpretation is grounded are generally not acknowledged and discussed, and therefore are not open to challenge. This situation is disturbing even when the relevant assumptions and values are shared by all members of the community, and it is unacceptable when they are not.

D. THE ROLE OF TEXTUAL ANALYSIS

As emphasized above, ordinary meaning is not dictionary meaning; but neither is it the meaning a court would attribute to a word or an expression after all the work of interpretation has been done. Rather, it is first-impression meaning, produced by interaction between a reader's knowledge of language and his or her knowledge of the world. This interaction is complex and difficult to describe, but a simple example will illustrate the sort of reasoning on which ordinary meaning formation relies. Consider the word "shower," which as a noun connotes a short rainfall, or by extension a copious short fall or discharge of any liquid, and by further extension a copious outburst or supply of anything (meteors, bullets, praise), and by still further extension a social gathering at which numerous gifts of a specified nature are bestowed on a single person (as in bridal shower or baby shower). "Shower" can also be a verb, with a corresponding range of connotations. In the sentences that follow, consider the reasoning process by which you determine which sense of "shower" is appropriate. Consider the range of

---

5   Such evidence could take the form of expert testimony by linguists, corpus-based linguistic analysis, or even opinion polls. For reliance on the latter in statutory interpretation, see C. Cunningham, J. Levi, and G. Green, "Plain Meaning and Hard Cases" (1994) 103 Yale L.J. 1561.

knowledge you draw on, where that knowledge came from, how it is relied on to fix the likely or possible meaning(s) of "shower," and how certain you are of your conclusion. For example,

1) Each morning, rain or shine, X showers.
2) When X's best friend became engaged, X gave her a shower.
3) The forecast today calls for showers.
4) According to the experts, we may soon experience an unusual shower.
5) Did X hear the shower?
6) X died in the shower.
7) X died in a shower.
8) Having exercised in the hot sun, X needed a shower.
9) Given all that, X needed a shower.

The range of possible denotations of "shower" is indicated by the dictionary, but our judgments about what "shower" means in these sentences, and how certain we are of its meaning, is rooted primarily in context — in what meanings are possible and plausible, given both the conventions of language and what we know of the world.

E. THE ROLE OF DICTIONARIES

Although the ordinary meaning of a text cannot be determined by looking up its words in a dictionary, dictionaries play an important role in statutory interpretation argument. They offer a useful starting point, one that is tangible and objective. An interpretation may seem less arbitrary if the private intuitions on which it is based are confirmed to some extent by a formal dictionary definition. It is common for judges to begin their analysis by noting the relevant definitions of the word or words to be interpreted. The impact of the immediate context is then taken into account by identifying particular features of the context that are relevant (such as punctuation, adjacent words, word order) and explaining how these features affect the meaning.[6]

In *R. v. McCraw*,[7] for example, the Supreme Court of Canada had to determine the meaning of "serious bodily harm" in section 264.1(1)(a) of the *Criminal Code* and whether on its true interpretation it included psychological harm. The *Code* itself defined "bodily harm" in section

---

6   For a survey of contextual features and how they are used to determine the meaning of a text, see Chapter 9.

7   *R. v. McCraw*, [1991] 3 S.C.R. 72.

267(2) as "any hurt or injury ... that interferes with the health or comfort of the complainant." *The Shorter Oxford English Dictionary* defined "serious" as "[w]eighty, important, grave; (of quantity or degree) considerable. b. Attended with danger; giving cause for anxiety." After reciting these definitions, Cory J. used them as an objective anchor for his own definition of "serious bodily harm":

> Giving the word "serious" its appropriate dictionary meaning, I would interpret "serious bodily harm" as being any hurt or injury that interferes in a grave or substantial way with the physical integrity or well-being of the complainant....[8]

On the basis of this definition, Cory J. then easily concluded that the words "serious bodily harm" were intended to encompass psychological harm.

Dictionaries also assist by establishing the limits of plausible interpretation. Although it is permissible to reject the ordinary meaning of a provision in favour of an interpretation that promotes the purpose or avoids unacceptable consequences, under the plausible meaning rule the interpretation that is adopted must normally be one that the words are capable of bearing.[9] By fixing the outer limits of meaning, dictionary definitions help to establish the range of plausible meanings a given word may bear. An interpretation that can be grounded in one of the meanings listed in a standard dictionary is more likely to be accepted as plausible than one that cannot.

In *R. v. Hasselwander*,[10] for example, the Supreme Court of Canada had to determine whether a semi-automatic machine gun that could be made fully automatic through minor adjustments was "capable of firing bullets in rapid succession" within the meaning of section 84(1)(c) of the *Criminal Code*. If so, it was a "prohibited weapon" as defined in the *Code*. The majority wrote:

> What then, should "capable" mean as it is used in the s. 84(1) definition of prohibited weapon? It should not be restricted to the narrow meaning of immediately capable... .
>
> The word "capable" as it is defined in the *Oxford English Dictionary* (2nd ed. 1989) includes an aspect of potential capability for conversion. It is defined as:

---

8   *Ibid.* at 80–81.
9   For an account of the plausible meaning rule, and the several qualifications and exceptions to the rule, See Chapter 7.
10 [1993] 2 S.C.R. 398.

3. Able or fit to receive and be affected by; open to, susceptible

...

5. Having the needful capacity, power, or fitness for (some specified purpose or activity).

From this, it is clear that "capable" does in fact include a potential for conversion. It is then fair and reasonable to interpret the definition of "prohibited weapon" as including a gun that has the potential to be readily converted to a fully automatic weapon.[11]

The dictionary is here used to establish that the interpretation preferred by the court is within the range of plausible meaning.

In interpreting bilingual legislation, interpreters rely on both French and English dictionaries. In looking up English words, it is common to consult British and American dictionaries. In looking up French words, it is common to consult dictionaries made in France. Canadian dictionaries are used less often by the courts.

F. HOW THE ORDINARY MEANING PRESUMPTION IS APPLIED

A good example of how the presumption in favour of ordinary meaning rule operates in statutory interpretation is found in the judgment of the Supreme Court of Canada in *Thomson v. Canada (Deputy Minister of Agriculture)*.[12] The *Canadian Security Intelligence Service Act* established a scheme for dealing with security matters in the federal public service. Under this scheme, a person denied security clearance by a deputy minister could complain to the Security Intelligence Review Committee and request a full investigation. Under section 52(2) of the Act, upon completion of the investigation, the committee had to provide the complainant and the deputy minister with "a report containing any recommendations that the Committee considers appropriate." The issue was whether the recommendations contained in such a report were binding on the deputy minister. In the view of both Cory J., who wrote for the majority, and L'Heureux-Dubé J., who wrote in dissent, the case turned on the meaning of the word "recommendations." Cory J. wrote:

---

11   *Ibid.* at 415–16.
12   [1992] 1 S.C.R. 385.

The simple term "recommendations" should be given its ordinary meaning. "Recommendations" ordinarily means the offering of advice and should not be taken to mean a binding decision.... .

There is nothing in either the section or the Act as a whole which indicates that the word "recommendations" should have anything other than its usual meaning.[13]

To justify his conclusion that "recommendations" ordinarily means non-binding advice, Cory J. relied on dictionaries and his own intuitions. To justify his conclusion that the ordinary meaning should be adopted, he looked at a full range of indications. He considered the purpose of the legislation. He looked at the provision to be interpreted in the context of the Act as a whole and of common law. He explored relevant policy considerations. He looked at case law interpreting the word "recommendation" in other contexts. Because he found nothing in this material sufficiently compelling to make him depart from the ordinary meaning, that meaning prevailed.

Although L'Heureux-Dubé J. arrived at a different conclusion, her approach was much the same. She too looked at context, at the scheme and purpose of the Act, at policy, and at relevant case law. In her view, the ordinary meaning of "recommendations" could not be adopted because it was inconsistent with the overall scheme of the Act and it violated a fundamental principle of natural justice—namely, a party cannot be a judge in his or her own case. To avoid these unacceptable results, she found it necessary to interpret "recommendations" as meaning "binding advice." Although this was a departure from the ordinary meaning, it was a well-motivated one and the result was not too implausible. Therefore it was not inconsistent with the ordinary meaning rule.[14]

G. THE LIMITS OF ORDINARY MEANING

When legislation is in the form of specific rules or directives expressed in concrete and precise language, the ordinary meaning is apt to be

---

13   *Ibid.* at 399–400.
14   Another way of understanding L'Heureux-Dubé's judgment is to rely on the doctrine of jurisdiction by necessary implication. Although the Act did not contain a provision that explicitly obliged the deputy minister to follow the recommendation, that obligation was necessary for the scheme to operate in a coherent and efficacious way. For an explanation of this doctrine, see *ATCO Gas & Pipelines Ltd. v. Alberta (Energy & Utilities Board)*, [2006] 1 S.C.R. 140 at paras. 51 and 73, discussed in Chapter 7, Section D.

clear and to leave little room for competing plausible interpretations. In such cases the presumption in favour of ordinary meaning is difficult to rebut. On the other hand, if the language used is vague or abstract or incorporates concepts that are complex or call for a judgment, ordinary meaning is not very helpful. Consider, for example, a provision conferring power on a board to establish prices that are "reasonable and fair" or that "do not unduly burden the consumer." The ordinary meaning of these terms is so vague that it is unlikely to prove helpful in resolving the question of whether a given price is within the power of the board.

Even when the language of a provision is relatively precise and clear, ordinary meaning may not take the courts very far. Suppose, for example, that under an amendment to the *Employment Insurance Act* insurance benefits became payable to any person over the age of twenty who is "unable to work." Suppose a court was asked to apply this provision to a single mother who is a high school drop-out and who at the age of twenty-two quit her job and returned to school full-time. Is she "unable to work" within the meaning of the Act? The answer to this question cannot turn on the meaning of the word "unable" or the phrase "unable to work." The court must rely on something other than word meaning to decide whether the reason for the applicant's inability to work is acceptable — that is, whether persons in the applicant's position were intended to have access to insurance benefits, or if that question is unanswerable, whether they should have access to such benefits.

Ordinary meaning cannot resolve this interpretation problem because the phrase "unable to work" could be used by competent language speakers to refer to persons in the applicant's position or, equally, to exclude them. There would be nothing strained or peculiar in saying, "Persons whose time is taken by other commitments are unable to work." Nor is there anything strained or imprecise in saying, "Persons who deliberately choose to give their time to other commitments are not unable to work." Which meaning is adopted depends on factors other than linguistic intuition. It depends on the court's understanding of the purposes of the legislation, relevant contextual considerations and its view of acceptable outcomes, whether or not these things are mentioned in the judgment.

H. THE PLAIN MEANING RULE

When judges are satisfied that the ordinary meaning of legislation is the meaning that should be adopted, they sometimes invoke the plain meaning rule. This rule originated in a passage from the judgment of Lord Tindal in the *Sussex Peerage* case. He wrote:

> If the words of the statute are in themselves precise and unambiguous, then no more can be necessary than to expound those words in their natural and ordinary sense. *The words themselves alone do, in such case, best declare the intention of the lawgiver.* But if any doubt arises from the terms employed by the legislature, it has always been held a safe means of collecting the intention, to call in aid the ground and cause of making the statute, and to have recourse to the preamble ... and "the mischiefs which [the makers of the Act] intended to redress."[15]

Lord Tindal says that resort to the purpose or the larger context is *unnecessary* if the meaning of the words is clear. In some formulations of the rule, resort to other factors is said to be *impermissible* if the meaning of the words is clear. On either approach, considerations like purpose, context, consequence, and the extrinsic aids to interpretation are taken into account only if the ordinary meaning is ambiguous. Furthermore, these considerations and aids may not be used to create the ambiguity in the first place. The provision to be interpreted must be looked at in isolation: if its meaning is clear, that's the end of it; if its meaning is doubtful, only then may interpretation begin.

In both formulations, the plain meaning rule draws a sharp distinction between reading a legislative text and interpreting it. It presupposes that meaning is a matter of fact, captured by the words of the text and therefore invariable from one reader to the next. When a court reads a text, it uses the rules of language to discover this pre-existing meaning, which is more or less clear. However, when a court interprets a text, it must choose from a range of possible meaning, relying on factors other than the meaning of the text. While this choice is constrained by the rules of interpretation, there is nonetheless a creative dimension in interpretation that is absent in mere reading. The plain meaning rule tells judges that they should engage in the more creative process of interpretation only if the less creative process of reading yields uncertain results.

There are problems with the plain meaning rule. In the first place, the distinction it draws between reading and interpretation is illusory. Establishing the ordinary meaning of a text is a creative, interpretive activity that involves more than the simple application of language rules. Considerations of purpose and consequence, as well as the common sense

---

15   (1844), 11 Cl. & Fin. 85 at 143, 8 E.R. 1034 at 1057. [Emphasis added.]

on which interpreters necessarily draw, have a role to play in every act of reading. And where the language is vague or complex, these non-linguistic factors are determinative, whether or not they are acknowledged.

Second, the plain meaning rule expressly requires courts to distinguish between clear or plain meaning on the one hand and ambiguous or doubtful meaning on the other. This distinction has no solid basis. Whether a text is more, or less, clear is a judgment that may vary widely from one person to the next. The courts do not say how clear a text must be, what qualities it must have, to be "plain." They do not reveal the tests or criteria they use to decide that one text is sufficiently clear while another is not. In many cases the labels "plain" and "not plain" appear to be either arbitrary or result driven.

The chief objection to the plain meaning rule, however, is that it imposes artificial constraints on interpretation. The rule developed at a time when legislation was drafted in a detailed, concrete style — in contrast to modern drafting, which prefers a more general style. The rule reflects a view of language and the communication of meaning that to modern sensibilities seems simplistic and dated. Above all, if the courts were to take the rule seriously, it would prevent them from carrying out their work of interpretation in a sensible and transparent way. If the task is to give effect to the intention of the legislature, interpreters need to look at all relevant evidence of that intention. There is no cogent reason to limit one's consideration to the words to be interpreted, isolated in their immediate context. An interpretation that takes into account the full context of legislation, its purpose, and its possible consequences, along with any relevant interpretive aids, is superior to one that looks to a limited context only and ignores, or purports to ignore, all other considerations.

As a rule of statutory interpretation, the plain meaning rule is unsatisfactory. However, it appears that in practice the courts rely on it less to constrain their own interpretive practice and more as a reason to discount the arguments of the other side. In other words, it functions primarily as a rhetorical strategy designed to discount the weight of the arguments that favour alternative interpretations. The court says, in effect, "Since my interpretation is dictated by the plain meaning, other considerations (which don't support my interpretation) should be ignored." But in most instances the court has not reached this conclusion simply through reading the text. In most instances the court has in fact considered many or all of the relevant contextual factors and concluded that there is nothing to rebut the presumption favouring ordinary meaning. Only then is this meaning labelled "plain" and other evidence of intent dismissed as unnecessary or inadmissible.

This rhetorical use of the plain meaning rule is illustrated by the *Thomson* case.[16] Cory J. began and ended his analysis of the ordinary meaning of "recommendations" by saying that nothing further was needed. Since the meaning of the word was clear and unambiguous, no other step need be taken to identify Parliament's intention.[17] The rules of language by themselves were sufficient to dispose of the appeal.[18] But in fact Cory J. was not content simply to identify the ordinary meaning of "recommendations" and to conclude that it was clear. He carried out purposive and contextual analyses and he addressed at least some of the arguments raised by the appellant. Had he not done so, his judgment would not have been persuasive.

In recent years, particularly in the United States, the plain meaning rule has become associated with a conservative attitude towards interpretation and a preference for minimizing state interference in the marketplace and in private life.[19] The "new textualists," as proponents of this school of interpretation are called, refuse to extend legislative provisions to any facts that are not plainly within the scope of the law maker's language. If the drafter has failed to produce a competent text, if the provision does not do all that the legislature apparently hoped for, the solution lies with the legislature and not with the courts.

This attitude towards interpretation and its connection to the plain meaning rule can be seen in the judgment of Lamer C.J. in *R. v. McIntosh*. The issue in the case was whether the defence of self-defence as set out in section 34(2) of the *Criminal Code* was available to an initial aggressor—a person who provoked the attack from which he then sought to defend himself. Both the majority and the dissenting judges agreed that there was nothing in the wording of the provision to preclude an initial aggressor from invoking it. In this sense, the provision plainly applied. However, both the majority and the dissenting judges also agreed that permitting an initial aggressor to have the benefit of section 34(2) would create a conflict with section 35 and would lead to absurd results. Faced with this dilemma, Lamer C.J. relied on the plain meaning rule. He wrote: "Section 34(2) is clear, and I fail to see how anyone could conclude that it is, on its face, ambiguous in any way. Therefore, taking s. 34(2) in isolation, it is clearly available to an in-

---

16   Above note 12.
17   *Ibid.* at 399.
18   *Ibid.* at 400.
19   In the United States, those who favour textualism also tend to favour an originalist approach to constitutional interpretation. See Antonin Scalia, *A Matter of Interpretation: Federal Courts and the Law* (Princeton: Princeton University Press, 1997).

itial aggressor."[20] Because the meaning was clear, the arguments of the Crown based on common law, legislative evolution, context, purpose, and consequences were dismissed as irrelevant.

In the *McIntosh* case, the majority relies on the plain meaning rule not simply to express its preference for the ordinary meaning of the provision in a rhetorically emphatic way but also to deny the Court's jurisdiction to correct errors, resolve conflicts, and avoid absurd consequences. Lamer C.J. wrote:

> Even though I agree with the Crown that the interpretation of s. 34(2) which makes it available to initial aggressors may be somewhat illogical in light of s. 35, and may lead to some absurdity, I do not believe that such considerations should lead this Court to narrow a statutory defence. Parliament, after all, has the right to legislate illogically …. And if Parliament is not satisfied with the judicial application of its illogical enactments, then Parliament may amend them accordingly.[21]

A similar attitude is found in many cases interpreting fiscal legislation. In these cases, the plain meaning rule is similar in effect to strict construction: the provision is applied as broadly as its ordinary meaning requires, but no further, regardless of other considerations suggesting that a broader application may have been intended.

---

20   *R. v. McIntosh*, [1995] 1 S.C.R. 686 at para. 19.

21   *Ibid.* at 697. Arguably the majority's use of the plain meaning rule is ill-conceived and misleading. The jurisdiction of courts to cure internal contradictions and avoid absurdity is well-established and should not be made to depend on an artificial and highly manipulable distinction between provisions that are ambiguous and those that are plain.

CHAPTER 4

TECHNICAL MEANING AND MEANINGS FIXED BY LAW

In statutory interpretation the expression "ordinary meaning" is used in two overlapping, but distinguishable senses. In the presumption in favour of ordinary meaning examined in chapter 3, "ordinary meaning" refers to the meaning that spontaneously comes to mind of an interpreter when he or she reads a legislative text. In this chapter, "ordinary meaning" refers to the popular, non-technical meaning of a word or expression contained in a legislative text.

Generally speaking, it is presumed that words should be given their ordinary, non-technical meaning subject to two exceptions. First, when words are defined in an Act or regulation, or the meaning of legislation is otherwise declared by the legislature, this meaning prevails over the ordinary meaning to the extent of any inconsistency. Second, some words or expressions have technical as well as ordinary meanings and on occasion it is the technical rather than the ordinary meaning that the law maker intends to use. Some technical meanings are legal, derived from common law, the *Civil Code* or from commercial usage.

A. PRESUMPTIONS APPLICABLE TO TECHNICAL MEANING

A technical meaning is a meaning understood by a group of speakers who are engaged in a specialized activity. Technical meanings are helpful because they permit insiders to refer to aspects of their activity in a precise and functional way. To other insiders, technical meanings are clear and present little interpretative challenge; they facilitate accurate, efficient communication. To outsiders, however, such meanings are obscure and unnatural.

Because technical meanings are not familiar to the average language user, they do not meet the test for judicial notice.[1] They must be proven through the testimony of expert witnesses. In *R. v. Perka*,[2] for example, to prove the meaning of "*Cannibis sativa* L" in the *Narcotic Control Act*, both the Crown and the defence relied on the testimony of professional botanists. Experts may also be relied on to establish that a term does not have a technical meaning within a given specialization.[3]

It is important to distinguish technical meanings from technical terms. Technical terms are words or expressions that have a technical meaning only. In such cases, the possibility of ambiguity between technical and ordinary meaning cannot arise and there is no need for a presumption. A court determines the meaning of technical terms by receiving relevant expert evidence and making a finding of fact.[4]

A more difficult problem arises when legislation contains words that have both a technical and an ordinary meaning. In such cases, a court must decide which meaning should prevail. In addition to the usual techniques for resolving ambiguity, such as purposive and consequential analysis, the courts draw on two special rules. The first is a presumption in favour of the ordinary, non-technical meaning of words. The other is a presumption in favour of the meaning that would be understood by the audience to which the legislation is addressed, given the matter dealt with. Where legislation is addressed to the public at large, these presumptions complement one another, but where legislation is addressed to a specialized audience they may be at odds.

The presumption in favour of ordinary, non-technical meaning was applied by the Supreme Court of Canada in *Pfizer Co. v. Deputy Minister of National Revenue (Customs & Excise)*.[5] The issue in the case was whether the drug imported by the appellant was a "derivative" of tetracycline within the meaning of the *Customs Tariff Act*. The ordinary meaning of "derivative," established through judicial notice, was "drugs

---

1   For an explanation of judicial notice, see Chapter 3.
2   [1984] 2 S.C.R. 232.
3   See, for example, *Canadian Pacific Ltd. v. Canada*, [1994] F.C.J. No. 933 (C.A.).
4   The ordinary or technical meaning of a word or expression is a matter of fact; whether that meaning has been adopted by the legislature is a matter of law.
5   [1977] 1 S.C.R. 456.

originating in or obtained from other drugs." The technical meaning of "derivative" was "drugs of the same group." This meaning was established through the expert testimony of academic and professional chemists. Even though the matter dealt with in the legislation was technical, and even though "derivative" was linked to "tetracycline," clearly a technical term, the court opted for the ordinary meaning. It relied on the presumption in favour of the ordinary, non-technical meaning of words. Pigeon J. wrote: "The rule that statutes are to be construed according to the meaning of the words in common language is quite firmly established and it is applicable to statutes dealing with technical or scientific matters, such as the *Patent Act*."[6]

Although the drug imported by the appellant belonged to the same group as tetracycline and was thus within the technical meaning of "derivative," because it had not been physically derived from that drug as required by the ordinary meaning, it was not a derivative within the meaning of the Act.

The other presumption relied on by courts in resolving ambiguity favours the meaning that would naturally occur to the audience whose activities are governed by the legislation. This principle is explained in a leading passage from the judgment of Lord Esher in *Unwin v. Hanson*:

> If the Act is directed to dealing with matters affecting everybody generally, the words used have the meaning attached to them in the common and ordinary use of language. If the Act is one passed with reference to a particular trade, business, or transaction, and words are used which everybody conversant with that trade, business, or transaction, knows and understands to have a particular meaning in it, then the words are to be construed as having that particular meaning, though it may differ from the common or ordinary meaning of the words.[7]

Along similar lines, Baron Pollock wrote in *Granfell v. Commissioners of Inland Revenue* that words are to be construed in their popular sense, "meaning, of course, by the words 'popular sense' that sense which people conversant with the subject matter with which the statute is dealing would attribute to it."[8] Relying on this "audience understanding" principle, the courts have adopted technical meanings for such common words as "sex" (in British Columbia's *Horse Racing*

---

6   *Ibid.* at 460.
7   [1891] 2 Q.B. 115 at 119 (C.A.).
8   (1876), 1 Ex. D. 242 at 248.

Act),[9] "earthenware" (in a tariff item under the *Customs Tariff Act*),[10] and "concentrators" (in Ontario's *Assessment Act*).[11]

It is not always clear whether legislation is addressed to a specialized audience or to the public at large. The federal *Income Tax Act*, for example, is addressed to everyone, but particular provisions of it target a specialized audience. In these circumstances, which presumption (if any) should apply? A further problem arises when a provision is addressed to several specialized audiences who would, or might, assign different technical meanings to a word or expression it contains. May each specialty rely on its own understanding of the provision? Or in the absence of a uniform technical meaning, must the ordinary meaning prevail? The courts are still grappling with these questions and no definitive answers can be given.[12]

However, it appears that the courts currently put less emphasis on the presumptions dealing with technical meaning than in the past. In dealing with all interpretation issues, the starting point is Driedger's modern principle, which emphasizes the total context of the words to be interpreted.[13] Also, regard must always be given to the other language version of the legislation, which may be capable of bearing only one meaning, whether technical or ordinary.[14]

B. LEGAL TERMINOLOGY

Legal meaning is a subcategory of technical meanings. It is the meaning that legal insiders assign to the special vocabulary of the law, the terms and expressions used to identify legal interests, responsibilities,

---

9   See *Re Witts and Attorney-General for British Columbia* (1982), 138 D.L.R. (3d) 555 (B.C.S.C.).

10 See *Olympia Floor and Wall Tile Co. v. Deputy Minister of National Revenue for Customs and Excise* (1983), 49 N.R. 66 (F.C.A.).

11 See *Township of Waters v. International Nickel Co. of Canada*, [1959] S.C.R. 585.

12 See, for example, *Northern and Central Gas Corp. v. Canada Ltd.*, [1985] F.C.J. No. 111 (T.D.), aff'd [1987] F.C.J. 1006 (C.A.); *Nova, an Alberta Corp. v. Canada*, [1987] F.C.J. No. 218 (T.D.), aff'd [1988] F.C.J. No. 636 (C.A.); and *Pacific Northern Gas Ltd. v. the Queen* (1990), 90 D.T.C. 6252 (F.C.T.D.), aff'd (1991), 91 D.T.C. 5287 (F.C.A.), all interpreting the word "pipeline" in the capital cost allowance provisions in schedule B of the federal *Income Tax Regulations*.

13 See *Barrie Public Utilities v. Canadian Cable Television Assn*, [2003] 1 S.C.R. 476.

14 See, for example *Azdo v. Canada (Minister of Employment and Immigration)*, [1980] 2 F.C. 645 (C.A.), where the English word "guardian" could have referred to a legal or a social relationship, but the French word "*tuteur*" could refer to a legal relationship only.

remedies, procedures, and the like. Legal meanings may originate in the common law or the *Civil Code*, in statute law, or in the practice of lawyers, judges, and accountants.

Legal terms are words or expressions that have a legal meaning only. As Finch J.A. noted in *McRae v. Canada (Attorney-General)*, for example, "subrogation" refers to a doctrine developed in law and equity and is a word used almost exclusively in a legal context.[15] However, as often as not, key vocabulary is ambiguous, that is, capable of bearing both a technical legal meaning and an ordinary, non-technical meaning. In *Citibank Canada v. Canada*,[16] for example, the court had to decide whether the arrangement under which the bank received certain shares amounted to a "form of guarantee" of the shares' value. The bank relied on the technical meaning of guarantee — a promise to cover another's debt — while the Minister relied on the ordinary meaning — a promise to cover any loss, regardless of how it arose. To resolve this ambiguity, Malone J.A. relied primarily on the purpose of the provision, but he also invoked the presumption in favour of audience meaning: "where legislation applies to a narrow commercial context, Parliament must make clear its intention to apply a meaning other than that ascribed by settled commercial law."[17]

As the *Citibank* case illustrates, the presumption in favour of ordinary meaning applies to terms that have both an ordinary and a technical legal meaning. However, a number of factors complicate the interpretation of such terms and favour the adoption of legal over ordinary meaning, even in statutes aimed at the general public. First, in dealing with legal terminology, it is not always easy to distinguish technical from ordinary meaning. Words like "property" or "spouse" or "agent" have meanings in ordinary language that are closely related to, although not necessarily identical to, their technical legal meanings. This can be a source of confusion. Courts sometimes resort to *Black's Law Dictionary* to determine the ordinary meaning of words and occasionally to the *Shorter Oxford English Dictionary* in search of legal meanings.

A second factor is the expertise of legal interpreters. Because lawyers and judges are themselves legal experts, they do not require the assistance of expert witnesses to establish the legal meaning of terms. Technical legal meanings are established through judicial notice. And because lawyers and judges are legal insiders, they naturally tend to draw on their technical vocabulary when reading legislation. Although

---

15   [1997] B.C.J. No. 2497 at paras. 19 and 25 (C.A.).
16   [2002] F.C.J. No. 496 (C.A.).
17   *Ibid.* at para 29.

the presumption in favour of ordinary meaning may point one way, familiarity with legal meanings leans the other way.

Finally, because the purpose of legislation is to set out the law applicable to a matter, reliance on legal meanings often seems appropriate. Suppose, for example, that legislation dealing with taxation refers to "property given on trust." In ordinary conversation, this expression might well be understood as describing a transfer of possession without benefit of a receipt or other security. But in the context of legislation, it is more plausible to treat it as a reference to the legal institution of trust.

For these reasons, the presumption in favour of ordinary meaning may be ignored or readily rebutted in the case of words with legal meanings. In *Hawboldt Hydraulics (Canada) Inc. (Bankrupt) v. M.N.R.,*[18] for example, the issue was whether the manufacture of replacement parts for use in a repair business could be considered "manufacturing … goods for sale" within the meaning of the *Income Tax Act Regulations*. Isaac C.J. wrote:

> We are invited by the modern rule of statutory interpretation to give those words their ordinary meaning. But we are dealing with a commercial statute and in commerce the words have a meaning that is well understood. In the common law, "for sale" does not mean "for use in a repair process." And I doubt that any informed commercial person would seriously say that the manufacture of parts to be used to repair a customer's defective equipment was a manufacture of those parts for sale.[19]

Although the ordinary understanding of "sale" was broad enough to apply to facts such as these, Isaac C.J. preferred a narrower technical meaning. He took judicial notice of the legal meaning of "sale" and found, again on the basis of judicial notice, that this meaning would be understood by the community of informed commercial persons who made up the audience for these provisions of the *Income Tax Act.*[20]

C. MEANINGS FIXED BY LAW

Meanings fixed by law are meanings assigned to words used in legislation by the law maker, by legal drafting convention, or by precedent.

---

18   (1994), 174 N.R. 6 (Fed. C.A.).

19   *Ibid.* at 17.

20   See also *Will-Kare Paving & Contracting Ltd. v. Canada*, [2000] 1 S.C.R. 915. But note the strong dissent of Binnie J.

When the meaning of a word is fixed by the legislature, usually in the form of statutory definitions, it prevails over other possible meanings. When the meaning is fixed by a court in interpreting the legislation, this interpretation is a precedent that may bind future courts. Meanings fixed by drafting convention are not legally binding, although repeated usage can give such conventions a strong presumptive force.

1) Statutory Definitions

Many statutes and regulations begin with a section or subsection, sometimes quite a long one, setting out definitions of words or expressions that are used in the Act. Definitions may also be found at the beginning of divisions or parts or of individual sections.[21] Because the legislature is sovereign, it may assign meanings to words that bear little or no relation to their ordinary meaning. It can deem "red" to mean blue, or "land" to include sky and ocean. But legislatures generally have little interest in major departures from conventional usage, and most definitions incorporate, clarify, or only slightly modify the ordinary meaning, or in some cases the technical meaning, of the defined words.

The federal *Interpretation Act*[22] sets out a number of rules applicable to statutory definitions. Similar rules apply to provincial and territorial legislation as well.

> **15.** (1) Definitions or rules of interpretation in an enactment apply to all the provisions of the enactment, including the provisions that contain those definitions or rules of interpretation.
>
> (2) Where an enactment contains an interpretation section or provision, it shall be read and construed
> (*a*) as being applicable only if a contrary intention does not appear; and
> (*b*) as being applicable to all other enactments relating to the same subject-matter unless a contrary intention.
>
> **16.** Where an enactment confers power to make regulations, expressions used in the regulations have the same respective meanings as in the enactment conferring the power.

a) Exhaustive versus Non-Exhaustive Definitions
It is important to distinguish between statutory definitions that are exhaustive and those that are non-exhaustive.

---

21 In older Acts and in some jurisdictions definitions are set out at the end of Acts, parts, or sections.
22 R.S.C. 1985, c. I-21.

Exhaustive definitions are usually introduced by the word "means," followed by a definition that comprises the sole meaning the word may bear throughout the statute and throughout any regulations made under it. For example:

In this section,

"fishing gear" means any tackle, netting, or other device designed or adapted to catch fish or marine mammals.

The meaning assigned to "fishing gear" by this definition may not be varied or supplemented by ordinary usage or by other convention.

Non-exhaustive definitions are usually introduced by the expression "includes," or "does not include," followed by a directive which adds to or subtracts from the ordinary (or technical) meaning of the defined term. For example:

In this Part,

"nets" includes crab pots and lobster traps but does not include gill nets.

This definition presupposes that the interpreter knows or will be able to determine the ordinary meaning of "nets" in this context. The point of the definition is not to fix the meaning of "nets" but to ensure that the provisions governing the use of nets apply equally to crab pots and lobster traps, which are functional equivalents, and do not apply to gill nets, which are meant to be governed by different rules.

Note that it is common in legislation to use the word to be defined as part of the definition. This does not indicate a lack of skill on the part of the drafter; it simply reflects the fact that statutory definitions have a different function than dictionary definitions.

b) Uses of Statutory Definitions

Statutory definitions are used for a variety of purposes. One important use is to create a short form of reference for lengthy or awkward expressions. For example:

In this Act,

"investigation" means an investigation carried out by the Competition Commissioner pursuant to s. 19 of the *Competition Act*;

"Minister" means the Minister of Employment and Immigration.

When readers come across the term "investigation" or "Minister" in the Act, they are expected to fill in the details identifying the relevant investigation or minister. This relieves drafters of the need to repeat these details each time a reference is made.

Statutory definitions are also used to narrow the usual scope of a word or expression. For example:

In this Part,

"grain" does not include rice or wild rice;

"employee" means an employee who is not a member of a union;

"will" means a will made before 1 January 1957.

These definitions rely on the ordinary (or technical) meanings of the defined terms, which are then narrowed by excluding things that might normally fall within the meaning (the first example) or by adding qualifying words or expressions that describe a subclass within the meaning (the next two examples).

Statutory definitions are also used to expand the usual scope of a word or expression. For example:

In this section,

"fish" includes shell fish, crustaceans, and marine mammals;

"sale" includes a promise to sell;

"will" means any writing signed by a person, whether witnessed or not, that contains a direction respecting the disposition of their property to take effect after their death.

In these examples, the statutory definition enlarges the ordinary (or technical) meaning of the defined terms by including things that might normally be thought to fall outside their denotation. The first two examples are non-exhaustive; the verb "includes" is used to extend the defined term to the things singled out for special mention—shell fish and some mammals, mere promises to sell—so that they are subject to the same rules as the things within the ordinary scope of the terms—standard types of fish, enforceable contracts of sale. In the third example, an exhaustive definition is used to expand the defined term to writings that are not ordinarily considered as wills—an insurance contract naming the beneficiary of life insurance, for example.

Finally, statutory definitions are used to resolve possible doubt or ambiguity:

In this Act,

"mammal" includes whales and other marine mammals;

"fruit" does not include tomatoes;

"counsel" means a member of the Law Society of Upper Canada;

"vehicle" means any car, cart, truck, motorcycle, tractor, or other convey-ance capable of travelling on roadways at a speed of 30 k.p.h. or more.

These definitions are meant to clarify rather than qualify the or-dinary (or technical) meaning of the defined terms—to create precise meanings and sharp distinctions, to resolve doubt. They are often in-cluded by drafters in an effort to anticipate and resolve the interpreta-tion issues that are likely to arise in the application of the legislation. Sometimes they are added to legislation by way of amendment in re-sponse to complaints or unsatisfactory judicial interpretations.

As these examples indicate, statutory definitions do not necessar-ily lighten the interpreter's load. Many simply add to the ordinary or technical meaning of the defined term, which must still be determined in the usual way. And since all consist of words, all require interpreta-tion, like any other legislative text. In the definition of "vehicle" set out above, for example, although the interpreter is given help in determin-ing the scope of the defined term, he or she must now tackle "convey-ance," "roadway," and "capable."

2) Interpretation Acts

Each Canadian jurisdiction has an Interpretation Act that applies to all the statute law enacted by that jurisdiction. Although there are some significant variations in the Acts of the different jurisdictions, in many respects they are similar or identical. All include provisions about enactment, the coming into force of legislation and its temporal and territorial application; all have a smattering of interpretation rules. In addition, there are rules for making appointments, conferring powers, tabling reports, taking oaths, computing time, and other miscellan-eous matters. And finally, there are numerous definitions of particular words—words like "Act", "bank", "contravene", "standard time" and "writing"—that might occur in legislation dealing with any subject. These definitions apply to the entire statute book of a jurisdiction, "un-less a contrary intention appears."

In the federal Act, for example, "person" is defined to include cor-porations, while "corporation" is defined to exclude partnerships, even partnerships that are considered separate legal entities under provin-cial law. This means that each time the word "person" is used in a fed-eral enactment, it is presumed to refer to individuals and corporations, but not to partnerships.

Most Interpretation Acts have definitions of the auxiliary verbs "may" and "shall" or "must."

3) Legislative Interpretation

As the sovereign law-making authority within a jurisdiction, the legislature can not only enact binding legislation but can also give binding instructions on how to interpret it. On occasion the legislature enacts declaratory provisions, which establish the true meaning of the law on a particular point. Declaratory provisions are usually enacted in response to judicial decisions that the legislature finds unacceptable and wishes to reverse. The distinctive feature of a declaratory provision is that it does not make new law, but rather it declares what the law has been all along, notwithstanding the court's defective interpretation.

In 1899, for example, Quebec's legislature enacted the following provision:

> 4. All ... grants of Crown lands made since the 1st June, 1884, are ... subject to the reserve for fishing purposes of three chains in depth.

Some years later a dispute arose concerning the extent of the Crown's rights under the three–chain reserve. In 1919 the legislature enacted a provision that substituted the words "in full ownership by the Crown" for the words "for fishing purposes." In *Quebec (Attorney General)* v. *Healey*,[23] the Supreme Court of Canada decided that this legislation was a declaration rather than an amendment; that is, it declared the true meaning of the 1899 provision rather than introducing new law. This meant that Crown grants since 1884 were subject to the full ownership reserve.

Although particular definition and application sections are common in legislation, binding directives concerning the proper interpretation of a previously enacted text are rare. Statutory interpretation is a judicially managed operation and courts are not always receptive to taking instruction from the legislature. For this reason, perhaps, courts generally are slow to label a provision declaratory of the law.

D. DRAFTING CONVENTIONS

Certain words or expressions are used by drafters repeatedly in legislation to signal particular meanings. For example, the use of the word

---

23 [1987] 1 S.C.R. 158.

"knowingly" in a regulatory offence indicates that *mens rea* is required for a conviction. The use of the word "deems" indicates that the legislature is declaring the law with respect to a matter even though the declaration may be contrary to common understanding. The use of the word "or" inclusively to mean "and/or" is another example, examined below. The effect of these conventions is to establish accepted legal meanings or usages for the relevant terms. Although these meanings are not binding, they are strongly presumed.

1) "May" and "Shall"

Section 11 of the federal *Interpretation Act* provides that the meaning of "may" is permissive and "shall" is imperative.[24] Other Interpretation Acts have similar provisions. Section 29 of B.C.'s *Interpretation Act* includes the following definitions:

> "**may**" is to be construed as permissive and empowering;

> "**must**" is to be construed as imperative;

> "**shall**" is to be construed as imperative.

Despite these definitions, both "may" and "shall" (or "must") are a recurring source of ambiguity. "May" is ambiguous because it may or may not be coupled with a duty; "shall" is ambiguous because it may be either mandatory or directory.

a) "May" Confers Powers: Discretionary versus Obligatory

"May" is generally used in legislation to confer a power or legal authority on a person or a body. The expression "X may do y" means that X has a legal authority to do y and cannot be found guilty of an offence or liable in damages for doing y. The interpretation question that arises in connection with "may" is not whether it is permissive, but whether the power it confers must be exercised. If the power is discretionary, the person or body on whom it is conferred must decide whether to exercise it and may choose not to. If it is obligatory, the recipient of the power must exercise it and has no choice but to do so. The difficulty lies in determining when a power is discretion and when it is obligatory.

The leading authority on this problem is the judgment of Lord Cairns in *Julius v. Lord Bishop of Oxford*.[25] In that case the court had to

---

24   In French, "*pouvoir*" is permissive and the use of the present indicative tense of verbs is imperative.

25   (1880), 5 App. Cas. 214 (H.L.).

interpret the phrase "it shall be lawful," which was used by drafters of the day as "may" now is used, to confer powers. Lord Cairns wrote:

> The words "shall be lawful" [or "may"] confer a faculty or power, and they do not of themselves do more than confer a faculty or power. But there may be something in the nature of the thing empowered to be done, something in the object for which it is to be done, something in the title of the person or persons for whose benefit the power is to be exercised, which may couple the power with a duty, and make it the duty of the person in whom the power is reposed, to exercise that power when called upon to do so.[26]

In the absence of evidence to the contrary, powers conferred by "may" are taken to be discretionary. But where failure to exercise the power would tend to defeat the purpose of the legislation, undermine the legislative scheme, create a contextual anomaly, or otherwise produce unacceptable consequences, the courts readily conclude that the power was meant to be exercised, that it is a power coupled with a duty. In particular, where exercising a power is made conditional on specific findings or the fulfilment of a set of conditions, the courts are apt to conclude that the power must be exercised once all the relevant findings are made or the conditions all are met.

In *Julius v. Lord Bishop of Oxford* Lord Cairns emphasizes that words of permission (such as "may") do not themselves impose obligation; the obligation (if any) arises from the context in which the words appear. Strictly speaking, then, it is incorrect, though commonplace, to say that "may" is sometimes imperative or that "may" sometimes means "shall." "May" is always permissive, in the sense that it always confers a power. The power is presumed to be discretionary unless something in the context obliges its recipient to exercise it.

The way in which the courts respond to "may" is well illustrated in the case law interpreting section 17(1) of the *Divorce Act*.

> 17(1) A court of competent jurisdiction *may* make an order varying, rescinding or suspending, prospectively or retroactively,
> (a) a support order ...
> ...
>
> (4) Before the court makes a variation order in respect of a child support order, the court shall satisfy itself that a change in circumstances as provided for in the applicable [child support] guidelines

---

26   *Ibid.* at 222–23.

has occurred since the making of the child support order or the last variation order made in respect of that order.

...

(6.1) A court making a variation order in respect of a child support order shall do so in accordance with the applicable [child support] guidelines.

The child support guidelines set out a formula to determine the amount each parent must contribute to the support of their child. Section 14 of the guidelines provides:

14. For the purposes of subsection 17(4) of the Act, any one of the following constitutes a change of circumstances:

...

(c) in the case of an order made before May 1, 1997, the coming into force of section 15.1 of the Act.

One of the issues that arose in interpreting section 17(1) of the Act was whether a court could refuse to vary a support order made before 1 May 1997 for which the coming into force of section 15.1 is deemed to constitute a change of circumstances. The following from the judgment of Laskin J.A. in *Bates v. Bates* sets out the reasoning of the Ontario Court of Appeal:

Provincial appellate courts have divided on this issue. The British Columbia Court of Appeal, in a series of cases beginning with Wang v. Wang ... has held that the courts maintain a discretion not to vary despite the coming into force of the Guidelines. ... The panel in Sherman came to the same view, as did the Alberta Court of Appeal in Laird v. Laird. ... But the Saskatchewan Court of Appeal reached the opposite conclusion in Dergousoff v. Dergousoff ..., rejecting the reasoning in Wang and holding that the court has no discretion, but must vary the previous order to comply with the Guidelines. The New Brunswick Court of Appeal in Parent v. Pelletier ... partly rejected the reasoning in Wang and Sherman, holding that, though the court had a narrow discretion not to apply the Guidelines, it could do so only where varying the existing order would cause significant harm to the child.[27]

...

Those who argue in favour of giving the court an overriding discretion to refuse to apply the Guidelines focus on the word "may" in

---

27   (2000), 49 O.R. (3d) 1 at para. 13 (C.A.).

s. 17(1) of the Act: "[a] court ... may make an order varying ... a support order." ... But the word "may" has to be read in its context.

In the context of the new child support regime under s. 17 of the *Divorce Act* and the Guidelines it seems to me "may" in s. 17(1) is not permissive but authorizing or empowering, in the sense that if the condition of the section is met—if there has been a change in circumstances—the court must vary the child support order to comply with the Guidelines. Because the mere coming into force of the Guidelines is a change in circumstances, on application, a court must vary a previous child support order to comply with the Guidelines....

...

This interpretation of the word "may" best reflects the purpose of the Guidelines. Their purpose is to promote uniformity, fairness, objectivity and efficiency in child support orders by curtailing, not expanding, judicial discretion.

...

Assuming the Guidelines reflect what Parliament considers "fair" support, adopting an interpretation of s. 17 of the *Divorce Act* that gives judges an open-ended discretion to refuse to apply the Guidelines does not promote fair support. Expanding the scope of judicial discretion to permit judges to refuse to apply the only objective standard of child support available, the Guidelines, will increase, not reduce, conflict and tension between spouses. Permitting judges to ignore the Guidelines will make the resolution of family disputes less efficient, not more efficient. And giving judges broad discretion to refuse to vary previous child support orders to comply with the Guidelines regime will not ensure that spouses and children in similar circumstances are treated consistently, because their treatment will differ depending on the wholly arbitrary factor of when separation or divorce took place.[28]

The courts have similarly divided over the proper interpretation of the dangerous offender provision in the *Criminal Code*,[29] which is in the following terms:

753. (1) The court *may* ... find the offender to be a dangerous offender if it is satisfied

(a) that the offence for which the offender has been convicted is a serious personal injury offence ... and the offender constitutes a

---

28   *Ibid.* at para. 24.

29   A list of the relevant cases is set out in *R. v. Johnson*, [2003] 2 S.C.R. 357 at para. 25.

threat to the life, safety or physical or mental well-being of other persons. ...

(b) that the offence for which the offender has been convicted is a serious personal injury offence ... and the offender, by his or her conduct in any sexual matter ... has shown a failure to control his or her sexual impulses and a likelihood of causing injury, pain or other evil to other persons through failure in the future to control his or her sexual impulses. [Emphasis added.]

Iacobucci and Arbour JJ. wrote:

> The language of s. 753(1) indicates that a sentencing judge retains a discretion whether to declare an offender dangerous who meets the criteria for that designation. As mentioned above, s. 753(1) provides that the court _may_ find an offender to be a dangerous offender if it is satisfied that the statutory criteria set out in paras. (*a*) or (*b*) are met. On its face, the word "may" denotes a discretion, while the word "shall" is commonly used to denote an obligation: see for example *R. v. Potvin*, [1989] 1 S.C.R. 525, at p. 549. Indeed, s. 11 of the *Interpretation Act*, R.S.C. 1985, c. I-21, requires "shall" to be construed as imperative and "may" to be construed as permissive. If Parliament had intended that an offender _must_ be designated dangerous if each of the statutory criteria have been satisfied, one would have expected Parliament to have used the word "shall" rather than "may."
>
> That said, cases do exist in which courts have found that the power conferred by "may" is coupled with a duty once all the conditions for the exercise of the power have been met.
>
> ...
>
> In this case, there is no indication of a duty to find an offender dangerous once the statutory criteria have been met. As we will elaborate, neither the purpose of the dangerous offenders regime, nor the principles of sentencing, nor the principles of statutory interpretation suggest that a sentencing judge must designate an offender dangerous if the statutory criteria in s. 753(1)(*a*) or (*b*) have been met.[30]

In examining the relevant purpose and principles, the court emphasized the need for judicial discretion in sentencing to ensure that the goals of punishment are appropriately balanced in each individual case. In these circumstances, there was no basis for coupling the power conferred by "may" with a duty.

---

30   *Ibid.* at paras. 16–18.

b) "Shall" Imposes Duties: Mandatory versus Directory

The word "shall" also causes problems of interpretation. "Shall" is used in legislation to impose a duty on persons or to indicate the binding character of conditions or rules.[31] "Shall" is always imperative in the sense that it always imposes binding duties or requirements. The interpretation question that arises in connection with "shall" is what are the consequences of breaching the binding duty or ignoring the binding requirement. Often the legislation itself stipulates what the consequences are, but when the legislation is silent, the courts or other interpreters must decide. If "shall" is judged to be mandatory, the result of the breach is total nullity. If "shall" is judged to be directory, the result is an irregularity that can be cured.[32]

The leading authority on the distinction between mandatory and directory "shall" is a passage from the judgment of the Privy Council in *Montreal Street Railway Co. v. Normandin*:

> The question whether provisions in a statute are directory or imperative [mandatory] has very frequently arisen in this country, but it has been said that no general rule can be laid down, and that in every case the object of the statute must be looked at… . When the provisions of a statute relate to the performance of a public duty and the case is such that to hold null and void acts done in neglect of this duty would work serious general inconvenience, or injustice to persons who have no control over those entrusted with the duty, and at the same time would not promote the main object of the Legislature, it has been the practice to hold such provisions to be directory only, the neglect of them, though punishable, not affecting the validity of the acts done.[33]

Generally, "shall" is taken to be mandatory unless this interpretation would lead to unacceptable consequences or is otherwise inappropriate. The *Montreal Street Railway* case describes one type of unacceptable consequence—causing gratuitous hardship to innocent parties or to the public at large. The courts look at other things as well, including context and purpose, to arrive at an appropriate result. As Iacobucci J. wrote in *British Columbia (Attorney General) v. Canada (Attorney General)*,

---

31   Note that "shall" is never used to indicate future action.

32   Courts sometimes use the word "imperative" as a synonym for "mandatory"; but this is confusing and misleading given the use of "imperative" to mean "binding" in the *Interpretation Act*.

33   [1917] A.C. 170 at 174–75 (P.C.).

[T]he court which decides what is mandatory, and what is directory, brings no special tools to bear upon the decision. The decision is informed by the usual process of statutory interpretation. But the process perhaps evokes a special concern for "inconvenient" effects, both public and private, which will emanate from the interpretive result.[34]

The courts also rely on a distinction between procedural requirements, which are likely to be considered directory, and substantive requirements, which are mandatory.

Judicial reasoning in response to "shall" is well illustrated by *Canada v. Harbour*,[35] in which the Federal Court of Appeal concluded that "shall" in section 55(4) of the *Unemployment Insurance Act* and in section 34(1) of the *Regulations* is directory rather than mandatory. The relevant parts of the Act provide:

54.(1) No person is entitled to any benefit for a week of unemployment ... until he makes a claim for benefit for that week in accordance with section 55.

55.(4) A claim for benefit for a week of unemployment in a benefit period *shall* be made within such time as is prescribed [by regulation]. [Emphasis added.]

Section 34(1) of the *Regulations* provided:

34.(1) ... a claim for benefit for a week of unemployment ... *shall* be made within three weeks of the week for which benefit is claimed. [Emphasis added.]

In this case the claimant filed his claim after the lapse of the three-week period. The issue was whether this late submission was an irregularity that could be cured or a nullity that could not.

The court first drew attention to the unfairness that might result from a mandatory reading of these requirements. In this case, for example, the claimant was late through no fault of his own but because the Unemployment Insurance Commission had failed to supply him with the necessary forms. The court also drew attention to the purpose of the requirements, distinguishing between substantive and procedural prerequisites to statutory rights. Because substantive prerequisites are conditions precedent to the right, they must be strictly complied with or the right does not arise. However, this reasoning does not apply to procedural requirements the purpose of which is merely to facili-

---

34   [1994] 2 S.C.R. 41 at 123–24.
35   (1986), 26 D.L.R. (4th) 96 (Fed. C.A.).

tate efficient administration of the statutory scheme. Finally, the court relied on context. It pointed out that treating these provisions as mandatory would be inconsistent with other provisions of the Act which clearly contemplated the possibility of payment for late claims. In light of these considerations, the court found that "shall" in this context was directory rather than mandatory and that the claimant's missed deadline could therefore be cured.

Not all procedural requirements are held to be directory. In *Doucet v. British Columbia (Adult Forensic Psychiatric Services, Director)*,[36] for example, Lambert J.A. concluded that the "shall" in section 672.47(1) of the *Criminal Code* is mandatory and a review board's untimely disposition under the section was therefore a nullity. The section reads as follows:

> 672.47 (1) Where a verdict of not criminally responsible on account of mental disorder or unfit to stand trial is rendered and the court makes no disposition in respect of an accused, the Review Board *shall*, as soon as is practicable but not later than forty-five days after the verdict was rendered, hold a hearing and make a disposition. [Emphasis added.]

The accused in the case received a verdict of not criminally responsible on account of mental disorder, but the review board did not hold a hearing and make a disposition until seventy-three days after the verdict was rendered. Lambert J.A. wrote:

> If s-s. 672.47(1) stood alone within the section, it might well be difficult to determine whether the provision was intended to be directory, involving no loss of jurisdiction if the time limit were not met, or mandatory, in the sense that failure to comply entails nullity and a loss of jurisdiction. But s-s. 672.47(1) does not stand alone. It is immediately followed by s-s. 672.47(2) which provides that the time limit of 45 days set by s-s. (1) may be extended by the Court to give a total period of up to 90 days under these conditions: "Where the court is satisfied that there are exceptional circumstances that warrant it." ... It is contrary to one of the most fundamental principles of statutory interpretation to suppose that Parliament enacted a totally ineffective provision. If the "shall" in s-s. 672.47(1) were directory only, and involved no loss of jurisdiction if the time limit was not met, then s-s. 672.47(2) would be wholly ineffective and unnecessary. In my opinion, against the background of s-s. 672.47(2), the imperative "shall" must be construed as being mandatory in the sense that

---

36   [2000] B.C.J. No. 586 (C.A.).

failure to comply entails nullity. If no extension is granted, then the Review Board's initial jurisdiction is lost after the lapse of 45 days from the date of the verdict.[37]

Lambert J.A. also pointed out that treating "shall" as directory would have reduced the protection available to an accused suffering from mental disorder, something Parliament would not have intended.

2) "And" and "Or"

a) Joint or Joint and Several "and"

Both "and" and "or" are inherently ambiguous. "And" is always conjunctive in the sense that it always signals the cumulation of the possibilities listed before and after the "and." However, "and" is ambiguous in that it may be joint or joint and several. In the case of a joint "and," every listed possibility must be included: both (a) and (b); all of (a), (b), and (c). In the case of a joint and several "and," all the possibilities may be, but need not be, included: (a) or (b) or both; (a) or (b) or (c), or any two, or all three. In other words, the joint and several "and" is equivalent to "and/or."[38]

Which meaning is appropriate depends on the context. When "and" is used before the final item in a list of powers, for example, it is joint and several:

> To carry out the purposes of this Act, the Governor in Council may make regulations respecting
> (a) the conditions on which licences may be issued;
> (b) the information and fees that firearm vendors may be required to furnish; and
> (c) the annual fees that firearm owners may be charged.

In this provision the Governor in Council is empowered to make regulations on any one or more of the listed subjects. However, notice what happens if "may" is replaced by "shall." If the Governor in Council is obliged to make regulations respecting (a) conditions (b) information *and* (c) fees, the joint and several "and" becomes joint.

b) Exclusive or Inclusive "or"

"Or" is always disjunctive in the sense that it always indicates that the things listed before and after the "or" are alternatives. However, "or"

---

37   *Ibid.* at para. 13.
38   In this book, "and/or" is equivalent to "and or or."

is ambiguous in that it may be inclusive or exclusive. In the case of an exclusive "or," the alternatives are mutually exclusive: (a) or (b), but not both; (a) or (b) or (c), but only one of them to the exclusion of the others. In the case of the inclusive "or," the alternatives may be cumulated: (a) or (b) or both; (a) or (b) or (c), or any two, or all three.

Like the joint and several "and," the inclusive "or" expresses the idea of "and/or." In the provision conferring powers on the Governor in Council set out above, "and" could be replaced by "or" without changing the meaning. In this context, joint and several "and" is equivalent to inclusive "or."

In legislation, "or" is presumed to be inclusive, but the presumption is rebutted when it is clear from the context that the listed alternatives are meant to be mutually exclusive. For example, many *Criminal Code* provisions say that a person who acts in a certain way is guilty of an indictable offence *and* is liable to imprisonment for a stipulated number of years *or* is guilty of an offence punishable on summary conviction. In this context, the "and" is joint: the person is both guilty of an offence and also liable to punishment. However, the presumption of inclusive "or" is rebutted. Since a given *Code* violation cannot be handled simultaneously through both indictable and summary conviction procedures, the "or" in this provision is exclusive: an indictable offence or a summary conviction offence, but not both.

In referring to the inclusive "or," courts sometimes say that the "or" is conjunctive or, worse still, that "or" means "and." "Or" is always disjunctive and, unless the drafter has made a mistake, "or" should never be understood to mean "and."

CHAPTER 5

BILINGUAL AND BIJURAL LEGISLATION

Canada is both a bilingual and a bijural country. The legislation of the Parliament of Canada and of some provincial legislatures is bilingual in that it is enacted in both French and English. And federal legislation is bijural in that it applies in both a civil law context in Quebec and a common law context in other provinces and the territories. In some respects, like many nations, Canada is becoming a multilingual, multijural nation. For example, international agreements currently exert an important influence on domestic law at both the federal and provincial levels. Legislation designed to implement such agreements may incorporate or adapt provisions that have been drafted in several languages and reflect diverse legal systems. To date, neither federal nor provincial legislation is enacted in any of the First Nations languages, nor does it take into account First Nations law. However, Aboriginal languages are used in the legislative assemblies of the territories. In Nunavut, elders participate in the legislative process, traditional knowledge is sometimes incorporated into legislation, and the statutes of Nunavut are published in Inuktituk as well as English and French. It is evident that First Nations' law will play a role in the government of Aboriginal peoples in the future. These developments contribute to a growing national and international law on the drafting and interpretation of multilingual, multicultural legal instruments.[1]

---

1   For further discussion of these issues, see Ruth Sullivan, "The Challenges of Interpreting Multilingual, Multijural Legislation" (2004) 29 Brook. J. Int'l L. 1–82.

A. BILINGUAL LEGISLATION

Under the Constitution of Canada, Acts of the Parliament of Canada and of the legislatures of Quebec, New Brunswick, and Manitoba must be printed and published in both French and English.[2] Under Ontario's *French Language Services Act*, the legislation of Ontario is now enacted in French as well as English.[3] The purpose of enacting bilingual legislation is to permit Canadians who are English or French speaking to have access to the law in their own language.

The Supreme Court of Canada has held that when legislation must be enacted in two languages, both language versions have equal status and are equally authoritative.[4] This is known as the equal authenticity rule, and it is well established. The implications of the rule, however, are open to debate. In the view of Michael Beaupré, who wrote extensively on the subject, equal authenticity means that by itself a single language version of a bilingual statute is incomplete; its true meaning can be determined only by reading and correctly interpreting both language versions.[5] It is also possible to argue that equal authenticity means that each reader can rely on the version of the statute written in his or her own language. While this understanding is more in keeping with the evident purpose of the rule, courts to date have preferred the former view: the meaning of a bilingual provision is the meaning of both versions read together. This approach is preferred because it ensures that the meaning of the provision is the same for both language groups. It would violate the principle of equality under the law if the same provision could be understood to say something different in English and in French.

Because the two versions of bilingual legislation are equally authentic, neither can be given paramountcy over the other. If the two versions do not appear to say the same thing, the discrepancy must be resolved in a way that does not automatically give priority to one or the other version. In the *Manitoba Language Reference*, for example, the Supreme Court of Canada struck down a provision of *An Act Re-*

---

2   See the *Constitution Act, 1867* (U.K.), 30 & 31 Vict., c. 3, s. 133; the *Manitoba Act, 1870* (U.K.), 33 Vict., c. 3, s. 23; the *Constitution Act, 1982*, being Schedule B to the *Canada Act 1982* (U.K.), 1982, c. 11, s. 18.

3   R.S.O. 1990, c. F.32, ss. 3–4.

4   See *Reference Re Language Rights Under s. 23 of Manitoba Act, 1870 and s. 133 of Constitution Act, 1867*, [1985] 1 S.C.R. 721 at 774–75 [*Manitoba Language Reference*]. Section 18 of the *Constitution Act, 1982* codifies the equal authenticity rule for federal and New Brunswick legislation.

5   See R.M. Beaupré, *Interpreting Bilingual Legislation*, 2d ed. (Toronto: Carswell, 1986).

specting the Operation of s. 23 of the Manitoba Act in Regards to Statutes,[6] which said that to resolve any conflict between the French and English versions of Manitoba legislation, the original enactment (invariably drafted in English) should prevail over the subsequent translation (invariably the French version). As the court explained, any mechanism that effectively attributes paramountcy to either version, however formulated, violates the equal authenticity rule. Discrepancies between the two versions can be resolved only by reading them both together and formulating a meaning that works for both.

1) Shared Meaning Rule

The primary tool used by the courts in reading bilingual legislation is the shared meaning rule.[7] Under this rule, the meaning that is shared by the French and English versions is presumed to be the meaning intended by the legislature. It may be the ordinary meaning of the words as read in one or both versions, or it may be a technical or restricted meaning. The fact that it is common to both versions is cogent evidence that it captures the intention of the legislature.

The operation of the shared meaning rule is illustrated in the majority judgment of the Supreme Court of Canada in *Chrysler Canada Ltd. v. Canada (Competition Tribunal)*.[8] The court there had to interpret a provision in the *Competition Tribunal Act* conferring jurisdiction on the Tribunal to hear applications for orders under Part VIII of the *Competition Act*. Section 8(1) provided:

> 8.(1) The Tribunal has jurisdiction to hear and determine all applications made under Part VIII of the *Competition Act* and any *matters relating thereto*.

> 8.(1) Le Tribunal entend les demandes qui lui sont présentées en application de la partie VIII de la *Loi sur la concurrence* de même que toute *question s'y rattachant*. [Emphasis added.]

At the end of a hearing, the Competition Tribunal made a Part VIII order against Chrysler with which the latter did not comply. The question

---

6   S.M. 1980, c. 3, s. 2.

7   This is a judge-made rule. In 1969, Parliament attempted to codify the rules for interpreting bilingual legislation in s. 8(2) of the *Official Languages Act*, R.S.C. 1970, c. O-2. The attempt was deemed unsuccessful and these provisions were repealed in 1988: see S.C. 1988, c. 38, s. 110. Courts still occasionally invoke the repealed statutory rules.

8   [1992] 2 S.C.R. 394 [*Chrysler*]. See also *R. v. Daoust*, [2004] 1 S.C.R. 217; *R. v. Mac*, [2002] 1 S.C.R. 856.

for the court was whether under this section the tribunal had jurisdiction to enforce its order by holding Chrysler in contempt for its failure to comply. The answer turned on the meaning of the phrase "matters relating thereto."

In English, "thereto" is ambiguous. It might refer to the act of hearing and determining applications, in which case the tribunal's jurisdiction would end as soon as the order applied for under Part VIII was granted or rejected. Enforcing such an order would not be a "matter relating to the hearing and determination of applications under Part VIII." Alternatively, "thereto" might refer to the applications themselves, in which case the tribunal's jurisdiction could extend to enforcement. Enforcing a Part VIII order could well be a "matter relating to applications under Part VIII." This ambiguity was resolved when the court looked at the French version. Gonthier J. wrote:

> In English, the phrase "any matters related thereto" may refer to the applications or to their hearing and determination .... In French, "s'y rattachant" can only refer to the noun "demandes," and not to the verb "entend," or otherwise the clause would read "toute question se rattachant aux auditions."[9]

The court resolved the ambiguity in English by adopting the meaning that corresponded to the clear French version. This was the sole meaning that was common to both languages. Since both must state the same law, and each has an equal claim to be an authoritative formulation of the law, the best interpretation was one grounded in a shared meaning.

2) Limits of Shared Meaning

Although it is sometimes heavily relied on, the presumption in favour of shared meaning is rebuttable. The courts must consider the provision in context, taking into account the legislative purpose, relevant policy concerns, and relevant external evidence. If the shared meaning is inappropriate in light of these factors, it may be rejected in favour of a more appropriate interpretation. The preferred interpretation may correspond to the English version only, to the French version only, or on rare occasions to neither.

In rejecting the shared meaning, the court effectively finds that one version was improperly drafted and therefore does not express the true meaning of the legislation as determined by the court. Such errors are not uncommon and are normally put down to "bad translation." In

---

9   *Chrysler, ibid.* at 409–10.

fact, neither version has the status of a translation and, at the federal level at least, legislation is simultaneously drafted in both languages rather than translated from one to the other. Despite the best efforts of the drafters, inadvertent discrepancies between the versions sometimes occur. Although the courts may refer to these discrepancies as translation errors, strictly speaking they are drafting errors.

Rejection of the shared meaning is illustrated in the judgment of the Supreme Court of Canada in *R. v. Cie Immobilière BCN*.[10] The issue in this case was whether a taxpayer, by extinguishing a lease and demolishing a building, had disposed of property or *a aliéné des biens* within section 1100(2) of the *Income Tax Act Regulations*. It provided:

> 1100.(2) Where ... all property of a prescribed class ... has been disposed of ... the taxpayer is hereby allowed a deduction ....

> 1100.(2) Lorsque ... tous les biens d'une catégorie ... ont été aliénés ... il est par les présentes accordé au contribuable une déduction.

The English expression "has been disposed of" is broad enough to include not only transfers of title but any means, legal or physical, by which a person is dispossessed of property. However, the French expression "*ont été aliénés*" is narrower and unlikely to extend to extinguishment or physical destruction. In the Federal Court of Appeal, Jackett C.J. applied the shared meaning rule. He wrote:

> Regardless of whether the expression "disposed of" would have been given some other sense if the English version were read alone, in my view, when the two versions are read together, "disposed of" must be read in the sole relevant sense that that expression has in common with the French word "*aliénés*". In my view, this sense would include any transfer, by way of sale, gift or otherwise, of legal title, to some other person but would not include the bringing about of the destruction or extinguishment of the property.[11]

In the Supreme Court of Canada the shared meaning was rejected because it did not express the true meaning of the provision. Pratte J. wrote:

> [The shared meaning rule] should not be given such an absolute effect that it would necessarily override all other canons of construction. In my view ... the narrower meaning of one of the two versions should not be preferred where such meaning would clearly run con-

---

10   [1979] 1 S.C.R. 865.
11   [1976] 2 F.C. 433 at 436.

trary to the intent of the legislation and would consequently tend to defeat rather than assist the attainment of its objects.[12]

The intent of the legislation was established by the court primarily through contextual analysis. Pratte J. examined the use of the words "disposition" and "dispose of" in related provisions of the Act and the *Regulations*. He noted that these words were uniformly used in English in the broadest possible sense. He also noted that in the French version of these provisions the drafter generally used the words "*disposition*" and "*disposer*," which were broad in scope, rather than the narrower "*aliénation*" and "*aliéner*." He concluded:

> A detailed examination of these provisions has convinced me that the expressions "disposition", "proceeds of disposition" and "disposed of" must, throughout, receive the same meaning respectively, regardless of the fact that in a limited number of cases the French text taken in isolation would convey a more restrictive meaning. Such a narrow meaning cannot however be held to control the much broader meaning of the English expressions, especially when it is apparent that such was not the intent.[13]

On the face of it, the court violated the equal status rule by relying exclusively on the English version of the provision and adopting a meaning that was inconsistent with the French version. In reality, however, the court did not reject the French version but rather corrected it so that it would reflect the legislature's true intent. Having been appropriately interpreted, the French version now said exactly what the English version said.

3) Absence of Shared Meaning

Sometimes the English version of a provision differs so greatly from the French version that there is no shared meaning. This occurs, for example, when a word or an expression appearing in one version has no counterpart in the other. In such cases, since the versions have equal status, there is no basis for preferring one to the other. The court must rely on the usual techniques and aids to determine the most appropriate or intended meaning.

This problem arose in *Slaight Communications Inc. v. Davidson*,[14] where the Supreme Court of Canada had to consider the extent of the remedial powers conferred on adjudicators by section 61.5(9) of the

---

12   Above note 10 at 871–72.
13   *Ibid.* at 874–75.
14   [1989] 1 S.C.R. 1038.

Canada Labour Code. Under the section an adjudicator could order an employer to (a) pay compensation, (b) reinstate an employee, or (c) "do any other like thing that it is equitable to require"/"*faire toute autre chose qu'il juge équitable d'ordonner.*" In the court's analysis, the presence of the word "like" in the English version suggested that any orders made under paragraph (c) would have to be similar to compensation or reinstatement orders, while the absence of a comparable word in French suggested that no such limitation was intended. In deciding which interpretation to adopt, the court relied on a variety of factors. Lamer J. wrote:

> [The meaning found in the French version] is much more consistent with the general scheme of the *Code,* and in particular with the purpose of Division V.7, which is to give non-unionized employees a means of challenging a dismissal they feel to be unjust and at the same time to equip the adjudicator with the powers necessary to remedy the consequences of such a dismissal. Section 61.5 is clearly a remedial provision and must accordingly be given a broad interpretation .... I believe that the legislator intended to vest in the adjudicator powers that would be sufficiently wide and flexible for him to adequately perform the duties entrusted to him .... I therefore consider that the meaning to be given to both versions is what clearly appears on the face of the French version.[15]

The court here repairs the faulty English version by notionally striking out the word "like." The English version now says exactly the same thing as the French version.

4) Methodology

The methodology for interpreting bilingual legislation was considered by the Supreme Court of Canada in *R. v. Daoust.* Speaking for the court, Bastarache J. wrote:

> I would ... draw attention to the two-step analysis proposed by Professor Côté in *The Interpretation of Legislation in Canada* (3d ed. 2000), at p. 324, for resolving discordances resulting from divergences between the two versions of a statute:
>
> > Unless otherwise provided, differences between two official versions of the same enactment are reconciled by educing the meaning common to both. Should this prove to be impossible, or if the common meaning seems incompatible

---

15   *Ibid.* at 1072.

with the intention of the legislature as indicated by the ordinary rules of interpretation, the meaning arrived at by the ordinary rules should be retained.

There is, therefore, a specific procedure to be followed when interpreting bilingual statutes.[16]

Bastarache J. then set out in some detail the steps to be followed. The first step is to compare the two versions to determine whether they say the same or different things. If they say different things, there are several possibilities.

1) There may be ambiguity in one version but not the other. In this case, the shared meaning is the meaning of the plain version that is also found in the ambiguous version. (This possibility is illustrated by the *Chrysler* case, discussed above.)
2) If neither version is ambiguous or they both are, and one meaning is broader than the other, the shared meaning is normally the narrower version. (This possibility is illustrated by *Daoust* itself.)
3) If the two versions are irreconcilable, there is no shared meaning and the interpreter must rely on other principles. (This possibility is illustrated by the *Slaight Communications* case, discussed above.)

"The second step," Bastarache J. explains, " is to determine whether the common or dominant meaning is, according to the ordinary rules of statutory interpretation, consistent with Parliament's intent: Côté, *supra*, at pp. 328–329."[17] (This step led to the rejection of the shared meaning in *R. v. Cie Immobilière BCN*, discussed above.)

In *Daoust*, the court was concerned with section 462.31 of the *Criminal Code*. Compare the English and French versions:

462.31 (1) Every one commits an offence who uses, transfers the possession of, sends or delivers to any person or place, transports, transmits, alters, disposes of *or otherwise deals with*, in any manner and by any means, any property or any proceeds of any property with intent to conceal or convert that property or those proceeds … [Emphasis added.]	462.31 (1) Est coupable d'une infraction quiconque—de quelque façon que ce soit—utilise, enlève, envoie, livre à une personne ou à un endroit, transporte, modifie ou aliène des biens ou leurs produits—ou en transfère la possession—dans l'intention de les cacher ou de les convertir …

---

16   [2004] 1 S.C.R. 217 at paras. 26–27.
17   *Ibid.* at para. 30.

The italicized words are missing in the French version, creating a significant discrepancy between the two versions. Bastarache J. rightly points out that neither version is ambiguous and the two versions are "obviously irreconcilable."[18] Arguably, in such a case there is no shared meaning and resort must be had to other principles of interpretation—see possibility 3 above. Yet, because the English version is broader in scope than the French version, the court relied on possibility 2. Bastarache J. wrote:

> As I have already mentioned, when one of the two versions of a provision of a bilingual statute has a broader meaning than the other, the common meaning of the two versions is normally the one that is derived from the version with a more restricted meaning. This rule is especially relevant in a criminal context, as the accused may, depending on which version he or she reads, form a different conception of the elements of the offence in question[19]

Bastarache J. appropriately invokes rule of law considerations here. Although the strict construction of penal legislation is most often treated as a presumption of last resort, in a case such as this, giving effect to the broader version, even if it proved to be the one intended by Parliament, would seriously mislead anyone relying on the narrower French version. Such a person would not have fair notice of the law.

B. BIJURAL LEGISLATION

Bijural or multijural legislation is legislation drafted to apply to jurisdictions that have different legal systems. In Canada, under sections 91–92 of the *Constitution Act, 1867* Parliament enacts legislation for the whole of Canada, while the provinces enact legislation that applies within their own territories. One of the subjects assigned to the provinces is property and civil rights, an area of law that is based on the *Civil Code* in Quebec and on the common law in the rest of Canada. Therefore, when Parliament legislates over matters like taxation, bankruptcy, or banking, which impinge on property and civil rights in the province, it must adjust its legislation so as to harmonize with the civil law regime of Quebec and the common law regime prevailing elsewhere in Canada.

18　*Ibid.* at para. 34.
19　*Ibid.* at para. 35.

So long as Parliament does not exceed its powers under section 91, it may enact a uniform law for the whole of Canada, drawing on whatever legal sources seem appropriate, including not only common and civil law but also Aboriginal law, foreign law, or international law. In practice, however, most federal legislation draws on common law sources. This makes for relatively easy harmonization in the common law provinces, but historically it has created significant problems for Quebec, not to mention Aboriginal peoples.

The drafting of federal legislation in Canada is complicated by the fact that it must be bilingual as well as bijural. There is a natural tendency to associate the French version of federal legislation with the civil law system and the English version with the common law. But as a matter of constitutional law, both versions must address both legal systems. The French version is as applicable in British Columbia as it is in Quebec and must speak to francophones throughout common law Canada as well as those in civil law Quebec. Similarly, the English version applies in Quebec and must be comprehensible to anglophone Quebeckers whose private law matters are governed by the *Civil Code*. For this reason, interpreters cannot assume that the French version incorporates or refers to the civil law while the English version does the same with common law. A more nuanced approach is required.

1) Recent Reforms

On 1 January 1994 the *Civil Code of Lower Canada*, which had been in force in Quebec since 1866, was replaced by the *Civil Code of Québec*. The new code extensively changed Quebec's law, introducing new concepts and institutions and new legal terminology. These changes created significant disharmony with existing federal legislation and led to the establishment of a *Civil Code* section within the Department of Justice whose mandate was to develop the tools necessary to harmonize existing and future federal legislation with the private law of Quebec. To carry out this mandate the section commissioned research into various aspects of bijuralism, devised a set of drafting techniques suited to bilingual, bijural legislation, and formulated a set of bijural interpretation principles. It also undertook a review of the federal statute book to identify existing harmonization problems and propose solutions. This work led to enactment of a series of Federal Law–Civil Law Harmonization Acts, the first of which amended the federal *Interpretation Act* by introducing rules for the interpretation of bijural legislation. It also led to the development and publication of so-called bijural terminology records.[20] These describe the bijuralism problems that have been detected in a federal statute, summarize the research carried out in response, and explain the reasoning behind each solution adopted.

2) Drafting Conventions

In developing appropriate techniques for drafting bilingual bijural legislation, there are two competing concerns: (1) communicating directly to francophones in Quebec, anglophones in Quebec, francophones outside Quebec, and anglophones outside Quebec; and (2) producing texts that are readable and concise. The first concern is most easily met by lengthy complex provisions, while the second calls for short, simple ones. Table 5.1 sets out the techniques developed by the Department of Justice in an effort to meet both concerns.

Table 5.1 Drafting Bilingual Bijural Legislation

Technique	English Illustration/Explanation	French Illustration/Explanation
Bijural term	contract	contrat
	The text uses a single term "contract" that works for both legal systems.	The text uses a single term "contrat" for both legal systems.
	"Contract" is the correct English term for both civil law and common law contracts. It should be understood to refer to civil law contracts in Quebec and common law contracts elsewhere.	"Contrat" is the correct French term for both civil law and common law contracts. It should be understood to refer to civil law contracts in Quebec and common law contracts elsewhere.
Doublet	real property or immovables	immeubles ou biens réel
	The text uses a phrase that includes two legal terms, one common law and one civil law.	The text uses a phrase that includes two legal terms, one civil law and once common law.
	"Real property" is the English term for the common law concept whereas "immovables" is the English term for the analogous civil law concept. In the English version, the common law term comes first.	"Immeubles" is the French term for the civil law concept whereas "biens réel" is the French term for the analogous common law concept. In the French version, the civil law term comes first.

---

20   See, for example, Department of Justice, *Bijural Terminology Records* (Ottawa: Department of Justice, 2001). These records are also available online: www.justice.gc.ca/en/ps/bj/harm/liste.html.

Technique	English Illustration/Explanation	French Illustration/Explanation
Partial doublet	mortgage or hypotheque	hypothèque
	In English, "mortgage" refers to a common law security interest in real property whereas "hypotheque" refers to an analogous civil law security interest in immovables or movables.	In French, a single expression "hypothèque" is used to refer to the civil law security interest and the analogous common law interest.
Paragraphed doublet	(a) in the Province of Quebec, … (b) in any other province, …	(a) dans la province de Québec, … (b) dans les autres provinces, …
	This technique is used to define words, giving them different meaning in common law and civil law provinces.	This technique can also be used to set out different rules for different provinces.
Generic language	accept security for payment	accepter des garanties pour le paiement
	This language is broad and generic enough to encompass both common law and civil law ways of securing payment as these may exist from time to time.	Using a single generic expression is less cumbersome than doublets and eliminates the need to amend federal law when provincial law changes

To avoid mistakes, interpreters must be familiar with these techniques; they must understand their purpose and how they work. This necessity is clearly demonstrated in *Schreiber v. Canada (Attorney General)*.[21] In 1999, Schreiber was jailed in Ontario pursuant to a request by Germany to arrest and detain him for the purpose of extradition. Schreiber later brought a civil action against Germany and Canada, seeking damages for the loss of liberty and reputation caused by his detention. Germany moved for dismissal of this action on the ground of sovereign immunity, but Schreiber maintained that his action was within an exception to this immunity set out in section 6 of the *Sovereign Immunity Act*.

Before harmonization:

6. A foreign state is not immune from the jurisdiction of a court in any proceedings that relate to (a) any death or *personal injury*, or (b) any damage to or loss of property that occurs in Canada.	6. L'État étranger ne bénéficie pas de l'immunité de juridiction dans les actions découlant: a) des décès ou *dommages corporels* survenus au Canada; b) des dommages matériels survenus au Canada.

---

21   *Schreiber v. Canada (Attorney General)*, [2002] 3 S.C.R. 269.

After harmonization:

6. A foreign state is not immune from the jurisdiction of a court in any proceedings that relate to	6. L'État étranger ne bénéficie pas de l'immunité de juridiction dans les actions découlant :
(a) any death or *personal or bodily* injury, or	a) des décès ou *dommages corporels* survenus au Canada;
(b) any damage to or loss of property that occurs in Canada.	b) des dommages aux biens ou perte deceux-ci survenus au Canada.
[Emphasis added.]	[Emphasis added.]

The drafting technique used here to harmonize the federal Act with Quebec's civil law is the partial doublet. In English, "personal injury" is the common law term whereas "bodily injury" is the civil law term. In French, "dommages corporels" covers both common law and civil law concepts.

Before the Supreme Court of Canada, counsel for Schreiber argued that in keeping with the presumption against tautology, distinct meaning must be given to the terms "person injury" and "bodily injury." The court rightly rejected this argument. LeBel J. Wrote:

> The appellant submits that "personal injury" must mean something more than just "bodily injury", otherwise its inclusion in the English version of the *Harmonization Act* would be redundant. In particular, it must mean injury to such interests as mental integrity, dignity and reputation....
>
> I am of the view that the *Harmonization Act* amendment does not help the appellant's position. Instead, I agree with the proposition ... that that the term "bodily injury" was added to s. 6(*a*) to clarify the limited scope of the exception for the anglophone civil law audience by using wording that better reflects the civil law tradition.[22]

The court also relied on the *Bijural Terminology Records* prepared by the department which expressly indicated that the words "or bodily" were added to the English version of the text to reflect the relatively narrow scope of damages available in civil law.

The *Schreiber* case affirms that the Federal Law–Civil Law Harmonization Acts operate primarily as statute revisions, in that they are designed to improve the form of federal legislation without changing the substance of the law.[23]

---

22 *Ibid.* at paras. 68–69.
23 *Ibid.* at paras. 69 and ff.

3) Interpretation Rules

The *Federal Law–Civil Law Harmonization Act, No. 1* added the following provisions to the federal *Interpretation Act.*

8.1. Both the common law and the civil law are equally authoritative and recognized sources of the law of property and civil rights in Canada, and unless otherwise provided by law, if in interpreting an enactment it is necessary to refer to a province's rules, principles or concepts forming part of the law of property and civil rights, reference must be made to the rules, principles or concepts in force in the province at the time the enactment is being applied.	8.1. Le droit civil et la common law font pareillement autorité et sont tous deux sources de droit en matière de propriété et de droits civils au Canada et, s'il est nécessaire de recourir à des règles, principes ou notions appartenant au domaine de la propriété et des droits civils en vue d'assurer l'application d'un texte dans une province, il faut, sauf règle de droit s'y opposant, avoir recours aux règles, principes et notions en vigueur dans cette province au moment de l'application du texte.
8.2. Unless otherwise provided by law, when an enactment contains both civil law and common law terminology, or terminology that has a different meaning in the civil law and the common law, the civil law terminology or meaning is to be adopted in the Province of Quebec and the common law terminology or meaning is to be adopted in other provinces.	8.2. Sauf règle de droit s'y opposant, est entendu dans un sens compatible avec le système juridique de la province d'application le texte qui emploie à la fois des termes propres au droit civil de la province de Québec et des termes propres à la common law des autres provinces, ou qui emploie des termes qui ont un sens différent dans l'un et l'autre de ces systèmes.

Section 8.1 begins by affirming the principle that common law and civil law are equally legitimate sources of law in Canada. Thus, in interpreting federal legislation it must not be assumed that the rules, concepts, and principles found in the legislation are necessarily derived from the common law. The Supreme Court of Canada has pointed out that the *Canadian Shipping Act* is based on English admiralty law, which is "an amalgam of principles deriving in large part from both the common law and the civilian tradition."[24] Similarly, the protection afforded the moral rights of an author under Canada's *Copyright Act* derives from the civil law.[25] Civil law concepts and principles may also enter federal law through the implementation of international treaties.

---

24   See *Orden Estate v. Grail*, [1998] 3 S.C.R. 437 at para. 71.
25   See *Théberge v. Galerie d'Art du Petit Champlain*, [2002] 2 S.C.R. 336.

The second part of section 8.1 is generally understood to embody, or at least to presuppose, what has become known as the principle of complementarity. In exercising its jurisdiction under section 91 of the *Constitution Act, 1867*, Parliament may legislate different rules for different regions of the country or it may impose a uniform regime.[26] As mentioned above, so long as it does not exceed its jurisdiction, it may impose common law–based rules on Quebec and civil law–based rules on the rest of Canada. Alternatively, it may try to establish a complete set of rules that draws from or is more or less independent of both systems. However, in the area of property and civil rights federal legislation necessarily depends on provincial law. It would be impossible to regulate bankruptcy or implement the policies of the *Income Tax Act* without acknowledging and working with provincial laws governing the creation of property interests, the formation and enforcement of contracts, the requirements for a valid gift and the like. The principle of complementarity addresses this reality. More particularly, it addresses two common problems. First, in formulating federal rules that relate to property or civil rights, Parliament may use undefined legal language. Second, in the application of federal legislation, questions may arise concerning property or civil rights in the province which Parliament has failed to address. In either case, under the principle of complementarity, the incomplete federal legislation must be supplemented by resort to the relevant provincial law.

Section 8.2 addresses the problem of interpreting bijural legal terminology. As explained above, to facilitate harmonization with provincial law, federal drafters may use single terms, doublets, or generic language in each language version. If they use doublets, the text will contain both civil law and common law terminology. If they use single terms or generic language, the text will contain terminology that has a different meaning in the civil law and the common law. In either case under section 8.2, unless otherwise provided by law, the terminology must be understood to refer to civil law concepts in Quebec and common law concepts elsewhere in Canada.

The significance of these rules is illustrated by *D.I.M.S. Construction Inc. (Trustee of) v. Quebec (Attorney General)*,[27] where the Supreme Court of Canada had to determine how to apply section 97(3) of the federal *Bankruptcy and Insolvency Act* to a bankruptcy occurring in Quebec.

---

26 Under the constitutional law doctrine of federal paramountcy, if validly enacted federal legislation comes into conflict with provincial law, the federal legislation prevails.

27 [2005] 2 S.C.R. 564 [*D.I.M.S.*]. See also *St.-Hilaire v. Canada (Attorney General)*, [2001] 4 F.C. 289 (C.A.) leave to appeal to S.C.C. refused, [2001] C.S.C.R. no 296.

97 (3) The law of set-off applies to all claims made against the estate of the bankrupt and also to all actions instituted by the trustee for the recovery of debts due to the bankrupt in the same manner and to the same extent as if the bankrupt were plaintiff or defendant, as the case may be.

Speaking for the court, Deschamps J. wrote:

The BIA [Bankruptcy and Insolvency Act] thus incorporates, although without defining it, a compensation mechanism. To delimit this mechanism, it is necessary to refer not only to the BIA itself, but also to provincial law. Since the enactment of the Federal Law–Civil Law Harmonization Act, No. 1, S.C. 2001, c. 4, [amending the Interpretation Act] it has been clear that in the province of Quebec, the civil law of Quebec is the suppletive law in bankruptcy matters. This means that in respect of aspects not governed by the BIA, the civil law rules of compensation apply.[28]

At trial the trustee in bankruptcy had argued that section 97(3) introduces the law of equitable set-off into Quebec in matters of bankruptcy. In response to this argument Deschamps J. wrote:

The applicability of equitable set-off was questionable even before the Federal Law–Civil Law Harmonization Act, No. 1: … Since that Act came into force, however, it has been clear that s. 97(3) BIA must be applied in Quebec on the basis of civil law and not common law rules. Equitable set-off cannot make up for the non-application of civil law compensation and cannot be introduced into Quebec law by s. 97(3) BIA. In Quebec, the suppletive law is Quebec civil law and, more specifically in this case, the rules governing compensation under the C.C.Q. [the Civil Code of Québec].[29]

Deschamps J. here makes very clear exactly what the rules in sections 8.1 and 8.2 were meant to achieve—an end to the backdoor erosion of civil law in Quebec, by recognizing that in Quebec the supplemental law is to be found in the Civil Code of Québec and not the common law.

While the general thrust of sections 8.1 to 8.2 is clear, a number of questions remain to be answered by the courts. Section 3(1) of the Interpretation Act provides that its provisions apply to every federal enactment "unless a contrary intention appears." In other words, the

---

28   D.I.M.S., ibid. at para 34.
29   Ibid. at para 64.

rules of the *Interpretation Act* operate as presumptions, rebuttable by any admissible evidence of legislative intent. Given this general provision, why did Parliament add to sections 8.1 and 8.2 the words "unless otherwise provided by law." Did it intend to impose a higher standard for rebutting sections 8.1 and 8.2 than other provisions in the Act?

A second issue is how an interpreter is to determine when "it is necessary to refer to a province's rules, principles or concepts."[30] Is the interpreter to apply the full range of interpretive tools to the federal legislation before concluding that reference to provincial law is necessary?

Finally, in cases that have connections with more than one province, how is an interpreter to know which province's rules, principles, and concepts must be referred to? Are interpreters meant to rely on conflict of laws rules? And if so, whose conflict rules apply?

---

30   On this issue, see *Re Canada 3000 Inc.*, [2006] SCC 24 at para. 80 and ff.

CHAPTER 6

ORIGINAL MEANING

A. THE ORIGINAL MEANING RULE

It is generally assumed that the meaning of a legislative text is stable. Unless there is a reason to suppose that the meaning has changed, the current understanding of legislation is assumed not to differ from the understanding that would have prevailed when the legislation was first enacted. However, when this assumption is challenged, the courts must decide whether to insist on the original meaning of the legislation, which is the meaning the enacting legislature would have had in mind, or to adopt the current meaning, which is the meaning relied on by those whose conduct or interests are currently governed by the legislation.

In responding to this problem, Canadian courts distinguish between ordinary legislation, which (in principle) is easily amended,[1] and constitutional texts, which are not. In the interpretation of ordinary legislation, the original meaning rule prevails. It assumes that the meaning of legislation is fixed when the legislation is first enacted and, once fixed, nothing short of amendment or repeal can change it. In the interpretation of the *Charter* and other constitutional documents, the courts adopt a "dynamic" or "organic" approach. Under this approach, meaning is not tied to the framer's original understanding but

---

1   In fact, it is often very difficult to get amendments on the legislative agenda, which tends to be controlled by short-term political considerations.

is permitted to evolve in response to both linguistic and social change.[2] In the interpretation of "quasi-constitutional" legislation like Human Rights Acts, although adaptation to change remains primarily a legislative responsibility, the judicial approach appears to be more flexible and responsive to an evolving external context than is the case for ordinary legislation.

B. CRITICISM OF THE ORIGINAL MEANING RULE

The original meaning rule is criticized by most commentators, and their criticism seems well justified. Although courts must take care not to exceed their institutional role, it is essential that legislation be adapted to changing social and material circumstances. It is not realistic to expect the legislature to engage in continuous monitoring and adaptation of its enactments. The courts, on the other hand, are ideally suited to this role, having performed it for centuries in the context of the common law. It is arguable that adapting legislation to an evolving reality lies at the heart of the judicial role and complements rather than encroaches on the policy-setting and allocative role of the legislature.

Those who defend the original meaning rule emphasize, in keeping with traditional theory,[3] that the job of the court is to give effect to the real intention of the legislature. This is taken to imply that interpreters are confined to the meanings and contexts current when the legislation was enacted. However, the conclusion does not follow from the premise. It is equally plausible to assume that the legislature intended its enactment to operate over time in a sensible and effective way so as to achieve its purposes. This intention is likely to be thwarted if interpreters are not permitted to adapt the legislation to evolving circumstance.

Although the courts tend to be conservative in their account of the theory, in practice they usually strike a careful balance between allegiance to the original meaning of a text and the need to respond to change. Significant innovation is reserved to the legislature, but judicial adaptation, in which the original purposes and policies of the legislation are applied to new facts, is a daily occurrence.

---

2   For the classic formulation of this rule, see *Edwards v. Attorney-General for Canada*, [1930] A.C. 124 at 136. For its application to the *Charter*, see *Re s. 94(2) of the Motor Vehicles Act*, [1985] 2 S.C.R. 486 at 500*ff.*

3   The traditional theory of statutory interpretation is explained in Chapter 2.

C. DYNAMIC VERSUS STATIC APPROACH

The leading case on the original meaning rule is *R. v. Perka*, where Dickson J. wrote:

> The doctrine of *contemporanea expositio* is well established in our law. "The words of a statute must be construed as they would have been the day after the statute was passed ..." *Sharpe v. Wakefield* (1888) 22 Q.B.D. 239 at p. 242 (*per* Lord Esher, M.R.). See also Driedger, *Construction of Statutes* (2nd ed. 1983) at p. 163: "Since a statute must be considered in the light of all circumstances existing at the time of its enactment it follows logically that the words must be given the meanings they had at the time of enactment, and the courts have so held".[4]

As this passage indicates, there are two ways of formulating the original meaning rule: (1) words must give the meanings they had at the time of enactment—their original *sense*; and (2) words must be construed as they would have been the day after the statute was passed—their original *interpretation*. These formulations do not necessarily mean the same thing:

1) The original sense of a word or expression is its abstract meaning, its dictionary definition in effect, at the time the legislation was passed. This understanding of original meaning permits a relatively dynamic approach to interpretation. Although the sense of the legislative text is fixed, the material facts to which it applies can change with the times. Suppose, for example, that in 1920, long before the Internet was dreamed of, the legislature enacted legislation prohibiting the "publication" of certain classes of information. Suppose that in 1920 "publication" would have been defined as "making known to the public at large." If original meaning refers to original sense, "publication" in this legislation must continue to mean "making known to the public at large," but it would readily embrace novel means of publication such as posting on a website.

2) The original construction or interpretation of a word or expression refers to the way it would have been applied by interpreters to the facts in question had those facts occurred when the legislation was first passed. This formulation of the original meaning rule leads to a static approach. Unlike definitions, which are abstract, interpretations are rooted in a particular time and place, a particular way of seeing the world. If courts are bound by past interpretations, as op-

---

4   [1984] 2 S.C.R. 232 at 264–65. [Citations in original.]

posed to past definitions or sense, their ability to respond to change is greatly restricted. Suppose, for example, in 1890 the legislature enacted a provision prohibiting the publication of "pornography," and "pornography" would have been defined both in 1890 and now as a depiction of sexual activity that offends community standards. Obviously the sort of material embraced by such a definition would change significantly from time to time. If original meaning refers to original interpretation, a court would have to rely on the standards of 1890 when judging the offensiveness of material published in 2005.

As these examples show, the difference between the two formulations of the original meaning rule turns on which context the courts refer to in establishing the meaning of the legislative text. If original meaning refers to original interpretation, the court must read the text in its original context, with regard to contemporaneous conditions and cultural assumptions. If original meaning refers to original sense, the court reads the text in its current context, in light of current conditions and assumptions.

The significance of the distinction between these two under-standings of the rule can be illustrated by considering the expression "expense ... incurred by the taxpayer for the purpose of gaining or producing income from ... [a] business" in section 18(1)(a) of the *Income Tax Act*. In *Symes v. Canada*,[5] the Supreme Court of Canada was asked to determine whether this language applied to expenditures for child care. Section 18(1)(a) was part of the original *Income Tax Act* enacted in 1917.[6] In the course of the last seventy-five years, the sense of the words used in this section has not undergone significant change. "Expense" still means a payment of money; "for a purpose" requires that the payment be motivated by and causally related to a particular goal; "income" is defined in the Act. If original meaning refers to original sense, there is nothing in the original meaning rule to prevent the court from applying the provision to payments made by parents for child care so long as the payments are closely enough related to the gaining of income. The fact that this connection had not been made in the past could be explained by historical attitudes toward child-rearing and women's limited access to the income-generating activities contemplated by section 18. The only question for the court is whether the connection should now be made having regard to current attitudes and conditions. However, if original meaning refers to original inter-

---

5   [1993] 4 S.C.R. 695 [*Symes*].
6   See *Income War Tax Act*, S.C. 1917, c. 28, s. 3(1).

pretation, the court must assess the connection between expense and income in light of the attitudes and conditions prevailing in 1917. There can be little doubt that in 1917 most courts would have refused to apply section 18(1)(a) to expenditures for child care.

In practice, the courts rely on one or the other formulation of the original meaning rule, depending on the circumstances. This gives them maximum flexibility in responding to problems of change. However, there are a number of factors that, alone or in combination, tend to favour either a dynamic or a static approach.

D. FACTORS AFFECTING WHICH APPROACH IS ADOPTED

1) Legislative Intent

In some cases there is evidence that the legislature itself had an intention respecting the dynamic or static character of a particular enactment. This intention might be set out in a preamble or recorded in *Hansard*.[7] Or it may be apparent from the purpose of the legislation. For example, legislation that has been designed to regulate a general activity for the indefinite future would imply a dynamic approach, whereas legislation that is meant to deal with a specific set of facts or implement a particular agreement would lend itself to a static approach. In *Bogoch Seed Co. Ltd. v. Canadian Pacific Railway Co.*,[8] for example, the Supreme Court of Canada ruled that rapeseed (canola) was not a "grain" within the meaning of the *Crow's Nest Pass Act, 1897*.[9] This Act authorized the *Crow's Nest Pass Agreement* between Canada and the Canadian Pacific Railway for the purpose of subsidizing the transport of grain. At the time, canola was not grown in Canada. Invoking the original meaning rule, the Court ruled that canola was therefore not within the scope of the subsidy. In its view, the Act addressed the particular situation existing on the prairies in 1897, and its duty was to give effect to the language of the Act as Parliament would have understood it at that time.

Although courts normally feel comfortable applying general language to new facts, they will take a static approach if the new facts have been addressed by the legislature. If there is evidence suggesting

---

7   *Hansard* is the name of the journal in which legislative debates and proceedings are recorded.

8   [1963] S.C.R. 247.

9   S.C. 1897, c. 5.

that before the most recent enactment the legislature in fact considered and rejected the proposed adaptation, the court will not second-guess this legislative decision. This was an important factor in the judgment of Lamer C.J. in *Canada (Attorney General) v. Mossop*.[10] The issue there was whether the failure to extend family benefits to a homosexual couple was discrimination on the basis of "family status," contrary to the *Canadian Human Rights Act*. While this was a plausible reading of "family status," the majority of the court adopted a narrow approach because it was convinced that Parliament had considered and rejected the possibility of prohibiting discrimination on the grounds of sexual orientation. Lamer C.J. wrote:

> It is interesting to note in this regard that there was a recommendation by the Canadian Human Rights Commission that sexual orientation be made a prohibited ground of discrimination. Nevertheless, at the time of the 1983 amendments to the *CHRA* [*Canadian Human Rights Act*], no action was taken to implement this recommendation.
>
> It is thus clear that when Parliament added the phrase "family status" to the English version of the *CHRA* in 1983, it refused at the same time to prohibit discrimination on the basis of sexual orientation in that Act. In my opinion, this fact is determinative. I find it hard to see how Parliament can be deemed to have intended to cover the situation now before the Court in the CHRA when we know that it specifically excluded sexual orientation from the list of prohibited grounds of discrimination contained in the Act.[11]

2) Politics versus Law

Generally, the dynamic approach is avoided when it would involve the court in balancing competing interests, developing policy, or allocating resources. These are considered political tasks that are best left to the legislature, not only because the legislature is elected but also because of its superior institutional resources. However, when it comes to matters such as the law of evidence or the administration of justice, the courts generally take a dynamic approach. In matters of law, where the courts have common law experience and specialized expertise, there is less reason to defer to the legislature.

---

10   [1993] 1 S.C.R. 554.
11   *Ibid.* at paras. 31–32. See also *Symes*, above note 5 at paras. 99–100.

Judicial reluctance to take on what are essentially political tasks is well illustrated by the majority judgment in the *Harvard Mouse* case.[12] The issue in that case was whether the so-called oncomouse, a type of mouse whose genes had been altered to make it more susceptible to cancer, came within the definition of "invention" in Canada's *Patent Act*: "[I]nvention means any new and useful art, process, machine, manufacture or composition of matter, or any new and useful improvement in any art, process, machine, manufacture or composition of matter."[13]

Although the oncomouse clearly was new and useful and arguably was a "composition of matter," the majority ruled that it was not within the scope of the definition. It pointed out that the decision to patent higher life forms is a matter of great complexity that raises a range of moral, social, and political issues. For this reason, in its view, the matter must be dealt with by Parliament. Bastarache J. wrote: "In my view, this Court does not possess the institutional competence to deal with issues of this complexity, which presumably will require Parliament to engage in public debate, a balancing of competing societal interests and intricate legislative drafting."[14]

3) The Type of Language to Be Interpreted

General or relative terms, abstract concepts, and legal norms such as "fair" or "reasonable" all require the exercise of discretion and therefore invite the interpreter to adopt a dynamic approach. A general term like "mammal" or "vehicle" refers to a class of things and is apt to embrace new members of the class as they are discovered or invented from time to time. That is one reason for using a general term rather than listing known members. When new members come within the purpose of the provision in which the general term appears and there is no reason to exclude them from its scope, the courts are almost sure to adopt a dynamic approach. Similarly, normative terms like "reasonable," "equitable," or "undue" implicitly require the interpreter to examine and evaluate relevant contextual factors as they arise from time to time. In recent years, in dealing with such language the courts have sometimes relied on the following provision, found in most Interpretation Acts, to justify a dynamic approach:

---

12 *Harvard College v. Canada (Commissioner of Patents)*, [2002] 4 S.C.R. 45 [*Harvard*].
13 R.S.C. 1985, c. P-4, s. 2.
14 *Harvard*, above note 12 at para. 183. See also *Bishop v. Stevens*, [1990] 2 S.C.R. 467.

10. The law shall be considered as always speaking, and where a matter or thing is expressed in the present tense, it shall be applied to the circumstances as they arise, so that effect may be given to the enactment according to its true spirit, intent and meaning.[15]

Conversely, technical terms and language that is precise and concrete call for a static approach. Provisions drafted in this type of language are often aimed at a particular set of circumstances and are not readily adapted to other contexts. Numerous examples are found in the legislation establishing railways and providing for the provision of adequate rail service across the country. Terms like "continuous line," "branch line," and "lay-out" had specific local meanings, which the courts attempt to discover and apply so as to give effect to the original intent of the legislature.[16]

4) Functional Equivalence

When new facts are functionally equivalent or analogous to facts that were within the ambit of the legislation when it first came into force, the courts tend to adopt a dynamic approach. The adaptation of rules to new circumstances by way of analogy is a classic common law technique that lends itself readily to the application of statutory provisions. Thus, rules designed to ensure safety in down-hill skiing would likely be applied without question to snow boarding, which takes place on the same terrain and creates the same sort of risks.[17]

E. HOW THE APPROACHES ARE APPLIED

The flexibility that results from these principles and their interaction in particular cases is illustrated in the following examples. In the *Perka* case,[18] the term to be interpreted was "*Cannibis sativa* L.," the botanical term for marijuana. When this drug was first added to the list of prohibited drugs under the *Narcotic Control Act*, botanists believed that all

---

15 R.S.C. 1985, c. I-23, s. 10.

16 See, for example, *Reference re Canadian Pacific Railway Co. Act (Canada)*(1905), 36 S.C.R. 42.

17 A classic example of functional equivalence reasoning is found in *Attorney General v. Edison Telephone Co. of London* (1880), 6 Q.B.D. 244, in which provisions of U.K.'s *Telegraph Act* were applied to newly invented telephones. The *Perka* case, above note 4, could also be understood in this light.

18 Above note 4.

cannibis belonged to the same species, namely *Cannibis sativa* L. By the time the defendants were charged with possession, at least some botanists had come to believe that there are several species of cannibis. The defendants argued that they should be acquitted in the absence of proof that the cannibis in their possession was *sativa* L. The court concluded, however, that "*Cannibis sativa* L." should be interpreted to refer to all species of cannibis since that was how the term was understood and how it would have been interpreted the day the legislation was passed. Dickson J. wrote:

> Broad statutory categories are often held to include things unknown when the statute was enacted .... This kind of interpretive approach is most likely to be taken, however, with legislative language that is broad or "open-textured" .... But where, as here, the legislature has deliberately chosen a specific scientific or technical term to represent an equally specific and particular class of things, it would do violence to Parliament's intent to give a new meaning to that term.... It is clear that Parliament intended in 1961, by the phrase "*Cannibis sativa* L.", to prohibit all cannibis.[19]

The court here adopts the static approach. It accepts the interpretation that would have been adopted by a court considering the phrase in 1961.

The *Perka* case may be contrasted with *Apple Computer Inc. v. Macintosh Computers Ltd.*[20] and *Tataryn v. Tataryn Estate.*[21] In the *Apple Computer* case, the court had to determine whether computer programs originating in text format continued to be protected by the *Copyright Act* when converted into electronic code and embedded in a silicon chip. The question, more specifically, was whether this conversion amounted to reproducing a work within the meaning of section 3: "3 (1) For the purposes of this Act, 'copyright', in relation to a work, means the sole right to produce or reproduce the work or any substantial part thereof in any material form whatever."[22]

In reasons later adopted by the Supreme Court of Canada, Reed J. pointed out that when the *Copyright Act* was first enacted, Parliament could not have contemplated facts of this sort:

> No one disputes, of course, that when the present Copyright Act was originally enacted by Parliament in 1921 no thought could have been

---

19   *Ibid.* at 265–66.
20   (1986), [1987] 1 F.C. 173 (T.D.), aff'd (1987), [1988] 1 F.C. 673 (C.A.), aff'd [1990] 2 S.C.R. 209 [*Apple Computer*].
21   [1994] 2 S.C.R. 807.
22   R.S.C. 1985, c. C-42.

given to computer programs and whether they would be covered by the provisions of the Act. This is not a relevant consideration, since the only question is whether the terms of the Act as drafted can fairly be said to cover such programs as encoded in the ROM chip.[23]

In the end, she found that "the opening words of subsection 1(2), now section 3 of the Act, were purposely drafted broadly enough to encompass new technologies which had not been thought of when the Act was drafted."[24] This conclusion is supported by the general and unqualified language used in the provision—"a work," "produce or reproduce," and especially "any material form whatever." It is also supported by the nature of the Act—one designed to deal with innovation occurring from time to time.

In the *Tataryn Estate* case, the issue was the meaning of section 2(1) of British Columbia's *Wills Variation Act*, providing that when a testator dies leaving a will that does not adequately provide for his or her dependants, the court may override the will and order whatever "provision that it thinks adequate, just and equitable" to be made out of the estate. The Supreme Court of Canada ruled that the meaning of this language should not be tied to conditions existing in 1920 when the statute was first enacted, but should be understood in a modern context. McLachlin J. wrote:

> The language of the Act confers a broad discretion on the court. The generosity of the language suggests that the legislature was attempting to craft a formula which would permit the courts to make orders which are just in the specific circumstances and in light of contemporary standards. This, combined with the rule that a statute is always speaking (*Interpretation Act*, R.S.B.C. 1979, c. 206, s.7), means that the Act must be read in light of modern values and expectations. What was thought to be adequate, just and equitable in the 1920s may be quite different from what is considered adequate, just and equitable in the 1990s .... Courts are not necessarily bound by the views and awards made in earlier times. The search is for contemporary justice.[25]

Here, the legislature delegated discretion to the court to do justice in the particular case. The court interprets this authority as a mandate to adapt the provision to changing circumstances so as to achieve its basic purpose.

---

23   *Apple Computer*, above note 21 at para. 28 (T.D.).
24   *Ibid.* at para 33.
25   Above note 22 at 814–15.

F. OBSOLESCENCE

Legislation becomes obsolete when it is addressed to facts that no longer exist or is based on assumptions that are no longer true. Obsolesence does not affect the status of legislation—it remains in force as valid law and must be applied by the courts to the extent this is possible. Only an Act of the legislature can repeal legislation or render it inoperative.

In some cases obsolescence is not a problem. A statute regulating the sale of a discontinued product or conferring powers on an office that no longer exists has nothing to apply to and therefore interpretation problems cannot arise. On occasion, however, only a particular aspect of the legislation is obsolete, leaving the courts with difficult interpretive challenges. In *Re Vabalis*,[26] for example, the court was asked to apply a provision in Ontario's *Change of Name Act* which required married persons applying for a change of surname to join their spouse and children in the application. This provision was enacted at a time when women automatically took their husband's surname upon marrying. Given this assumption, the provision makes perfect sense. Given current social practices, however, it leads to serious absurdities. Suppose Tom Ramsbottom is married to Jai Percy and the couple has two children whose last name is Ramsbottom. If Tom Ramsbottom later wants to change his name to Tom Ramsey, he is required not only to change his children's name from Ramsbottom to Ramsey, but also to get his wife to change her name from Percy to Ramsey. If Jai Percy wants to change her name to Jai Persaud, she must get Tom and their children to change their name to Persaud too. The Ontario Court of Appeal found these consequences to be foolish and refused to apply the provision:

> We are all agreed that the literal interpretation of s. 4(1) as requiring a change of name of the applicant's spouse in the present situation would lead to an obvious absurdity. A statute enacted by the Legislature of this province should not be so interpreted....
>
> We are satisfied that in a society where it is not uncommon for married persons to use a name other than the name of the spouse, it would not be reasonable to require that the spouse whose name is different should adopt the change of surname.[27]

---

26 (1983), 43 O.R. (2d) 609 (C.A.). See also *R. v. Paul*, [1982] 1 S.C.R. 621.
27 *Ibid.* at 610–11.

Although the court did not refer to the problem of obsolescence in so many words, it effectively modernized the provision by creating an exception for spouses who do not have the same surname.

CHAPTER 7

PLAUSIBLE INTERPRETATION, GAPS, AND MISTAKES

A. THE PLAUSIBLE MEANING RULE

Under the plausible meaning rule, a court may adopt an interpretation that departs from the ordinary meaning of the legislative text, but the interpretation adopted must be one that the text can reasonably bear. The following passage from the judgment of Estey J. in *Bernadelli v. Ontario Housing Corp.* is typical of the many occasions on which this rule is invoked:

> When one interpretation can be placed upon a statutory provision which would bring about a more workable and practical result, such an interpretation should be preferred if the words invoked by the Legislature can reasonably bear it.[1]

It follows, as Arbour J. explains in *Ruby v. Canada (Solicitor General)*, that an interpretation that cannot reasonably be borne by the words of the text must be rejected; there is no discretion in the court to accept such an interpretation:

> [T]he Solicitor General's interpretation of s. 51(2)(a) is not one that the statute can reasonably bear. Section 51(2)(a) *mandates* that the hearing ... be heard in camera.... It is not open to the parties, even on consent, to bypass the mandatory in camera requirements of s.

---

1   [1979] 1 S.C.R. 275 at 284.

51. Nor is open to a judge to conduct a hearing in open court in direct contradiction to the requirements of the statute, regardless of the proposal put forth by the parties. Unless the mandatory requirement is found to be unconstitutional and the section is "read down" as a constitutional remedy, it cannot otherwise be interpreted to bypass its mandatory nature.[2]

The notion of plausible meaning figures other ways in statutory interpretation and in administrative law as well. In *Bell ExpressVu Limited Partnership v. Rex*, for example, the Supreme Court of Canada offered the following definition of ambiguity: "What, then, in law is an *ambiguity*? To answer, an *ambiguity* must be 'real'. ... The words of the provision must be 'reasonably capable of more than one meaning.'"[3] In cases involving applications for judicial review, the Supreme Court of Canada has distinguished among three standards of review. Depending on a number of factors, a decision of an inferior tribunal must be set aside by the reviewing court if it is (1) merely incorrect, (2) unreasonable, or (3) patently unreasonable. As explained by Arbour J. in *Moreau-Bérubé v. New Brunswick (Judicial Council)*, an interpretation that is unreasonable or patently unreasonable is one that the words of the text cannot reasonably bear.[4]

The plausible meaning rule is invoked by courts as a justification for rejecting an interpretation that may be appropriate in some respects—it may fit the context or avoid bad consequences or otherwise appear to have been intended. But it puts too great a strain on the words of the text. The court says, in effect, that because the legislature is a competent language user it would not have chosen *these* words to express *that* meaning; if *that* is what the legislature meant, it would have said so in different terms or in a different way. In *Forget v. Quebec (Attorney General)*, for example, in connection with section 35 of the *Charter of the French Language*, Lamer J. wrote:

> If the legislator had intended that knowledge of French be assessed by only one method of proof ... he would have stated that intent clearly. For example, the statute might have imposed ... a duty to measure knowledge of French by holding an examination .... [B]ut that is not the case here. Section 35 of the Act provides that the Office [de la langue française] may, but is not required to, hold an examination.[5]

---

2   [2002] 4 S.C.R. 3 at para. 58.
3   [2002] 2 S.C.R. 559 at para. 29. [Citations omitted. Emphasis added.]
4   See [2002] 1 S.C.R. 249, especially paras. 61–62.
5   [1988] 2 S.C.R. 90 at 106–7.

The plausible meaning rule is meant to express an important limitation on judicial interpretation. Courts are not free to disregard the language of the legislative text. Any interpretation adopted by a court must be plausible from a linguistic point of view, however implausible it may be from the point of view of sound policy or other considerations.

It is worth noting the assumptions on which the plausible meaning rule is based. It assumes, first of all, that the jurisdiction of the courts is limited to interpretation and does not extend to amending the rules enacted by the legislature. The legislature alone can amend or repeal its own law. Second, it assumes that textual meaning is the primary means by which the intention of the legislature can be discerned. Thus, in the event of a conflict between textual meaning and other indicators of legislative intent, the former must prevail. Finally, it assumes that the linguistic intuitions of judges provide a sound basis for judgments of plausibility, even though judges need have no special linguistic expertise and often disagree among themselves about the meaning of a text.

B. PROBLEMS WITH THE PLAUSIBLE MEANING RULE

There are problems with the plausible meaning rule which to some extent undermine its ability to function as a serious constraint on judicial interpretation. First, because it is used primarily for its rhetorical impact, the concept of plausibility has been given little definite content by the courts. Second, the rhetoric associated with the plausible meaning rule is misleading. And third, the rule is subject to a number of significant but ill-defined exceptions.

1) Unclear Concept of Plausibility

Judgments of plausibility are highly personal, intuitive, and difficult to pin down. What strikes one person as plausible may strain the credulity of another. In *Thomson v. Canada (Deputy Minister of Agriculture)*, L'Heureux-Dubé J., dissenting, was prepared to interpret "recommendation" as meaning a binding directive or order.[6] Was this plausible? In *Kannata Highlands Ltd. v. Kannata Valley (Village)*, Wakeling J.A. was prepared to interpret the words "shall have regard to" as "shall ensure

---

6   [1992] 1 S.C.R. 385 at 409.

compliance with."[7] Was this plausible? There is no obviously correct answer to these questions.

Although courts are accustomed to giving content to difficult concepts by applying them in successive circumstances, the idea of plausible meaning has not benefited from this process. Little effort has been made to explore plausibility as a legal or a linguistic concept or to develop a workable test.

2) Misleading Rhetoric

Courts often say that they cannot change or add words to a text because that would amount to an amendment. The following passage from the judgment of Lamer C.J. in *R. v. McIntosh* is typical:

> The Crown is asking this Court to read words into s. 34(2) which are simply not there. In my view, to do so would be tantamount to *amending* s. 34(2), which is a legislative and not a judicial function. The contextual approach provides no basis for the courts to engage in legislative amendment.[8]

This rhetoric may be effective, but it is also misleading. In fact, courts "read words into" legislation or "rewrite" it on a daily basis through the use of paraphrase.

Although courts are not allowed to amend legislation, they are allowed to paraphrase it. A paraphrase of a legislative text restates the rule enacted by the legislature using different words. Often a paraphrase spells out qualifications or exceptions or inclusions that are found to be implicit in the legislation, even though they are not expressly mentioned in the text.

In *Jahnke v. Wylie*,[9] for example, the Alberta Court of Appeal had to interpret section 142 of Alberta's *Workers' Compensation Act*. This provision made the documents and files of the Workers' Compensation Board inadmissible as evidence "in any action or proceeding without the consent of the Board." The court pointed out that if the provision were applied without qualification, it would lead to unacceptable results. For example, the board might use the section to insulate itself from civil actions or even judicial review. Kerans J.A. wrote: "I conclude that actions in which the Board is a party are necessarily outside the scope of the provision. In other words, I would read down 'any' in

---

7   (1987), 61 Sask. R. 292 at 297 (C.A.).
8   [1995] 1 S.C.R. 686 at 701.
9   (1994), 162 A.R. 131 (C.A.).

'any action or proceeding' to mean *any action other than one in which the Board is a party*, and thus give effect to a meaning that, in my view, is necessarily implicit."[10] In this passage the court "reads words into the section which are simply not there." As Kerans J.A. indicates, every time a court adopts an interpretation that excludes any application within the ordinary meaning of the text, it effectively adds words of qualification or exception. In principle, this does not change the rule enacted by the legislature, but rather clarifies the rule; it gives effect to a meaning that the court has found to be implicit in the text. This is interpretation, not amendment. To suggest that an interpretation is unacceptable because it "adds words" to the legislation or "rewrites" it is thus a misleading thing to say. In fact, an interpretation is unacceptable only if the changes or additions supplied by the interpreter cannot be justified as a paraphrase of the text that gives effect to legislative intent.

This point is well made by McLachlin C.J., speaking for the majority, in *Montreal (City) v. 2952-1355 Québec Inc.*[11] The issue in that case was the scope of article 9(1) of Montreal's *By-law concerning noise*, which prohibited "where [it] can be heard from the outside ... noise produced by sound equipment, whether it is inside a building or installed or used outside." The majority of the Court interpreted this provision to mean that noise was prohibited only if it interferes with the peaceful enjoyment of the environment. In his dissenting judgment Binnie J. characterized this interpretation as amendment:

> In my view, with respect, my colleagues resort to a combination of reading expressions "up", reading expressions "down", reading words "out" and reading words "in" that goes beyond what a court is authorized to do by way of interpretation and amounts to impermissible judicial amendment.[12]

McLachlin C.J. wrote:

> The historical and purposive analysis of the provision enabled us to determine that the lawmaker's purpose was to control noises that interfere with peaceful enjoyment of the environment. ... The delimination of the By-law's scope does not, as Binnie J. claims, constitute judicial amendement that is inconsistent with the plain meaning of the provision. Rather, it is the result of a judicious interpretation that

10   *Ibid.* at 135. [Emphasis added.]
11   [2005] 3 S.C.R. 141.
12   *Ibid.* at para. 110.

resolves the provision's ambiguity in accordance with the modern approach to interpretation.[13]

Rhetoric about judicial amendment is ubiquitous in the case law. When an interpreter prefers to stick to ordinary meaning, he or she typically characterizes departures from that meaning as amendment rather than interpretation. In fact, the majority in the *Montreal* case does not read up or out or in, but it does read down, significantly narrowing the scope of the provision to bring it in line with its purpose. Reading down to bring a provision in line with its purpose is a well-established interpretive technique that is perfectly legitimate, provided it can be adequately justified. In the *Montreal* case, the dissenting judges clearly thought the justification offered by the majority was inadequate.

3) Ill-Defined Exceptions

Yet another problem with the plausible meaning rule is that it is subject to a number of ill-defined exceptions. First, to avoid absurdity, courts sometimes adopt interpretations that are implausible by anybody's standard. Second, while courts ordinarily deny any jurisdiction to fill a gap in a legislative scheme, there are a number of strategies that permit the court to do indirectly what it could not do directly. Finally, courts have a jurisdiction to correct any errors that may have occurred in the drafting of legislation. This jurisdiction is well established and the grounds for exercising it are reasonably clear. Yet it is not uncommon for a court to deny this jurisdiction or to refuse to exercise it, preferring to leave the correction of errors to the legislature.

These exceptions to the plausible meaning rule are examined in greater detail below. They are problematic because they are applied inconsistently and with little explanation. When the courts invoke the rule, they tend to ignore the exceptions. When they invoke an exception, they more or less ignore the rule.

4) Varying Judicial Views

Because the concept of plausibility is so nebulous and the exceptions to the plausibility rule are so ill defined, there is considerable inconsistency in the case law. To a significant degree, the willingness of a court to depart from ordinary meaning or to correct a drafting error is a matter of personal style. Judges have different views about their role as in-

---

13   *Ibid.* at para. 34.

terpreters and different attitudes towards language. These factors affect their attitude towards plausibility, gap filling, and the correction of errors. But personal style aside, it is not uncommon for the same judge to express different views about plausibility in different cases. This can be illustrated by comparing the judgment of Lamer C.J. in *R. v. McIntosh*[14] with his judgment in *Michaud v. Quebec (Attorney General)*.[15]

In *R. v. McIntosh* the issue was how to interpret section 34(2) of the *Criminal Code*, which provided that a person "who is unlawfully assaulted and who causes death or grievous bodily harm in repelling the assault" can successfully plead self-defence if certain conditions are met. These conditions were more lenient than those set out in section 35 dealing with provoked assaults. Relying on purposive and scheme analysis, consequential analysis, legislative evolution, and the jursidiction of the court to correct drafting errors, the Crown argued that the provision should be understood to mean that only a person who is unlawfully assaulted *without having provoked the assault* can rely on section 34(2). Lamer C.J. rejected this interpretation as amendment rather than interpretation.

In *Michaud v. Quebec (Attorney General)*, by contrast, Lamer C.J. relied on purposive analysis to add an exception to section 187(1)(a) of the *Criminal Code*. It prohibited the opening of sealed evidence packets without a judicial order. The issue was whether a judge hearing an application to open a packet could, in the course of his or her deliberations, open the packet in question. Lamer C.J. wrote:

> [A] stark, literal reading of the provision would appear to suggest that the court must rule on such a motion while turning a blind eye to the contents of the packet.
>
> ...
>
> In my view, the provision should be interpreted as permitting a judge to examine the contents of the packet in private for the restricted purpose of adjudicating a s. 187(1)(a)(ii) application. The confidentiality interests underlying the provision are simply not triggered when a competent judicial authority examines the contents of the packet in camera.[16]

In this case, in contrast to the position he took in *McIntosh*, Lamer C.J. was willing to abandon literal interpretation to ensure a sensible outcome.

---

14   Above note 8.
15   *Michaud v. Quebec (Attorney General)*, [1996] 3 S.C.R. 3.
16   *Ibid.* at paras. 27–28. See also *R. v. Paul*, discussed below at note 18.

C. IMPLAUSIBLE INTERPRETATIONS

Courts have long grappled with the question whether it is permissible to adopt an implausible interpretation to avoid an absurdity.[17] It is important to notice when and how this question arises. Courts adopt interpretations that strain language to some extent, by some standards, on a daily basis. In such cases one presumes that, to the adopting court at least, the interpretation in question seemed plausible. Such cases do not depend on there being an exception to the rule; they depend on the court having a low threshold of plausibility. The question of an exception arises only when the interpretation to be adopted is one that the court itself finds to be implausible. Some courts are unwilling to adopt implausible interpretations under any circumstances. Others are willing to do so in some circumstances, where the absurdity to be avoided warrants it.

In *R. v. Paul*,[18] for example, the Supreme Court of Canada had to interpret section 645(4)(c) of the *Criminal Code* governing consecutive sentencing. It provided that where an accused is found guilty of multiple offences, consecutive sentences may be imposed only if the accused was "convicted ... before the same court at the same sittings." The court interpreted the words "before the same court at the same sittings" to mean "before the same judge." Lamer J. acknowledged that this was not a plausible reading of the words in question, but he found it to be justified in the circumstances. It was not possible to give the words their ordinary meaning: due to changes in the structure of the courts and the administration of criminal trials, the reference to "same sittings" had become meaningless. The court was invited to interpret these words as meaning "before the same judge on the same occasion." This interpretation was plausible from a linguistic point of view. However, it led to absurd results. The purpose of the provision was to permit judges to impose consecutive sentences on persons who committed multiple offences, while excluding the possibility of double sentencing. If the plausible interpretation were adopted, the power to impose consecutive sentences would be severely curtailed and part of the purpose would be defeated. To avoid this unacceptable outcome, an implausible interpretation was preferred. In effect, the reference to "same sittings"

---

17 Absurdity here covers a wide range of undesirable consequences, from defeating the purpose of the legislation or creating internal inconsistencies to producing outcomes that are foolish or unfair. For further discussion of absurdity and the question raised in the text, see Chapter 11.

18 [1982] 1 S.C.R. 621.

was struck from the text. Lamer J. wrote: "I am not unmindful of the stress I am suggesting we put on Parliament's words and the fact that little or no meaning is being given to the words 'at the same sittings'; but I am encouraged in this endeavour when considering the absurd results we are led into by the alternative."[19]

Lamer J. does not explain what it is about this absurdity that warrants departure from the plausible meaning rule. The absurdity here was due to changes that could not have been foreseen by the legislature at the time of enactment. This may have been a relevant and important consideration. The area of law dealt with may also have been a factor. Generally speaking, courts are more likely to "legislate" on matters involving the administration of justice or in traditional common law areas where they can draw on judicial experience and expertise. Whatever the reasons in *R. v. Paul*, the court was prepared to reject the plausible interpretation in favour of an implausible one to avoid the unacceptable result.[20]

D. GAPS IN THE LEGISLATIVE SCHEME

There is said to be a "gap in the legislative scheme" if the legislation to be interpreted is underinclusive. Legislation is underinclusive if it fails to extend to something that should have been included in order to achieve the legislature's purpose. A provision is omitted that needs to be there; or a provision is too narrowly drafted and cannot plausibly be extended to facts that should have been covered. As explained below, the courts have a jurisdiction to cure *drafter's* errors. However, gaps in the legislative scheme are attributed to the legislature. Gaps may be the result of a considered decision or the result of an oversight or mistake, but in either case the court has no jurisdiction to cure the problem. The technique required to remedy this problem, namely reading in, is perceived as going beyond interpretation and impinging on the legislative role.

The terms "reading down" and "reading in" are used in both statutory interpretation and *Charter* application. In both contexts, reading down refers to narrowing the scope of a legislative text, while reading in refers to expanding its scope. Reading down or reading in as used in statutory interpretation is an interpretive technique designed to give effect to the true intention of the legislature. By contrast, reading down or reading in as used in *Charter* application is a remedy designed to

---

19   *Ibid.* at 664.
20   See also *R. v. Monney*, [1999] 1 S.C.R. 652.

cure a *Charter* violation. The remedy is necessary because the true intention of the legislature violates one or more *Charter* norms in a way that cannot be demonstrably justified in a free and democratic society.

It is important to notice that reading in cannot be equated with adding words to the legislative text. In fact, both reading down and reading in effectively add words to the legislative text. Reading down adds words of restriction or qualification. For example, in *Montreal (City) v. 2952-1355 Québec Inc.*,[21] in interpreting article 9(1) of Montreal's noise by-law, which prohibited the production of noise by sound equipment if the noise could be heard outside a building, the court added the words "but only if the noise interferes with the peaceful enjoyment of the environment." The effect of adding these words was to narrow the scope of the provision so that not all noise heard outside a building was captured, but only disruptive noise. Reading in, by contrast, adds words of expansion. In *Gell v. Canadian Pacific Ltd.*,[22] the court added words stipulating the deadline for appeals to the Supreme Court of Canada from the Federal Court of Appeal, a matter overlooked in both the *Federal Court Act* and the *Supreme Court of Canada Act*. In effect, the court added a new provision to this legislation.

At first glance, reading down and reading in may seem to be symmetrical techniques or remedies, two sides of the same coin. However, the courts are right to distinguish them and to be much more cautious in using the reading in technique or remedy. As an interpretation technique, reading down merely makes explicit what the court finds to be implicit in the legislative text. It would be impossible for drafters to spell out every single qualification and caveat—or provisions might go on for pages. Particularly when legislation is drafted in general or abstract terms, every act of interpretation is necessarily an exercise in reading down. However, reading in is different. It does not purport to operate within the scope of the legislative text, but rather to expand that scope to matters that are neither implicit nor explicit in the legislation.

A good example of underinclusiveness is found in Prince Edward Island's *Judicial Review Act*, which was considered by the Prince Edward Island Supreme Court in *National Farmers Union v. Prince Edward Island (Potato Marketing Council).*[23] Section 2 of the Act provided that "the purpose of this Act is to substitute an application for judicial review for the following existing proceedings," including applications for orders of *certiorari*. However, nothing in the remaining sections of the

---

21 This case is discussed above at note 11.
22 This case is dicussed below at note 28.
23 (1989), 74 Nfld. & P.E.I.R. 64 (P.E.I.S.C.T.D.).

Act actually provided for the abolition of *certiorari* and its replacement by judicial review. Sections 3 through 9 of the Act set out the procedures to be followed in an application for judicial review. Section 10 provided that a reference to *certiorari* in other enactments should also be read as a reference to judicial review. Section 11 abolished the writ of *quo warranto*. In the view of McQuaid J. this was not enough. Although the purpose was clear, in this case "the reach of Parliament exceeded its grasp."[24] There was a gap in the legislative scheme that could not be filled.[25]

It is important to distinguish gaps (that is, underinclusive legislation) from interpretation problems that arise because the legislature failed to anticipate a particular fact scenario arising within the scope of the legislative scheme. In *Canada (Attorney General) v. Ward*,[26] for example, the court had to apply the definition of "Convention refugee" in Canada's *Immigration Act* to a person with dual citizenship. To be a Convention refugee, a person must have a well-founded fear of persecution that prevents them from from returning to the country of their nationality. The question was whether a person with dual citizenship had to fear return to the initial country of nationality, the subsequent country of nationality, or both. The Act did not address this issue, so in one sense there was a gap in the legislative scheme. However, the problem was not underinclusiveness; the court could not resolve the issue by saying that the facts fell outside the scope of the legislation and therefore did not apply. The court had to determine whether Ward was a convention refugee and to do so it had to apply the existing definition which contemplated single citizenship to a dual citizenship situation.[27]

Although the courts ordinarily say they lack the power to cure underinclusiveness, they sometimes do so. As mentioned above, in *Gell v. Canadian Pacific Ltd.*,[28] the Supreme Court of Canada was confronted with a gap in the legislation governing appeals to its own court. The issue was whether the Court had jurisdiction to extend the time for leave to appeal applications from the Federal Court of Appeal, as it did for applications from provincial Courts of Appeal. As it happened, there was nothing in either the *Supreme Court of Canada Act* or the

---

24   *Ibid.* at 66.
25   For a more recent example, see *Beattie v. National Frontier Insurance Co.* (2003), 68 O.R. (3d) 60 (C.A.).
26   [1993] 2 S.C.R. 689 [*Ward*].
27   For another example, see *Pointe-Claire (City) v.Quebec (Labour Court)*, [1997] 1 S.C.R. 1015.
28   [1988] 2 S.C.R. 271.

Federal Court Act addressing leave for appeal from the Federal Court of Appeal. Speaking for the court, Beetz J. wrote:

> These provisions appear to create a jurisdictional gap. While section 31(2) and (3) of the *Federal Court Act* give the Federal Court of Appeal and the Supreme Court the power to grant leave to appeal from a judgment of the Federal Court of Appeal, neither the *Federal Court Act* nor the *Supreme Court Act* prescribe a time period during which an application for leave to appeal must be brought. Furthermore, if such a time period does exist, neither statute grants express authority to extend time for a late application.[29]

These gaps were filled by reading new rules into the legislation, based on analogy to the rules governing other time limits. The court did not explain why it was permissible to fill these particular gaps, but the fact that the legislation dealt with appeals to itself was probably an important factor.

Some legislative gaps are filled by relying on the doctrine of jurisdiction by necessary implication. Bastarache J. explained this doctrine in *ATCO Gas & Pipelines Ltd. v. Alberta (Energy & Utilities Board)*:

> [W]hen the "doctrine of jurisdiction by necessary implication" [is applied], the powers conferred by an enabling statute are construed to include not only those expressly granted but also, by implication, all powers which are practically necessary for the accomplishment of the object intended to be secured by the statutory regime created by the legislation.
>
> …
>
> When legislation attempts to create a comprehensive regulatory framework, the tribunal must have the powers which by practical necessity and necessary implication flow from the regulatory authority explicitly conferred upon it.[30]

In the *ATCO* case the court concluded that the test for invoking the doctrine was not met. However, the court left no doubt that in a proper case it would not hesitate to read in the necessary powers. It appears that courts rely on a comparable doctrine of necessity in cases like *Ward*, where the issue not dealt with in the legislative scheme *must* be resolved in order to dispose of the case.

---

29   *Ibid.* at para. 9.
30   [2006] 1 S.C.R. 140 at para. 51 [*ATCO*]. See para. 73 for a list of conditions that must be met for the doctrine to apply.

Even when the courts refuse to fill a gap, they may achieve much the same result by relying on the common law, and particularly the inherent powers of superior courts. The leading case is *Beson v. Newfoundland (Director of Child Welfare)*.[31] In that case, the Director of Child Welfare for Newfoundland removed a child from the home of its adoptive parents, the Besons, shortly before the expiry of the probationary period for the adoption. The Besons wished to contest this decision, but the Act did not afford them a right of appeal. Speaking for the Supreme Court of Canada, Wilson J. wrote:

> [Assuming] the Besons had indeed no right of appeal under the statute from the Director's removal of Christopher from their home, then I believe there is a gap in the legislative scheme which the Newfoundland courts could have filled by an exercise of their parens patriae jurisdiction. Noel J., in other words, could have done more than recommend that the Director give Christopher the chance of the good home available with the Besons. ... If it were not in Christopher's best interests that he be removed from the appellants' home, then in the absence of any statutory right of appeal through which his interests might be protected, Noel J. had an obligation to intervene.[32]

Gaps in legislation may be filled not only through the exercise of inherent jurisdiction but also through reliance on ordinary common law rules and principles. However, there is a significant difference between the two. Inherent jurisdiction is more readily relied on to supplement legislation, especially elaborate regulatory schemes, than ordinary common law.[33]

E. DRAFTING ERRORS

The courts have a well-established jurisdiction to cure legislative drafting errors. These errors occur when the language chosen by the drafter fails to express the rule that the legislature intended to enact. Errors may be corrected provided the court is confident that it knows what the legislature intended and what it would have said had the mistake not occurred.

Drafting errors tend to fall into one or more of the following categories: (a) use of language for which no plausible interpretation is pos-

---

31   [1982] 2 S.C.R. 716.
32   *Ibid.* at XX.
33   For further discussion of the relation between statute law and common law, see Chapter 15 .

sible because it is meaningless or contradictory or nonsensical; (b) use of language that leads to a glaring absurdity, the origin of which is evident—for example, a translation error or a mistake made in preparing an amendment or a statute revision; or (c) use of language that defeats the clear intention of the legislature as established through standard interpretive techniques.

Drafting errors in the first category are usually easy to detect and cure. In *Morishita v. Richmond (Township)*,[34] for example, the British Columbia Court of Appeal was asked to apply section 8 of a municipal by-law which directed the municipal clerk to proceed "as provided … in section 4 of this By-law." Southin J.A. pointed out that this was impossible to do: "The difficulty arising on s. 8 is its reference to s. 4. The simple fact is, the reference to s. 4 makes no sense at all."[35] In reviewing the legislative evolution of the by-law, the court found that in previous versions the municipal clerk was directed to proceed in accordance with section 5, not section 4, and that a reference to section 5 in the current by-law would make sense of the provision. It concluded that the reference to section 4 was a drafting error that should be corrected by reading the section as if it referred to section 5.

Drafting errors in the second and third categories call for more judgment on the part of the courts. In *R. v. McIntosh*[36] the Supreme Court of Canada was invited to correct a mistake in section 34(2) of the *Criminal Code*. Sections 34 and 35 of the *Code* both dealt with self-defence. Section 34(1) applied to "[e]very one who is unlawfully assaulted without having provoked the assault." Section 34(2) applied to "[e]very one who is unlawfully assaulted and who causes death or grievous bodily harm in repelling the assault." Section 35 applied to persons who provoked the assault from which they then sought to defend themselves. The Crown argued that section 34(2), like section 34(1), was meant to apply only to persons who did not provoke the assault; the absence of express words to that effect was a mistake made by a drafter. A majority of the court did not accept this analysis. However, in a strong dissent McLachlin J. wrote:

> The Court's task is to determine the intention of Parliament. The words of the section, taken alone, do not provide a clear and conclusive indication of Parliament's intention. It is therefore necessary to look further to determine Parliament's intention to the history of the

---

34   (1990), 67 D.L.R. (4th) 609 (B.C.C.A.).
35   *Ibid.* at 618.
36   Above note 8.

section and the practical problems and absurdities which may result from interpreting the section one way or the other. These considerations lead, in my respectful view, to the inescapable conclusion that Parliament intended s. 34(2) to apply only to unprovoked assaults.[37]

Since the words of section 34(2) did not express that intention, the drafting was faulty and required correction.

McLachlin J. established the discrepancy between Parliament's clear intention on the one hand and the drafter's wording on the other by relying on a number of techniques. First, she traced the evolution of the self-defence provisions back to their origins in the common law. This provided evidence of Parliament's original intention. She then followed the provisions forward through successive statute revisions. This enabled her to pinpoint exactly when and how the mistake in drafting occurred. In the 1955 *Criminal Code*,[38] the opening words of what was then section 53(2), later section 34(2), were reformulated to bring the provision in line with a more modern drafting style. In effecting this reformulation the reference to unprovoked assault, which had been clear in the previous version, was inadvertently dropped. This change in wording was not meant to be an amendment to the rules governing self-defence. It was the result of sloppy work in the statute revision office. To undo the damage, the reference to unprovoked assault had to be put back into the provision.

McLachlin J. also looked at contextual features like marginal notes and she reviewed the apparent scheme of the self-defence provisions. Under this scheme, unprovoked assaults were dealt with leniently in section 34, while provoked assaults were dealt with more harshly in section 35. Subsection 34(1) dealt with minor injuries whereas subsection 34(2) covered death or grievous bodily harm. However, after the change in wording introduced in 1955, this scheme was disrupted. After 1955, an accused who provoked an assault would benefit from the lenient treatment provided by section 34 if he caused death or grievous bodily harm, while an accused who caused less serious forms of harm would be subject to the more onerous requirements of section 35. This absurdity was further evidence that the change in wording introduced in the 1955 *Code* was a mistake and not a change in legislative policy.

Lamer C.J. wrote the majority judgment. Like McLachlin J., he emphasized how badly drafted the section was and he acknowledged the

---

37   *Ibid.* at 714.

38   Although the 1955 enactment of the *Criminal Code* included some amendments as well as revision, the internal evidence suggested that the sections governing self-defence were revised rather than amended.

absurdity that would result if the wording were not changed. There were several techniques at his disposal to get around the bad drafting and bad outcome, had he wished to do so. He could have found that the words "not having provoked the attack" were implicit in the provision. He could have found that in this case the need to avoid a bad outcome warranted the adoption of an implausible interpretation. The absurdity here seems every bit as compelling as it was in R. v. Paul.[39] Or he could have adopted the approach of McLachlin J. and corrected the drafting error that occurred in the preparation of the 1955 Code. However, because Lamer J. was moved by other considerations, which were for him more compelling, he preferred to rely on the plausible meaning rule.

---

39   Above note 18.

CHAPTER 8

THE ENTIRE CONTEXT

A. INTRODUCTION

As Driedger's modern principle tells us,[1] to achieve a sound interpretation of a legislative text, the words to be interpreted must be read in their entire context. More precisely, they must be read not only in their immediate context,[2] so as to determine their ordinary meaning, but also in a larger context that may include the Act as a whole, other legislation, the legal system as a whole, and the social conditions in which the legislation operates. It is necessary to look at this larger context for two reasons. The first is to determine whether a provision is ambiguous. As McLachlin C.J. asserts in *Montreal (City) v. 2952-1366 Québec Inc.*:

> Words that appear clear and unambiguous may in fact prove to be ambiguous once placed in their context. The possibility of the context revealing a latent ambiguity ... is a logical result of the modern approach to interpretation.[3]

---

1   For an account of Driedger's modern principle, see Chapter 2.
2   The immediate context consists of as much of the text surrounding the words to be interpreted as is needed to make sense of those words. Usually the immediate context consists of the section in which the words appear. For further discussion, see Chapter 3, Sections B & C.
3   [2005] 3 S.C.R. 141 at para 10. See also *Re Canada 3000 Inc.*, [2006] 1 S.C.R. 865 at paras. 44–45.

The second reason is to establish which interpretation of an ambiguous provision should be adopted. An interpretation that accords with the features of this larger context is preferred over one that does not. Coherence with the context suggests that a proposed interpretation is appropriate, whereas inconsistency or disharmony suggests that there is a problem.

It is obvious that in practice courts cannot scrutinize the entire context of a legislative provision, including the entire Act, the entire statute book, the legal context, and relevant external conditions. Of necessity, courts work with particular features of this larger context, features that are brought to its attention and appear to offer insight into legislative intention.

The type of analysis in which a court engages depends on the type of context it is looking at. When a court looks at the words to be interpreted in light of the entire Act or the entire statute book, its analysis is largely literary. Literary analysis treats the statute as a distinct literary genre and the statute book as the *oeuvre* of a single author — the legislature. It uses textual analysis techniques, similar to those used by scholars to explore the meaning of a poem or a play by a particular author. These techniques assume that the text has been written with care, that each word has a specific function to perform, and that the parts all fit together harmoniously to form a coherent whole.[4] They also assume that the Act (or part of the Act, or several Acts together)[5] is an action plan designed to implement a particular mix of objects. The challenge for the interpreter here is to identify the objects to be implemented, understand the scheme designed to implement them, and determine how the provision to be interpreted fits into the overall scheme.[6]

When courts look at the larger legal system to which a statute contributes, its analysis is legal. The purpose of legal analysis is to identify the established and emerging legal norms that a legislature has in mind when devising legislation and interpreters would have in mind when interpreting it. Legal norms are values or ways of proceeding that are accepted as important in a legal system and therefore to be observed as a matter of course. Most legal norms are grounded in the entrenched

---

4   These techniques are examined in detail in Chapter 9.

5   Some major Acts (for example, the *Criminal Code*) contain multiple schemes, and sometimes a number of Acts (for example, the *Broadcasting Act* and the *Radiocommunications Act* or the *Privacy Act* and the *Access to Information Act*) operate together to regulate a matter or problem. Statutes that relate to the same matter or problem are known as statutes *in pari materia*.

6   For a detailed account of purposive and scheme analysis, see Section B(4), below in this chapter.

constitution, in international law, or in common law, but such norms can also emerge from recurring themes in the relevant statute book or in the legislation of jurisdictions with a similar legal system.

Within each Canadian jurisdiction, there are four distinct sources of law: the Constitution, legislation, common law, and international law. There is presumed harmony among these several sources of law: legislation is presumed to comply with constitutional law and with Canada's obligations at international law; legislation is presumed to preserve rather than change the common law. Even though in principle these sources of law form an integrated "system," they don't form a single text. Statutes (and regulations) issue from a different "author" than the entrenched constitution, international law, or the common law. This creates a potential for conflict, which is resolved through paramountcy rules: in the event of conflict, the entrenched constitution trumps legislation, but legislation trumps international and common law. Ideally, however, the norms emerging from these sources work together to help infer legislative intent and guide interpretive as well as administrative discretion.

The final context in which legislation is examined is the so-called external context. This consists first of all of the original setting in which legislation was enacted—its social, cultural, economic, and political background. Here judicial analysis depends not on law, but on knowledge of the world. Courts assume that legislatures are well informed about the conditions existing when legislation is enacted and that this information is reflected in the preparation and drafting of statutes and regulations. This same information is then used by interpreters to draw inferences about the likely meaning and purpose of the text.[7]

The other aspect of external context, which is not always formally recognized by the court, is the operational context—the social, economic, political, and institutional context in which the legislation operates over time. Canadian courts began to explicitly address the operational context in the course of interpreting and applying the *Charter*. In dealing with *Charter* cases, it is well established that the meaning of protected rights and freedoms can only be understood in the context of current realities, that the courts must respond to changing conditions. When it comes to interpreting ordinary legislation, however, there is disagreement about the proper judicial role. Many judges insist that their sole task in interpretation is to discover and

---

7   The external context can be established through legislative history materials: see Chapter 14, Section B. Often, however, it is established through judicial notice.

carry out the intention of the legislature. Since that intention was fixed at the moment of enactment, subsequent change is irrelevant. Others reject this narrow conception and suggest that to achieve an appropriate interpretation of legislation the courts must consider its meaning in relation to the world in which it actually operates from time to time.[8]

B. THE ACT AS A WHOLE

Courts often say that the meaning of a word or expression can be fully understood only if it is read in the context of the Act as a whole. In *Garland v. Canada (Employment & Immigration Commission)*, for example, Heald J. wrote: "[I]t is necessary to read the statute containing the words in issue in its entirety as an initial step. Only after that has been done can it be determined with any precision whether or not the words being interpreted are clear and unambiguous."[9] Although commonplace, this advice is somewhat misleading. In the first place, it is not necessary to read every word of an enactment to get a sense of an Act as a whole. What one looks for when considering an Act in its entirety is (1) provisions elsewhere in the Act that are in some way related to the provision to be interpreted; (2) internal groupings; (3) relevant structural components; and (4) the overall legislative scheme.

In the second place, a court does not simply read legislation, the way it might read a report or some other piece of expository prose. In so far as the whole of an Act or other legislation is relevant, it is read with unusual care and attention to detail, and with conscious regard to assumptions about the way it is drafted. Lord Reid mentions one of these assumptions in *Inland Revenue Commissioners v. Hinchy*: "[O]ne assumes that in drafting one clause of a Bill the draftsman had in mind the language and substance of other clauses, and attributes to Parliament a comprehension of the whole Act."[10] One also assumes that:

- the enacting legislature had a purpose, and each provision contributes in some cogent way to accomplishing the purpose;[11]

---

8   The use of current context to interpret legislation is discussed in Chapter 6.

9   [1985] 2 F.C. 508 at 515 (C.A.). This point has been made in recent judgments of the Supreme Court of Canada. See in particular *Re Canada 3000 Inc.*, above note 3 at paras. 44–45.

10   [1960] A.C. 748 at 766 (H.L.).

11   This is the basic assumption underlying scheme analysis. For further discussion, see Section B(4), below in this chapter.

- the legislation has been competently drafted, in a straightforward and elegant style, taking care to avoid tautology, inconsistency, or stylistic variation;[12]
- provisions are set out in an orderly fashion, to reflect a coherent plan; and
- non-substantive components of the legislation (preambles, titles, headings, and the like) have been used conventionally.[13]

By reading a statute in light of these assumptions, it is possible to draw inferences about the intention of the legislature.

1) Related Provisions Elsewhere in the Act

Initially, one tackles a statute in its entirety by skimming through it, with an eye to keywords, concepts, or issues. Acts often follow a conventional order, so a reader knows where to look for certain types of provisions; headings and marginal notes (often set out in a table of contents) also facilitate quick perusal of an Act. This initial reading should give a sense of the overall structure of the Act and also turn up other provisions that may have some significant relation to the provision to be interpreted. By reading related provisions together, the court uncovers aspects of what the legislature intended.[14]

Reliance on this form of textual analysis is illustrated by Sopinka J. in *Willick v. Willick*.[15] Section 17(4) of the *Divorce Act* provided that before a support order made under the Act could be varied, there must have been a material change in the "circumstances of either former spouse or of any child of the marriage." The question was whether this condition was met when a former husband received a pay increase but the circumstances of the former wife and the children had not changed. Sopinka J. wrote:

---

12   These assumptions are explained and discussed in Chapter 9.
13   The role of these components in interpreting legislation are explained and discussed in Section B(3), below in this chapter.
14   See *Chieu v. Canada (Minister of Citizenship and Immigration)*, [2002] 1 S.C.R. 84 at para. 5, where Iabobucci J. wrote:

> There are three statutory provisions which are at the heart of this appeal—ss. 70(1), 52 and 114(2) of the Act, which are set out below. Many other provisions are relevant to the particular facts of this case and to the overall scheme of the Act. They will be cited as they become relevant throughout the course of these reasons.

15   [1994] 3 S.C.R. 670.

With respect to the application of the contextual approach advocated by the respondent, the objective is to interpret statutory provisions to harmonize the components of legislation inasmuch as is possible.... If one peruses s. 15, other subsections of s. 17 and the overall pattern of the *Divorce Act*, especially compared with the 1970 version of the Act, it is my view that the interpretation advocated by the appellant must prevail. In rendering original divorce orders pursuant to s. 11(1), courts are to ensure that reasonable arrangements have been made for the children.... Under s. 15, in granting support orders, courts are to consider, among other things, the needs of the children.... This suggests a child-centred approach to rendering support orders.[16]

What Sopinka J. noticed was a common theme found in each provision of the Act dealing with support orders — namely, concern for the children of the marriage. This recurring and consistent preoccupation suggested that maximum support of children was an important goal of the legislature. Since the appellant's interpretation was more in keeping with this goal, it was preferred.[17]

In *McClurg v. M.N.R.*,[18] La Forest J. relied on textual analysis of the Act as a whole to help determine the meaning of section 24 of Saskatchewan's *Business Corporations Act*. The section listed matters that had to be included in a corporation's articles of association. Section 24(4)(a) provided that where a corporation's articles of association allowed for more than one class of shares, the rights attaching to each class had to be "set out therein." The question was whether this requirement was met if the articles of association stated that dividends on a class of shares were payable at the sole discretion of the directors. La Forest J., dissenting, said no. On his interpretation, to comply with the section, the full substance of the rights had to be spelled out in the articles. He wrote: "I note that this interpretation of s. 24(4)(a) appears to be the most consistent with other provisions of the Act."[19] He went on to compare section 24(4)(a) to various other provisions that gave directors discretion over shareholders' rights. Where such discretion was granted elsewhere in the Act, he noted, it was expressly conferred and carefully limited. The absence of any such limitation in section 24 suggested that no discretion was intended here. This inference was based on the pre-

---

16   *Ibid.* at 689–90.
17   A similar analysis is found in *Gosselin v. Quebec (Attorney General)*, [2002] 4 S.C.R. 429 at para. 89*ff* [*Gosselin*] and in *Re Canada 3000 Inc.*, above note 3 at para. 49*ff*.
18   [1990] 3 S.C.R. 1020.
19   *Ibid.* at 1066.

sumption of uniform expression: once a legislature adopts a particular form to express a particular idea, it uses the same form each time to express that idea. One is therefore justified in inferring that if this form is not used, the legislature did not intend to express that idea.

La Forest J. also noted the relationship between section 24(4)(*a*) and other provisions in the Act which were designed to protect the rights of shareholders. If directors could be given discretion under section 24, these protections could easily be undermined. Of course, the legislature would not introduce protections in one section of an Act only to undermine them in another. To do so would violate the presumptions in favour of coherence and against tautology: the legislature does not contradict itself, nor does it enact futile or self-defeating provisions. In light of these considerations, the more restrictive interpretation was preferred.

2) Internal Groupings

Provisions tend to be grouped together when they deal with the same theme, share a single idea, contribute to a shared purpose, or perform the same or analogous functions. Attention may be drawn to these connections through the use of structural components such as headings and marginal notes. Or they may be signalled in more subtle fashion through the use of subsections and paragraphs, through reliance on repetition and parallel structures, or simply through proximity.

In *Committee for the Commonwealth of Canada v. Canada*,[20] for example, the Supreme Court of Canada had to determine whether section 7(b) of the *Government Airport Concession Operations Regulations* applied to a group whose members wished to deliver a political message by carrying signs and distributing literature in airport terminals. Section 7 provided that, without the permission of the minister, no person could

    (a)   conduct any business or undertaking, commercial or otherwise, at an airport;

    (b)   advertise or solicit at an airport on his own behalf or on behalf of any person; or

    (c)   fix, install or place anything at an airport for the purpose of any business or undertaking.

The language of paragraph (b) was broad and unqualified, yet Lamer J. found that section 7 was aimed at business and other commercial activity and was never intended to apply to political activities. This finding was based on an analysis of the group of provisions in which section

---

20   [1991] 1 S.C.R. 139.

7 was placed. This analysis revealed a common theme — namely, the provisions all dealt with commercial operations: section 6 dealt with gas stations, while sections 8 to 20 dealt with passenger transportation. Lamer J. concluded:

> In my view, it would be surprising to find that, in these provisions dealing essentially with commercial passenger transportation, the legislature intended to prohibit any form of political propaganda in s. 7(*b*) of the Regulations. Thus, the context in which the language of this paragraph is found also leads to the conclusion that ... [it prohibits only] operations of a commercial nature.[21]

3) Components

Legislation is made up primarily of provisions, which are drafted in the form of sentences and set out in numbered sections and subsections. Legislation also includes other elements, usually called "components," which may not be in sentence form and are not set out in sections and subsections. The traditional components are titles, headings, preambles, marginal notes, and schedules. Current legislation often includes purpose statements.[22] And in recent years, there has been much discussion of using examples, footnotes, and other types of explanatory aids in legislation.

Acts are given short titles for ease of reference and long titles that indicate the subject and scope of the Act.[23] Each section of an Act is given a short descriptive label, historically called a marginal note, which is set out above or next to the relevant section or in a table of contents at the beginning of the Act. In addition, many Acts have internal titles, headings, and subheadings. They indicate the subject or purpose of the provisions that follow and help to indicate the structure and scheme of the Act. Some Acts have preambles, which set out the primary considerations that moved the legislature to enact the legislation. Occasionally, Acts have schedules or appendices. They contain material which, because of its form, cannot conveniently be included in the body of the

---

21   *Ibid.* at 163.
22   Strictly speaking, purpose statements should not be classified as "components" because they are sentences in numbered sections or subsections. Purpose statements are properly understood as interpretive provisions, that is, provisions that tell users of legislation how to understand and apply legislation. Other examples of interpretive provisions are definition sections and application provisions.
23   In some jurisdictions the convention of long and short titles has been abandoned and Acts receive a single title.

Act—for example, lists, tables, maps, or forms to be used in administering the Act. Schedules are also used to set out texts or instruments that are relevant to the legislation, such as a treaty that is implemented or a contract that is validated in the main body of the Act.

There is no doubt that components can sometimes shed light on the meaning or purpose of legislation, and courts have taken advantage of this assistance on countless occasions. Nonetheless, the rules governing the use of components are technical, complex, inconsistent, and uncertain. There are three main sources of difficulty.

First, there is the distinction drawn between the internal and external components of legislation. This distinction originated in the peculiarities of Anglo-Canadian parliamentary procedure. Historically, under this procedure the provisions of legislation were included in bills when they were tabled in the legislature. These provisions were considered to be internal—that is, part of the legislation. They could therefore be relied on in interpretation for whatever insight they might yield. However, other components were added to legislation by parliamentary clerks after enactment. These were the so-called external components. Because they did not form part of the legislation at the time of enactment, their use in interpretation was considered inappropriate. Nowadays all components of legislation are present in bills from the outset, and the internal/external distinction is no longer important for purposes of interpretation. It nonetheless lingers, in part because of the plain meaning rule.

According to the plain meaning rule (or some versions of the rule), where the meaning of legislative language is plain, nothing outside the provision to be interpreted—in other words, nothing "external"—should be looked at.[24] Resort to things like headings or preambles is permissible only in cases of ambiguity. Furthermore, under the plain meaning rule these external components must not be relied on to help "create" ambiguity in the first place. To determine whether the meaning is plain, the provision must be read in isolation from its context. Although the plain meaning rule has been discredited on many occasions, and is inconsistent with Driedger's modern principle, it is still invoked by some judges when dealing with aids to interpretation that are considered to be "extrinsic" or "external."

Finally, to add to the confusion, the rules governing components have been partially and inconsistently codified in Canadian Interpretation Acts. Since the various provincial and federal Interpretation Acts

---

24   For a complete account of the plain meaning rule and its limitations, see Chapter 3.

are not all uniform in their treatment of these components, it is necessary to consult the relevant Act to know which rules apply.

Despite these difficulties, Anglo-Canadian courts are moving towards adoption of a single general principle. Under this principle, all components of legislation are considered part of the legislative context and may be taken into account in interpreting a text, not only to resolve ambiguity but generally to help determine the intended or appropriate meaning. On this approach, it is not necessary to find that a text is ambiguous before looking at a heading or a preamble. As Viscount Simonds wrote in *Attorney-General v. Prince Ernest Augustus of Hanover*, speaking of preambles: "[N]o one should profess to understand any part of a statute or of any other document before he has read the whole of it. Until he has done so he is not entitled to say that it or any part of it is clear and unambiguous."[25]

a) Titles

The title of an enactment, whether long or short, is relied on in interpretation to indicate the purpose or scope of legislation. In *Hudon v. United States Borax & Chemical Corp.*,[26] a Saskatchewan court relied on the title of Saskatchewan's *Act to Regulate the Operation of Vehicles on Highways* to limit the scope of its gratuitous passenger provision. This provision limited the liability of vehicle owners and drivers for injuries or death suffered by non-paying passengers "being carried in … or entering … or alighting from the motor vehicle." The issue was whether the provision applied when the gratuitous passenger was injured in an accident occurring on a private parking lot. Although the provision itself contained no words limiting its application to accidents occurring in a particular place, the court relied on the title to read in this limitation. Disberry J. wrote: "The long title of a statute is itself an important part of an Act and should be taken into consideration in determining the scope and purview of the Act."[27] He concluded that the Act was meant to apply to events occurring on highways, to the exclusion of other places. Since this restriction was clearly set out in the title, it was not necessary for the drafter to mention the restriction expressly in each section of the Act. The restriction implicitly applied to the entire Act.

Titles are also relied on as evidence of legislative purpose. In *R. v. Thompson*, Wilson J. wrote: "When Parliament enacted the amendments

25   [1957] A.C. 436 at 463 (H.L.).
26   (1970), 11 D.L.R. (3d) 345 (Sask. Q.B.).
27   *Ibid.* at 348.

to the *Criminal Code* to establish Part IV.1, they did so through the *Protection of Privacy Act....* This legislation, in my view, was enacted to do just that, protect privacy."[28] Along similar lines, La Forest J. wrote: "The primary purpose of the Act, as is evident from its original name (the *Protection of Privacy Act ...*), is to protect the privacy of individuals from electronic interceptions of their private communications."[29]

In constitutional cases, the title may be used to help identify the primary purpose of legislation for *Charter* analysis or the "pith and substance" for classification under sections 91 and 92 of the *Constitution Act, 1867.* In *R. v. Swain,*[30] for example, the Supreme Court of Canada relied on the title of British Columbia's *Heroin Treatment Act* to conclude that even though the Act provided for the involuntary detention of addicts, its pith and substance was treatment rather than punishment. It was therefore valid as legislation in relation to health, a provincial matter.

b) Preambles

Preambles are set out at the beginning of enactments, immediately after the title and before the enacting clause. They set out the reasons why the legislature thought it necessary or appropriate to enact the legislation. These reasons may recite the social or economic evils the Act was meant to combat, the aspirations that motivated the legislature, the concerns it was attempting to meet, the principles that guided it in preparing the legislation, and the ultimate goals it hoped to achieve.

Preambles are not an essential element of legislation and many statutes do not have one. Most drafters regard them as too vague to be useful, or "too political." To the extent they offer a concise and useful explanation of purpose, they can be replaced by purpose statements which, unlike preambles, are enacted as part of the Act. However, the free-ranging and overtly political character of preambles often serves political needs, and for this reason they are unlikely to soon disappear.

Preambles are relied on most often to reveal legislative purpose, either directly by setting out the purposes of the legislation or indirectly by describing the evils or concerns that motivated the legislature. In

---

28 [1990] 2 S.C.R. 1111 at 1158. [Citations omitted.]

29 *Ibid.* at 1160. [Citations omitted.] See also *CCH Canadian Ltd. v. Law Society of Upper Canada,* [2004] 1 S.C.R. 339 at para. 20., in which the title is relied on to illuminate the governing conception of the legislation.

30 [1991] 1 S.C.R. 933.

Finlay v. Canada (Minister of Finance), for example, in dealing with the *Canada Assistance Plan*, LeDain J. wrote:

> It is a spending statute. This is confirmed by reference to its preamble which ... identifies Parliament's specific aim in enacting this legislation—"the Parliament of Canada ... is desirous of encouraging the further development and extension of assistance and welfare service programs throughout Canada *by sharing more fully with the provinces in the cost thereof*".[31]

In this instance the preamble provided a direct description of the legislature's goal, the development and extension of national programs, as well as the instrument chosen to achieve the goal—namely, cost sharing.[32]

Preambles can also be a source of legislative values and principles on which courts and other interpreters may draw, particularly to guide the exercise of any powers or discretion conferred by the Act. In *New Brunswick (Minister of Health & Community Services) v. C. (G.C.)*,[33] for example, the issue was how the court should determine the "best interests" of a child under New Brunswick's *Family Services Act*, and in particular what weight should attach to the interests of parents in deciding what to do with the child. L'Heureux-Dubé J. referred to the preamble to justify her understanding of the child's best interests. She wrote: "Even if the Act did transfer to the Minister 'all parental rights' ... it provides some means for the conservation of the relationship between the child and its natural parent or guardian when in the former's best interests. Indeed, the preamble of the Act declares that 'children should only be removed from parental supervision either partly or entirely when all other measures are inappropriate.'"[34] Here the preamble was helpful in indicating how competing interests might be balanced in an appropriate way.

---

31   [1993] 1 S.C.R. 1080 at 1123. [Emphasis in original.]
32   See also *Re Application under s. 83.28 of the Criminal Code*, [1991] S.C.J. No. 69 at paras. 37–38:

> The Preamble to the Act ... provide[s] insight into the purpose of the Act in general, and of s. 83.28 in particular .... The Preamble to the Act speaks to the "challenge of eradicating terrorism", the requirement for the "strengthening of Canada's capacity to suppress, investigate and incapacitate terrorist activity", and the need for legislation to "prevent and suppress the financing, preparation, facilitation and commission of acts of terrorism".

33   [1988] 1 S.C.R. 1073.
34   *Ibid.* at 1080.

Preambles are also relied on to help resolve ambiguity or to determine the scope of legislative language. In *R. v. C.D.*,[35] for example, the issue was whether the term "violent offence" in the *Youth Criminal Justice Act* extended to every offence in which the offender used or threatened to use force or was limited to offences in which the offender caused or threatened to cause bodily harm. The Supreme Court of Canada opted for the narrower interpretation because it was more in keeping with the purposes of the legislation. Speaking for the court, Bastarache J. wrote:

> While the Act may be generally concerned with the protection of the public, it also has some specific goals, including restricting the use of custody for young offenders. This particular goal is evidenced in the preamble of the Act, as well as in s. 38(2).[36.]
>
> Turning first to the preamble, there are two parts that demonstrate that the Act is aimed at restricting the use of custody for young persons. First, there is the part of the preamble that states that "Canada is a party to the United Nations Convention on the Rights of the Child.... This reference to the Convention ... is important because art. 37(b) of the Convention provides that:
>
> > No child shall be deprived of his or her liberty unlawfully or arbitrarily. The arrest, detention or imprisonment of a child shall be in conformity with the law and shall be used only as a measure of last resort and for the shortest appropriate period of time;

The second part of the preamble that demonstrates that the Act is aimed at restricting the use of custody for young offenders reads as follows:

> WHEREAS Canadian society should have a youth criminal justice system that commands respect, takes into account the interests of victims, fosters responsibility and ensures accountability through meaningful consequences and effective rehabilitation and reintegration, and *that reserves its most serious intervention for the most serious crimes and reduces the over-reliance on incarceration for non-violent young persons.*[37] [Emphasis added.]

---

35   [2005] 3 S.C.R. 668.
36   *Ibid.* at 690. Section 38(2) sets out the principles that are to govern the sentencing of youth under the Act.
37   *Ibid.* at 691.

Finally, courts may look to the preamble of one statute to help interpret another related statute.[38] They may also look to the preamble to an international instrument for help in interpreting the legislation enacted to give domestic effect to that instrument.[39]

c) Purpose Statements

Purpose statements can take different forms, from a short introductory phrase to elaborate, multiparagraphed provisions.[40] Like preambles, purpose statements reveal the purpose of legislation and draw attention to the principles and policies that should inform the exercise of discretion conferred by the Act. However, unlike preambles, purpose statements are set out in the body of the statute as a numbered provision (or part of a numbered provision) and they unquestionably form an integral part of the legislation in which they appear. They are to be relied on in every interpretive exercise.

The use of purpose statements is illustrated by the Supreme Court of Canada in *LeBlanc v. LeBlanc*.[41] The issue in the case was whether New Brunswick's *Marital Property Act* conferred discretion on the courts to deny a spouse an equal share in the couple's marital property upon marriage breakdown. In holding that it did, the Supreme Court of Canada relied on the purpose statement set out in section 2 of the Act. La Forest J. wrote:

> Section 2 is an interpretative provision in the nature of a preamble announcing the general framework and philosophy of the legislation. It reads:
>
> > "2. Child care, household management and financial provision are joint responsibilities of spouses and are recognized to be of equal importance in assessing the contributions of the respective spouses to the acquisition, management,

---

38   See *Bell ExpressVu Limited Partnership v. Rex*, [2002] 2 S.C.R. 559 at paras. 45–46 [*Bell ExpressVu*]. In *Bell ExpressVu*, the court relied on s. 3 of the Act setting out the governing principles of Canadian broadcasting policy; this is the sort of material that is often found in preambles.

39   See *Canada (Attorney General) v. Ward*, [1993] 2 S.C.R. 689 at para. 63; *Baker v. Canada (Minister of Citizenship and Immigration)*, [1999] 2 S.C.R. 817 at para. 71.

40   Because purpose statements appear as sentences or parts of sentences within sections or subsections, they are not really components. They are appropriately classified as interpretive provisions. However, it is customary in statutory interpretation texts to examine them in conjunction with preambles, which perform a similar function.

41   [1988] 1 S.C.R. 217.

maintenance, operation or improvement of marital property; and *subject to the equitable considerations recognized
elsewhere in the Act the contribution of each spouse to the fulfilment of these responsibilities entitles each spouse to an equal
share of the marital property* and imposes on each spouse,
in relation to the other, the burden of an equal share of the
marital debts." [Emphasis added.]

...

In common with similar provisions in other jurisdictions, s. 2
establishes the general principle that each spouse is entitled to an
equal share of marital property.... The principle must be respected.
In applying that principle, the courts are not permitted to engage in
measurements of the relative contribution of spouses to a marriage.
Nevertheless ... the principle is expressly made subject to the equitable considerations recognized elsewhere in the Act.[42]

The purpose statement made it clear that the Act was animated by more
than one guiding principle, that the ideal of partnership and pooling
between spouses might in appropriate circumstances be tempered by
concerns of fairness and of avoiding unjust enrichment.

As purpose statements become more commonplace in legislation,
they figure ever more prominently in interpretation.

d) Headings

The majority of Canadian Interpretation Acts state that headings are
not part of the enactment in which they appear, the implication being
that they should not be taken into account (at least not in the absence
of ambiguity). Other Interpretation Acts say nothing of headings. In
practice, courts often ignore the Interpretation Acts and rely on case
law to decide what use should be made of headings. In the older cases,
courts emphasize the external nature of headings and refuse to rely
on them unless the language of the legislation is ambiguous. In more
recent cases, there is a tendency to treat headings as an integral part of
the context, to be relied on like any other contextual feature. This is the
approach taken by the Supreme Court of Canada towards the headings
that appear in the *Charter.* In *Law Society of Upper Canada v. Skapinker,*
Estey J. wrote:

The *Charter,* from its first introduction into the constitutional process,
included many headings including the heading now in question.... It

---

42   *Ibid.* at 221–22.

is clear that these headings were systematically and deliberately included as an integral part of the *Charter* for whatever purpose. At the very minimum, the Court must take them into consideration when engaged in the process of discerning the meaning and application of the provisions of the *Charter*.[43]

This approach to headings has been adopted in interpreting ordinary legislation as well.

In *R. v. Lohnes*,[44] for example, the Supreme Court of Canada relied on headings in adopting a restrictive reading of section 175(1)(a) of the *Criminal Code*. That section made it an offence to cause a disturbance in or near a public place. It was one of several sections grouped under the heading "Disorderly Conduct." The issue was whether the word "disturbance" should be read broadly to include mental or emotional upset or should be limited to overt, publicly exhibited disorder. McLachlin J. wrote:

> [H]eadings and preambles may be used as intrinsic aids in interpreting ambiguous statutes. Section 175(1)(a) appears under the section "Disorderly Conduct". Without elevating headings to determinative status, the heading under which s. 175(1)(a) appears supports the view that Parliament had in mind, not the emotional upset or annoyance of individuals, but disorder and agitation which interfere with the ordinary use of a place.[45]

Headings are also useful in exploring the structure of legislation. In *Charlebois v. Saint John (City)*,[46] in concluding that the term "institution" in New Brunswick's *Official Languages Act* did not include municipalities, a majority of the Supreme Court of Canada relied on the presumption that statutes are coherent structures, in which all the parts work together to advance a legislation scheme. To reveal the structure of the Act, the court analyzed the headings and their relation to the provisions set out beneath each heading. Charron J. wrote:

> A reading of the *OLA* reveals two main structural features. First, the word "institution", as defined in s.1, acts as a central provision that identifies those public bodies on which the Legislature imposes

---

43 [1984] 1 S.C.R. 357 at 376. See also *B.(R.) v. Children's Aid Society of Metro Toronto*, [1995] 1 S.C.R. 315 at paras. 25–26.

44 [1992] 1 S.C.R. 167.

45 *Ibid.* at 179. See also *R. v. Kelly*, [1992] 2 S.C.R. 170 and *R. v. Zundel*, [1992] 2 S.C.R. 731.

46 [2005] S.C.J. No. 77 [*Charlebois*].

particular language obligations in other provisions of the *OLA*. ... Second, the *OLA* groups under various headings different areas of activity or services which fall under the purview of the public administration of the province and imposes specific language obligations under each heading. "Municipalities" (which by definition includes cities, towns and villages) is one such heading.[47]

After examining the nature and scope of the obligations imposed under each heading, Charron J. concluded that interpreting "institution" to include municipalities would lead to "incoherent and illogical consequences" whereas if "institution" is read as not including municipalities, "the internal coherence is restored."[48]

e) Marginal Notes

Both the common law and Canadian Interpretation Acts say that marginal notes do not form part of the legislation in which they appear. For this reason, the courts have traditionally refused to rely on them in statutory interpretation. In a number of recent cases, however, the Supreme Court of Canada has adopted a new rule. It says that marginal notes may be used in interpretation, but should receive only minimal weight. The leading case is *R. v. Wigglesworth*, where Wilson J. looked at the marginal note accompanying section 11 of the *Charter*.[49] Since then her approach has been applied to both federal and provincial legislation.

In her dissenting judgment in *R. v. McIntosh*,[50] for example, McLachlin J. traced the evolution of the marginal notes accompanying sections 34 and 35 of the *Criminal Code* to show that a drafting error occurred in the preparation of the 1954–55 revision. In her view, the self-defence provision set out in section 34 afforded a defence only if the accused had not provoked the assault from which he then defended himself. The section itself did not expressly mention a non-provocation requirement, but only because the relevant words had been inadvertently eliminated from the section during the revision process. On the subject of marginal notes, McLachlin J. wrote:

> The marginal notes accompanying ss. 34 and 35 support the view that the omission of the phrase "without having provoked the assault" in the 1955 *Code* was inadvertent and that Parliament continued to intend

---

47   *Ibid.* at para. 16.
48   *Ibid.* at para. 19
49   [1987] 2 S.C.R. 541 at 556.
50   [1995] 1 S.C.R. 686.

that s. 34 would apply [only] to unprovoked assaults.... The note for s. 34 is "Self-defence against unprovoked assault/Extent of justification", for s. 35 "Self-defence in case of aggression", namely assault or provocation. While marginal notes are not part of the legislative act of Parliament, and hence are not conclusive support in interpretation ... they may be of some limited use in gleaning the intention of the enactment. Inasmuch as they do indicate an intention, they clearly support the interpretation suggested by the above discussion.[51]

McLachlin J.'s position has been adopted by the court in a number of cases.[52]

f) Schedules

Schedules include materials that could not conveniently be put into the form of sentences, such as lists, tables, charts, and maps. They are also used to set out copies of documents, instruments, or other texts that are relevant to the legislation, such as forms to be used in administering the legislation or an international convention to be implemented. Often the executive branch is given delegated authority to add or delete items from a schedule, thereby enabling the government to respond to change without having to go back to the legislature.

Although schedules are considered internal rather than external, not all scheduled materials have the force of law. To be considered part of what is enacted into law, the scheduled material must be incorporated into the Act either expressly or by implication. Once incorporated, scheduled material is as much a part of an Act as its sections and subsections, and it has the same significance and use in interpretation. An example of this type of schedule is found in federal legislation creating illegal drug offences. As the Supreme Court of Canada explains in *R. v. Malmo-Levine*,

> Section 2 of the *NCA* [*Narcotics Control Act*] defines "marihuana" as *Cannabis sativa* L. and a "narcotic" as "any substance included in the schedule or anything that contains any substance included in the schedule". Marihuana became a scheduled drug when *The Opium and Narcotic Drug Act*, 1923, S.C. 1923, c. 22 (the predecessor to the *NCA*) was enacted by Parliament.[53]

---

51 *Ibid.* at 717.
52 See, for example, *Francis v. Baker*, [1999] 3 S.C.R. 250 at paras. 22 and 42; *Imperial Oil Ltd. v. Canada*, [2006] 2 S.C.R. 447 at para. 57.
53 [2003] 3 S.C.R. 571 at para. 12.

So long as marihuana remains in the schedule, possession of it will remain an offence under section 3(1) of the *Narcotics Control Act*.[54]

Scheduled material that is not incorporated into the Act is not part of the law, and is included for convenience only. Although unincorporated material is not law, it is considered internal to the statute and may be relied on to help determine its meaning and purpose. Thus "extrinsic materials"[55] that might otherwise be inadmissible become admissible for all purposes if they are included in a schedule.

Reliance on scheduled material is illustrated in the judgment of the Supreme Court of Canada in *Composers Authors and Publishers Assn. of Canada Ltd. v. CTV Television Network*.[56] The court had to determine whether the right to communicate musical works by "radio communication" included transmitting works on video taped television programs by microwave. Although microwave transmission could be considered a form of radio communication, the court concluded that the expression "radio communication" was in fact a drafter's error, based on a mistranslation of *"communication ... par la radiodiffusion."* This conclusion was reached after examining the official French version of the *Rome Convention on Copyright* set out in a schedule to the Act. Pigeon J. wrote:

> [T]he intention must be gathered from the statute as a whole and this certainly includes the Schedule that is referred to in the body of the Act and is printed with it. Upon such consideration it becomes apparent that ... [the reference to "radio communication" in the Act] is intended to achieve the result contemplated in ... [article 11*bis* of the Convention].[57]
>
> It will be noted that where the Convention speaks of *"radiodiffusion"* i.e. radio broadcasting, the unfortunate translation reads "radio-communication". The error in translation of the Convention was obviously carried into the statute intended to implement it.[58]

Because the Convention was set out in the Schedule, it was unnecessary for the court to worry about the rules governing the admissibility and use of extrinsic materials.

---

54 The *Narcotics Control Act* has been replaced by the *Controlled Drugs and Substances Act*. It adopts the same approach, setting out the controlled substances in a number of schedules and making it an offence to possess a scheduled substance.
55 For the rules governing the use of extrinsic materials, see Chapter 14.
56 [1968] S.C.R. 676.
57 *Ibid.* at 682.
58 *Ibid.* at 681.

4) The Legislative Scheme

All legislation is enacted for a purpose — to reach imagined goals or to produce specific effects. The most challenging part of preparing legislation lies in devising a plan that will actually achieve the intended purpose. The government must decide what kind of resources it is willing to commit to its goals and it must choose appropriate implementation mechanisms, taking into account many factors: efficacy, efficiency, constraints imposed by the *Charter* and the rule of law, public opinion, interest group pressures, party politics, and more. Once a plan is formulated, it must be approved by Cabinet. Then it goes to the drafter.

The process just described is the standard protocol at the federal level. However, there are many variations on this process. For example, bills introduced by private members do not receive Cabinet approval, and regulations made by independent bodies like administrative boards may respond to different constraints. But regardless of process, the essentials are the same. They include the need for a coherent relation between means and goals, an implementation plan that takes into account the relevant constraints, and a drafter to put it all into legislative form.

The drafter's primary job is to transform the proposed plan into a legislative scheme by formulating a series of provisions which, if acted upon as written, will create the necessary structures and offices, confer the necessary powers, issue appropriate directives and prohibitions, and establish suitable procedures. If the plan is a good one and the circumstances in which it must operate do not materially change, the purpose should be achieved.

In analyzing the Act as a whole, the court tries to discern the scheme implicit in the legislation and how the words to be interpreted fit into this scheme. Competing interpretations are tested to see which is more consistent with the apparent function of the words in the overall scheme, which better facilitates the efficient operation of the scheme.

A good example of this type of analysis is found in the judgment of Deschamps J. in *Monsanto Canada Inc. v. Ontario (Superintendent of Financial Services)*,[59] where the Supreme Court of Canada had to determine the meaning of section 70(6) of Ontario's *Pension Benefits Act*:

> 70. (6) On the partial wind up of a pension plan, ... persons entitled to benefits under the pension plan shall have rights and benefits that are not less than the rights and benefits they would have on a full wind up of the pension plan on the effective date of the partial wind up.

---

59   [2004] 3 S.C.R. 152 [*Monsanto*]. See also *Gosselin*, above note 17 at para. 89*ff.*

Monsanto's proposal to partially wind up its pension plan did not provide for the immediate distribution of surplus assets. Monsanto argued that section 70(6) did not require immediate distribution, that the effect of the section was merely to create a vested right in persons entitled to benefits to participate in the eventual distribution of surplus assets if and when the plan was fully wound up. The Superintendent of Financial Services argued that the section required distribution on the effective date of the partial wind up.

Relying on the ordinary meaning of the words, the court concluded that the latter interpretation was correct. In support of this conclusion Deschamps J. carried out a careful scheme analysis in which she explored the underlying logic of the various provisions dealing with the winding up of plans. She began by noting that the definitions of "wind up" and "partial wind up" in the Act were nearly identical and both required a distribution of assets:

> "partial wind up" means the termination of part of a pension plan and *the distribution of the assets of the pension fund related to that part of the pension plan*;

> "wind up" means the termination of a pension plan and the distribution of the assets of the pension fund.[60] [Emphasis added.]

She then drew attention to provisions in both the Act and the Regulations that clearly contemplated the immediate distribution of assets on a partial wind up. For example, under section 70(1)(c) of the Act both partial and full wind-up reports had to set out "the methods of allocating and distributing the assets of the pension plan." Similarly, under section 28.1(2) of Reg. 909, each person entitled to participate in a partial wind up was to receive a pension statement setting out "[t]he method of distributing the surplus assets amount allocated to the person." She concluded that "delaying the distribution would not be consonant with these provisions that make distribution of surplus assets an intended part of the wind-up process, whether the wind-up is in whole or in part."[61]

Having noted that the rights and procedural requirements set out in the Act are the same for both partial and full wind ups, Deschamps J. then turned her attention to the different treatment afforded continuing plans on the one hand and winding-up plans (whether partial or full) on the other. She wrote:

---

60   *Monsanto, ibid.* at para. 32.
61   *Ibid.*

[I]n s. 78(1) the general rule is established that "[n]o money may be paid out of a pension fund to the employer without the prior consent of the Superintendent." Sections 79(1) and 79(3) then provide for exceptions to this rule depending on whether the application for payment is being made with regard to a plan that is continuing or one that is winding up. [Under both the Act and the Regulations] it is much more difficult to justify surplus withdrawal from a continuing plan than from a plan winding up in whole or in part. The interpretation of s. 70(6) herein proposed is consistent with the logic of this aspect of the statutory scheme and the legislature's choice to treat partial wind-ups in the same manner as full wind-ups.[62]

As Deschamps J. suggests, there is a logic underlying the provisions that comprise an Act. Scheme analysis is based on the assumption that the legislature creates coherent, workable schemes that promote the legislative purpose, that all the provisions have a role in the scheme and there are no contradictions or inconsistencies. Therefore, interpretations that fit the logic of the scheme and avoid internal inconsistency or conflict are to be preferred.[63]

An interesting aspect of Deschamps J.'s analysis is her treatment of the Act and its regulations as constituting an integrated scheme. Even though regulations are a subordinate form of legislation that issue from the executive branch, the courts recognize that they often play an essential role in the legislative scheme.[64]

C. RELATED STATUTES (STATUTES *IN PARI MATERIA*)

A legislature may enact more than one statute on the same subject or may enact provisions in one statute that touch on a matter dealt with in another. A single legislative scheme may be embodied in more than one enactment. Statutes, or portions of statutes, that deal with the same subject or contribute to an integrated scheme are said to be in pari materia. As Gonthier J. explains in Re Therrien: "Interpretations favouring harmony between the various statutes enacted by the same govern-

---

62   *Ibid.* at para. 33.
63   For an excellent example of a judgment in which the outcome turns on the majority's conclusion that a restrictive interpretation must be adopted to avoid incoherence in the legislative scheme, see *Charlebois*, above note 46 at para. 16*ff.*
64   See, for example, *Re Canada 3000 Inc.*, above note 3 at para. 50.

ment should indeed prevail. This presumption is even stronger when the statutes relate to the same subject matter."[65]

When statutes are closely related, a court may also find it appropriate to rely on definitions or other interpretive provisions found in one statute to help interpret the other. This practice is partially codified in section 15(2) of the federal *Interpretation Act* which provides that the interpretation provisions of an enactment are applicable to all other enactments relating to the same subject matter.[66]

An example of multistatute scheme analysis is found in *Canada (Attorney General) v. Public Service Alliance of Canada*[67] This case concerned the status of workers who were formally employed by a private-sector corporation but whose services were performed exclusively for the federal government. The question was whether these workers were government employees for collective bargaining purposes. Although the answer turned on the meaning of "employee" in section 33 of the *Public Service Staff Relations Act*, the court found it necessary to examine three other related enactments: the *Canada Labour Code*, the *Public Service Employment Act*, and the *Financial Administration Act*. On the basis of this examination, a majority of the court concluded that the expansive interpretation of "employee" urged by the union would disrupt the scheme of labour relations put in place by the several Acts. Sopinka J. wrote:

> The three statutes referred to above when read with the *Canada Labour Code* reveal a scheme to create two separate and distinct labour regimes for two categories of federal employees. The legislation treats each category as mutually exclusive....
>
> In ... [this] scheme of labour relations ... there is just no place for a species of *de facto* public servant who is neither fish nor fowl.[68]

Sopinka J. went on to outline a number of problems and anomalies that would arise if the broader interpretation were adopted. Since legislative schemes are presumed to be coherent and internally consistent, an interpretation that creates anomalies and inconsistencies is unlikely to have been intended. Such an interpretation is less appropriate than one that fits the context without disruptive effect.

---

65   [2001] 2 S.C.R. 3 at para. 121.

66   *Interpretation Act*, R.S.C. 1985, c. I-21, s. 15(2). Provincial Interpretation Acts do not contain a comparable provision.

67   [1991] 1 S.C.R. 614 [*Public Service Alliance*]. See also *Bell ExpressVu*, above note 38 at paras. 45–46; *H.J. Heinz Co. of Canada Ltd. v. Canada (Attorney General)*, [2006] 1 S.C.R. 441 at para. 22*ff*.

68   *Public Service Alliance*, *ibid.* at 632–33.

A more subtle example of reliance on related legislation is found in *Maurice v. Priel*.[69] The question put to the Supreme Court of Canada was whether a judge of the Court of Queen's Bench for Saskatchewan was a member of the Law Society of Saskatchewan within the meaning of *The Legal Profession Act*. As part of its analysis, the court looked through the *Judges Act* and the *Rules of the Law Society of Saskatchewan*, picking out any provisions that had some bearing on this question. Although none of the provisions expressly addressed the point, all were consistent with the assumption that judges were not members, and some were inconsistent with the assumption that they were. Since statutes are presumed to operate together harmoniously and to reflect a consistent view of the subject dealt with, it was appropriate to conclude that judges were not members under the *Legal Profession Act*.

D. THE STATUTE BOOK AS A WHOLE

The principles that apply to reading the Act as a whole are also relevant to the statute book as a whole. It goes without saying that no one would read the entire statute book of a jurisdiction to come up with a better interpretation of a single provision. Interpreters read selectively, looking for provisions that are relevant because of their form, the matter dealt with, or a particular word or turn of phrase.

This approach is well illustrated in *Law Society of Upper Canada v. Ontario (Attorney General)*.[70] The court there had to determine the scope of the power conferred by Ontario's *Law Society Act* on the Convocation of the Law Society to make rules providing for the election of benchers. Section 15 of the Act provided for the election of benchers every four years and stipulated that half the benchers must be members from the metropolitan Toronto region and half from outside that region. Section 62(1) of the Act provided:

> 62.(1) Convocation may make rules relating to the affairs of the Society and, without limiting the generality of the foregoing, [it may make rules]
>
> ...
>
> 6. providing for the time and manner of and the methods and procedures for the election of benchers.

---

69   [1989] 1 S.C.R. 1023.
70   (1995), 21 O.R. (3d) 666 (Gen. Div.).

Convocation sought to make a rule dividing the metropolitan Toronto region into two divisions and the rest of the province into seven divisions, each of which would be ensured representation. The issue was whether this rule was within Convocation's powers. The court concluded that it was not, that the power to provide for regional representation in Convocation had been retained by the legislature.

In reaching this conclusion, Borins J. relied on a survey of Ontario's legislation dealing with the self-governing professions. He found that in other self-government schemes, the power to provide for regional representation in elections to the governing council was conferred expressly when it was conferred at all. Section 50(a) of the *Health Disciplines Act*, for example, provided that the Lieutenant Governor in Council may make regulations "fixing the number of members to be elected ... and establishing electoral districts for elections." The *Veterinarians Act* provided that the self-governing body itself could make by-laws regarding the election of members, including defining constituencies and fixing numbers. Borins J. concluded:

> Thus, it can be seen that with all of the self-governing professions referred to above, with the exception of the veterinarians, the legislation is in lock-step in retaining in the legislature, or in the Lieutenant Governor in Council by regulation, the power to legislate with respect to the election of the members of the governing councils, including their regional election. As for the veterinarians, specific powers are conferred on the governing council to deal with the election by the passing of by laws. In my view, for Convocation to have the power to pass rules providing for the regional election of benchers provisions similar to ... [those in] the *Veterinarians Act* would be required.[71]

The pattern apparent in the legislation dealing with other self-governing professions created expectations about whether the legislature was likely to delegate certain powers and what mechanism and language it would use if it wished to do so. This pattern suggested that the legislature is reluctant to put the power to define electoral districts into the hands of professional bodies like the committee. It also suggested that when this reluctance is overcome, as it was in the case of the veterinarians, the legislature signals its intention by conferring a power to make by-laws establishing representative electoral districts. The absence of

71   *Ibid.* at 679.

a similar provision in the *Law Society Act* therefore suggested the absence of any intention to depart from the usual pattern.[72]

E. THE LAW OF OTHER JURISDICTIONS

Legislation from other jurisdictions is often relied on in interpretation, especially if the other jurisdiction is Canadian or British or shares Canada's past as a British colony. Sometimes the domestic legislation to be interpreted has been modelled on the foreign legislation.[73] In other cases, both are derived from a common external source. Interpreters may compare the domestic and foreign enactments, drawing inferences on the basis of their similarities and differences. Or they may look at case law interpreting the foreign enactment. When a provision enacted by jurisdiction A is interpreted in a particular way and is later copied and enacted by jurisdiction B, courts sometimes presume that the provision was adopted by legislature B as interpreted by A's courts.

1) Comparison of Legislative Texts

When a foreign enactment has served as a model for domestic legislation, the courts are alert for any departures from the model, for these require an explanation that may be suggestive of the legislature's intent. In *Reference Re Canada Labour Code*,[74] for example, the Supreme Court of Canada relied on a comparison of Canadian and American legislation on sovereign immunity to determine the scope of the words "commercial activity" as used in the Canadian Act. Cory J. (dissenting on another point) wrote:

> The Canadian definition of commercial activity differs from the American in that it does not explicitly bar a consideration of the purpose of an activity as does the American statute.... The material shows that the drafters of the Canadian Act were aware of the particular wording of the American legislation. I would infer that they departed from it intentionally. By not prohibiting the consideration

---

72 For other examples, see also *Chrysler Canada Ltd. v. Canada (Competition Tribunal)*, [1992] 2 S.C.R. 394 at 412; *Poulin v. Serge Morency et Associés Inc.*, [1999] 3 S.C.R. 351 at para. 33.

73 The term "foreign" is used to describe legislation enacted by other Canadian legislatures as well as non-Canadian legislation.

74 [1992] 2 S.C.R. 50.

of the purpose of an activity, the drafters avoided an overly narrow interpretation of the definition.[75]

Even when there is no reason to suppose that legislation is based on a foreign model, the foreign legislation may be used as an exemplar of how particular meanings are normally expressed in legislative form. In *R. v. McIntosh*,[76] for example, in interpreting the sections governing self-defence in Canada's *Criminal Code*, a majority of the Supreme Court of Canada compared the Canadian provisions with similar ones in New Zealand's *Crimes Act 1961*. The issue was whether a person who grievously harmed another could rely on section 34(2) of the Canadian *Code* even where he provoked the attack in the first place. Section 34(2) provided:

> 34 (2) Every one who is unlawfully assaulted and who causes death or grievous bodily harm in repelling the assault is justified if ...

The New Zealand Act provided:

> 48. (2) Every one unlawfully assaulted, not having provoked the assault, is justified in repelling force by force although in so doing he causes death or grievous bodily harm, if ...

Lamer J. wrote:

> When Parliament revised the *Criminal Code* in 1955, it could have included a provocation requirement in s. 34(2). The result would then be similar to s. 48(2) of the New Zealand *Crimes Act 1961* ... which was virtually identical to s. 34(2) save that it included an express non-provocation requirement.... The fact that Parliament did not choose this route is the best and only evidence we have of legislative intention.[77]

Given the absence of any reference to provocation in the Canadian version, it was fair to infer that Parliament did not intend to make non-provocation a requirement of the defence. This inference was reinforced by the New Zealand legislation, even though it was enacted six years after the Canadian revision, because it showed what legislation looks like when a legislature intends to include a non-provocation requirement.

---

75   *Ibid.* at 106.
76   Above note 50.
77   *Ibid.* at 700–1.

2) Case Law Interpreting the Legislation of Other Jurisdictions

When a legislature adopts language from an existing Act, whether domestic or foreign, it is presumed to be aware of any case law interpreting that language. If it adopts the language without significant change, it is presumed to adopt the interpretation put on the language by the courts.

The reasoning underlying this presumption is illustrated in the judgment of the Ontario Court of Appeal in *Coderre v. Lambert*.[78] In the *Coderre* case the court was asked to interpret the word "entitled" in paragraph 267(1)(*c*) of Ontario's *Insurance Act*. This provision was added to section 267(1) by way of a 1983 amendment. Prior to the amendment, the word "entitled" in paragraph 267(1)(*a*) had been interpreted to exclude any rights to payments that were claimed but disputed by the insurance company. When the legislature amended the section by adding paragraph (*c*), it used the same term "entitled." Austin J.A. wrote:

> The objective of … [s. 267(1)(*a*)], like that of s. 267(1)(*c*), is to avoid or prevent double recovery. As "entitled" in … s. 267(1)(*a*) has been consistently interpreted in a "narrow" fashion, it is reasonable to assume that when the legislature added s. 267(1)(*c*) to the Act in 1989 and used the same word, it intended that word to be interpreted the same way.[79]

Given the legislature's presumed knowledge, both of the case law interpreting the Act and of the rules of interpretation, it is reasonable to infer that by using the same word the legislature intended to adopt the same meaning; if it had intended to include disputed claims within the concept of entitled it would have used language that signalled this intent.

F. THE LEGAL CONTEXT

Canadian legislation operates in a legal context that includes levels of law both above and beneath it in the hierarchy of laws. At the top of the hierarchy is the Canadian Constitution, as defined in section 52 of the *Constitution Act, 1982*. Next is the legislation, both statutes enacted by the federal Parliament and the legislatures and delegated legisla-

---

78   (1993), 14 O.R. (3d) 453 (C.A.).
79   *Ibid.* at 459.

tion. Below legislation is the common law and international law, both conventional and customary. The role of the customary law of First Nations in this hierarchy is an important and evolving area of law.

In interpreting legislation, the ideal is to achieve consistency and harmonious interaction with the other levels of law. This ideal is the basis for several of the presumptions of legislative intent. It is presumed that legislation is meant to comply with constitutional law and with international law and that it is informed by constitutional and international law values. Similarly, it is presumed that the legislature does not intend to change the common law or to take away common law rights.[80]

Like all the presumptions of statutory interpretation, these are rebuttable. At times it is perfectly clear that the legislature meant to disregard or contradict existing law. In such cases, the courts apply the appropriate paramountcy rule: conflicts between legislation and the Constitution are resolved in favour of the Constitution, while conflicts between legislation and international law, common law, or customary law are resolved in favour of the legislation.[81]

One issue that has not been satisfactorily resolved is the role of these presumptions of harmony in statutory interpretation. When courts were committed to the plain meaning rule, these presumptions could not be relied on unless the legislation to be interpreted was ambiguous on its face. With the demise of the plain meaning rule, some courts recognized the legal norms embodied in constitutional law, common law, and international law as part of the context in which legislation is enacted and operates. Under Driedger's modern principle, the "entire context" is to be taken into account in every interpretive exercise, with an eye to achieving harmony. Ambiguity in the text to be interpreted is not a prerequisite.

L'Heureux-Dubé J. was a leading exponent of the latter approach, which is well illustrated by her judgment in *114957 Canada Ltée (Spraytech, Société d'arrosage) v. Hudson (Town).*[82] The issue in the case was whether Hudson's By-law 270 was within the authority conferred on Quebec municipalities by section 410(1) of the *Cities and Towns Act.* By-law 270 prohibited the use of pesticide in the Town of Hudson, subject to certain exceptions. Section 410(1) of the Act authorized municipal councils to make by-laws to "secure peace, order, good government,

---

80   For further discussion of these and other presumptions of legislative intent, see Chapter 12.

81   For further discussion of the rules governing overlap and conflict between different sources of law, see Chapter 15.

82   [2001] 2 S.C.R. 241 [*Spraytech*].

health and general welfare in the territory of the municipality." The court held that this omnibus enabling power was broad enough to authorize the pesticide by-law. In the majority reasons L'Heureux-Dubé J. wrote:

> The interpretation of By-law 270 contained in these reasons respects international law's "precautionary principle", which is defined as follows at para. 7 of the Bergen Ministerial Declaration on Sustainable Development (1990):
>
>> In order to achieve sustainable development, policies must be based on the precautionary principle. Environmental measures must anticipate, prevent and attack the causes of environmental degradation. Where there are threats of serious or irreversible damage, lack of full scientific certainty should not be used as a reason for postponing measures to prevent environmental degradation.
>
> Canada "advocated inclusion of the precautionary principle" during the Bergen Conference negotiations.
>
> ...
>
> Scholars have documented the precautionary principle's inclusion "in virtually every recently adopted treaty and policy document related to the protection and preservation of the environment" .... The Supreme Court of India considers the precautionary principle to be "part of the Customary International Law" .... In the context of the precautionary principle's tenets, the Town's concerns about pesticides fit well under this rubric of preventive action.[83]

Because the language of section 410(1) of the *Cities and Towns Act* is highly general and abstract, it grants a broad discretion to both the municipal council on which the power is conferred and the courts that may review its exercise. There is no need to invoke a presumption. The values that appropriately inform legislative, administrative, and judicial discretion include international law norms.

Although this approach is consistent with Driedger's modern principle, and avoids the problems of the plain meaning rule, in a number of recent cases the Supreme Court of Canada has asserted that the presumptions of compliance with constitutional and international law are to be ignored unless, after reading the disputed text in its statutory and external contexts, it remains ambiguous. In effect, the norms embod-

---

83   *Ibid.* at 266–67.

ied in these other levels of law are afforded a secondary status, and the plain meaning rule is re-introduced through the back door.[84]

The debate between the two approaches to legal norms is well illustrated in the majority and concurring judgments of the Supreme Court of Canada in *Baker v. Canada (Minister of Citizenship and Immigration)*.[85] Under regulations made under the *Immigration Act*, the minister of citizenship and immigration had discretion to exempt persons from certain regulations or to facilitate their admission to Canada if satisfied "owing to the existence of compassionate or humanitarian considerations" that this was the proper course to take. The issue in *Baker* was whether the minister had exercised his discretion properly when he refused to intervene in the deportation of a woman who had four children born and residing in Canada. A majority found the exercise of discretion unreasonable, in part because it disregarded important international legal norms. L'Heureux-Dubé J. wrote:

> Another indicator of the importance of considering the interests of children when making a compassionate and humanitarian decision is the ratification by Canada of the *Convention on the Rights of the Child*, and the recognition of the importance of children's rights and the best interests of children in other international instruments ratified by Canada. International treaties and conventions are not part of Canadian law unless they have been implemented by statute.
>
> ...
>
> *Nevertheless, the values reflected in international human rights law may help inform the contextual approach to statutory interpretation and judicial review.*[86] [Emphasis added.]

A minority of the court objected to reliance on norms that had not been expressly incorporated into Canadian law. Iacobucci J. wrote:

> It is a matter of well-settled law that an international convention ratified by the executive branch of government is of no force or effect within the Canadian legal system until such time as its provisions have been incorporated into domestic law by way of implementing legislation.... I do not agree with the approach adopted by my colleague, wherein reference is made to the underlying values of an unimplemented international treaty in the course of the contextual approach to statutory interpretation and administrative law, because such an approach is not

---

84   The leading case is *Bell ExpressVu*, above note 38 at paras. 63–66. For other relevant authorities and further discussion, see Chapter 12.

85   Above note 39.

86   *Ibid.* at paras. 69–70.

in accordance with the Court's jurisprudence concerning the status of international law within the domestic legal system.[87]

In this passage, Iacobucci J. effectively excludes international law from the "entire context" in which legislation must be read.

G. THE EXTERNAL CONTEXT

The external context of legislation refers to its factual and ideological setting. This setting is multifaceted and includes the historical, social, political, cultural, and economic conditions in which legislation is enacted and continues to operate. Most often, external context is relied on to reveal the "mischief" the legislation was meant to address. As Binnie J. writes in *Re Canada 3000 Inc.*,

> [T]he issues of interpretation are, as always, closely tied to context. The notion that a statute is to be interpreted in light of the problem it was intended to address is as old at least as the 16th century....[88]
>
> As this Court noted in 1915,[89] part of the context is "the condition of things existent at the time of the enactment."[90]

After examining the conditions existing at the time of enactment, Binnie J. then turns to context in which the legislation actually operates. He emphasizes the vital importance of "the commercial reality" in which a statute functions.[91]

1) Proof of External Context

In the law of evidence, information about external context is referred to as "legislative facts" because it is the sort of information a legislature requires to make sound policy choices and to create effective schemes.[92] Legislative facts may be brought to the attention of a court through formal or informal judicial notice, through expert testimony,

---

87   *Ibid.* at para. 79.
88   See *Heydon's Case* (1584), 3 Co. Rep. 7a, 76 E.R. 637.
89   *Grand Trunk Railway Co. of Canada v. Hepworth Silica Pressed Brick Co.* (1915), 51 S.C.R. 81 at 88.
90   *Re Canada 3000 Inc.* above note 3 at paras. 36–37.
91   *Ibid.* at paras. 38 and 40.
92   For discussion of legislative facts, social facts, and judicial notice, see *R. v. Spence*, [2005] 3 S.C.R. 458.

through so-called Brandeis briefs (explained below), and through legislative history materials.

In formal judicial notice the court expressly indicates that it is taking into account certain facts that are presumed to be true. Because they are so well established, evidence verifying the truth of these facts is unnecessary.[93] In informal notice, judges draw on their beliefs about the world and how it operates without going through the exercise of taking formal judicial notice. If a judge were to think about it, he or she would probably characterize these beliefs as "basic common sense."[94] But in most cases the question of truth or legitimacy does not even arise. Because informal notice occurs automatically and often without conscious thought, it is simply taken for granted that the noticed beliefs are valid.

Judicially noticed facts and common sense beliefs may be challenged through the testimony of expert witnesses and through the submission of Brandeis briefs. In a Brandeis brief, counsel provides the court with documentary evidence of legislative facts in the form of statistics, reports, studies, surveys, analyses, and the like. The use of such materials to attack cultural stereotypes and to introduce non-traditional perspectives has become more common in recent years, particularly in the *Charter* context, but in statutory interpretation cases as well.[95]

Legislative facts may also come before the court as part of the legislative history of an enactment. Legislative history consists of materials that were brought to the attention of the legislature during the enactment process and which therefore formed part of the understanding on which the legislation was enacted. In so far as these materials are admissible, they provide particularly strong evidence of the knowledge and concerns of the legislature at the relevant time.[96]

2) Use of External Context

Once established, the external context is relied on by courts in several ways. First, by studying conditions existing at the time of enactment, it may be possible to identify the particular "evils" addressed by the legislation and on this basis to infer its purpose. Second, the meaning of particular words or expressions may be illuminated by taking into account

---

93   The rules governing formal judicial notice are explained in Chapter 3.
94   The important role of common sense in interpretation is discussed in Chapter 2.
95   See *R. v. Seaboyer*, [1991] 2 S.C.R. 577; *R. v. Williams*, [1998] 1 S.C.R. 1128.
96   The law governing the admissibility and use of legislative history materials is dealt with in Chapter 14.

the circumstances existing at the time of enactment. Finally, knowledge of external context helps the court in its own policy decisions.

In *R. v. Chartrand*,[97] the Supreme Court of Canada relied on external context in concluding that certain amendments to the *Criminal Code* were meant to enhance the ability of parents to safeguard their children against abduction. This purpose was inferred from reading the amended legislation in the light of relevant social conditions. L'Heureux-Dubé J. wrote:

> That purpose is still more apparent from the social context in which those amendments were adopted and the mischief they were intended to cure....
>
> Each year, in Canada, hundreds of children are abducted by strangers from playgrounds, parks, school yards and streets.[98]

This claim was substantiated by excerpts from Statistics Canada and from the RCMP's *Annual Report* for 1993. The court also relied on the legislative history of the amendments, noting that prior to their adoption, Parliament heard from numerous groups who expressed concern over the increasing vulnerability of children to both parental and stranger abduction. The court used this material to infer that Parliament's purpose in amending the *Code* was to introduce measures that would prevent and deter such abductions. Given this purpose, a liberal reading of the provision was appropriate, despite its penal nature:

> The purpose of s. 281 — to protect children from abduction — reflects a societal interest in the security of children.... This accords with public policy. Viewed in the light of its purpose and context, such legislation has a broad scope and the restrictive interpretation ... proposed by the respondent does not seem to be particularly attractive.[99]

In the *Chartrand* case the court relied on evidence of conditions in the 1990s to establish the concerns of Parliament in 1982. Reliance on evidence of post-enactment conditions is not uncommon in the cases. This reliance is justified by the assumption that conditions have not changed significantly during the intervening years.

In *Agricultural Credit Corp. of Saskatchewan v. Novak*,[100] the Saskatchewan Court of Appeal relied on its personal knowledge of conditions in Saskatchewan to help determine how section 66 of the *Saskatchewan*

---

97   [1994] 2 S.C.R. 864.
98   *Ibid.* at 880–81.
99   *Ibid.* at 882.
100 (1985), 134 Sask. R. 87 (C.A.).

Farm Security Act applied to farmers who owned both an urban and a rural residence. Section 66 provided:

> 66. The following property of a farmer and his family is declared free from seizure
>
> ...
>
> (h) the house and buildings occupied by the farmer as his bona fide residence;
>
> ...
>
> (k) the homestead [defined in the Act as "the house and buildings occupied by a farmer as his bona fide farm residence"].

A majority of the court concluded that given the circumstances existing in Saskatchewan in 1988 the legislature must have considered the possibility of a farmer occupying both urban and rural residences and must have meant to provide for the exemption of both. Bayda C.J.S. wrote:

> Before examining the language of the statute ... one ought to remind oneself of and consider the social and economic conditions at the time the *SFSA* was enacted and the societal context into which it was thrust and expected to operate, that is to say, to remind oneself of and consider the realities of the farming community in Saskatchewan in 1988–89 when the *Act* was passed.[101]

Bayda C.J.S. then pointed out, as "[n]early everyone in Saskatchewan knows," that many, if not the majority, of farmers in the province lived partly on a farm and partly in an urban residence. After exploring the economic and social pressures that favoured dual occupancy, Bayda C.J.S. emphasized that these pressures would not have escaped the notice of Saskatchewan's legislators, many of whom represented rural constituencies and all of whom were likely to have some sort of "farming connection." He concluded: "[I]t is my respectful view that in order to find that the *SFSA* does not contemplate as a real life possibility a farmer having both an urban and a farm residence at the same time would require virtually an express statement in the *SFSA* to that effect."[102]

The court then engaged in a careful textual analysis of the provision and its immediate context in the Act. Having considered the provision in both its internal and external contexts, the court concluded that both residences were meant to be exempt.

---

101 *Ibid.* at 91.
102 *Ibid.* at 94.

In *R. v. McCraw*[103] the Supreme Court of Canada relied on external context to ensure that the perspective of women was taken into account in deciding whether a threat of rape was a threat of "serious bodily harm" within the meaning of section 243.4 of the *Criminal Code*. The court looked at a number of contemporary reports and studies examining the impact of rape on women. Cory J. wrote:

> It seems to me that to argue that a woman who has been forced to have sexual intercourse has not necessarily suffered grave and serious violence is to ignore the perspective of women....
>
> The psychological trauma suffered by rape victims has been well documented. It involves symptoms of depression, sleeplessness, a sense of defilement, the loss of sexual desire, fear and distrust of others, strong feelings of guilt, shame and loss of self-esteem. It is a crime committed against women which has a dramatic, traumatic impact.[104]

These facts may not have been foremost in the minds of the legislators who voted to make threats of serious bodily harm a crime in 1985. They are nonetheless relevant because they supply the information base necessary for reaching a plausible and appropriate conclusion. Given the purpose of section 243.4—to permit individuals to live in security, without fear of harmful attack—and given knowledge of the impact of rape on women, the court was able to infer that a threat of rape was a threat of "serious bodily harm" within the meaning of the section.

---

103 [1991] 3 S.C.R. 72.
104 *Ibid.* at 83–84.

CHAPTER 9

TEXTUAL ANALYSIS

A. ASSUMPTIONS UNDERLYING TEXTUAL ANALYSIS

The meaning of a legislative text is determined by analyzing the words to be interpreted in context. Words are analyzed in their immediate context by focusing on the specific provision in which the words appear and attempting to understand the reasons why the legislature has chosen this combination of words, this structure, this punctuation, and so on. Words are also analyzed in larger contexts by comparing the wording of the provision to be interpreted with the wording of provisions elsewhere in the same or other Acts and by considering the role of the provision in the scheme to which it belongs.[1]

In both types of analysis the interpreter depends on a number of assumptions about the knowledge and competence of the legislature, its use of language, and its fidelity to the conventions of legislative structure and style. Some of these assumptions are acknowledged and discussed by the courts. Others are rarely mentioned but are nonetheless implicit in judicial reasoning.

---

1   For discussion of the larger context in which words are analyzed, including the Act as a whole, the statute book as a whole, and the legislation of other jurisdictions, see Chapter 8.

The assumptions relied on by courts in analyzing legislative texts paint an idealized picture of the legislature and its work, one that is often belied by the finished product. Given the pressures of the job and the limitations of language, drafters of legislation are unlikely to achieve anything like the complete knowledge or perfect clarity and consistency that is attributed to them by the conventions.[2] Nevertheless, these are the virtues to which they aspire, and the courts frequently invoke them in analyzing legislative texts.

1) Linguistic Competence

It is assumed that the legislature is an accomplished user of language and has fully mastered the linguistic conventions through which meaning is communicated to an audience. Like the courts themselves, the legislature understands the impact of context on meaning, the significance of word choice and word order; it appreciates the nuances of sophisticated language use.

It is also assumed that the legislature is a careful user of language, that it says what it means exactly and therefore means exactly what it has said. Its texts are scrutinized, analyzed, and often much revised before the final version is enacted into law. During this drafting process, particular attention is paid to the ways that meaning is controlled through

- the use of one word rather than another;
- the arrangement of words within a structure;
- the conjunction of words with similar meanings or different levels of generality within a structure;
- the creation of parallel structures and other distinct patterns of expression; and
- departure from established patterns.

This high level of attention to linguistic detail is meant to minimize inadvertence and mistakes so that the final text captures the desired meaning.

2) Drafting Competence

It is assumed that the legislature is an accomplished drafter of legislation. This assumption implies, first of all, that the legislature is able to devise effective legislative schemes and to formulate directives and

---

2   See, for example, *Canada (Attorney General) v. Savard*, [1996] Y.J. No. 4 at paras. 35–38 (C.A.).

rules that will provide adequate guidance to those who must implement and obey the law. Secondly, it implies mastery of the conventions of legislative drafting. These conventions address such matters as the correct way to draft a legislative sentence; what style to use; when to paragraph;[3] and the appropriate use of definitions, purpose statements, amending formulae, and the like. Finally, as a competent drafter, the legislature is assumed to be aware of the rules of interpretation and to draft with them in mind.

3) Encyclopedic Knowledge

Another aspect of its competence as a drafter is the legislature's presumed knowledge of whatever information or data is relevant to the law it enacts. This includes knowledge of the law existing at the time of enactment — common law, international law, federal and provincial legislation, the legislation of foreign jurisdictions, and the case law interpreting legislation. It also includes knowledge of the world. In dealing with any subject, the legislature is presumed to have acquired the information and understanding needed to devise appropriate rules or an appropriate regulatory scheme. This knowledge may be highly technical and dependent on specialized expertise. However, the legislature is also credited with the sort of general knowledge referred to as "legislative facts."[4] This consists of data and studies concerning economic and social conditions, an understanding of history and culture, and an appreciation of the human condition. This is the sort of knowledge one receives from the social sciences and the liberal arts.

4) Straightforward Expression

The legislature is presumed to prefer a clear, simple, and straightforward manner of expression. Drafters avoid metaphor and language that is allusive, convoluted, or indirect. The goal is to make the legislative directive as clear and as concise as possible. If there is a simple combination of words that can be used to make a point, but the legislature has not used that combination of words, then chances are that is not the point the legislature was trying to make.

---

3 "Paragraphing" (sometimes called "tabulation") refers to the convention of using bullets, introduced by letters, to list the parallel elements of legislative sentences.

4 For discussion of legislative facts, see Chapter 8.

5) Orderly Arrangement

The provisions included in legislation are presumed to be ordered in a coherent and systematic way. By convention, each subsection of a statute contains a single complete idea. Related ideas are grouped together within the same section or series of sections. Parallel structures are used to express functionally equivalent or analogous meanings. The nature of the connection among provisions is also suggested by headings, marginal notes, and other components. As much as possible, the sequence of provisions is methodical and follows a conventional order or reflects an intelligible plan.

6) Coherence

It is presumed that legislation is internally consistent and coherent. The legislature does not contradict itself or enact inconsistent provisions.[5] Its policies, and the procedures and rules for implementing those policies, are meant to work together harmoniously so that the entire body of legislation forms a single coherent and consistent system. This body of legislation must be made consistent with entrenched constitutional law, just as the common law must be made consistent with it.

7) No Tautology

It is presumed that every feature of a legislative text has been deliberately chosen and has a particular role to play in the legislative design. The legislature does not include unnecessary or meaningless language in its statutes; it does not use words solely for rhetorical or aesthetic effect; it does not make the same point twice. This is what is meant when it is said that the legislature "does not speak in vain."

8) Consistent Expression

It is presumed that the legislature uses words and patterns of expression in a consistent way. Once the legislature has adopted a particular way of expressing a meaning, it avoids stylistic variation and prefers to express the same meaning in the same way, and parallel meanings in parallel ways, throughout the legislative text.

---

5   The techniques for dealing with conflicts among legislative provisions are discussed in Chapter 15.

The presumption of consistent expression applies not only to words and phrases but to any structure or feature of expression. Having done a thing once, the legislature is inclined to use the same or a comparable method when it sets out to do the same or a similar thing again. As this method is repeatedly used for a particular purpose, a convention is established. The more distinctive the convention, the more frequent the repetition, the more justified the conclusion that this convention is always used to accomplish this purpose and any departure from it signals a different intent. These assumptions about the way legislation is drafted underlie many of the rules and techniques relied on by courts in analyzing legislative texts. The use of these rules and techniques is explained and illustrated in the sections that follow.

B. TECHNIQUES USED IN TEXTUAL ANALYSIS

The ordinary meaning of a legislative text is its meaning on first impression, the meaning that naturally and immediately comes to mind upon first reading the text. In forming this meaning, interpreters rely on the conventions of language use that are shared with others and also on the facts, beliefs, and values that together make up common sense.[6] In normal practice, the process of meaning formation is largely intuitive and unconscious. Through textual analysis, however, interpreters can explore, refine, and test their first impressions by reading the text more self-consciously—by identifying the conventions and assumptions relied on and spelling out the reasoning that justifies the intuitive outcome.

In analyzing legislative texts, interpreters draw not only on the ordinary conventions of language and common sense but also on the presumptions about legislative drafting described above:

- the legislature has flawless linguistic competence and encyclopedic knowledge;
- it has an intelligible goal and a rational plan;
- its choice of words, word order, and structure and its sequencing of material are careful and orderly, with an accurate appreciation of the impact on meaning;
- it uses a direct, straightforward style, avoiding rhetorical devices and relying on fixed patterns and pattern variations; and

---

6   For an explanation of the role of common sense in statutory interpretation, see Chapter 2.

- every feature of the text is there for a reason and has its own work to do.

These conventions of drafting operate in a manner similar to the ordinary conventions of language. In so far as they are shared by both drafter and audience, they facilitate clear and accurate communication.

The first step in textual analysis is to determine the grammatical structure of the legislative sentence by identifying the elements of subject, verb, object, and complement and by noting the relation of the modifying words, phrases, and clauses to these basic elements. The next step is to see what inferences can be drawn about the meaning of the sentence, having regard to the conventions of drafting described above. Here the interpreter looks for parallel structures and other patterns, for recurring themes, and for variations in wording, patterns, and themes. Above all, the interpreter asks the question "Why?": Why this choice of word, this combination of words, this arrangement?

A *Criminal Code* provision analyzed by Ontario's Court of Appeal in *R. v. Volante*[7] offers a good illustration of this approach. The accused in *Volante* owned six gambling machines, which he put in a café owned and operated by someone else. His contact with the machines consisted of visiting the café at least once a week to ensure that the machines were in working order and to pick up his portion of the proceeds. The issue was whether in so doing he "kept" the machines contrary to section 202(1)(b) of the *Criminal Code*. It provided:

> Every one commits an offence who
>
> ...
>
> (b) imports, makes, buys, sells, rents, leases, hires or keeps, exhibits, employs or knowingly allows to be kept, exhibited or employed in any place under his control any device or apparatus for the purpose of recording or registering bets or selling a pool, or any machine or device for gambling or betting.

Like all legislative sentences, this is a complete sentence; it describes the facts to which it is applicable, followed by a description of the legal consequences attaching to those facts. The grammatical structure of the sentence is as follows:

---

7   (1993), 14 O.R. (3d) 682 (C.A.). For other examples, see *Barrie Public Utilities v. Canadian Cable Television Assn.*, [2003] 1 S.C.R. 476 at para. 22*ff*; *Monsanto Canada Inc. v. Ontario (Superintendent of Financial Services)*, 2004 SCC 54 at para. 27*ff*.

(subject)	(verb)	(object)	(clause modifying "every one")
Every one	commits	an offence	who performs a prohibited act

The grammatical structure of the modifying clause is as follows:

(subject)	(verb)	
who	imports,	(Note the parallel structure here,
	makes,	indicating an analogous function
	buys,	among the parallel items.)
	sells,	
	rents,	
	leases,	
	hires *or*	(Note the inclusion of a grammat-
	keeps,	ically unnecessary "or": Why is it
	exhibits,	here? This calls for an explanation.)
	employs *or*	

allows to be kept,
exhibited *or*
employed

(adverb)
knowingly

(adverbial phrase)
in any place
under his control

> (object)
> any device or apparatus for ... pool, or
> any machine or device for ... betting

The subject of the sentence is "every one." It is modified by the clause beginning with "who": not every one is guilty of an offence; only those who engage in the conduct described in the clause. The verbs and objects set out in the clause are linked by inclusive "or's": this means an accused is within the clause if he or she engages in any one of the acts in relation to any one of the objects.[8]

The clause setting out the list of prohibited acts (from "imports" to "allows to be employed") contains an unnecessary "or" after "hires." This, in conjunction with the use of the variant "allows to be ...," tends to create three distinct groupings among the verbs. The first seven

---

8   The conventions governing the use of "or" are explained in Chapter 4.

verbs — beginning with "imports" and ending with "hires" — form the first group, followed by "or." The next three verbs — "keep," "exhibit," "employs" — form the second group, again followed by "or." The third group introduces a new pattern: "knowingly allows to be kept, exhibited, or employed." The similarities and differences among the three groupings should be noted. In group two it is an offence for a person to keep, exhibit, or employ, while in group three it is an offence for a person to knowingly allow another to perform any of those same three acts. In groups one and two, there is no express reference to "knowingly" as there is in group three.

The clause contains a significant ambiguity: the adverbial phrase "in any place under his control" might apply to all or to only some of the groupings. There are good reasons for supposing the adverbial phrase applies to the final grouping. The most obvious is proximity: the phrase is placed immediately after the final verb. It is also easy to discern a reason for attaching this phrase to the final grouping: although normally we think it unfair to penalize one person for the act of another, it is not so unfair where the first person knows of the act and by virtue of being in control of a place can prevent it from occurring. Clearly, then, the adverbial phrase applies to the final grouping of verbs.

There are reasons that suggest the phrase does not apply to the verbs in group one. First, it would be odd to say "imports in a place under his control." Importing takes place at borders that are not under the control of individual citizens. Second, although it is less strange to say "buys or leases or makes in a place under his control," it is still somewhat odd because there is no discernible connection between the apparent purpose of prohibiting these acts and the place where they might be performed. Finally, if the phrase is inapplicable to one or some of the verbs in this grouping, it is inapplicable to all. By grouping the verbs in this way, the legislature invites a uniform treatment of the items within each grouping.

The difficult question is whether the phrase "in any place under his control" modifies the verbs in the second grouping ("keeps, exhibits, or controls"). There is nothing odd from a linguistic point of view in applying the phrase to these verbs. It is normal to keep, exhibit, or use the things mentioned in a particular place that may but need not be under one's control. Moreover, if the phrase "in any place under his control" applied to "keeps," "exhibits," and "employs," but not to the previous seven verbs, this could explain why "or" was inserted between the two groupings. Finally, it is possible to identify a difference between the verbs in the two groupings which could explain on policy grounds why the legislature might wish to treat them differently. A person who does any of the acts described by the verbs in the first grouping is definitively implicated in the promotion of gambling. However, a person who keeps, exhibits, or employs a machine may be only peripherally involved. The manager of a restaurant, for example, might be said to "keep" or "exhibit" a gambling machine, even though he or she had nothing to do with its being there and derived no benefit from its operation. By adding the qualification "in a place under his control," the legislature ensured that only persons closely connected to or involved in the promotion of gambling would be captured by the section.

The Ontario Court of Appeal adopted a slightly different analysis. Austin J.A. drew attention to the following argument by the appellant:

> [T]he words of s. 202(1)(b) were calculated to follow a gambling machine through the hands of an importer or manufacturer into the hands of a user. The sequence of verbs from "imports" to "hires" supports that argument. The use of the word "or" followed by "keeps", "exhibits", "employs", it was argued, was intended to indicate a change in the character of the person involved from wholesaler (or producer) to retailer (or user).[9]

On the basis of this argument the court concluded that "keeps" should be interpreted as requiring some activity on the part of the accused aimed at making gambling machines available to the public:

> [T]he context in which "keeps" is found suggests that it is intended to signify something more than "owns" or "possesses". "Exhibits" suggests "displaying" or perhaps "advertising for sale" and "employs" suggests "using", that is, activities one might reasonably expect in the carrying out of the purpose of a gambling machine.[10]

In other words, the court suggests that "keeps" must be given a meaning that is distinct from "exhibits" and "employs" but also that accords with the subtheme of grouping two, namely, purposeful activities by the person in possession. The court then turns to the theme that is implicit in the section as a whole:

> The activity to be rendered criminal ... [is] not simply ... possession of a gambling machine, but being part of a process that makes them available for use by the public. Importing, making, buying, selling, renting, leasing, and hiring are, or could be, all parts of such a process. To "keep" gambling machines in this context would include

---

9   Above note 7 at 686.
10   *Ibid.*

having them available for use, directly or indirectly, for the purpose of gambling by the public.[11]

Given this definition of "keeps," the accused was found to have violated the section.

Another good example of textual analysis is found in the judgments of the Supreme Court of Canada in *R. v. Dunn*.[12] Section 44(e) of the federal *Interpretation Act* provided that where new legislation is enacted that repeals an existing punishment, penalty, or forfeiture and replaces it with a more lenient one, an accused is entitled to the benefit of the new legislation, provided the accused's "punishment, penalty or forfeiture" is "imposed or adjudged" *after* the new legislation comes into force.[13] Consider the following example:

Day 1: X and Y contravene the *Criminal Code*, committing an offence for which the maximum penalty is ten years imprisonment. Both are arrested and charged that very day.

Day 2: X is tried, convicted, and sentenced to ten years' imprisonment.

Day 4: The *Code* is amended, reducing the maximum penalty for the relevant offence to five years imprisonment.

Day 5: Y is tried, convicted, and sentenced.

Under section 44(e), X could be sentenced to the maximum ten years as provided by the *Code* at the time of the offence. He would not be entitled to the benefit of the reduced penalty because his sentence was imposed before the amendment came into force. Y, however, could not be sentenced to more than five years' imprisonment. She is entitled to the benefit of the amendment because her sentence was imposed after the amendment came into force.

The issue that arose in the *Dunn* case is what to do when an accused who is sentenced under existing legislation appeals his sentence and new, more lenient legislation comes into force while the appeal is pending. In terms of the above example, what happens if X appeals on Day

---

11   *Ibid.* at 687.

12   [1995] 1 S.C.R. 226.

13   R.S.C. 1985, c. I-23. The provision, in full, reads as follows:

44. Where an enactment, in this section called the "former enactment", is repealed and another enactment, in this section called the "new enactment", is substituted therefor,

…

(e)   when any punishment, penalty or forfeiture is reduced or mitigated by the new enactment, *the punishment, penalty or forfeiture if imposed or adjudged* after the repeal shall be reduced or mitigated accordingly …

3 and the appeal court renders its decision, affirming the sentence, on Day 5? In these circumstances, does section 44(e) ensure X the benefit of the lesser punishment?

The accused in *Dunn* could succeed only if in dismissing his appeal the appellate court had "adjudged" his punishment within the meaning of the provision. As L'Heureux-Dubé J. explained in her dissenting judgment: "What is clear here is that the word 'imposed' relates to the sentence 'imposed' at trial. The question then becomes why did Parliament believe it necessary to add the words 'or adjudged'? Is it … to cover the appeal, or is it for another reason which can be easily explained?"[14] The key question here, addressed by both the majority judges and those in dissent, is "Why?": Why did the legislature say "adjudge" in addition to "impose"? What work does "adjudge" do in the provision? The difference between the majority and the dissenting judgments lies in the different ways they answered this question.

The majority of the court said "adjudged" was added to include judgments on appeal. In reaching this conclusion it relied primarily on definitions of "adjudge" in language and law dictionaries. In both, the verb "adjudge" is broadly defined to encompass any judicial decision or pronouncement, including but not limited to the imposition of sentence. The majority found nothing in the context of section 44(2) to narrow the broad scope of the word. On the contrary, in order to avoid tautology, "adjudged" had to denote something in addition to sentencing;[15] otherwise the word would do no useful work.[16] Applying the word to judgments on appeal was a plausible solution.

L'Heureux-Dubé J. offered a different analysis; she wrote:

> I believe that had Parliament wanted the words "or adjudged" to connote appellate finality, it would have chosen clear wording to that effect. As the respondent points out, phrases such as "reviewed on appeal" or "finally decided" could presumably have been used by Parliament … had it in fact wished to … include appellate review.
>
> Furthermore, the use of the words "or adjudged" is grammatically necessary to encompass all conceivable judicial orders of a penal nature available at the trial level.[17]

---

14   Above note 12 at 246.

15   The presumption against tautology is discussed in section A(7), above in this chapter.

16   Of course, if the broad sense of "adjudge" is accepted, one must then wonder what work is done by "impose" since the imposition of a sentence is clearly covered by "adjudge."

17   Above note 12 at 247–48.

L'Heureux-Dubé J. went on to point out that when a court orders the forfeiture of property, the forfeiture is not said to be "imposed"; the conventional term is "adjudged." In her view, the word "adjudge" was included in the provision not to encompass appellate decision making, but to go with the word "forfeiture" earlier in the provision.

In this passage L'Heureux-Dubé J. appeals to the presumption of careful, straightforward expression.[18] She points out that Parliament would not use the vague term "adjudge" when it has more direct and precise ways of expressing the idea of judgment on appeal. She also relies on a form of word association known as collocation.[19] Although there is nothing grammatically or semantically wrong with saying that a sentence is "adjudged" or a forfeiture is "imposed," we are nonetheless accustomed to saying that sentences are "imposed" and forfeitures are "adjudged" at trial, while both sentences and forfeitures are "reviewed" on appeal.

Because of the more careful and considered engagement with the text, the dissent's answer to the question "Why include 'adjudged'?" is arguably more persuasive than the majority's.

C. THE ASSOCIATED WORDS RULE (*NOSCITUR A SOCIIS*)

When two or more words or phrases perform a parallel function within a provision and are linked by "and" or "or," the meaning of each is presumed to be influenced by the others. The interpreter looks for a pattern or a common theme in the words or phrases, which may be relied on to resolve ambiguity or to fix the scope of the provision.

The associated words principle was applied by Martin J.A. in *R. v. Goulis*.[20] The court was asked to interpret a provision of the *Criminal Code* making it an offence where a person, with intent to defraud his creditors,

(i) makes … a gift, conveyance, assignment, sale, transfer or delivery of his property, or

(ii) removes, conceals or disposes of any of his property.

---

18 The presumption of straightforward expression is discussed in section A(4), above in this chapter.

19 Collocation is discussed in Section E, below in this chapter.

20 (1981), 33 O.R. (2d) 55 (C.A.).

The accused was a bankrupt who failed to reveal the existence of certain property to his trustee in bankruptcy as required under the *Bankruptcy Act*. The question was whether his conduct violated the *Code*. It was clear that in failing to disclose the existence of property, the accused intended to defraud his creditors. It was also clear that a mere failure to disclose did not amount to a gift, conveyance, sale, transfer, delivery, removal, or disposal of the property. The question was whether such non-disclosure should be considered a form of concealment.

According to common understanding of the word "conceal," as reflected in its dictionary definition, it is broad enough to include a failure to disclose in some contexts. However, the court relied on the associated words principle to conclude that in this context a narrow meaning was intended. Martin J.A. wrote:

> When two or more words which are susceptible of analogous meanings are coupled together they are understood to be used in their cognate sense. They take their colour from each other, the meaning of the more general being restricted to a sense analogous to the less general....
>
> In this case, the words which lend colour to the word "conceals" are, first, the word "removes", which clearly refers to a physical removal of property, and second, the words "disposes of", which, standing in contrast to the kind of disposition which is expressly dealt with in subpara. (i) ..., namely, one which is made by "gift, conveyance, assignment, sale, transfer or delivery", strongly suggests the kind of disposition which results from a positive act taken by a person to physically part with his property. In my view the association of "conceals" with the words "removes" or "disposes of" in ... [subpara. (ii)] shows that the word "conceals" is there used by Parliament in a sense which contemplates a positive act of concealment.[21]

The reasoning here is exemplary. Martin J.A. first assumes that Parliament had an intelligible scheme in mind when it created the section and that each paragraph has a distinct function to perform. In effect, he finds that subparagraph (i) deals with the situation of a debtor defrauding his creditors by handing over his property to someone else, perhaps a family member or a friend, while subparagraph (ii) deals with the situation where the debtor retains the property but tries to keep it from the creditors. He also assumes that Parliament has chosen its words with care and is aware of the associated words rule. He infers

---

21   *Ibid.* at 61. See also *McDiarmid Lumber Ltd v. God's Lake First Nation*, 2006 SCC 58 at para 30*ff*; See also *R. v. Daoust*, [2004] 1 S.C.R. 217 at paras. 49, 51, and 60.

that by sandwiching the word "conceals" between two expressions that in this context at least emphasize physical activity, Parliament must have meant to limit the prohibition to positive acts of concealment. This interpretation is supported by the policy of giving penal provisions a narrow interpretation.

Although exemplary as far as it goes, arguably the reasoning of Martin J.A. does not go far enough. Both purposive and consequential analysis suggest that the case was wrongly decided. Failure by a bankrupt to reveal property to his or her creditors is certainly within the purpose of the provision, which is to ensure that all non-exempt property of a debtor is available to cover the debts. There is no rational basis for Parliament to prohibit debtors from wilfully defeating this purpose by moving their property while allowing them to do so through silence. An interpretation that results in defeating the purpose of the provision and produces irrational distinctions is likely to be incorrect.

The importance of supplementing textual analysis with other kinds of analysis is well illustrated in the judgment of the Supreme Court of Canada in *Brossard (Town) v. Quebec (Commission des droits de la personne)*.[22] The issue in the case was whether the town's anti-nepotism policy, which precluded it from hiring relatives of its own employees, violated the anti-discrimination provisions of the *Quebec Charter of Human Rights and Freedoms*. One of the questions on appeal was whether the town could defend its exclusionary policy on the grounds that a town is a political non-profit institution within the meaning of section 20 of the *Charter*:

> 20. A distinction, exclusion or preference ..., [if it is] justified by the charitable, philanthropic, religious, political or educational nature of a non-profit institution or of an institution devoted exclusively to the well-being of an ethnic group, is deemed non-discriminatory.

Beetz J. conceded that in some contexts a municipality might aptly be described as a non-profit political institution. In this context, however, a "political" institution must be understood as an institution espousing a particular political ideology. He wrote:

> the conclusion that "political" is limited to partisanship is founded upon a well-known rule of statutory interpretation *noscitur a sociis*. The word "political" is explained by the other examples of non-profit institutions given by the legislator [page 329] in s. 20: "... charitable, philanthropic, religious, political or educational nature of a non-profit

---

22   [1988] 2 S.C.R. 279.

institution." The concept of "vocation" [that is, a commitment to promoting a particular set of beliefs] appears to be implicit in each of the words "charitable," "philanthropic," "religious," "political" and "educational." An institution such as a church, for example, would be permitted to discriminate in hiring on the basis of religious conviction when that discrimination is justified by its religious nature. In this sense, an institution of a political nature would be one with a particular ideological or policy-oriented vocation, such as a political party.[23]

Having invoked the associated words rule, Beetz J. then pointed out the need to supplement his textual approach with a purposive analysis. In his view, the purpose of section 20 was to balance the right to equality protected by the anti-discrimination provision against the freedom to associate and espouse a cause:

> [Section] 20 is designed to promote the fundamental freedom of individuals to associate in groups, for the purpose of expressing particular views or engaging in particular pursuits, and for those individuals not to be inhibited, in so doing, by the anti-discriminatory norm.[24]

The section thus "strikes a specific balance between the freedom to associate and the right to be free from discrimination."[25] In this case, textual and purposive analysis were integrated and yielded a persuasive basis for the court's conclusion that the town could not rely on section 20 to justify its discriminatory hiring practice.

D. THE LIMITED CLASS RULE (*EJUSDEM GENERIS*)

When the legislature sets out a list of items followed by a general term embracing the listed items, the scope of the general term may be limited to any class to which the specific items all belong. A class is a grouping of items based on one or a set of characteristics that is shared by all items in the class.[26] Pens, pencils, and crayons, for example, could be grouped together as a class because they are all handheld instruments designed to make marks on paper.

---

23   *Ibid.* at 328–29.
24   *Ibid.* at 330–31.
25   *Ibid.* at 332.
26   In some recent cases, the courts have applied limited class analysis to lists of items that fall into two distinct classes: see *Nanaimo (City) v. Rascal Trucking Ltd.*, [2000] 1 S.C.R. 342 at paras. 21–22; *Walker v. Ritchie*, [2006] 2 S.C.R. 428 at para. 24*ff.*

Suppose a municipal by-law prohibited the consumption of beer, wine, gin, whisky, and other beverages on municipal playgrounds. Since the specific items listed in the provision have the characteristic of containing alcohol, they form a class—namely, beverages containing alcohol. Under the limited class rule, the general term "beverages" is "read down" or narrowed so that it applies only to other items in the same class—to tequila or vodka, for example, but not to juices or soft drinks.

Suppose a human rights code prohibited the publication of "any image, symbol, emblem, cartoon or other representation that is likely to expose a protected group to hatred." The term "representation" is ambiguous. In ordinary usage it may refer to a visual portrayal, as in the sentence "it's a representation of human suffering." It may also refer to verbal communications about a subject, as in the sentence "the lobbyist made representations to the committee." Or it may refer to acting as agent for another, as in the sentence "the lawyer provided effective representation for the client." In the provision set out above, "representation" follows a list of items that share a common feature: all communicate visually through pictures and images rather than verbally through sentences and argument. In this context, then, the limited class rule suggests that "representation" should be limited to portrayals of this type. A political cartoon or a product logo would be a "representation" within the meaning of the provision, but a news article or letter to the editor would not.[27]

A good example of the sort of provision that attracts the limited class rule is found in section 331 of the *Criminal Code* considered by the Supreme Court of Canada in *R. v. Nabis*:[28]

> 331. (1) Every one commits an offence who by letter, telegram, telephone, cable, radio, or otherwise, knowingly utters, conveys or causes any person to receive a threat [to their physical well being or property].

The issue for the court was whether the section extended to threats made orally in the presence of the threatened person. Although the words "or otherwise" were certainly broad enough to capture oral face-to-face threats, Parliament's use of the convention of listing specific items followed by a general term suggested that the general term should be read down in accordance with the limited class rule. As Beetz J. wrote for the majority:

---

27   This example is based on *Warren v. Chapman* (1985), 17 D.L.R. (4th) 261 (Man. C.A.).

28   [1975] 2 S.C.R. 485 [*Nabis*].

One can indeed ask why Parliament would take the trouble to enum-
erate, even in a manner which is not exhaustive, various means of
expressing or conveying threats if its purpose was to prohibit threats
by whatever means they are uttered....

. . .

The offence prohibited by s. 331 is of singular flexibility. One
may say that it consists of the simple expression of a thought. That
the expression of a thought, albeit a sinister one, should of itself constitute a serious crime, regardless of the form it takes, the motives of
its author, and its present or probable effects on the victim or on any
other individual, seems to me to be contrary to the general economy
of our criminal law and also likely to lead to many difficulties....
Such an offence must almost of necessity be delimited. To achieve
this result, two main techniques, among others, can be used, and
they are not mutually exclusive. The one consists of taking into consideration the intent of the person making the threat or his ability to
carry it out or to cause others to believe, on reasonable grounds, that
he is able to do so; ... and the other consists of taking into account
the means used in expressing the threat.[29]

Beetz J.'s analysis here is instructive. He rightly points out that
the basis for limited class reasoning is the presumption against tautology. Some role must be given to the words "letter, telegram, telephone,
cable, radio" in section 331. If Parliament had intended to criminalize
all threats, regardless of their means of delivery, it would have said "by
any means" or said nothing at all. Under the no tautology rule, Parliament is presumed to have had something in mind when it added the
list of specifics before the general reference. One common explanation
(although not the only explanation) is that Parliament intended to limit
the scope of the general reference.

The keys to effective use of the limited class rule are (a) identifying
as precisely as possible the shared characteristic or defining feature of
the class, (b) offering examples of additional specific items that are not
expressly mentioned in the list and (c) showing that the legislature's purpose is promoted by limiting the general words to the suggested class.
Identifying the defining feature of the class and relating it to the purpose
of the provision is important because it grounds the textual analysis in
purposive analysis, thus enhancing the plausibility of both analyses. Being able to offer additional specific examples of the class is important
because it shows that limiting the application of the general term will

---

29   *Ibid.* at 492–93.

not render it useless. The limited class rule cannot apply if the items expressly mentioned exhaust the class, leaving the general words with nothing to apply to. That too would violate the rule against tautology.

The courts have suggested that the limited class rule cannot apply where the general term or description is preceded by a single specific item. This observation is sound in that it is impossible to infer the defining features of a class from a sample of one. However, once again, given the presumption against tautology, the interpreter is bound to come up with some explanation for the legislature's choice of words. In *K.F. Evans Ltd. v. Canada (Minister of Foreign Affairs)*,[30] the Federal Court had to consider the expression "defense or other needs" in section 3(e) of the *Export and Import Permits Act*:

> 3. The Governor in Council may establish a list of goods, to be called an Export Control List, including therein any article the export of which the Governor in Council deems it necessary to control for any of the following purposes:
> (e) to ensure that there is an adequate supply and distribution of the article in Canada for defence or other needs.

The minister argued that under section 3(e) the Governor in Council could list for control raw materials whose export a province wished to restrict in order to promote provincial economic and environmental policies. Reed J. was unwilling to read the provision so broadly. She pointed out that the words "for defence or other needs" are not synonymous with the words "for any purpose." The defence concern must be a need, and needs other than defence must at least have a national or federal character.[31]

In my view, this analysis is sound. The pattern "x or other y" appears frequently in legislation. One inference that clearly flows from this pattern, specifically from the use of the word "other," is that x is a "hyponym" (that is, a subclass) of y, such that all x's are examples of y and share y's characteristics.[32] If I say "shoes and other footwear," I presuppose that all shoes are a type of footwear. However, the extent to which x limits y in this pattern is more difficult to establish. In each case, the interpreter must pose the question "Why?"—Why did the legislature single out this particular example of y? What inference can

---

30   [1997] 1 F.C. 405.
31   *Ibid.* at para. 32.
32   But see *Berardinelli v. Ontario Housing Corp.*, [1979] 1 S.C.R. 275, where the court held that "any statutory or other public duty" in s. 11 of Ontario's *Housing Development Act* did not imply that all statutory duties were public.

fairly be drawn, having regard to all relevant considerations? In the expression "shoes and other footwear," the prototypical case of shoes is probably mentioned to ensure that "footwear" will not be read down to shoes but construed broadly enough to include boots, slippers, and the like. However, in a provision prohibiting "stunts and other activities" on a highway, the reference to stunts would almost surely be relied on to limit the scope of prohibited activities to frivolous ones.

It has also been suggested that the limited class rule does not apply if the general words precede the list of specific items.[33] The basis for this observation is harder to discern. Arguably the crucial factor is not whether the list precedes or follows the general words, but the language used to connect the two. If I say "footwear, including skates, ski boots, and snow shoes," it would be inappropriate to limit footwear to specialized boots used in winter sports. The specific items have been mentioned not to narrow the class but to expand it, or at least to clarify that it extends to these potentially doubtful examples of footwear. However, if I say "footwear such as skates, ski boots, and snow shoes," the analysis might be different—simply because "such as" differs from "including." On occasion, even "including" has attracted a limited class analysis.[34]

E. COLLOCATION

Collocation is a term from linguistics that refers to associations between words that are based not on connotation, grammar, or logic but on mere habit or experience. Examples are "stubbed toe" (not "stubbed knee" or "stubbed leg") and "blond hair" (not "blond skin" or "blond wall").[35] Although there is no logical or experiential basis for it, we expect to see these words together. Their association seems natural, even inevitable.

Associations of this sort can be important in analyzing legislative texts. Compare the following provisions:

(1) The council may determine the *fees* to be charged for any service supplied by the municipality.

(2) The council may determine the *fares* to be charged for any service supplied by the municipality.

---

33   See *National Bank of Greece (Canada)* v. *Katsikonouris*, [1990] 2 S.C.R. 1029.

34   See *Aquasource Ltd.* v. *British Columbia (Information and Privacy Commission)*, [1998] B.C.J. No. 1927 at para. 39 (C.A.).

35   See F. Bowers, *Linguistic Aspects of Legislative Expression* (Vancouver: University of British Columbia Press, 1989) at 75–76.

In these examples, the impact of the words "fee" and "fare" on the meaning of the word "service" is striking. In example (1) "service" would likely be applied to the filing of applications for municipal parking permits and the like, because that is the sort of service we associate with the word "fee." Conversely, its application to the municipal bus service would be doubtful, because "fee" is not normally associated with the charge for riding a bus. We do not normally speak of "bus fee." In example (2), this analysis is reversed. "Service" is likely to include bus service but not the filing of applications. The linking of bus service with "fare" is natural; the linking of filing applications with "fare" is not.

An example of judicial analysis based on this sort of association is found in *Crupi v. Canada (Employment & Immigration Commission).*[36] The legislation to be interpreted was a provision of the *Unemployment Insurance Act* which prevented a claimant from receiving insurance benefits while "an inmate of any prison or similar institution." The question was whether the provision applied to a person who had been charged with an offence and then sent for observation to a psychiatric health centre equipped with a maximum security facility and located within a penitentiary complex. In concluding that the health centre was not a prison or similar institution within the meaning of the Act, Ryan J.A. wrote:

> The word "inmate" historically has had, and even now often has, rightly or wrongly, a pejorative ring. When used in conjunction with the words "prison" and "similar institution", it tars both expressions with the same brush. The words "inmate of any prison or similar institution" strongly suggest that the words "similar institution" must mean something very closely resembling a prison. Some common features, some points of resemblance could hardly be enough.[37]

There are several ways in which other institutions might resemble prisons: through their public funding, their restriction of free movement, their counselling and adult education services, their tasteless food. By using the word "inmate" the legislature narrows this range of possibility. The institution must be one whose clients are appropriately referred to as "inmates." One would not ordinarily speak of "hospital inmates" or "inmates of a nursing home."

---

36 [1986] 3 F.C. 3 (C.A.).
37 *Ibid.* at 17.

F. EVERY WORD MUST BE GIVEN MEANING

Every word in a legislative text must be given its own meaning. This rule follows from the assumption that the legislature avoids tautology and that every word of legislation has a sensible reason for being there. It is frequently invoked by the courts.[38] In *R. v. Kelly*,[39] it was relied on by the Supreme Court of Canada to help define the offence of taking a bribe. Section 426(1) of the *Criminal Code* provided that an offence occurs when a person acting as an agent "corruptly ... agrees to accept ... any reward, advantage or benefit" in connection with his or her task as an agent. The question was whether an agent would violate this provision simply by accepting a benefit or whether something more was required. Cory J. wrote:

> The interpretation of the word "corruptly" must take place within the context of s. 426 itself. It is a trite rule of statutory interpretation that every word in the statute must be given a meaning. It would be superfluous to include "corruptly" in the section if the offence were complete upon the taking of the benefit in the circumstances described by the section. The word must add something to the offence.[40]

The court found that "corruptly" in this context added the idea of secrecy. It concluded that an agent would not violate the provision unless the reward, advantage, or benefit was accepted surreptitiously.

The word "corruptly" is not given its usual meaning here. In ordinary usage, "corruptly" as it appears in this sentence would probably be understood not as a reference to secrecy, but as a rhetorical comment emphasizing the immoral quality of bribe taking by an agent. In legislation, however, words are not included for rhetorical emphasis. Each word is expected to make a distinct and meaningful contribution to the legislative rule or scheme. Since the idea of improper taking of benefit was already covered by other words in the provision, a different function had to be assigned to the word "corruptly." The word had to be given a distinct meaning as close as possible to its ordinary meaning, but one that fit the context and reflected some plausible idea or purpose. The court did well to adopt the notion of secrecy. Since under the law of agency it is possible for a principal to consent to an agent's self-serving conduct, it is plausible that such conduct would not

---

38   See, for example, *Placer Dome Canada Ltd. v. Ontario (Minister of Finance)*, [2006] 1 S.C.R. 715 at paras. 45–46; *Re Therrien*, [2001] 2 S.C.R. 3 at para 120.

39   [1992] 2 S.C.R. 170.

40   *Ibid.* at 188.

be considered wrongful or "corrupt" unless carried out surreptitiously and without consent.

G. SAME WORDS, SAME MEANING— DIFFERENT WORDS, DIFFERENT MEANING

As Sopinka J. wrote in *R. v. Zeolkowski*, "[g]iving the same words the same meaning throughout a statute is a basic principle of statutory interpretation."[41] In light of this principle, and the legislature's preference for uniform expression, it follows that different words appearing in the same statute should be given a different meaning. Thus, in *R. v. Frank*, Dickson J. wrote:

> I do not think "Indians of the Province" and "Indians within the boundaries thereof" refer to the same group. The use of different language suggests different groups. In my view, "Indians of the Province" means Alberta Indians. The words, "Indians within the boundaries," on the other hand, refer to a larger group, namely, Indians who, at any particular moment, happen to be found within the boundaries of the Province of Alberta, irrespective of normal residence.[42]

This analysis is well done because Dickson J. not only invokes the rule but also offers an explicit paraphrase of both expressions. He assures his audience that the words have different meanings, and he explains what they are. The next step in the analysis would be to identify a plausible reason for distinguishing the two groups. This may be done by noting how the two groups are treated differently under the Act, and then suggesting historical or desirable reasons for this difference in treatment.

A good example of the reasoning associated with the same words, same meaning rule is found in the judgment of Cory J. in *Thomson v. Canada (Deputy Minister of Agriculture)*.[43] The *Canadian Security Intelligence Act* established a Security Intelligence Review Committee with jurisdiction to review decisions denying persons security clearance. Section 52(2) provided that after finishing its investigation, the committee had to provide the deputy minister with a report "containing any recommendations that the Committee considers appropriate." The Act did not specify what use was to be made of this report. The issue

---

41   [1989] 1 S.C.R. 1378 at 1387.
42   (1977), [1978] 1 S.C.R. 95 at 101.
43   [1992] 1 S.C.R. 385.

for the Court was whether the recommendations of the committee were binding on the deputy minister. A majority of the Supreme Court of Canada concluded that in ordinary usage recommendations are not considered binding and that in this context ordinary usage should prevail. Cory J. wrote:

> The word ["recommendations"] is used in other provisions of the Act. Unless the contrary is clearly indicated by the context, a word should be given the same interpretation or meaning whenever it appears in an act....
>
> It would be obviously inappropriate to interpret "recommendations" in s. 52(1) as a binding decision. This is so, since it would result in the Committee encroaching on the management powers of CSIS. Clearly, in s. 52(1) "recommendations" has its ordinary and plain meaning of advising or counselling. Parliament could not have intended the word "recommendations" in the subsequent subsection of the same section [s. 52(2)] to receive a different interpretation. The word must have the same meaning in both subsections.[44]

The reasoning here is persuasive for a number of reasons. First, the meaning of "recommendations" in subsection 52(1) is clear. Its meaning is not clouded by the same doubts as arise in subsection (2). Cory J. emphasizes this advantage and explains the factors that render the use of "recommendations" in subsection (1) clear and certain. He then invokes the same word, same meaning presumption, pointing out the special force of the presumption where the same words appear in adjacent provisions and are part of a single section. It is highly unlikely that a legislature would use the same words to express different meanings within the same section or within provisions that are closely related.

Although the same word, same meaning presumption is frequently invoked, it does not always prevail. In *Bapoo v. Co-Operators General Insurance Co.*,[45] for example, the court had to determine the meaning of section 12(4) of the the statutory benefits schedule to Ontario's *Insurance Act*, which permitted an insurance company, when calculating the gross weekly income of an insured, to deduct "payments for loss of income ... received by or available to the insured person ... under any income continuation benefit plan." The issue was whether the amount to be deducted was the gross or the net payments received by or avail-

---

44   *Ibid.* at 400–1. For a judgment in which Dickson C.J. attached a different meaning to the same words in two paragraphs of the same section, see *Mitchell v. Peguis Indian Band*, [1990] 2 S.C.R. 85 at 105–6.

45   (1997), 36 O.R (3d) 616 (C.A.).

able to the insured. The insurer took the position that it was entitled to deduct the gross amount. Laskin J.A. wrote:

> The third argument advanced by Co-Operators is an argument of textual consistency. Section 15 of the Schedule provides:
>
> > 15. The insurer may deduct from any benefit payable under this Part 80 per cent of any income received or available from any occupation or employment subsequent to the accident.
>
> Like s. 12(4), s. 15 uses the words "received or available". Both parties on this appeal agree that the deduction permitted under s. 15 is a gross deduction. Otherwise, an injured person who earned income after the accident would be overcompensated under the Schedule. Co-Operators submits that if the words "received or available" permit gross deductions under s. 15, these same words must permit gross deductions under s. 12(4).
>
> Giving the same words the same meaning throughout a statute is a recognized principle of statutory interpretation.... The court ordinarily presumes that legislation is internally consistent and coherent and that the legislature does not enact inconsistent provisions.
>
> ...
>
> However, the principle of textual consistency is not an inflexible rule or an infallible guide to interpretation.... As with the interpretation of any statutory provision, the meaning of the words "received or available" in s. 15 can only be established by considering their context.... Because their contexts differ, the words "received or available ' should be interpreted differently in ss. 12(4) and 15.[46]

In rebutting the same words, same meaning presumption Laskin J.A. relied on both purposive and consequential analysis.

H. DEPARTURE FROM A PATTERN OR PRACTICE

Courts frequently reject a proposed interpretation by saying if *that* is what the legislature intended, it would have used different words or adopted a different approach. In reaching this conclusion the courts may appeal expressly, or more often by implication, to (a) an estab-

---

46   Ibid. at 626–27; See also *Newfoundland and Labrador Regional Council of Carpenters, Millwrights and Allied Workers v. Construction General Labourers, Rock and Tunnel Workers*, [2003] N.J. No. 127 at para 8 (C.A.).

lished drafting convention or practice, (b) a fixed pattern of expression, (c) a presumption of legislative intent, or (d) some other source of legitimate expectation.

The courts often reject an interpretation without fully explaining what convention has not been followed or what expectation has been upset. It is more effective, however, to offer this explanation and, where appropriate, to illustrate what the legislature would have said had it wished to express the rejected meaning.

This approach is illustrated by *University Hospital v. Boros*,[47] where the Saskatchewan Court of Appeal had to determine the application of a limitation provision in *The Hospital Standards Act of Saskatchewan*. It barred "actions ... against ... a hospital, nursing home or other institution ... for the recovery of damages, after the expiration of three months from the date on which the damages are sustained." The issue was whether this very short limitation period applied not only to actions arising out of the care of patients but to all actions, including those for breach of commercial contracts.

The court thought it unlikely that the legislature intended to affect commercial contracts. While there were reasons to impose short limitation periods on medical malpractice suits, and many legislatures had done so, those reasons did not apply to contracts with commercial suppliers. If the section applied to commercial contracts, it would mean that a contract to supply goods or services would be subject to a limitation period of several years if the contract were with a prison, a university, or a business, but to a period of several months if it were with a hospital. Despite this anomaly, the court was unwilling to narrow the scope of the section. Cameron J.A. wrote: "A comparison of other Saskatchewan statutes containing special limitation periods shows how, when the Legislature intends them to apply to some but not other classes of actions, it does so."[48] Specifically, the legislature does so by setting out explicit words of qualification after the word "action" or the word "damages." The existence of this drafting practice and the contrast between it and section 15 of *The Hospital Standards Act* was illustrated by Cameron J.A. by setting out in list form the relevant provisions:

The *Hospital Standards Act*:

15. No action shall be brought ... for the recovery of damages

...

---

47   (1985), 24 D.L.R. (4th) 628 [*Boros*]. See also *Temelini v. Ontario Provincial Police (Commissioner)* (1999), 44 O.R. (3d) 609 at 619–20 (C.A.).

48   *Boros, ibid.* at 631.

The *Vehicles Act*, 1983 (Sask.), c. V-3.1, s. 143(1):

> 143(1) No action may be brought ... for the recovery of damages *occasioned by a motor vehicle* ...

The *Medical Profession Act*, 1980-81 (Sask.), c. M-10.1, s.72:

> 72. No person registered under this Act is liable for damages in any action *arising out of the provision of professional services* unless ...

The *Urban Municipality Act*, R.S.S. 1978, c. U-10, s. 406(1):

> 406(1) No action shall be brought against the municipality for the recovery of damages *occasioned by default in its duty of repair* ...

The *Dental Profession Act*, R.S.S. 1978, c. D-5.1 (Supp.), s. 57:

> 57. No member shall be liable in any action for *negligence or malpractice by reason of services provided* by him as a dentist or dental surgeon unless the action is commenced within one year from the date of termination of those services.

The *Saskatchewan Railway Act*, R.S.S. 1978, c. S-33, s. 191(1):

> 191(1) All actions for indemnity for damages *sustained by reason of the construction or operation of* the railway shall be commenced within one year after the damages [sic] was sustained.[49] [Emphasis added.]

The court here implicitly assumes that the legislature is familiar with its own statute book and its own drafting practices. If it had intended to limit the scope of the protection introduced by section 15 of the *Hospital Standards Act*, it would have drafted a provision similar to those found in existing legislation, particularly in related legislation like the *Medical Profession Act* and the *Dental Profession Act*. It would have written, for example, that "no action shall be brought for the recovery of damages arising out of the provision of care" or that hospitals "shall not be liable in any action for negligence in the services provided." Its failure to do so is assumed to be deliberate and to reflect its intention *not* to limit the scope of section 15.

Another well-reasoned example is found in the judgment of Morden A.C.J.O. in *R. v. Harricharan*.[50] The issue there was whether a person

---

49   *Ibid.*
50   (1995), 23 O.R. (3d) 233 (C.A.).

could be found guilty of negligently failing to control a fire if the person's negligence was not the original cause of the fire. Section 436(1) of the *Criminal Code* was badly drafted and difficult to understand. It provided that a person who owns property is guilty of an offence where, by failing to exercise the care that "a reasonably prudent person would use to prevent or control the spread of fires or to prevent explosions, that person is *a cause of a fire* or explosion … that causes bodily harm … or damage to property" [emphasis added]. Morden A.C.J.O. wrote:

> The term "a cause" is significant. It recognizes that other "causes" may be contributing factors to the origin or spread of the fire.
>
> The significance of "a cause of a fire" is emphasized by its contrast with the wording contained in the immediately preceding four sections … which is "[e]very person who … causes damage by fire or explosion to property". If Parliament had intended in s. 436(1) to impose liability only where the person causes … [the] fire, as in these preceding provisions, it would not have departed from the key wording of these provisions. The syntax of s. 436(1) is such that the drafter could easily have used "that person causes a fire" in place of "that person is a cause of a fire".[51]

Morden A.C.J.O. concluded that the variation in phrasing was meant to signal a difference in meaning. In this provision, unlike the others, a person could be guilty of an offence even though the conduct for which the person is held criminally responsible was not the sole cause of the fire.

I. IMPLIED EXCLUSION (*EXPRESSIO UNIUS EST EXCLUSIO ALTERIUS*)

In English the form of argument known as *expressio unius* is called negative implication or implied exclusion. The latter expression is preferred here. An implied exclusion argument lies whenever the legislature sets out some but not all members of a category or class, or mentions some things but fails to mention others that are comparable. The reasoning goes as follows: if the legislature had intended to include all possible members or things, it would have mentioned them all or described them using general terms; it would not have mentioned one or some while saying nothing of the others, for that would be irrational and disorderly. Legislation is supposed to be drafted in a coherent and

---

51   *Ibid.* at 245.

orderly way. It thus follows from sound drafting practice that a partial enumeration of like things is meant to be exhaustive, and anything left off the list is by implication meant to be excluded.

This reasoning is illustrated in the majority judgment of the Supreme Court of Canada in *Zeitel v. Ellscheid*.[52] The case arose because, owing to a series of mistakes, the appellant had been occupying one parcel of land while registered and paying taxes as the owner of another. When the land occupied by the appellant was sold by the municipality for tax arrears, the appellant sought to assert title to it based on his adverse possession. The case turned on subsection 9(5) of Ontario's *Municipal Tax Sales Act*, which provided that once a tax sale was complete and the deed or notice of vesting was registered by the appropriate municipal official, title to the land vested in the new owner "free from all estates and interests, subject only to"

(a) easements and restrictive covenants that run with the land;

(b) any estates and interests of the Crown ... ; and

(c) any interest or title acquired by adverse possession by abutting landowners before the registration of the tax deed or notice of vesting.

The section made no mention of adverse possession by non-abutting occupiers. Major J. wrote:

> The maxim *expressio unius est exclusio alterius* stands for the proposition that where a statute specifies one exception to a general rule, other exceptions are excluded. In s. 9(5)(c), the legislature states that purchasers at tax sales take title subject only to one class of adverse possessors, i.e., abutting landowners.[53]

Since the appellants could not bring themselves within the only adverse possession exception mentioned by the legislature, and the exceptions set out in paragraphs (a) and (b) did not apply, they had no recourse. Had the legislature intended to protect other types of adverse possession claims, it would either have listed them or have chosen language broad enough to embrace them. It would not have singled out for special mention just one type of claim.

The *expressio unius* rule is formally invoked by courts primarily in this type of case, where the legislature has set out some but not all members of a class or comparable items. However, the reasoning on which implied exclusion is based is found everywhere in statutory

---

52 [1994] 2 S.C.R. 142.

53 *Ibid.* at 152.

interpretation. An intention to exclude may legitimately be implied whenever a thing is not mentioned in a context where, if it were meant to be included, one would have expected it to be expressly mentioned. Given an expectation of express mention, the silence of the legislature becomes meaningful. An expectation of express reference legitimately arises whenever a pattern or practice of express reference is discernible. Since such patterns and practices are common in legislation, reliance on implied exclusion reasoning is also common.

In *Prassad v. Canada (Minister of Employment & Immigration)*,[54] for example, the Supreme Court of Canada had to deal with an application for an adjournment of an inquiry under the *Immigration Act*. Section 35(1) provided that an adjudicator presiding at an inquiry has a discretion to adjourn proceedings at any time to ensure a full and proper inquiry. Section 37(1) provided that a person who is the subject of an inquiry could apply to the minister for permission to remain in Canada. The applicant argued that where an application was made to the minister under section 37(1), an adjudicator was *obliged* to adjourn proceedings under section 35(1). This obligation, he argued, was implicit in the scheme of the Act; it was necessary to ensure that the procedures for dealing with immigration applications operated in a reasonable and fair way.

Courts often respond favourably to this sort of argument. Because the legislature cannot be expected to provide expressly for every circumstance that might arise in the operation of a legislative scheme, courts must be prepared to work out the unspoken implications of what the legislature has said. Thus, there was nothing unusual or inappropriate in what the applicant was asking the court to do. However, in this case, because the *Immigration Act* contained a number of provisions that expressly obliged adjudicators to adjourn in certain circumstances, the court was reluctant to imply an obligation to adjourn. Sopinka J. wrote:

> [Section 37(1)] may be usefully contrasted with other provisions of the Act which explicitly require an adjournment for specified purposes. The adjudicator shall adjourn the inquiry if: the subject of the inquiry is under eighteen years of age and unrepresented by a parent or guardian (s. 29(5)); the subject of the inquiry who is to be removed from Canada claims, during the inquiry, to be a Canadian citizen (s. 43(1)); or the subject of the inquiry who is to be removed from Canada claims, during the inquiry, to be a Convention refugee (s. 45(1)).[55]

---

54   [1989] 1 S.C.R. 560.
55   *Ibid.* at 571. See also *R. v. Ulybel Enterprises Ltd.*, [2001] 2 S.C.R. 867 at para. 42.

Sopinka J. here draws attention to a pattern of express reference. In the *Immigration Act*, when the legislature wished to limit the discretion conferred on adjudicators by section 35(1), it did so expressly in the form of a mandatory directive to adjourn. Had the legislature intended to make adjournments obligatory for applications to the minister under section 37(1), it would have followed this pattern and included an express directive. In the absence of any such directive, it is reasonable to infer that the legislature intended the adjudicator to retain his or her discretion.

Like the other presumptions relied on in textual analysis, implied exclusion is merely a presumption and can be rebutted. In *Marche v. Halifax Insurance Co.*,[56] for example, the court had to interpret section 171 of Nova Scotia's *Insurance Act*, which provided that an exclusion, stipulation, condition, or warranty contained in an insurance contract is not binding on an insured if it is held to be unjust or unreasonable by a court. The issue was whether the section applied to statutory conditions, that is, conditions included in every contract of insurance by virtue of the Act, as opposed to optional conditions chosen by the parties. The insurer pointed out that there were only two provisions in the Act which relieved an insured from the terms of an insurance contract: section 33, providing relief against forfeiture, and section 171, providing relief against unjust or unreasonable terms. Since section 33 explicitly referred to statutory conditions, whereas section 171 did not, the insurer relied on implied exclusion to argue that section 171 was not intended to extend to statutory conditions. This argument did not succeed with the majority of the court. MacLachlin C.J. wrote:

> The explicit reference to statutory conditions [implies] that s. 33 alone applies to statutory conditions, and s. 171 only applies to optional contractual provisions. This conclusion, however, is of limited relevance given the different legislative histories and objects of the two provisions, the broad interpretations of "statutory conditions" in [the case law], and the generally imprecise use of the term "condition" throughout the *Insurance Act*.[57]

---

56   [2005] 1 S.C.R. 47.
57   *Ibid.* at para. 19.

CHAPTER 10

PURPOSIVE ANALYSIS

A. INTRODUCTION

To achieve a sound interpretation of a legislative text, interpreters must identify and take into account the purpose of the legislation. This includes the purpose of the provision to be interpreted as well as larger units—parts, divisions, and the Act as a whole. Once identified, the purpose is relied on to help establish the meaning of the text. It is used as a standard against which proposed interpretations are tested: an interpretation that promotes the purpose is preferred over one that does not, while interpretations that would tend to defeat the purpose are avoided.

Purposive analysis has become a staple of modern interpretation. It is used not only when the language of a text is found to be ambiguous but in every case and at every stage of interpretation. This reliance is justified by the interaction between language and purpose that is present in all communication, including legislation. The listener or reader infers the purpose from what is being said and the circumstances in which it is said, and at the same time understands what is being said in light of the purpose.

A strong emphasis on purpose is also justified by a number of legal considerations. First, a purposive approach has been mandated by the legislature. There is a provision in every Canadian Interpretation Act directing interpreters to give to every enactment "such fair, large and liberal construction and interpretation as best ensures the attainment of its objects." Second, much modern legislation is written in a form that lends itself to purposive analysis. Modern provisions tend to be drafted in general terms and many confer a broad discretion on officials. For courts to discern the proper scope of such provisions, they must know their purpose. A third factor is the *Canadian Charter of Rights and Freedoms*, which came into force in 1982. In its earliest *Charter* decisions the Supreme Court of Canada emphasized the need for purposive analysis both to give definite meaning to the broad language and complex ideas found in the *Charter* and to test whether legislation found to violate its provisions might be justified under section 1. In working with the *Charter*, Canadian courts have become accustomed to the techniques of purposive analysis.

B. WHAT IS MEANT BY LEGISLATIVE PURPOSE

"Legislative purpose" can refer to a number of different things. First, it may refer to the primary aim or object of an enactment—that is, the effect the legislature hopes to produce through the operation of its rules or scheme. This objective could be a social or economic goal, such as job creation, reducing air pollution, or finding a cure for disease. Or it could be the promotion of specific values or policies, such as multiculturalism or respect for privacy. Many statutes have several objects that complement or conflict with one another. In analyzing multipurpose legislation, the courts may have to rank or strike a balance between competing goals.

"Legislative purpose" may also refer to various secondary considerations. These are principles or policies that the legislature wishes to observe, or considerations it is obliged to take into account, in pursuing its primary goals. The legislature never pursues a goal single-mindedly, without qualification, at all costs. There are always additional or competing factors to be taken into account. These show up in legislation in a variety of ways:

- in words of restriction, qualification, or exception that limit the reach or effectiveness of the main goals;
- in provisions that confer discretion on officials, permitting them to respond to a range of factors; and
- in the choice of program design and enforcement mechanism, which may be more, or less, comprehensive and efficacious.

Finally, "legislative purpose" refers to the function performed by a provision or a series of provisions in a legislative scheme, or the contribution a provision makes to an existing body of law. It is assumed that every word of legislation, every feature of a legislative text, is there and takes the form it does because it contributes in some particular way to the scheme of the Act or the body of existing law. This contribution is its purpose, its *raison d'être*.

Even though we often speak of "the" purpose of legislation, as if there were only one, it is apparent that every piece of legislation has multiple purposes that operate at different levels of generality. In sophisticated purposive analysis the interpreter attempts to identify and work with the primary objects, the secondary considerations, and the specific functions of legislation at all levels, from the words to be interpreted and the provision in which they appear to larger units of legislation and the Act as a whole.

C. HOW LEGISLATIVE PURPOSE IS ESTABLISHED

Legislative purpose can be established either directly or indirectly. Direct evidence consists of explicit descriptions of purpose brought to the attention of the legislature. If a minister upon introducing legislation says that the purpose of the legislation is to find a cure for diabetes, the minister has offered direct evidence of the purpose. Indirect evidence consists of descriptions of facts or concerns brought to the attention of the legislature from which the purpose can be inferred. If the minister upon introducing legislation mentions statistics about harmful chemicals found in lakes and rivers, and the legislation imposes limits on the use or discharge of these chemicals, the minister has offered indirect evidence of purpose.

Currently in Canada the courts rely on three primary strategies to establish purpose: (1) through direct descriptions of purpose emanating from the legislature or another authoritative source; (2) through inference drawn from reading the legislative text; or (3) through inference drawn from examining the external context.

1) Authoritative Descriptions of Purpose

The most authoritative statements of purpose are found in purpose statements set out in the body of the statute or regulation and sometimes in preambles as well. Purpose statements normally list the primary goals that legislation is meant to achieve or the principles or policies that should be taken into account in interpreting it. Section 5 of the Yukon's *Environment Act* provides a good example:

5.(1) The objectives of this Act are
(a) to ensure the maintenance of essential ecological processes and the preservation of biological diversity;
(b) to ensure the wise management of the environment of the Yukon;
(c) to promote sustainable development in the Yukon;

...

(g) to facilitate effective participation by Yukon residents in the making of decisions that will affect the environment.

(2) The following principles apply to the realization of the objectives of this Act
(a) economic development and the health of the natural environment are inter-dependent;
(b) environmental considerations must be integrated effectively into all public decision-making;

...

(e) all persons should be responsible for the consequences to the environment of their actions.

(3) This Act shall be interpreted and applied to give effect to the objectives and principles of this section.[1]

Purpose statements are also included within provisions that confer powers or discretion, to help indicate the limits of the powers and to guide the exercise of discretion. For example, section 12 of the *Controlled Drug and Substances Act* provides:

12. For the purpose of exercising any of the powers described in section 11, a peace officer may
(*a*) enlist such assistance as the officer deems necessary; and
(*b*) use as much force as is necessary in the circumstances.[2]

Although this provision confers considerable discretion on peace officers, the scope of the discretion is limited by the statement of purpose. Any exercise of force that is not for the purpose of exercising a section 11 power would be illegal and tortious.

Preambles usually recite the facts or considerations that led to the enactment of legislation, leaving it to the interpreter to infer the purpose. However, some preambles more closely resemble purpose statements in directly setting out the governing principles or goals to be achieved. A good example is found in the *Youth Criminal Justice Act*:

---

1   S.Y. 1991, c. 5, s. 5. For a recent example from the federal statute book, see the *Sex Offender Information Registration Act*, S.C. 2004, c. 10.
2   S.C. 1996, c. 19.

WHEREAS communities, families, parents and others concerned with the development of young persons should, through multi-disciplinary approaches, take reasonable steps to prevent youth crime by addressing its underlying causes, to respond to the needs of young persons, and to provide guidance and support to those at risk of committing crimes;

WHEREAS information about youth justice, youth crime and the effectiveness of measures taken to address youth crime should be publicly available;

...

AND WHEREAS Canadian society should have a youth criminal justice system that commands respect, takes into account the interests of victims, fosters responsibility and ensures accountability through meaningful consequences and effective rehabilitation and reintegration, and that reserves its most serious intervention for the most serious crimes and reduces the over-reliance on incarceration for non-violent young persons;

NOW, THEREFORE, Her Majesty, by and with the advice and consent of the Senate and House of Commons of Canada, enacts as follows.[3]

While legislative statements of purpose can be helpful, they generally do not take interpreters very far. This is because they focus on primary aims and objects that tend to be formulated in vague, sometimes grandiose, language. Also, when more than one purpose is mentioned, they are almost never ranked. It is left to the courts to work out the relationship among the listed purposes and their connection to specific provisions and words.[4]

Direct descriptions of purpose may also be found in extralegislative sources such as the reports of law reform commissions, legislative background papers, the comments of ministers in the House, and legislative committee reports. It is now well established that these materials may be consulted by the courts for direct as well as indirect evidence of purpose. Courts also look to case law and to scholarly analyses of legislation for authoritative descriptions of purpose. Although rarely discussed, the authority accorded to legal textbooks, monographs, and law review articles is considerable.[5]

---

3   S.C. 2002, c. 1, preamble.
4   See *M. v. H.*, [1999] 2 S.C.R. 3 at para. 100.
5   These extrinsic materials are discussed in Chapter 14.

2) Purpose Inferred from Text Alone

Most often the purpose of legislation is established simply by reading the words of the legislation. Sometimes the focus is on the provision to be interpreted, read in the context of the interpreter's common sense[6] as well as his or her individual knowledge, values, and beliefs. Interpreters rely on this contextual material, first, to surmise what effects are likely to result from the operation of the legislation and, second, to conclude which possible effects are desirable. The desirable effects are presumed to be the intended goals of the legislation.

A simple example of this sort of reasoning is found in the judgment of Cory J. in *R. v. Heywood*.[7] The court there was concerned with a *Charter* challenge to section 179(1) of the *Criminal Code* which made it an offence for persons previously convicted of designated sexual crimes to be "found loitering in or near a school ground, playground, public park or bathing area." Cory J. wrote:

> The section is aimed at protecting children from becoming victims of sexual offences. This is apparent from the places to which the prohibition of loitering applies. School grounds, playgrounds, public parks and public bathing areas are typically places where children are likely to congregate. The purpose of the prohibition on loitering is to keep people who are likely to pose a risk to children away from places where they are likely to be found.[8]

In this passage Cory J. is able to identify the purpose of the section simply from reading its terms because of the knowledge he brings to the text: the vulnerability of children to the crimes designated in the section, the importance of protecting children from harmful interference by strangers, and the opportunity for such interference in places like beaches and parks. Drawing on this knowledge, he surmises that the effect of the provision would be to reduce the exposure of children to sexual predators. Since this is clearly a desirable goal, it may plausibly be imputed to the legislature. Since the information and values assumed by Cory J. are non-controversial and are likely to be shared by everyone, his analysis seems cogent and persuasive.

Although purpose can be inferred from reading the provision to be interpreted in isolation, it is usually helpful to consider the role

---

6   The importance of "common sense" in statutory interpretation is discussed in Chapter 2.

7   [1994] 3 S.C.R. 761.

8   *Ibid.* at 786.

of the provision in the context of the legislative scheme of which it is part. This entails analyzing its relationship to other provisions in the Act and related legislation. There may be a common theme that runs through a series of provisions, suggesting a shared aim or concern. Or there may be a division of labour implicit in the provisions, with each performing a distinct function. This type of reasoning and analysis is illustrated in the judgment of the Supreme Court of Canada in *R. v. Chartrand*.[9]

In this case the court had to decide what significance, if any, to attach to the word "unlawfully" that appeared in the English version of section 281 of the *Criminal Code*. That section made it an offence for a stranger to "unlawfully" take, entice away, detain, or harbour a child with intent to deprive the child's lawful guardian of possession. After reviewing the legislative evolution of the provision and noting that the word "*illégalement*" had been eliminated from the French version in a previous amendment, the court turned to purposive analysis. It identified the purpose of the provision by examining its place in the relevant legislative scheme. L'Heureux-Dubé J. wrote: "In this examination of the purpose of s. 281, it is necessary to look at the whole scheme designed by Parliament to deal with such related offences as kidnapping, hostage taking and abduction ... [which are set out in] ss. 279 to 286 of the *Code*."[10] Those sections, she went on to point out, offer a complete list of offences relating to the theme of abduction. Since legislative schemes are presumed to be coherent, where the legislature enacts a series of provisions dealing with similar or related matters, the interpreter may reasonably suppose that there are reasons why more than one provision was enacted, that each provision does distinct work, and that the parts comprise a sensible whole. In keeping with these presumptions, L'Heureux-Dubé J. turned to consider the role and function of each provision in the series.

She began by noting that sections 279 and 279.1 dealt with kidnapping and hostage taking generally, while sections 281 to 283 dealt with the abduction of children. She pointed out that in the first two sections, the consent of the abducted person was a defence, whereas in sections 281 to 283 the consent of the abducted child was not a defence. She also noted that in sections 281 to 283 the taking had to be done with intent to deprive the lawful guardian of the child. She then asked herself why. What idea or purpose did the legislature have in mind that could account for these similarities and contrasts? She reached the following conclusion:

---

9   [1994] 2 S.C.R. 864.
10   *Ibid.* at 879.

[I]n ss. 279 and 279.1, the focus is on the person abducted while, in ss. 281 to 283, the focus is on the parents (guardians, etc.) since only their consent, and not that of the taken child, could constitute a defence. Therefore, it would appear that ss. 279 and 279.1 are offences against the person abducted, while ss. 281 to 283 are mainly offences against the rights of the parents (guardians, etc.) of the abducted child.

...

Seen in that context, the purpose of s. 281 is to secure the right and ability of parents (guardians, etc.) to exercise control over their children (those children for whom they act as guardians, etc.) for the protection of those children.... It is also a recognition by Parliament that children are best protected by the supervision of their parents (guardians, etc.).[11]

To the extent L'Heureux-Dubé J. succeeds in connecting the legislature's purpose to specific details of the text and making sense of these details in terms of the legislative scheme, her account of the purpose is persuasive.

3) Purpose Inferred from Mischief to Be Cured

When carrying out a purposive analysis, courts sometimes refer to the mischief rule, also known as the rule in *Heydon's Case*.[12] *Heydon's Case* was decided in 1584 and has been cited ever since for the following passage:

[F]or the sure and true interpretation of all statutes ... four things are to be discerned and considered: —

1st. What was the common law before the making of the Act.

2nd. What was the mischief and defect for which the common law did not provide.

3rd. What remedy the Parliament hath resolved and appointed to cure the disease of the commonwealth.

And, 4th. The true reason of the remedy; and then the office of all the Judges is always to make such construction as shall suppress the mischief, and advance the remedy.[13]

On this approach, each new Act or amendment is to be understood as an attempt to solve a problem, suppress an evil, or deal with an inadequacy in existing law. The court discovers the purpose by locating

---

11   *Ibid.* at 879–80.
12   (1584), 76 E.R. 637.
13   *Ibid.* at 638.

the "mischief" it was meant to cure. More precisely, the court looks at the legal and external contexts existing at the time the legislation was enacted and it identifies the purpose by matching the "remedy"—the provisions adopted by the legislature—with the "mischief" to which it is a plausible response.

This approach was used by L'Heureux-Dubé J. dissenting in *R. v. St. Pierre*.[14] The issue was what should count as "evidence to the contrary" in rebutting the presumption of accurate breathalyzer testing created by section 258(1) of the *Criminal Code*. In urging an interpretation that would promote the purpose of the provision, she wrote:

> Parliament enacted the presumption in s. 258(1)(c) in clear recognition of the difficulty and expense of requiring expert evidence in virtually every alcohol-related driving offence. In Canada in 1992 alone, police recorded 132,377 impaired driving incidents, of which 105,766 persons were charged with impaired driving related offences.... The enormous burden on our court system posed by these offences must be appreciated. The presumption in s. 258(1)(c) is an important means by which Parliament has sought to address this problem. The presumption strikes a fair balance between collective and individual interests.[15]

The primary purpose of the provision according to L'Heureux Dubé J. is to facilitate the prosecution of alcohol-related driving offences by dispensing with the need for expert testimony in such cases. This purpose is inferred by looking at relevant social facts (the high incidence of drunk driving prosecutions and the burdens this generates) and by exploring the ways in which the content of the legislation (introducing a relatively cheap and easy method to prove blood alcohol content at trial) represents an appropriate response to those facts. In the passage quoted above, L'Heureux-Dubé J. notices not only the primary object of facilitating prosecutions (a collective interest), but also the qualifying concern of ensuring a fair trial (an individual interest). The balance struck between these competing purposes should be reflected in the court's understanding and application of the provision.[16]

---

14   [1995] 1 S.C.R. 791.
15   *Ibid.* at 843. [Citations omitted.]
16   For other recent examples, see *Re Canada 3000 Inc.*, [2006] 1 S.C.R. 865 at para 36*ff.*; *AstraZeneca Canada Inc. v. Canada (Minister of Health)*, [2006] 2 S.C.R. 560 at para 12*ff.*

4) Purpose Inferred from Legislative Evolution

The purpose of legislation can also be established by tracing its evolution from initial enactment through subsequent amendments and revisions to its current form. Generally, the court begins by inferring the original purpose of legislation, from its original terms or perhaps from the mischief it was originally designed to cure. It must then determine whether this purpose has changed in the course of subsequent amendments and revisions. It is possible to conclude some or all changes in the wording of legislation are merely stylistic improvements or adaptations to technological or institutional change.

In *Montréal v. 2952-1366 Québec Inc.*,[17] for example, a majority of the Supreme Court of Canada reviewed the evolution of the authority conferred on the city of Montreal to deal with nuisance caused by noise. McLachlin C.J. and Deschamps J. noted that since 1851 the City had the authority to adopt by-laws for the peace and welfare of the city and for the "prevention and suppression of all nuisances." Since 1865 the city had been legislating for the purpose of controlling noise. Its first effort was a single article in a By-law to Preserve Public Peace and Good Order, which prohibited the wilful use of "any bell, horn, or bugle, or other sounding instrument." In 1937 the city adopted the first by-law dealing exclusively with noise. It included a provision that prohibited "sounds produced by sound equipment and projected from a building into a public space." McLachlin C.J. and Deschamps J. wrote:

> The purpose of the provision was apparently to prohibit sounds produced by equipment located inside a building at a volume such that a court could conclude that the person in control of the building intended the sounds to be heard by people in public spaces. The purpose of the prohibition was to preserve the peaceful nature of public spaces.[18]

By 1994, Montreal's noise by-law had expanded to twenty-one sections. Section 9 prohibited "noise produced by sound equipment, whether it is inside a building or installed or used outside" if the noise "can be heard from the outside." On the basis of this review, McLachlin C.J. and Deschamps J. concluded:

> Although the wording [of this provision] has been modified over the years, all the provisions adopted since 1937 have had as their purpose the elimination of sounds emitted by sound equipment inside or outside a building at a volume such that they are audible and

---

17   [2005] 3 S.C.R. 141 [*Montréal*].
18   *Ibid.* at para. 20.

thus interfere with citizens' peaceful enjoyment of public spaces. The underlying objective of all these by-laws has been to preserve the peaceful nature of public spaces.[19]

In the Montreal case, the court concluded that the purpose of the provision in question had not changed since its initial enactment in 1937. However, sometimes changes in the wording of legislation reflect significant changes in legislative policy or a distinct evolution in legislative thought. In *Zeitel v. Ellscheid*,[20] for example, the Supreme Court of Canada concluded that an important purpose of the *Municipal Tax Sales Act* (MTSA) was to facilitate the sale of property for non-payment of municipal tax, and for this purpose sales had to be final and secure, with minimum risk of challenge by previous owners. However, as the court noted, the *MTSA* contained a number of provisions designed to protect the interests of previous owners by permitting challenges to tax sales on a number of grounds. Clearly, in enacting the *MTSA*, the legislature sought to strike a balance between the competing interests of previous and current owners. This was the primary purpose of the part of the legislation to be interpreted. The interpretive challenge here was to determine how that balance should be, or was intended to be, struck—what weight should attach to each competing interest.

In rising to this challenge in the *Zeitel* case, the court relied on the historical evolution of the Act. Major J. wrote:

> As purchasers must be assured of the integrity of title, the legislature has stated that, with few exceptions, once a tax deed is issued, it is final and binding. In recent years, the legislation has been amended to better ensure finality.... [Section] 13(1) was introduced to abolish the power of courts to declare tax sales invalid on the basis that an assessment was invalid.... Similarly, the *MTSA* does not contain a provision found in predecessor legislation which allowed a tax deed to be attacked within two years of issue.[21]

The common theme of the amendments was to minimize the opportunity of previous owners to recover land sold for arrears. This focus suggested an increasing legislative commitment to security of title. Although the interests of previous owners had not been totally abandoned, given the trend of the legislative evolution, it was fair to con-

---

19   *Ibid.* at para. 22.
20   [1994] 2 S.C.R. 142.
21   *Ibid.* at 152. A similar analysis is found in the dissenting judgment of Bastarache J. in *Bristol-Myers Squibb Co. v. Canada (Attorney General)*, [2005] 1 S.C.R. 533 [*Bristol-Myers*].

clude that protecting the interests of current owners had become the more pressing concern.[22]

D. USES OF PURPOSIVE ANALYSIS

Purpose is relied on in many ways in statutory interpretation. Competent language users inevitably have regard for the apparent purpose of a statement in constructing its ordinary meaning. It is relied on to clarify doubts about the scope of generally worded provisions or to establish limits on the exercise of statutory powers: a provision or a power extends only to things that are rationally related to its purpose. It is also relied on to resolve ambiguity: the meaning that better promotes the purpose is the one that is preferred.

Purpose may be used not only to resolve doubt or ambiguity but also to "create" it, or more precisely to reveal the presence of an interpretive problem. Where the ordinary meaning of a provision appears to be clear but conflicts with the legislature's apparent purpose, there is work to be done. An interpretation must be sought that accords with the purpose without imposing too great a strain on the text.

Probably the most common use of purposive analysis is to clarify the scope of general language.[23] The scope of a word or expression is the range of things to which it applies. In the prohibition "No vehicles are allowed in the park," the range of reference of the word "vehicle" is doubtful. Presumably it applies to cars and buses. But does it also apply to toy wagons? to bicycles? to motorized wheelchairs? Does it apply to an ambulance responding to an in-park emergency? Should "vehicle" be defined broadly to include any means of transport, or narrowly to include only some means of transport—those driven by an internal combustion engine or those that make a lot of noise? These are questions of scope.

Questions of scope are often answered by referring to the purpose of the provision. If the sole purpose of the "no vehicles in the park" prohibition were to minimize exhaust fumes, the broad definition should be rejected as overinclusive because it would make the prohibition applicable to vehicles like bicycles and wagons which, being fumeless, have no relation to the purpose. Conversely, if the park had no path-

---

22   For further discussion of the legislative evolution of provisions and its use in interpretation, see Chapter 14.

23   *Montréal*, above note 17 at para 23.

ways and the purposes were to protect the grass and ensure the safety of picnickers, the narrower definitions should be rejected as underinclusive. They would prevent the prohibition from applying to bicycles and wagons which, being capable of spoiling grass and interfering with picnics, are related to these purposes.

In *R. v. Hasselwander*[24] the Supreme Court of Canada offers a classic example of the use of purposive analysis to clarify the scope of a provision. The issue was whether a Mini-Uzi submachine gun was a "prohibited weapon" within the following definition: "*(c) any firearm ... that is capable of firing bullets in rapid succession during one pressure of the trigger.*" As it came off the assembly line, a Mini-Uzi submachine gun could not fire bullets in rapid discharge. However, by removing a certain part, something an owner could quickly and easily do, the gun could be made to fire rapidly. The trial judge thus found the gun to be readily capable, but not immediately capable, of rapid discharge. The question was whether such a gun was "capable of firing bullets in rapid succession" within the meaning of the section.

Cory J. wrote: "In my view, any uncertainty as to whether the word 'capable' means either 'immediately capable' or 'readily capable', is resolved as soon as the word is interpreted in light of the purpose and goals of the prohibited weapons provisions of the *Code*."[25] Cory J. determined the "purpose and goals" of the relevant provisions through inference, relying on certain facts about automatic weapons and the preferences of Canadian society:

> Let us consider for a moment the nature of automatic weapons.... These guns are designed to kill and maim a large number of people rapidly and effectively.... They are not designed for hunting any animal but man. They are not designed to test the skill and accuracy of a marksman.... There is good reason to prohibit their use in light of the threat which they pose and the limited use to which they can be put. Their prohibition ensures a safer society....
>
> Canadians, unlike Americans do not have a constitutional right to bear arms. Indeed, most Canadians prefer the peace of mind and sense of security derived from the knowledge that the possession of automatic weapons is prohibited.[26]

---

24   [1993] 2 S.C.R. 398 [*Hasselwander*]. For a recent illustration, in which the narrower reading of an ambiguous provision was preferred, see *R. v. C.D.; R. v. C.D.K.*, [2005] 3 S.C.R. 668 at paras. 34–38 .

25   *Hasselwander, ibid.* at 413–14.

26   *Ibid.* at 414.

In other words, the purpose of the provisions is to curtail the use of automatic weapons so that a majority of the population can be secure and feel secure. Since automatic weapons have virtually no meritorious uses (Cory J. does not mention collection), the balance between community protection and individual freedom weighs heavily on the side of protection.

Given this purpose, a majority of the court preferred an expansive rather than a narrow interpretation of "capable":

> What then, should "capable" mean as it is used in the s. 84(1) definition of prohibited weapon? It should not be restricted to the narrow meaning of immediately capable. Such a definition would mean that the simple removal of a part which could be replaced in seconds would take the weapon outside the definition. This surely could not have been the intention of Parliament. If it were, the danger from automatic weapons would continue to exist just as strongly as it did before the prohibition was enacted.[27]

If the definition of prohibited weapon did not apply to convertible near-automatic weapons, it would be a simple matter for gun manufacturers and owners to evade the legislation, thereby defeating Parliament's goal of protecting the public from the dangers of automatic weapons. Since that outcome would be unacceptable, the broader interpretation was adopted.

In *Hasselwander*, purposive analysis led the court to choose the broader of two plausible interpretations. This outcome is in keeping with the conventional rhetoric of statutory interpretation, which associates purposive analysis with liberal applications. In practice, however, a purposive approach often leads to a narrower rather than a broader interpretation. Modern legislation tends to be written in general terms with minimal qualifications and exceptions. The resulting style is likely to be overinclusive and to correct for this tendency, to bring the scope of the legislative language in line with the purpose, the court must read it down. It must, in effect, add words of limitation or qualification or exception to the provision. In this way the court ensures a rational connection between the purpose of the provision and the things to which it applies.

In *R. v. Lohnes*,[28] for example, the Supreme Court of Canada had to determine the meaning of "disturbance" in section 175(1)(a) of the *Criminal Code*. McLachlin J. wrote:

---

27   *Ibid.* at 415.
28   [1992] 1 S.C.R. 167.

The word "disturbance" encompasses a broad range of meanings. At one extreme, it may be something as innocuous as a false note or a jarring colour; something which disturbs in the sense of annoyance or disruption. At the other end of the spectrum are incidents of violence, inducing disquiet, fear and apprehension for physical safety. Between these extremes lies a vast variety of disruptive conduct. The question before us is whether all conduct within the broad spectrum elicits criminal liability under s. 175(1).[29]

In answering this question the court looked at many things, including the French version of the provision, its evolution, and its context, as well as its purpose. The purpose was identified by inference from reading the text in the light of legal knowledge and common sense. The idea, McLachlin J. concluded, was to strike an appropriate balance between an individual's freedom of self-expression and the collective right to peace: "The individual right of expression must at some point give way to the collective interest in peace and tranquillity, and the collective right in peace and tranquillity must be based on recognition that in a society where people live together some degree of disruption must be tolerated."[30] This purpose made adoption of a broad, expansive reading of "disturbance" inappropriate. To strike the right balance, something more than mere emotional upset was necessary. The court thus concluded that "disturbance" in this context must refer to a manifest and material disturbance, one that interferes with the ordinary use of public premises. McLachlin J. wrote:

> [T]he narrower "public disturbance" … permits a more sensitive balancing between the countervailing interests at stake …. [The meaning adopted] … should permit the court to weigh the degree and intensity of the conduct complained of against the degree and nature of the peace which can be expected to prevail in a given place at a given time. A … [meaning] which accepts mental or emotional disturbance as sufficient … does not permit such balancing …. ["Public disturbance"] strikes a more sensitive balance between the individual interest in liberty and the public interest in going about its affairs in peace and tranquillity.[31]

Here, the legislative purpose justified a narrow understanding of a broad, open-ended term.

---

29   *Ibid.* at 171.
30   *Ibid.* at 172.
31   *Ibid.* at 180–81. See also *Montréal*, above note 17 at para. 34; *Bristol-Myers*, above note 21 at para 65.

CHAPTER 11

CONSEQUENTIAL ANALYSIS

A. INTRODUCTION

In resolving problems in statutory interpretation, courts appropriately take into account the consequences of applying legislation to particular facts. Consequences that are judged to be good are generally presumed to be intended and are regarded as part of the legislative purpose. Consequences that are judged to be absurd or otherwise unacceptable are presumed not to have been intended. As much as possible, interpretations that lead to unacceptable consequences are avoided.

Two questions arise in the context of consequential analysis which are difficult to answer. First, when is a court entitled to label a particular consequence absurd or unacceptable? In other words, what sorts of consequences are bad? And how bad do they have to be? Second, assuming consequences are absurd or unacceptable, what is a permissible response? How far may courts go in their efforts to avoid absurdity?

B. WHEN MAY CONSEQUENCES BE LABELLED ABSURD?

In testing whether the consequences of an interpretation are acceptable, the courts work with norms of reasonableness, fairness, and plausibility derived from the culture to which they belong. This includes legal culture, especially the norms of the common law, as well as the culture of the social groups to which judges belong. To be considered absurd or unacceptable, consequences must violate a norm that is judged to be important to the legislature or to society in general, and this violation must be evident and serious.

Although there is no limit on the ways in which norms of reasonableness, fairness, and plausibility can be violated, certain types of absurdity are encountered over and over again in applying legislation to facts. One common form of absurdity consists of treating persons or things that are similar in a dissimilar way without an adequate reason for the difference in treatment. Courts have repeatedly found this form of inequality to be unacceptable or absurd. In *Hills v. Canada (Attorney General)*,[1] for example, the Supreme Court of Canada considered an interpretation of the *Unemployment Insurance Act* that would have made the eligibility of laid-off workers for insurance benefits under the Act turn on whether their union dues were deposited in union coffers at the local or at the international level. Because there was no rational connection between the place where the workers' dues were handled and their entitlement to unemployment insurance benefits, the distinction was judged to be absurd and the interpretation that led to it was rejected.

It is also considered absurd for the legislature to contradict itself, to create an incoherent scheme,[2] or to act in a futile or self-defeating way.[3] A legislature would not go to the trouble of enacting rules that cannot be enforced or whose enforcement would tend to defeat the very purpose for which they were enacted.[4] Nor would it enact provisions that interfere with the efficient administration of justice[5] or impose pointless inconvenience on its subjects.[6]

Avoiding interpretations that would defeat the purpose of the legislation was an important consideration in *R. v. Monney*,[7] where the issue was whether section 98 of the *Customs Act* allowed a person suspected of having ingested drugs to be detained in a "drug loo facility" until he or she urinated or defecated. Section 98 authorized a customs officer to "search" a person arriving in Canada "if the officer believes on reasonable grounds that the person has secreted on or about his person"

---

1   [1988] 1 S.C.R. 513.
2   See, for example, *Marche v. Halifax Insurance Co.*, [2005] 1 S.C.R. 47.
3   See, for example, *Bisaillon v. Concordia University*, [2006] 1 S.C.R. 666 at para. 94.
4   See, for example, *Rizzo & Rizzo Shoes Ltd., (Re)*, [1998] 1 S.C.R. 27 at para. 26.
5   See, for example, *R. v. Chase*, [1987] 2 S.C.R. 293 at 302–3.
6   See, for example, *Québec (Services de santé) v. Québec (Communauté urbaine)*, [1992] 1 S.C.R. 426.
7   [1999] 1 S.C.R. 652.

some type of contraband. The Supreme Court of Canada concluded that, properly interpreted, contraband secreted "on or about his person" extended to contraband inside the person. The Court found that the purpose of section 98 was "to grant officers the necessary authority to control the smuggling of contraband into Canada."[8] This purpose would be defeated if a narrower interpretation, excluding ingested drugs, were adopted. Iacobucci J. wrote:

> Parliament's intent in extending the authority of customs officers to search for any concealed material, whether located internal or external to the traveller's physical body, is further supported by the illogical outcome that would ensue if the Court were to adopt a more restrictive interpretation. A traveller intent on smuggling narcotics across the Canadian border would be able to defeat the purpose of the provision simply by concealing contraband inside his or her mouth rather than under his or her clothing or elsewhere on his or her body. Interpreting s. 98 in light of the provision's purpose, which is to restrict the entry of contraband material into Canada, the phrase "secreted on or about his person" cannot have been intended to permit such an absurd result.[9]

Outside these standard categories, consequences are labelled absurd if they are senseless or obviously harmful or otherwise inconsistent with our basic assumption that the legislature is a competent institution acting in the public interest. A good example is found in the judgment of Dickson J. in *R. v. Skoke-Graham*.[10] In that case the Supreme Court of Canada had to determine whether four church members who deliberately violated church protocol by kneeling to receive communion during a religious service contravened section 172(3) of the *Criminal Code*. Under this provision, it was an offence to "wilfully ... [do] anything that disturbs the order or solemnity" of a religious meeting. Dickson J. acknowledged that the conduct in question came within the ordinary meaning of "doing anything that disturbs." However, in this case the ordinary meaning had to be rejected because of the absurd consequences to which it would lead. In its place a more restrictive interpretation was adopted, one that limited the prohibition to conduct "disorderly in itself or productive of disorder."[11] Dickson J. explained:

---

8   *Ibid.* at para. 26.
9   *Ibid.* at para. 28.
10   [1985] 1 S.C.R. 106.
11   *Ibid.* at 119.

> If "disturb" in the context of s. 172(3) is taken to encompass annoyance, anxiety or emotional upset, then "anything", no matter how trivial, which would lead to such annoyance, anxiety or emotional upset would be caught by the provision: a man might be convicted under the section for failing to take his hat off in a church, or failing to keep it on in a synagogue.[12]

Dickson J. does not explain why it would be absurd to convict a person of a criminal offence for wearing, or not wearing, a hat in a place of worship. He doesn't have to. It is obvious to any rational person (who shares the judge's values and assumptions) that hatwear is not a matter for the *Criminal Code* and that, given the good sense of Parliament, any interpretation resulting in the criminalization of hats must be wrong.

The argument here is effective for several reasons. First, Dickson J. does not just reject the ordinary meaning of the provision but formulates a plausible alternative. He offers a neat, dictionary-like definition of "do anything that disturbs" that is narrower than the ordinary meaning but not so narrow as to be implausible. Second, he does not just assert, but offers a concrete illustration of the absurdity to which the broader definition would lead. In addition to the facts of this case—namely, kneeling instead of standing to receive communion—he mentions other examples of protocol violation which are apt to strike his audience as trivial. In the years since this case was decided, Canadians have been sensitized to the importance of appropriate headwear in some religions, and no doubt today Dickson J. would have chosen a different example. For most members of his audience, however, his allusion to hats would create an appropriate impression of the silliness that would result from adopting the broader interpretation.[13]

C. HOW SHOULD COURTS RESPOND TO ABSURDITY?

In cases of ambiguity, where a provision lends itself to more than one plausible interpretation, it is clearly appropriate for a court to reject the interpretation that would lead to absurdity in favour of one that avoids it. In *R. v. Paré*,[14] for example, the Supreme Court of Canada was con-

---

12   *Ibid.*
13   This technique is used to good effect by Binnie J. in *Montréal (City) v. 2952-1366 Québec Inc.*, 2005 SCC 62 at paras. 118–19.
14   [1987] 2 S.C.R. 618.

cerned with section 214(5) of the *Criminal Code*. It provided that homicide by a person "while committing" certain other offences, including indecent assault, was deemed to be first-degree murder. The question was whether the section applied where there was a momentary pause between the actions involved in the assault and those involved in the homicide. Did the words "while committing" mean (a) "committing simultaneously, at exactly the same instant" or (b) "committing on the same occasion, as part of a continuous sequence of events"? From a purely linguistic perspective, both interpretations were plausible. But when the consequences of adopting one or the other were looked at, interpretation (a) was problematic. Wilson J. wrote:

> The first problem with the exactly simultaneous approach flows from the difficulty in defining the beginning and end of an indecent assault. In this case, for example, after ejaculation the respondent sat up and put his pants back on. But for the next two minutes he kept his hand on his victim's chest. Was this continued contact part of the assault? It does not seem to me that important issues of criminal law should be allowed to hinge upon this kind of distinction. An approach that depends on this kind of distinction should be avoided if possible.
>
> A second difficulty with the exactly simultaneous approach is that it leads to distinctions that are arbitrary and irrational. In the present case, had the respondent strangled his victim two minutes earlier than he did, his guilt of first degree murder would be beyond dispute. The exactly simultaneous approach would have us conclude that the two minutes he spent contemplating his next move had the effect of reducing his offence to one of second degree murder. This would be a strange result. The crime is no less serious in the latter case than in the former.... An interpretation of s. 214(5) that runs contrary to common sense is not to be adopted if a reasonable alternative is available.[15]

In this case the words to be interpreted were vague and readily lent themselves to more than one interpretation. Furthermore, the competing interpretations presented to the court were both plausible readings of the provision. In these circumstances, it was easy for the court to avoid the absurdity of interpretation (a) by adopting interpretation (b).

The hard question is whether absurdity may be relied on to reject interpretations that appear to be clear or to adopt interpretations that are strained or implausible. Where the meaning of a provision appears to be clear from a linguistic point of view, is it permissible to cast doubt on

---

15   *Ibid.* at 631.

that meaning by pointing out the unacceptable consequences to which it may lead? And if so, how far can one go? Is it permissible to reject a plausible interpretation in favour of an implausible one? Can courts refuse to apply a provision to the facts of a case when, on any plausible reading of the section, it clearly applies? Can they carve out exceptions, read in qualifications, or fill gaps in the legislative scheme?[16]

Since the mid-nineteenth century the courts have been guided in these matters by the so-called golden rule. The best known formulation is Lord Wensleydale's in *Grey v. Pearson*:

> [I]n construing wills, and indeed statutes, and all written instruments, the grammatical and ordinary sense of the words is to be adhered to, unless that would lead to some absurdity or some repugnance or inconsistency with the rest of the instrument, in which case the grammatical and ordinary sense of the words may be modified so as to avoid that absurdity and inconsistency, but no further.[17]

This description says that to avoid absurdity courts may depart from the ordinary meaning of a text, even though from a purely linguistic perspective that meaning is clear and unequivocal. As La Forest J.A. wrote in *Re Estabrooks Pontiac Buick Ltd.*:

> The fact that the words as interpreted would give an unreasonable result ... is certainly ground for the courts to scrutinize a statute carefully to make abundantly certain that those words are not susceptible of another interpretation. For it should not be readily assumed that the Legislature intends an unreasonable result or to perpetrate an injustice or absurdity.[18]

Some courts accept that if the ordinary meaning leads to absurd results, it cannot really be considered "plain." More often, however, courts insist that if the meaning is clear, consequences are irrelevant and cannot be relied on to cast doubt on what is plain.

The passage from *Grey v. Pearson* also says that courts may depart from the ordinary meaning of legislation to the extent necessary to avoid absurdity, even if this means adopting an implausible interpretation. This approach is certainly evident in the case law. It is easy to find examples in which implausible interpretations have been adopted to avoid unacceptable results. In *Talbot v. Gan General Insurance Co.*,[19] for

---

16 These questions are explored in greater detail in Chapter 7.
17 (1857), 29 L.T.O.S. 67 at 71 (H.L.).
18 (1982), 44 N.B.R. (2d) 201 at 210 (C.A.).
19 (1999), 44 O.R. (3d) 252 (S.C.J.).

example, the court concluded that a provision in the *Insurance Act* that provided coverage for insured persons who were "hit or struck by a motor vehicle" extended to insured persons who experienced a near miss. More often, however, courts are reluctant to express such a cavalier attitude towards the legislative text and prefer Lord Blackburn's more conservative formulation of the rule. In *River Wear Commissioners v. Adamson*, Lord Blackburn wrote:

> [W]e are to take the whole statute together, and construe it all together, giving the words their ordinary signification, unless when so applied they produce an inconsistency, or an absurdity or inconvenience so great as to convince the Court that the intention could not have been to use them in their ordinary signification, and to justify the Court in putting on them some other signification, which, though less proper, is one which the Court thinks the words will bear.[20]

This formulation says that departure from the ordinary meaning is permissible, provided the interpretation adopted is one that the words can reasonably bear.

The courts are far from providing definitive answers to the questions raised in this chapter. Judicial attitudes vary from judge to judge and from case to case. However, despite the absence of anything like a consensus on these questions, it is possible to discern a pattern in the practice of the courts based on a principle of proportionality: the greater the absurdity to be avoided, the farther the court may stray from the constraints of the text; conversely, the clearer the provision and the plainer its meaning, the greater the absurdity required to justify departure from the text. In some cases, it may be acceptable for a court to effectively amend a provision or refuse to apply it, even though it appears to be applicable. But such liberties are not to be taken lightly.

D. JUSTIFICATION FOR AVOIDING ABSURD CONSEQUENCES

Although it is natural for judges to consider the impact of their decisions on litigants and others who may be affected by an outcome, this aspect of interpretation has generally proved difficult for the courts to acknowledge and to justify. There are reasons for this difficulty. By noticing the consequences of adopting one interpretation rather than another, and by

---

20   (1877), 2 App. Cas. 743 at 764–65 (H.L.).

allowing this to influence their decisions, courts appear to violate both the doctrine of parliamentary sovereignty and the rule of law.

Under the doctrine of parliamentary sovereignty, it is inappropriate for courts to second-guess the wisdom of the legislature. Once a directive has been duly enacted, courts are supposed to give effect to that directive as written, not distort it or refuse to apply it if the outcome is not to their liking.

Under the rule of law, courts must strive for transparency, predictability, consistency, and even-handedness. These values can be achieved only if everyone proceeds on the same basis. Since the apparent meaning of a provision is the basis on which everyone ordinarily and naturally proceeds, this meaning must be respected. If a court can reject or distort an apparent meaning because accepting it would lead to unsatisfying results, we have rule by whim of the decision maker, not rule of law.

The concerns raised by these objections are serious, but they can be addressed. In the first place, the norms relied on by courts in assessing consequences are not personal whims. Legislatures and courts are created and staffed from the same society, and they participate in the same legal tradition. They consequently work with similar ideas about what is fair and reasonable and plausible. These norms do not come out of the blue. They come out of common experiences and values, a shared culture and knowledge base, a shared body of "common sense."[21] It is therefore possible to suggest that in applying norms of fairness or right reason, a court is ensuring that legislation is applied in a way that conforms to the values of the legislature itself and the society it represents.

In the second place, it is arguable that an essential part of the court's role in statutory interpretation lies in adjusting the application of fixed rules to individual cases to avoid absurd or unjust results. This is the basis on which the equitable jurisdiction of English courts was originally founded and later expanded in subsequent centuries. Like the rigid forms of the early common law, statutory rules sometimes require qualification or exception to ensure justice in particular circumstances. This flexibility does not undermine the authority of the legislature, but complements it. As O'Halloran wrote in *Waugh v. Pedneault (Nos. 2 & 3)*:

> The Legislature cannot be presumed to act unreasonably or unjustly, for that would be acting against the public interest. The members of the Legislature are elected by the people to protect the public in-

---

21   See the discussion of common sense in Chapter 2.

terest, and that means acting fairly and justly in all circumstances. Words used in enactments of the Legislature must be construed upon that premise. That is the real "intent" of the Legislature. That is why words in an Act of the Legislature are not restricted to what are sometimes called their "ordinary" or "literal" meaning, but are extended flexibly to include the most reasonable meaning which can be extracted from the purpose and object of what is sought to be accomplished by the statute.[22]

While the legislation concerns itself with the adoption of broad policy initiatives and resource allocation, the courts supervise the appropriate implementation of the legislature's programs and rules on individual citizens.[23]

As for the rule of law, although any departure from the apparent meaning of a provision lessens predictability and consistency, these are not the only values worth striving for in our legal system. In some cases it is better to sacrifice predictability to fairness, consistency to a sensible and workable outcome. A measure of uncertainty may be expected and even planned for in a healthy legal system. The truly difficult issue here is trust. Can we trust our judges and the many other officials to whom we give a power of interpretation to "get it right"? Can they be trusted to recognize unfairness or irrationality when they see it, to balance fairness or right reason against predictability in an appropriate way? If the answer to these questions is no, then perhaps we need new interpreters.

---

22   (1948), [1949] 1 W.W.R. 14 at 15 (B.C.C.A.).
23   For further discussion of the separation of powers doctrine and how it affects understanding of the judicial role, see Chapter 2.

POLICY ANALYSIS

A. JUSTIFICATION FOR POLICY ANALYSIS

In determining the meaning of a provision in relation to particular facts, courts inevitably engage in policy analysis. That is, they take into account extratextual values or preferences that tend to favour one outcome over another. Although this aspect of interpretation is often played down by the courts, it is an essential and appropriate part of the interpretive process.

There are many ways in which extratextual values and preferences are introduced into interpretation. They form part of the basis for inferring the meaning and purpose of legislation in textual and purposive analyses and for distinguishing good from bad consequences in consequential analysis. In these types of analyses the appeal to policy is usually implicit and intuitive rather than formal and self-conscious. However, policy enters interpretation in more formal and direct ways as well: through the doctrine of strict and liberal construction, through presumptions of legislative intent, through direct appeals to policy and through non-application rules.[1] These are not rigid or tidy categories. The values and policies are expressed in various ways, and there is a good deal of overlap. For example, respect for private property rights figures largely in the strict construction doctrine and is also reflected directly and indirectly in several of the presumptions of legislative intent.

---

1   Non-application rules are described and discussed in Chapter 13.

Although policy analysis involves an appeal to values and preferences that are external to the text, it is a legitimate part of statutory interpretation in so far as the values and preferences relied on are rooted in legislation or the common law or in the evolving legal tradition. Such reliance is legitimate because these values and preferences make up the legal culture in which legislatures and courts both operate. It is appropriately assumed that the legislature has them in mind when it enacts legislation and that interpreters will take them into account when determining the meaning of a legislative text.

Objections to policy analysis in statutory interpretation are generally grounded in fear that judges will reach conclusions based on their own subjective preferences instead of giving effect to the intention of the legislature. However, when properly done, policy analysis is not grounded in subjective preference; rather it is grounded in what the Supreme Court of Canada has called "objectively defined norms."[2] This concept was elaborated in *R. v. Labaye*, which dealt with a prosecution under section 210(1) of the *Criminal Code* making it an offence to keep a common bawdy house. In section 197(1), bawdy house was defined to include a place resorted to for "the practice of acts of indecency." It was up to the courts to give meaningful content to the vague and value-laden notion of indecency. In *Labaye* the court held that for an act to be criminally indecent it must create a risk of harm incompatible with the proper functioning of society.[3] McLachlin C.J. wrote:

> Two general requirement emerge from this description of the harm required for criminal indecency. First, ... the harm must be grounded in norms which our society has recognized in its Constitution or similar fundamental laws. This means that the inquiry is not based on individual notions of harm, nor on the teachings of a particular ideology, but on what society, through its laws and institutions, has recognized as essential to its proper functioning. Second, the harm must be serious in degree.[4]

In *Labaye* the court clearly recognizes that a vague term in a provision obliges the interpreter to complete the legislative process by giving specific content to the term in the context of particular cases. Interpreters give content to terms by relying on (among other things) "objectively defined norms." There is no bright-line distinction between terms that are vague or value-laden and those that are not. Rather, there is a

---

2   *R. v. Labaye*, 2005 SCC 80 at para. 2.
3   *Ibid.* at paras. 23–24.
4   *Ibid.* at para. 29.

continuum. To the extent the language of a provision is specific and concrete, and rooted in the physical world, it requires relatively little judgment and leaves little room for appeal to extratextual norms. However, as terms become more general, more abstract, more dependent on beliefs and values, appeal to such norms is necessary. The job of courts is not to avoid reliance on extratextual norms but rather to justify them in terms of accepted legal principles and values.

Even though reliance on extratextual norms is legitimate, Canadian courts have shown a puzzling ambivalence towards policy analysis. Despite their repudiation of the plain meaning rule, courts often refuse to apply strict construction or a presumption of legislative intent unless, upon completion of the appropriate textual and purposive analyses, the text to be interpreted is found to be ambiguous. In effect, this excludes legal context from the "entire context" in which, under Driedger's modern principle, the legislation must be read.

B. STRICT AND LIBERAL CONSTRUCTION

Since the eighteenth century, English courts have distinguished between legislation that calls for a strict construction and legislation that should be interpreted liberally. The first category is comprised primarily of Acts that interfere with individual liberty or rights. This includes penal legislation, regulatory legislation, taxation and expropriation Acts, zoning by-laws, and the like. When legislation is strictly construed, it is applied as narrowly as possible. General terms are read down; conditions of application are carefully enforced. Doubts about the meaning or scope of the legislation are resolved in favour of non-application. When taking a strict approach, courts often say that if the legislature had intended to interfere with the rights or freedoms of the subject, it would have said so in explicit and precise terms. In the absence of such language, it is fair to presume that the legislature did not intend to interfere.

The category of legislation requiring a liberal construction is harder to define. Historically, it consisted of so-called remedial legislation, Acts for the advancement of religion, and Acts that promote the public welfare. In liberal construction the court takes a purposive and a benevolent approach. It does what it can to promote the social goals of the legislation, and doubts about the meaning or scope of the legislation are resolved in favour of the person seeking its benefit. Liberal construction often leads the court to adopt an expansive interpretation of provisions defining benefits and entitlements, while procedural requirements and other formalities are minimized.

The strict or liberal construction doctrine has been criticized on a number of grounds. First, it rests on a difficult distinction between legislation that is remedial or beneficial to the public and legislation that interferes with individual liberties and rights. Since much legislation fits both descriptions, there is often no basis for the distinction other than the preferences of the classifying court. If the court values the policies served by the legislation more than the rights interfered with, the legislation will attract a liberal construction; otherwise not. Historically, courts have tended to attach a high value to individual liberty and rights while attaching less importance to collective social goals. As a result, until recently, calls for a liberal construction were extremely rare.

This heavy reliance on strict construction has been criticized because it tends to put the courts into an adversarial relationship with the legislature. When a court takes a strict approach, instead of trying to carry out the legislature's goals as fully as possible, the court focuses on reasons to limit the scope and impact of the legislation. This tends to defeat the legislative purpose. On more than one occasion the strict construction doctrine has been used to thwart and obstruct the effective implementation of social reform legislation.[5]

In an effort to control strict construction, Canadian legislatures early on enacted provisions in their Interpretation Acts, which direct courts to take a liberal approach to all legislation. Section 12 of the federal Act provides:

> 12. Every enactment is deemed remedial, and shall be given such fair, large and liberal construction and interpretation as best ensures the attainment of its objects.[6]

Although in principle this provision effectively abolished the strict construction doctrine, in practice until recently it had little impact on the way courts interpreted legislation. Whether a provision was given a strict or a liberal construction depended on how the court balanced the benevolent goals of the legislation against its interference with individual liberties and rights.

In recent years, however, there has been a change in the attitude of courts. The change takes two forms. First, in keeping with the modern emphasis on purposive analysis, courts tend to give more weight to

---

5   For a classic exposition of the techniques used by courts to thwart legislative
     intent, see J.A. Corry, "Administrative Law and the Interpretation of Statutes"
     (1936) 1 U.T.L.J. 286
6   *Interpretation Act*, R.S.C. 1985, c. I-21, s. 12.

the benevolent goals of legislation and to classify legislation as remedial rather than penal, as calling for a liberal rather than a strict construction. Second, in dealing with legislation that interferes with individual liberties or rights, courts sometimes treat the strict construction doctrine as a rule of last resort. On this approach, strict construction is used only for the purpose of resolving any doubt or ambiguity remaining after the court has explored all the other ways of establishing legislative intent.

The view that presumptions of legislative intent should be limited to cases of stubborn ambiguity was championed by Iacobucci J. while serving on the Supreme Court of Canada. In *Bell ExpressVu Limited Patnership v. Rex*, he wrote:

> The preferred approach [to statutory interpretation] recognizes the important role that context must inevitably play when a court construes the written words of a statute.
>
> …
>
> Other principles of interpretation—such as the strict construction of penal statutes and the "Charter values" presumption—only receive application where there is *ambiguity* as to the meaning of a provision....
>
> What, then, in law is an *ambiguity*? To answer, an *ambiguity* must be "real." … The words of the provision must be "reasonably capable of more than one meaning" …. By necessity, however, one must consider the "entire context" of a provision before one can determine if it is reasonably capable of multiple interpretations.[7]

This passage clearly indicates that Iacobucci J. did not consider the norms embodied in the presumptions of legislative intent and the doctrine of strict and liberal construction to be part of the entire context in which legislation must be read.

Iacobucci's view has been adopted by other members of the court. In *Re Canada 3000 Inc.*, for example, Bastarache J. wrote:

> [O]nly if a provision is ambiguous (in that after full consideration of the context, multiple interpretations of the words arise that are equally consistent with Parliamentary intent), is it permissible to resort to intepretive presumptions such as "strict construction". The applicable principle is not "strict construction" but s. 12 of the Interpretation Act, which provides that every enactment "is deemed remedial, and shall be given such fair, large and liberal construction as best ensure the attainment of its objects".[8]

---

7   [2002] 2 S.C.R. 559 at paras. 27–29 [*Bell ExpressVu*]. [Footnotes omitted.]
8   [2006] 1 S.C.R. 865 at para. 84.

It is arguable that this approach to the presumptions of legislative intent misunderstands their role in interpretation and effectively re-introduces the plain meaning rule through the back door. As explained above, the so-called presumptions of intent reflect well-established legal norms, forming part of the context in which legislation is made. It is hard to see why they would not form part of the context in which legislation is interpreted.

1) Penal Legislation

Penal legislation includes not only offences set out in the *Criminal Code* but any prohibition or restriction on the freedom of the subject that is enforced through punishment. Under the strict construction doctrine, penal legislation is strictly construed; any doubts concerning the application of the legislation are resolved in favour of the accused.

Nowadays, legally imposed punishment takes the form of fine, forfeiture, or imprisonment. However, in the eighteenth century when the strict construction doctrine first evolved, even petty crimes were often punishable by death. Strict construction provided a way for courts to minimize the exposure of subjects to this ultimate interference with liberty. As Wilson J. explained in *R. v. Paré*:

> The doctrine [of strict construction] … reached its pinnacle of importance in a former age when the death penalty attached to a vast array of offences…. Over the past two centuries criminal law penalties have become far less severe. Criminal law remains, however, the most dramatic and important incursion that the state makes into individual liberty. Thus, while the original justification for the doctrine has been substantially eroded, the seriousness of imposing criminal penalties of any sort demands that reasonable doubts be resolved in favour of the accused.[9]

A second concern underlying the strict construction of penal legislation is rooted in the rule of law and the idea that subjects must know in advance what conduct is proscribed by the state. This concern was explained by Lamer C.J. in *R. v. McIntosh*:

> [T]he overriding principle governing the interpretation of penal provisions is that ambiguity should be resolved in a manner most favourable to accused persons. Moreover, in choosing between two possible interpretations, a compelling consideration must be to give

---

9   [1987] 2 S.C.R. 618 at 630.

effect to the interpretation most consistent with the terms of the provision. As Dickson J. noted in ... [*Marcotte v. Canada (Deputy Attorney General)*[10]], when freedom is at stake, clarity and certainty are of fundamental importance .... Our criminal justice system presumes that everyone knows the law. Yet we can hardly sustain such a presumption if courts adopt interpretations of penal provisions which rely on the reading-in of words which do not appear on the face of the provisions. How can a citizen possibly know the law in such a circumstance?[11]

Lamer C.J. here refers to the strict construction of penal legislation as an "overriding principle." In the *McIntosh* case, in keeping with this emphasis, he gave it precedence over contextual and consequential analysis and the legislation's evolution, all of which tended to suggest that the interpretation less favourable to the accused was the one actually intended by Parliament. Lamer C.J. believed this approach was justified by the importance that we as a society attach to liberty interests. He wrote:

The *Criminal Code* ... is qualitatively different from most other legislative enactments because of its direct and potentially profound impact on the personal liberty of citizens. The special nature of the *Criminal Code* requires an interpretive approach which is sensitive to liberty interests. Therefore, an ambiguous penal provision must be interpreted in the manner most favourable to accused persons, and in the manner most likely to provide clarity and certainty in the criminal law.[12]

In other cases the courts have not been willing to attach so much weight to the strict construction doctrine. Some have noted the inconsistency between the doctrine and the *Interpretation Act* provisions that require courts to adopt a liberal purposive approach to all legislation. In a conflict between a statutory provision and a common law rule, the statutory provision is supposed to win.[13] Many courts have suggested that the strict construction rule should be invoked only as a last resort to resolve ambiguity when other methods of determining legislative intent have been tried and failed.[14] Certainly there are countless cases

10   [1976] 1 S.C.R. 108 at 115.
11   [1995] 1 S.C.R. 686 at 705 [*McIntosh*].
12   *Ibid.* at 705–6.
13   See, for example, *Canadian Oxy Chemicals Ltd. v. Canada (Attorney General)*, [1999] 1 S.C.R. 743 at paras. 18–19.
14   See, for example, *R. v. Mac*, [2002] 1 S.C.R. 856 at para. 4.

where strict construction has *not* prevailed, where ambiguities in penal provisions have been resolved against the accused because this outcome fit the context or avoided absurdity or better promoted the purpose. In *R. v. Chartrand*, for example, speaking for the Supreme Court of Canada, L'Heureux-Dubé J. wrote:

> The purpose of s. 281 — to protect children from abduction — reflects a societal interest in the security of children in that it both prevents and deters the abduction of children by strangers. This accords with public policy. Viewed in the light of its purpose and context, such legislation has a broad scope and the restrictive interpretation of s. 281 of the *Code* proposed by the respondent does not seem to be particularly attractive.[15]

2) Interference with Rights

Under the strict construction doctrine, legislation that interferes with the rights of subjects is strictly construed; any doubts concerning the application of such legislation are resolved in favour of the subject and the preservation of his or her rights. This idea is also expressed in the form of a presumption: it is presumed that the legislature does not intend to interfere with individual rights. This includes both common law and statutory rights. It includes rights of action and defences, rights of appeal and judicial review, real and personal property rights, contractual rights, and Aboriginal treaty rights.

In *GMAC Commercial Credit Corporation–Canada v. T.C.T. Logistics Inc.*,[16] the right in question was a statutory right to bring an action before the Ontario Labour Relations Board to determine whether the corporation to which T.C.T.'s assets had been sold by its interim receiver in bankruptcy was a successor corporation within the meaning of section 69 of Ontario's *Labour Relations Act, 1995*. Section 47(2) of the federal *Bankruptcy and Insolvency Act* provided that a court may direct an interim receiver to (1) take possession of the debtor's property, (2) control that property as the court considers advisable, and (3) take such other action as the court considers advisable. The issue was whether the actions of the interim receiver taken under section 47(2)(c) were immune from a challenge under section 69 of the Ontario Act. Abella J. wrote:

---

15   [1994] 2 S.C.R. 864 at para. 36. See also *R. v. Hasselwander*, [1993] 2 S.C.R. 398 at 413.

16   [2006] 2 S.C.R. 123.

If the s. 47 net were interpreted widely enough to permit interference with all rights which, though protected by law, represent an inconvenience to the bankruptcy process, it could be used to extinguish all employment rights if the bankruptcy court thinks it "advisable" under s. 47(2)(c). Explicit language would be required before such a sweeping power could be attached to s. 47.... As Major J. stated in *Crystalline Investments Ltd. v. Domgroup Ltd.*, [2004] 1 S.C.R. 60, 2004 SCC 3:

> explicit statutory language is required to divest persons of rights they otherwise enjoy at law.... The language of s. 47(2) falls well short of this standard. The bankruptcy court can undoubtedly mandate employment-related conduct by the receiver, but as s. 47(2) of the *Bankruptcy and Insolvency Act* is presently worded, the court cannot, on its own, abrogate the right to seek relief at the labour board.[17]

Although the range of protected rights is broad, some rights are judged to be more fundamental and therefore to warrant greater protection than others. In recent years, for example, the courts have emphasized the importance of Aboriginal treaty rights. Legislation that purports to limit or affect such rights is read as narrowly as possible. In *R. v. Simon*, Dickson C.J. explained the thinking of the courts: "Given the serious and far-reaching consequences of a finding that a treaty right has been extinguished, it seems appropriate to demand strict proof of the fact of extinguishment in each case where the issue arises."[18]

The extent and impact of the feared interference is also relevant. For example, a zoning by-law that prohibits the use of urban property for pig farming or other specified purposes would be a less serious interference with rights than outright expropriation. In *Leiriao v. Val-Bélair (Town)*, L'Heureux-Dubé J. wrote:

> Expropriation constitutes a drastic interference with an individual's right to property. It allows a government to deprive a person of his or her land. In some cases this may mean that an individual loses a home, a "safest refuge". In other cases, such as the case at bar, expropriation may lead to the loss of one's livelihood.
>
> Because property is a fundamental legal right, and because expropriation is such an exorbitant power, Canadian law has con-

---

17   *Ibid.* at para. 51.
18   [1985] 2 S.C.R. 387 at 405–6. See also *R. v. Sparrow*, [1990] 1 S.C.R. 1075 at para. 36.

sistently favoured a restrictive interpretation of statutes enabling expropriation.[19]

In the *Leiriao* case, the public good served by the expropriation was insufficient to outweigh the evil of expropriation, and the court therefore adopted a strict construction. In *Bayshore Shopping Centre Ltd. v. Nepean (Township)*, on the other hand, Spence J. wrote:

> No authority need be cited for the proposition that a man's property is his own which he may utilize as he deems fit ... and therefore by-laws restrictive of that right should be strictly construed. Yet it has been said that modern zoning provisions have been enacted to protect the whole community and should be construed liberally having in ... [mind] the public interest.[20]

Here, given a less serious interference with property rights, the public good prevailed. The by-law received a liberal, purposive construction.

3) Exceptions to General Law

Historically, courts have tended to take a strict approach to provisions that create exceptions to the general law. This tendency was especially evident in interpretations of fiscal legislation. Until recently, the rule was that provisions imposing a tax on subjects were strictly construed against the government, while provisions creating exemptions or exceptions were strictly construed against the taxpayer. This type of mechanical approach to interpretation has been repudiated by modern courts, in the tax area and elsewhere. Nowadays courts determine the scope of exceptions primarily through purposive analysis. Nonetheless, the idea that departures from the general rule should be strictly construed has not entirely disappeared.

In *Barrette v. Crabtree Estate*,[21] for example, the Supreme Court of Canada adopted a narrow interpretation of section 114 of the *Canada Business Corporations Act* (*C.B.C.A.*). This provision made corporate directors personally liable for the wages of employees in certain circumstances. L'Heureux-Dubé J. wrote:

> While its purpose is to ensure that certain sums, including wages, are paid to employees in the event the corporation becomes bankrupt or insolvent, s. 114 *C.B.C.A.* constitutes a major exception to the fun-

---

19   [1991] 3 S.C.R. 349 at 356–57.
20   [1972] S.C.R. 755 at 764.
21   [1993] 1 S.C.R. 1027.

damental principles of company law applicable to directors' liability. As we have seen, it also overrides the more general principles that no one is liable for the debts of another.[22]

In this passage the court's discomfort with exceptions to fundamental principles and well-established policies is evident. Such principles and policies create expectations that are relied on by subjects to guide their conduct and manage their affairs. Exceptions undermine these legitimate expectations, and the individuals affected may be taken by surprise. Exceptions may also exclude some individuals from protections or benefits available to others, contrary to the principle of equality. Where concerns of fair notice or fair treatment arise, the reasons for creating an exception must be cogent and compelling; otherwise, the courts take a strict approach.

4) Fiscal Legislation

Historically, the doctrine of strict construction was regularly invoked by courts when interpreting fiscal legislation. Like expropriation, taxation is considered a serious interference with the property rights of subjects; it is, in effect, a form of appropriation. In the past, courts have insisted on sticking to the literal meaning of fiscal legislation, ignoring purpose and context and construing the words of the text as narrowly as possible. In a series of recent cases, however, the Supreme Court of Canada has fashioned a new approach. Nowadays, the interpretation of tax legislation is to follow the ordinary rules of statutory interpretation. The court is to consider the purpose of the legislation, its context, and all relevant evidence of legislative intent. After exhausting these interpretive resources, if the intention of the legislature is still unclear, the court may then adopt the interpretation that favours the taxpayer. On this approach, the policy of favouring the taxpayer, of protecting individual rights from interference by the state, comes into play only as a last resort when other means of resolving ambiguity have failed.[23]

For some years the adoption of this new judicial rhetoric appeared to have little impact on the practice of the courts. Although taxing provisions were no longer strictly construed, they were "literally" construed, which in practice amounted to much the same thing. The

---

22   *Ibid.* at 1044. But see also *Macdonell v. Quebec (Commission d'accès à l'information)*, [2002] 3 S.C.R. 661 at para. 18.

23   The new approach is summarized in *Québec (Communauté Urbaine) v. Corp. Notre-Dame de Bon-Secours*, [1994] 3 S.C.R. 3.

following frequently cited passage from *Antosko v. Canada* captured the thinking of the Supreme Court of Canada:

> While it is true that the courts must view discrete sections of the *Income Tax Act* in light of the other provisions of the Act and of the purpose of the legislation, and that they must analyze a given transaction in the context of economic and commercial reality, such techniques cannot alter the result where the words of the statute are clear and plain.[24]

In other words, when it came to interpreting taxing provisions, the court applied the plain meaning rule. If the language of the text was clear and plain, purpose and context became irrelevant – they could not alter the result of the meaning based on reading the text in isolation from the rest of the context. Conversely, when it came to provisions that favour the taxpayer, the court adopted a purposive and liberal interpretation. In *Québec (Communauté urbaine) v. Corp. Notre-Dame de Bon-Secours,* Gonthier J. wrote:

> I should like to stress that it is no longer possible to apply automatically the rule that any tax exemption should be strictly construed. … [A]dhering to the principle that taxation is clearly the rule and exemption the exception no longer corresponds to the reality of present-day tax law. Such a way of looking at things was undoubtedly tenable at a time when the purpose of tax legislation was limited to raising funds to cover government expenses. In our time it has been recognized that such legislation serves other purposes and functions as a tool of economic and social policy.
>
> …
>
> The teleological [purposive] approach makes it clear that in tax matters it is no longer possible to reduce the rules of interpretation to presumptions in favour of or against the taxpayer or to well-defined categories known to require a liberal, strict or literal interpretation. … it is the teleological interpretation that will be the means of identifying the purpose underlying a specific legislative provision and the Act as a whole; and it is the purpose in question which will dictate in each case whether a strict or a liberal interpretation is appropriate or whether it is the tax department or the taxpayer which will be favoured.[25]

---

24   [1994] 2 S.C.R. 312 at para. 25.
25   Above note 23 at para. 22.

In the practice of the Supreme Court of Canada, it appeared that taxing provisions were subject to the plain meaning rule, while exemptions received a purposive approach. From the point of view of the taxpayer, this was a win-win situation.

Recent case law suggests a subtle but potentially significant evolution in the Supreme Court's approach. The clearest illustration of this evolution is the judgment of the Court in *Placer Dome Canada Ltd. v. Ontario (Minister of Finance)*,[26] written by LeBel J. The issue in the case was whether the definition of "hedging" in Ontario's *Mining Tax Act* extended to financial transactions that did not involve physical delivery of the output of an Ontario mine. The appellant mining company argued for a narrow interpretation, one that would exclude such transactions. However, the court adopted the broader interpretation favoured by the minister, largely because this interpretation avoided tautology. The most interesting aspect of the judgment (apart from the fact that the taxpayer lost) is the Court's résumé of the principles governing the interpretation of fiscal legislation. LeBel J. wrote:

> In *Stubart Investments Ltd. v. The Queen*, [1984] 1 S.C.R. 536, this Court rejected the strict approach to the construction of taxation statutes and held that [page728] the modern approach applies to taxation statutes no less than it does to other statutes. That is, "the words of an Act are to be read in their entire context and in their grammatical and ordinary sense harmoniously with the scheme of the Act, the object of the Act, and the intention of Parliament" (p. 578) .... However, because of the degree of precision and detail characteristic of many tax provisions, a greater emphasis has often been placed on textual interpretation where taxation statutes are concerned: *Canada Trustco Mortgage Co. v. Canada*, [2005] 2 S.C.R. 601, 2005 SCC 54, at para. 11. Taxpayers are entitled to rely on the clear meaning of taxation provisions in structuring their affairs. Where the words of a statute are precise and unequivocal, those words will play a dominant role in the interpretive process.
>
> On the other hand, where the words of a statute give rise to more than one reasonable interpretation, the ordinary meaning of words will play a lesser role, and greater recourse to the context and purpose of the Act may be necessary: *Canada Trustco*, at para. 10. Moreover, as McLachlin C.J. noted at para. 47, "[e]ven where the meaning of particular provisions may not appear to be ambiguous at first glance, statutory context and purpose may reveal or resolve latent

---

26   [2006] 1 S.C.R. 715.

ambiguities." The Chief Justice went on to explain that in order to resolve explicit and latent ambiguities in taxation legislation, "the courts must undertake a unified textual, contextual and purposive approach to statutory interpretation."

The interpretive approach is thus informed by the level of precision and clarity with which a taxing provision is drafted. Where such a provision admits of no ambiguity in its meaning or in its application to the facts, it must simply be applied. Reference to the purpose of the provision "cannot be used to create an unexpressed exception to clear language": see P.W. Hogg, J.E. Magee and J. Li, *Principles of Canadian Income Tax Law* (5th ed. 2005), at p. 569 .... Where, as in this case, the provision admits of more than one reasonable interpretation, greater emphasis must be placed on the context, scheme and purpose of the Act. Thus, legislative purpose may not be used to supplant clear statutory language, but to arrive at the most plausible interpretation of an ambiguous statutory provision.

Although there is a residual presumption in favour of the taxpayer, it is residual only and applies in the exceptional case where application of the ordinary principles of interpretation does not resolve the issue .... Any doubt about the meaning of a taxation statute must be reasonable, and no recourse to the presumption lies unless the usual rules of interpretation have been applied, to no avail, in an attempt to discern the meaning of the provision at issue.[27]

There are several noteworthy, and potentially significant, features of this account of the principles governing the interpretation of fiscal legislation. First, the court here grounds the weight accorded to textual analysis not on the fact that a provision to be interpreted imposes a tax but rather on the fact that it is detailed and precise. On this approach, language operating at a higher level of generality or abstraction would not attract the same textual emphasis, even though it appeared in a taxing provision. Furthermore, on this approach, while the clear meaning of a detailed text receives significant weight, reliance on other considerations is not excluded. Finally, the court emphasizes that judgments about whether a provision is ambiguous cannot be made in isolation from statutory context and purpose. On this approach, the court cannot conclude that a given provision is unambiguous until it is considered in light of these other features.[28]

---

27   *Ibid.* at paras. 21–24.

28   Note that the account of fiscal legislation interpretation offered in the text does not address the issue of sham transactions or the anti-avoidance provision set out in s. 245 of the *Income Tax Act*. For a comprehensive analysis of the anti-

5) Remedial Legislation

It is impossible to offer a precise definition or description of remedial legislation. Under Canadian Interpretation Acts, of course, all legislation is deemed remedial. In practice, however, some tyes of legislation are more likely to attract this label than others. The best example is legislation enacted to protect vulnerable groups in society. This includes groups that are inherently vulnerable, such as children. It also includes groups that find themselves on the vulnerable side of an unequal relationship, such as shareholders or consumers.[29]

Legislation labelled remedial is entitled to a broad, purposive interpretation. In *Genereux v. Catholic Children's Aid Society of Metropolitan Toronto (Municipality)*,[30] for example, the Ontario Court of Appeal had to determine how to interpret section 43(8) of Ontario's *Child Welfare Act*. It conferred a power on appeal courts to receive fresh evidence relating to any issue brought forward on appeal. Although this power was a significant departure from long-standing common law practice, the court was not prepared to limit the reach or impact of the new provision. Cory J.A. wrote:

> It can be seen that the judge hearing the appeal is granted a very wide discretion [to receive new evidence] with no restrictions imposed. This is remedial legislation dealing with the welfare of children. It should be broadly interpreted. Undue restrictions should not be placed upon it. Specifically, narrow restrictions should not be read into the section when they do not appear in the legislation.[31]

As often happens, the legislation in *Genereux* might have attracted either a strict or a liberal construction: strict because it introduced an exception to the general rule that new evidence is not admissible upon appeal; liberal because it was designed to ensure that children's interests are fully understood and protected in custody disputes. It is often difficult to say what combination of linguistic, legal, cultural, and

---

avoidance provision, see *Canada Trustco Mortgage Co. v. Canada*, [2005] 2 S.C.R. 601.

29   See, for example, the case law dealing with legislation regulating the insurance industry. The judicial attitude is expressed in *Marche v. Halifax Insurance Co.*, [2005] 1 S.C.R. 47 at para. 13.

30   (1985), 53 O.R. (2d) 163 (C.A.) [*Genereux*].

31   *Ibid.* at 164–65. This passage was quoted and adopted by the Supreme Court of Canada in *Catholic Children's Aid Society of Metropolitan Toronto (Municipality) v. M.(C.)*, [1994] 2 S.C.R. 165 at 187, to justify its liberal interpretation of a similar provision in Ontario's *Child and Family Services Act*.

personal considerations is responsible for a court's decision to label legislation remedial rather than exceptional, penal, disruptive of private rights, or the like.

6) Social Welfare Legislation

In recent years, largely because of the modern emphasis on purposive analysis, the liberal construction doctrine has enjoyed a revival. The context in which this revival first occurred was the legislation creating Canada's social safety net. In *Canada (Attorney General) v. Abrahams*[32] decided in 1983, the Supreme Court of Canada was asked to determine whether a claimant was entitled to benefits under the *Unemployment Insurance Act*. The outcome turned on whether the claimant had been "regularly engaged" in a new occupation after leaving his previous occupation on account of a strike. Wilson J. found this expression to be vague and ambiguous, but in the end she preferred the outcome that favoured the claimant. She wrote:

> Since the overall purpose of the Act is to make benefits available to the unemployed, I would favour a liberal interpretation of the re-entitlement provisions. I think any doubt arising from the difficulties of the language should be resolved in favour of the claimant.[33]

This passage has been relied on in subsequent cases to justify a liberal reading of social welfare legislation at both the federal and the provincial levels.[34]

7) Legislation Relating to Aboriginal Rights

Another context in which the liberal construction doctrine has experienced a comeback is legislation relating to Aboriginal peoples. The leading case here is *R. v. Nowegijick*,[35] another Supreme Court of Canada judgment from 1983. This case concerned section 87 of the *Indian Act* which provided that "the personal property of an Indian … situated on a reserve" was exempt from taxation. The appellant was an Indian who resided on a reserve and whose employer's offices were also on the reserve. The issue was whether the wages he received for logging that

---

32   [1983] 1 S.C.R. 2.
33   *Ibid.* at 10.
34   See, for example, *Beothuk Data Systems Ltd. v. Dean*, [1998] 1 F.C. 433 at paras. 34–35 (C.A.).
35   [1983] 1 S.C.R. 29.

took place off reserve were exempt under section 87. In concluding that such wages were exempt, Dickson J. wrote:

> It seems to me ... that treaties and statutes relating to Indians should be liberally construed and doubtful expressions resolved in favour of the Indians. If the statute contains language which can reasonably be construed to confer tax exemption that construction, in my view, is to be favoured over a more technical construction which might be available to deny exemption.[36]

It has been suggested that liberal construction in this context should incorporate the audience understanding principle applied by courts when choosing between the ordinary and the technical meanings of words.[37] Using this approach, the court would adopt the meaning that is most likely to be understood by the Aboriginal audience to which the legislation is addressed. Although this approach makes sense and has been applied in cases interpreting treaties with First Nations, to date it has not been accepted in cases interpreting the *Indian Act*.[38]

8) Legislation Relating to Human Rights

It is now well established that human rights legislation, including legislation designed to protect linguistic and cultural rights, should receive a liberal construction. The case law establishing this approach was summarized by Weiler J.A. in *Roberts v. Ontario*. She wrote:

> A human rights code is not like an ordinary law. It is a fundamental law which declares public policy.... Because a human rights code is not an ordinary statute, rules of statutory interpretation which advocate a strict grammatical construction of the words are not the proper approach to take in interpreting its provisions; focusing on the limited words of the section itself would ignore the dominant purpose of human rights legislation.... A human rights code is remedial legislation and is to be given such interpretation as will best ensure its *objects* are attained.[39]

The case concerned a complaint about a government program that provided special assistance to visually impaired persons under the age of

---

36   *Ibid.* at 36.
37   This principle is explained in Chapter 3.
38   See, for example, the judgment of La Forest J. in *Mitchell v. Peguis Indian Band*, [1990] 2 S.C.R. 85 at 143.
39   (1994), 19 O.R. (3d) 387 at 394 (C.A.). [Emphasis in original.]

eighteen. The complainant, a man of seventy-one, argued that the program discriminated against him on account of age, contrary to section 1 of Ontario's *Human Rights Code*. The government claimed that the program was exempt from section 1 because it was a special program designed to assist disadvantaged persons. Section 14(1) provided:

> 14.(1) A right under ... [section 1] is not infringed by the implementation of a special program designed to ... assist disadvantaged persons or groups to achieve ... equal opportunity.

Even though the vision aid assistance program was admittedly a special program within the meaning of the section, the court concluded that the section did not apply. Weiler J.A. explained:

> [T]o say that s. 14(1) exempts the *age discrimination* in the vision aids ... program from review, is to interpret the section so as to permit substantive equality to be undermined, when substantive equality is one of the section's very purposes. It is to permit unfairness which is antithetical to the overall purposes of the *Code*. Fairness, and the recognition of substantive equality, require that discrimination, in the provision of a service to a person who is a member of a disadvantaged group for whom a special program is designed, not be tolerated.[40]

The liberal construction doctrine is here relied on to justify a strict approach to the section 14(1) exemption. By reading down the exemption, the principle of equal treatment embodied in section 1 of the *Code* received a broad application in keeping with the purpose of both provisions and the *Code* as a whole.

In a more recent case,[41] L'Heureux-Dubé J., speaking for the Supreme Court of Canada, offered the following résumé of the principles governing the interpretation of human rights legislation, at both the federal and provincial levels:

> [G]iven its fundamental and quasi-constitutional status, human rights legislation prevails over other legislation. That principle has been reiterated by this Court on several occasions .... The Court has also held that because of its quasi-constitutional status, the *Charter* must be interpreted in light of both its context and objectives ....

---

40   *Ibid.* at 402. [Emphasis in original.]

41   *Quebec (Commission des droits de la personne et des droits de la jeunesse) v. Montréal (City); Quebec (Commission des droits de la personne et des droits de la jeunesse) v. Boisbriand (City)*, [2000] 1 S.C.R. 665.

More generally, in *Driedger on the Construction of Statutes* (3rd ed. 1994), at pp. 383–84, Professor R. Sullivan summarized as follows the rules of interpretation that apply to human rights legislation:

(1) Human rights legislation is given a liberal and purposive interpretation. Protected rights receive a broad [page 684] interpretation, while exceptions and defences are narrowly construed.

(2) In responding to general terms and concepts, the approach is organic and flexible. The key provisions of the legislation are adapted not only to changing social conditions but also to evolving conceptions of human rights.[42]

C. PRESUMPTIONS OF LEGISLATIVE INTENT

The presumptions of legislative intent are a means by which extratextual values and policies are introduced into interpretation. More particularly, they are the means by which the values and policies of international law, constitutional law, and the common law can reach and influence legislation. While the content of legislative programs may change from time to time, these values and policies are thought to be important and enduring. They are the foundation on which our legal culture is built. Therefore, in the absence of some indication to the contrary, interpreters presume that the legislature intends to observe them when it enacts legislation. An interpretation that promotes or complies with these values is preferred over one that does not.

The presumptions of legislative intent are rebuttable. Within the limits of the entrenched constitution, the legislature is sovereign and may enact legislation that disregards *Charter* values or violates international law. But since we presume that it does not intend to do so, the legislature must use clear and explicit language if it wants to do these things. It must make its intention clear; and the more important the court thinks the value or policy is, the clearer the language must be.

Like the doctrine of strict construction, the presumptions of legislative intent are conservative in thrust and they have sometimes been used by courts to resist change and undermine progressive legislative initiatives. In their desire to preserve established values, the courts

---

42　*Ibid.* at paras. 27–29. [Some footnotes omitted.]

have sometimes used Catch-22 reasoning. Where the legislative language is detailed and precise, it is given minimal application using the strict construction approach. But where the legislature has used broad general terms to ensure a wide application, this language is found to be vague and is read down in accordance with the presumptions designed to protect established law. In the face of determined judicial resistance, there is little a drafter can do.

Although it is possible for courts to misuse tools like the strict construction doctrine or the presumptions of legislative intent, properly used they are an important part of sound interpretive practice. They indicate what values are considered important in legal culture and therefore likely to influence judicial understanding of a text. This is useful information to have. They also ground judicial interpretation in "law" as opposed to personal whim, for they are the officially recognized values of our legal culture rather than personal preferences of the judge.

The thinking that underlies the presumptions of legislative intent is set out very clearly in the judgment of La Forest J.A. in *Re Estabrooks Pontiac Buick Ltd.*[43] In this case the New Brunswick Court of Appeal had to determine whether the legislature of New Brunswick in enacting the *Social Services and Education Tax Act* really meant to treat the property of one person as security for another's debts. La Forest J.A. wrote:

> There is no doubt that the duty of the courts is to give effect to the intention of the Legislature as expressed in the words of the statute. And however reprehensible the result may appear, it is our duty if the words are clear to give them effect. This follows from the constitutional doctrine of the supremacy of the Legislature when acting within its legislative powers. The fact that the words as interpreted would give an unreasonable result, however, is certainly ground for the courts to scrutinize a statute carefully to make abundantly certain that those words are not susceptible of another interpretation.[44]

If words can be read in two ways, the court will choose the way that produces harmony between the legislation and established legal principles, like the principle that A's property cannot be taken to pay B's debt:

> [W]hen we are asked to construe a statute as taking the property of one person to pay the debts of another, as we are here, it is our duty

---

43   (1982), 44 N.B.R. (2d) 201 (C.A.).
44   *Ibid.* at 210.

to scrutinize the legislation with great care to see whether the Legislature really intended to do this.

. . .

In performing this duty, the courts should not be looked upon as being at odds with the Legislature. Rather they are working along with the Legislature to ensure the preservation of our fundamental political values.[45]

The provision in question expressly imposed a lien on all property used in connection with a business to secure the payment of sales tax collected in the course of operating the business. The provision was not expressly limited to property belonging to the debtor (the owner of the business). Moreover, its purpose was to ensure that sales tax collected on behalf of the government pursuant to a statutory obligation did not go astray. Despite this and other evidence that the legislature intended its lien to apply to all property used in the business, regardless of ownership, the court reached the opposite conclusion. It could not believe that the legislature really intended to make the property of one person liable for the debts of another.

1) Presumed Compliance with Constitutional Law, Including *Charter* Norms

It is presumed that the legislature does not intend to violate the constitutional limits on its jurisdiction. These limits include the matters legislation may deal with as well as limits on government interference with *Charter*-protected rights. When faced with a choice, courts prefer interpretations that are consistent with these limits and avoid interpretations that would render legislation invalid. As Cartwright J. wrote in *McKay v. Canada*: "[I]f words in a statute are fairly susceptible of two constructions of which one will result in the statute being *intra vires* [within the limited powers of the legislature] and the other will have the contrary result the former is to be adopted."[46]

In *McKay*, the Supreme Court of Canada was concerned with a municipal by-law, authorized by provincial legislation, which prohibited the display of signs on residential property. The issue was whether the by-law could be relied on to prevent the display of signs advertising candidates for federal office. Since property is a provincial matter under section 92 of the *Constitution Act, 1867*, it was valid for the province to exercise

45 *Ibid.* at 214.
46 [1965] S.C.R. 798 at 804 [*McKay*].

regulatory authority over land use or, as was done here, to delegate this authority to municipalities. Thus, most applications of the by-law would have been perfectly valid. However, the regulation of federal elections is a matter within the exclusive jurisdiction of Parliament. Any attempt by a province to interfere with the display of federal election signs would therefore exceed its powers. In these circumstances the court faced a dilemma. Given the ordinary meaning of its language, the by-law must apply to all signs, including federal election signs. But if the by-law were applied to federal election signs it would be *ultra vires*. By presuming that the legislature did not intend to violate the limits on its jurisdiction, the dilemma was solved. The scope of "signs" was narrowed or "read down" to exclude application to federal election signs. In this way the by-law was given maximum effect within jurisdictional limits.

As the *McKay* case illustrates, the presumption in favour of valid interpretations is easy to apply in the context of challenges to validity based on sections 91 and 92 of the *Constitution Act, 1867*. It has also been invoked in the context of challenges to validity based on the *Charter*. In R. v. Bernshaw,[47] for example, the Supreme Court of Canada had to determine the meaning of "forthwith" in section 254(2) of the *Criminal Code*. It provided that a peace officer who reasonably suspects that a driver is under the influence of alcohol may, by demand made forthwith, require the person to furnish a sample of breath for a roadside test. The Crown argued that "forthwith" should be interpreted to mean "immediately." The accused argued that "forthwith" should be interpreted to mean "after the lapse of the 15 to 20 minutes necessary to ensure that any alcohol in the mouth of the driver has evaporated." Cory J. pointed out that detaining a driver for fifteen to twenty minutes without any opportunity to instruct counsel would be contrary to section 10(b) of the *Charter*, and that such a serious violation might not be saved by section 1. In light of this point, he concluded that the Crown's interpretation was better. He wrote:

> Where a statute is open to more than one interpretation, one of which is constitutional and the other of which is not, the interpretation which is consistent with the constitution should be adopted.... In my view, to interpret "forthwith" as meaning "immediately" is consistent with the *Charter* and should therefore be adopted.[48]

---

47   [1995] 1 S.C.R. 254.

48   *Ibid.* at 275. See also *Re Application under s. 83.28 of the Criminal Code*, 2004 SCC 42 at paras. 34–35.

Although it is appropriate to presume that the legislature does not intend to violate the *Charter*, the court must take into account the role played by section 1. As Cory J. later acknowledges, legislation is not invalid unless it violates *Charter*-protected rights *and the violation cannot be justified under section 1*. The courts must allow for the possibility that the legislature wanted to curtail *Charter* rights, believing this curtailment to be justified in a free and democratic society. In such a case it would be inappropriate to invoke the presumption in favour of valid interpretations to avoid a *Charter* challenge. The government must be given the opportunity to justify its curtailment of rights with a section 1 defence.[49]

In some recent cases, in an effort to avoid the section 1 problem, the presumption of validity has been recast as a presumption of compliance with *Charter* values. This formulation of the presumption relies on a different justification. The underlying idea is not to automatically favour the validity of legislation, but rather to recognize the fundamental nature of *Charter* values in the legal system. Given their importance, it is plausible to assume that the legislature had them in mind when drafting its legislation. While this assumption is most certainly valid, it does not avoid the section 1 problem. Recent case law has therefore emphasized that if the language of a text does not lend itself to ambiguity, the presumption of compliance with *Charter* values should not be applied. The leading case is *Bell ExpressVu Limited Partnership v. Rex*, where Iacobucci J. wrote:

> [W]hen a statute comes into play during judicial proceedings, the courts (absent any challenge on constitutional grounds) are charged with interpreting and applying it in accordance with the sovereign intent of the legislator. In this regard, although it is sometimes suggested that "it is appropriate for courts to prefer interpretations that tend to promote those [*Charter*] principles and values over interpretations that do not" ..., it must be stressed that, to the extent this Court has recognized a "*Charter* values" interpretive principle, such principle can <u>only</u> receive application in circumstances of genuine ambiguity, i.e., where a statutory provision is subject to differing, but equally plausible, interpretations.
>
> ...
>
> [I]f courts were to interpret all statutes such that they conformed to the *Charter*, this would wrongly upset the dialogic balance [between courts and legislatures]. Every time the principle were applied, it would pre-empt judicial review on *Charter* grounds, where resort

---

49   See *Symes v. Canada*, [1993] 4 S.C.R. 695 at 752.

to the internal checks and balances of s. 1 may be had. In this fashion, the legislatures would be largely shorn of their constitutional power to enact reasonable limits on *Charter* rights and freedoms, which would in turn be inflated to near absolute status.[50]

Iacobucci J. adds that a court cannot know whether a text is ambiguous until it has considered the ordinary meaning of the text in light of its purpose and entire context.[51]

2) Presumed Compliance with International Law

International law is composed of both customary international law and international conventions (treaties and agreements). Customary international law is received into domestic common law automatically in so far as it does not conflict with fundamental common law principles or existing statute law. However, international conventions, even those ratified by Canada, do not automatically form part of Canadian domestic law. As Iacobucci J. wrote in *Baker v. Canada (Minister of Citizenship and Immigration)*:

> It is a matter of well-settled law that an international convention ratified by the executive branch of government is of no force or effect within the Canadian legal system until such time as its provisions have been incorporated into domestic law by way of implementing legislation.[52]

Although neither customary nor conventional international law is binding on Canadian legislatures, it is nonetheless presumed that legislation is meant to be consistent with international law—that the legislature intends to respect international law values and principles and to comply with Canada's obligations under both customary law and convention. An interpretation that produces compliance with international law is preferred over one that does not.

This presumption was relied on in *R. v. Zingre*[53] to interpret section 43 of the *Canada Evidence Act*. It provided that where "any court

---

50 *Bell ExpressVu*, adopting this position, above note 7 at paras. 62 and 66. For discussion and a review of subsequent authorities adopting this position, see *R. v. Rodgers*, [2006] 1 S.C.R. 554 at paras. 18–19.

51 *Bell ExpressVu, ibid.* at para. 29. See also *AstraZeneca Canada Inc. v. Canada (Minister of Health)*, [2006] S.C.J. No. 49 at para. 30.

52 *Baker v. Canada (Minister of Citizenship and Immigration)*, [1999] 2 S.C.R. 817 at para. 79 [*Baker*], citing *Capital Cities Communications Inc. v. Canadian Radio-Television and Telecommunications Commission*, [1978] 2 S.C.R. 141.

53 [1981] 2 S.C.R. 392.

or tribunal of competent jurisdiction ... in any foreign country, before which any ... matter is pending, is desirous of obtaining ... testimony," a Canadian court may "upon an application for that purpose" order the relevant witnesses to appear for examination. In the course of investigating a fraud, the Swiss Federal Office for Police Matters requested the examination of a number of Canadian residents. This request was made in accordance with an 1880 extradition treaty that was binding on Canada. The issue was whether the request of the Federal Office could be considered an application by a "court or tribunal of competent jurisdiction." Dickson J. wrote:

> In responding affirmatively to the request which has been made the Court will be recognizing and giving effect to a duty to which Canada is subject, by treaty, under international law.... It is the duty of the Court, in interpreting the 1880 Treaty and s. 43 of the *Canada Evidence Act* to give them a fair and liberal interpretation with a view to fulfilling Canada's international obligations.[54]

In keeping with this principle, the court found that the Federal Office for Police Matters was a court within the meaning of the section and that its request, following the procedures set out in the treaty, was a proper application. Dickson J. concluded: "Since the request complied with the Treaty, I would consider it sufficient for the purposes of s. 43 of the Act."[55]

Another role international law plays in the interpretation of domestic legislation is illustrated in the judgment of McLachlin C.J. in *Canadian Foundation for Children, Youth and the Law v. Canada*.[56] One issue in the case was the meaning of the expression "reasonable under the circumstances" in section 43 of the *Criminal Code*:

> 43. Every schoolteacher, parent or person standing in the place of a parent is justified in using force by way of correction toward a pupil or child, as the case may be, who is under his care, if the force does not exceed what is reasonable under the circumstances.

In an effort to give meaningful content to the vague and evaluative word "reasonable," McLachlin C.J. wrote:

> [F]urther precision on what is reasonable under the circumstances may be derived from international treaty obligations. Statutes should

---

54   *Ibid.* at 410.
55   *Ibid.* at 406.
56   [2004] 1 S.C.R. 76.

be construed to comply with Canada's international obligations. ...
Canada's international commitments confirm that physical correction that either harms or degrades a child is unreasonable.[57]

MacLachlin C.J. went on to note that "neither the Convention on the
Rights of the Child nor the International Covenant on Civil and Political Rights explicitly require state parties to ban all corporal punishment
of children."[58] This assisted the majority in concluding that section 43
of the *Code* did not violate section 7 of the *Charter*. One of the interesting aspects of this and other recent case law from the Supreme Court
of Canada is that the international law materials relied on came into
existence *after* the provision to be interpreted was enacted.[59] Yet the
norms embodied in these materials are considered legitimate aids to
achieving an appropriate interpretation. These materials are part of the
operating context in which domestic legislation is interpreted.

This point is emphasized in the judgment of L'Heureux-Dubé J. in
Baker v. Canada (Minister of Citizenship and Immigration),[60] where the
issue was whether the minister of citizenship and immigration had
properly exercised her discretion under *Immigration Act* Regulations
that empowered her "to exempt any person from any regulation made
under under under subsection 114(1) ... where the Minister is satisfied
that the person should be exempted from that regulation ... owing to
the existence of compassionate or humanitarian considerations."[61] The
appellant sought exemption from deportation on the grounds that it
would be detrimental to her Canadian-born children if she were separ-
ated from them.

The majority concluded that the minister's refusal to grant an
exemption was an improper exercise of discretion because (among
other reasons) the minister had failed to give sufficient weight to the
best interests of the appellant's children. The importance of this norm
was evidenced in part by the international Convention on the Rights
of the Child, which provided that "in all actions concerning children,
... the best interests of the child shall be a primary consideration."[62]
Even though this Convention was ratified long after subsection 114 was
originally enacted (in 1976), and even though the Convention had not

---

57   *Ibid.* at para. 31.
58   *Ibid.* at para. 33.
59   For another example, see *114957 Canada Ltd. (Spraytech, Société d'arrosage) v.
     Hudson*, [2001] 2 S.C.R. 241 at 266–67.
60   Above note 52.
61   *Immigration Regulations*, 1978, S.O.R./78-172, as amended by S.O.R./93-94.
62   Convention on the Rights of the Child, Can. T.S. 1992 No. 3, art. 1.

been implemented by any Canadian legislature, it was nonetheless evidence of the importance that should attach to the welfare of children. As L'Heureux-Dubé J. wrote:

> Another indicator of the importance of considering the interests of children when making a compassionate and humanitarian decision is the ratification by Canada of the Convention on the Rights of the Child, and the recognition of the importance of children's rights and the best interests of children in other international instruments ratified by Canada. International treaties and conventions are not part of Canadian law unless they have been implemented by statute.
>
> …
>
> Nonetheless, the values reflected in international human rights law may help inform the contextual approach to statutory interpretation and judicial review.
>
> …
>
> The principles of the Convention and other international instruments place special importance on protections for children and childhood, and on particular consideration of their interests, needs, and rights. They help show the values that are central in determining whether this decision was a reasonable exercise of the H & C power.[63]

3) Presumed Compliance with Common Law

It is presumed that the legislature does not intend to change the common law. This presumption was used historically to shelter the common law from unwanted statutory intrusions. It is used by modern courts to resist any weakening or exclusion of common law principles that are considered important by the courts.

In *R. v. McIntosh*[64] the presumption against change was relied on by McLachlin J. in interpreting the self-defence provisions of the *Criminal Code*. At common law and initially in the *Criminal Code*, a sharp distinction was drawn between provoked and unprovoked assaults. Where an accused sought to defend himself from an attack that he had provoked, the defence of self-defence would lie only if the accused showed that he had tried to retreat. This duty of retreat did not arise, however, if the attack was unprovoked. After a revision of the *Code* in 1955, section 34(2) appeared to eliminate this distinction. It provided that a person who

---

63 *Baker*, above note 52 at paras. 69–71. See also *Suresh v. Canada*, [2002] 1 S.C.R. 3 at para. 98.

64 Above note 11.

harmed another in repelling an assault was justified if he reasonably believed that that level of violence was necessary to defend himself; it imposed no duty of retreat. On its face, this provision applied equally to provoked and unprovoked attacks. However, in a dissenting judgment, McLachlin J. found evidence in the legislative evolution of the provision that section 34(2) was in fact intended to deal with unprovoked assaults only and that its failure to say so expressly was due to a drafting error in the 1955 revision. She wrote:

> Taking all this into account, can it be said that Parliament intended to change the meaning of s. 34(2) in the 1955 codification, thus abrogating sixty years of statutory criminal law, based on hundreds of years of the common law? I suggest not. To effect such a significant change, Parliament would have made its intention clear. This it did not do.[65]

The presumption against change is heavily weighted here. It is warranted in part by the long-standing character of the distinction and in part by the importance of the values it reflects. In concluding her judgment McLachlin J. wrote:

> The common law has for centuries insisted that the person who provokes an assault and subsequently kills the person he attacks when that person responds to the assault must retreat if he wishes to plead self-defence.... People who provoke attacks must know that a response, even if it is life-threatening, will not entitle them to stand their ground and kill. Rather, they must retreat. The obligation to retreat from provoked assault has stood the test of time. It should not lightly be discarded.[66]

McLachlin J.'s analysis illustrates quite clearly how the presumptions of legislative intent operate in interpretation as tools of policy analysis.

D. DIRECT APPEAL TO POLICY

Courts need not rely on formal non-application rules or the presumptions of legislative intent to introduce policy analysis into statutory interpretation. Increasingly courts feel comfortable making direct appeal to policies that are relevant to the text to be interpreted. In *Marzetti v. Marzetti*,[67] for example, the Supreme Court of Canada relied on poli-

---

65   *Ibid.* at 718.
66   *Ibid.* at 722. See also *United Taxi Drivers' Fellowship of Southern Alberta v. Calgary (City)*, [2004] 1 S.C.R. 485 at para. 11; *Waldick v. Malcolm*, [1991] 2 S.C.R. 456.
67   [1994] 2 S.C.R. 765.

cies favouring support for single mothers in interpreting a provision of the *Bankruptcy Act*. Under sections 67 to 68 of this Act, the wages of a bankrupt were exempt from seizure unless a court decided, "having regard to the family responsibilities and personal situation of the bankrupt," that the wages should be shared with the creditors. The issue was whether a refund of income tax deductions from wages, received by the taxpayer after declaring bankruptcy, should be considered exempt. In concluding that it should be, the court relied on textual analysis of the relevant provisions and on policy analysis as well. Iacobucci J. wrote:

> My opinion is, furthermore, fortified by public policy considerations.... [W]hen family needs are at issue, I prefer to err on the side of caution. In s. 68 of the *Bankruptcy Act*, Parliament has indicated that, before wages become divisible among creditors, it is appropriate to have "regard to the family responsibilities and personal situation of the bankrupt". This demonstrates, to my mind, an overriding concern for the support of families.
>
> ...
>
> Moreover, there are related public policy goals to consider. As recently recognized by L'Heureux-Dubé J. in *Moge v. Moge*, ... "there is no doubt that divorce and its economic effects"[68] ... are playing a role in the "feminization of poverty"[69].... A statutory interpretation which might help defeat this role is to be preferred over one which does not.[70]

In the first paragraph above, Iacobucci J. derives the policy appealed to from the text itself. In the second paragraph, however, the policy is derived from common law in-the-making. In the *Moge* case the court looked at a large body of social science data and scholarly literature focusing on the economic impact of divorce on women and seeking ways to avoid the feminization of poverty. By adopting these factual and analytical materials and the attitudes that informed it, the *Moge* court gave official legal recognition to certain new values and set the stage for the development of new policies in the family law area. The *Marzetti* case takes this interpretation principle from the family law area and extends it to interpretation of legislation generally.

---

68 [1992] 3 S.C.R. 813 at 854.
69 *Ibid.* at 853.
70 Above note 67 at 800–1.

CHAPTER 13

THE PRESUMED APPLICATION OF LEGISLATION

A. INTRODUCTION

Some statutory interpretation rules provide for the non-application of provisions that would otherwise apply. A number of presumptions of legislative intent deal with the temporal, territorial, and personal application of legislation. The function of these presumptions is to prevent legislation from being applied in circumstances where, for one reason or another, its application would be inappropriate. Consider, for example, a provision that says "any person who does x is liable to y." On its face, this provision applies to *everyone* who does x, regardless of who the person is and regardless of when or where they acted. However, for policy reasons, many potential applications must be excluded as unacceptable, namely:

- retroactive or retrospective applications or applications that interfere with vested rights;
- extraterritorial applications; and
- applications to the Crown or to foreign states.[1]

Like many rules based on policy considerations, application rules take the form of presumptions rebuttable by the evidence of a contrary legislative intent.

---

1   Crown immunity is dealt with below, but sovereign immunity is not.

The presumptions dealing with the extraterritorial application of legislation and its application to Crown or foreign agents are relatively straightforward. However, the presumptions dealing with the temporal application of legislation are difficult to analyze and apply. For this reason, they are dealt with at length in this chapter.

B. THE TEMPORAL APPLICATION OF LEGISLATION

1) Overview

The common law governing the temporal application of legislation is comprised of a number of presumptions and rules:

- It is strongly presumed that the legislature does not intend its law to apply retroactively.
- It is presumed that the legislature does not intend its law to apply retrospectively.
- It is presumed that the legislature does not intend its law to interfere with vested rights.
- The presumption against retrospective application does not apply to purely procedural law, to law that merely confers a benefit on persons, or to law that is designed to protect the public.
- There is no presumption against the immediate application of legislation. Concerns arising from such applications are generally covered by the presumption against interference with vested rights.
- Legislation that simply declares the law may be applied "retroactively." Such applications are not really retroactive, however, since in fact the law has not changed; it has simply been re-enacted in clearer or more explicit terms.

These rules are partially codified in the federal and provincial Interpretation Acts. Sections 43 and 44 of the federal Act provide:

43. Where an enactment is repealed in whole or in part, the repeal does not

(a) revive any enactment or anything not in force or existing at the time when the repeal takes effect,

(b) affect the previous operation of the enactment so repealed or anything duly done or suffered thereunder,

(c) affect any right, privilege, obligation or liability acquired, accrued, accruing or incurred under the enactment so repealed, (*d*) affect any offence committed against or contravention of the provisions of the enactment so repealed, or any punishment, penalty or forfeiture incurred under the enactment so repealed, or

(*e*) affect any investigation, legal proceeding or remedy in respect of any right, privilege, obligation or liability referred to in paragraph (*c*) or in respect of any punishment, penalty or forfeiture referred to in paragraph (*d*),

and an investigation, legal proceeding or remedy as described in paragraph (*e*) may be instituted, continued or enforced, and the punishment, penalty or forfeiture may be imposed as if the enactment had not been so repealed.

44. Where an enactment, in this section called the "former enactment", is repealed and another enactment, in this section called the "new enactment", is substituted therefor,

(*a*) every person acting under the former enactment shall continue to act, as if appointed under the new enactment, until another person is appointed in the stead of that person;

(*b*) every bond and security given by a person appointed under the former enactment remains in force, and all books, papers, forms and things made or used under the former enactment shall continue to be used as before the repeal in so far as they are consistent with the new enactment;

(*c*) every proceeding taken under the former enactment shall be taken up and continued under and in conformity with the new enactment in so far as it may be done consistently with the new enactment;

(*d*) the procedure established by the new enactment shall be followed as far as it can be adapted thereto

(i) in the recovery or enforcement of fines, penalties and forfeitures imposed under the former enactment,

(ii) in the enforcement of rights, existing or accruing under the former enactment, and

(iii) in a proceeding in relation to matters that have happened before the repeal;

(*e*) when any punishment, penalty or forfeiture is reduced or mitigated by the new enactment, the punishment, penalty or forfeiture if imposed or adjudged after the repeal shall be reduced or mitigated accordingly;

(*f*) except to the extent that the provisions of the new enactment are not in substance the same as those of the former enactment, the new enactment shall not be held to operate as new law, but shall be construed and have effect as a consolidation and as declaratory of the law as contained in the former enactment;

(g) all regulations made under the repealed enactment remain in force and are deemed to have been made under the new enactment, in so far as they are not inconsistent with the new enactment, until they are repealed or others made in their stead; and

(h) any reference in an unrepealed enactment to the former enactment shall, with respect to a subsequent transaction, matter or thing, be read and construed as a reference to the provisions of the new enactment relating to the same subject-matter as the former enactment, but where there are no provisions in the new enactment relating to the same subject-matter, the former enactment shall be read as unrepealed in so far as is necessary to maintain or give effect to the unrepealed enactment.[2]

2) Definitions and Distinctions

The law governing the temporal application of legislation is complex and the case law dealing with it is often inconsistent or unclear. Some courts take a rule-governed approach; others rely more heavily, or more overtly, on policy. It is often difficult to predict how a court will react to a given set of facts. Following are a number of definitions, distinctions, and explanations that should assist in understanding this area of law.

a) The Difference between Temporal Operation and Temporal Application

It is important to distinguish between the temporal operation of a statute or regulation and its application in time. Temporal operation refers to the period during which the rules embodied in legislation are legally effective—from the time the legislation comes into force to the time it is repealed or expires.[3]

The temporal application of legislation refers to the range of facts to which legislation may appropriately be applied. Suppose a legislature enacts the following rule, which comes into force on 1 January 2005 and is repealed on 31 December 2005:

> No person shall sell tobacco to a person who has not reached the age of majority.

On its face this prohibition applies to every sale of tobacco to a minor regardless of when it took place. But it is presumed that the legislature did not intend to punish sales that were completed before 1

---

2   R.S.C. 1985, c. I-21.
3   For analysis of the temporal operation of legislation, see Chapter 1.

January 2005 or commenced after 31 December 2005. The application of the legislation is limited to sales occurring while the legislation was in force. In this example, the temporal application coincides with the temporal operation, largely because a sale is a short-term event that is easily situated in time. But consider the following example. On 1 January 2000 a provision comes into force in the following terms: "Any person who is convicted of a criminal offence is ineligible to be called to the Bar of British Columbia."

It is safe to assume that the provision will apply to anyone convicted of a criminal offence after 1 January 2000 who subsequently goes to law school and seeks a call to the Bar. But what of a person whose conviction occurred in 1990 and who started law school in 1998? What of a person whose conviction occurred in 1990 and who had fulfilled all the requirements for his or her call to the Bar before the new legislation came into force? Does the new legislation apply to these facts, so as to preclude a call to the Bar after 1 January 2000? In these circumstances, there is a real possibility that the temporal application of the legislation will not coincide with its temporal operation.

b)   The Unit of Analysis Used in Determining Temporal Application
When analyzing the temporal operation or application of legislation, it is usually necessary to think in terms of provisions rather than entire statutes or regulations. Although the provisions constituting statutes and regulations initially are enacted together and become law at the same time, they do not necessarily come into force at the same time. The legislature may provide different commencement dates for different provisions. Also, as a result of amendment, some sections of an Act may be wholly or partially repealed or changed while others continue to operate uninterrupted. It is possible for a single section to have two or more commencement dates, reflecting successive amendments. Finally, a statute may provide for the expiry of some of its provisions but not others.

Similarly, in the case of regulations, the commencement dates of different regulations under the same Act, and provisions within regulations may differ.

c)   Terminology
A major source of confusion in temporal law is the absence of a clear and consistent terminology. In the past, the terms "retrospective" and "retroactive" were used interchangeably to refer to legislation that applied to past events. No attempt was made to distinguish the different ways in which this might occur or the different effects it might produce. The first step out of the morass was to distinguish sharply between

retroactive or retrospective applications on the one hand and applications that interfere with vested rights on the other.

The leading case establishing this distinction is *West v. Gwynne*, where Buckley J. wrote:

> During the argument the words "retrospective" and "retroactive" have been repeatedly used, and the question has been stated to be whether s. 3 of the *Conveyancing Act, 1892* is retrospective. To my mind ... the question is not whether the section is retrospective. Retrospective operation is one matter. Interference with existing rights is another. If an Act provides that as of a past date the law shall be taken to have been that which it was not, that Act I understand to be retrospective. That is not this case. The question here is whether a certain provision as to the contents of leases is addressed to the case of all leases or only of some, namely, leases executed after the passing of the Act.[4]

Under this analysis, if applying new legislation to a set of facts would have the effect of changing the law for the past as well as the future, of effectively deeming the law to have been different from what it was when the facts occurred, then that application is retroactive or retrospective. If applying new legislation to a set of facts would have the effect of diminishing or destroying rights possessed by a person when the legislation came into force, that application interferes with vested rights.[5]

The next step occurred in 1978, when Elmer Driedger published an article in which he introduced a distinction between retroactive and retrospective:

> A retroactive statute is one that operates as of a time prior to its enactment. A retrospective statute is one that operates for the future only. It is prospective, but it imposes new results in respect of a past event. A retroactive statute operates backwards. A retrospective statute operates forwards, but it looks backwards in that it attaches new consequences for the future to an event that took place before the statute was enacted. A retroactive statute changes the law from what it was; a retrospective statute changes the law from what it otherwise would be with respect to a prior event.[6]

---

4   [1911] 2 Ch. 1 at 11–12 (C.A.).

5   This distinction has been adopted by the Supreme Court of Canada on many occasions. The leading Canadian case is *Gustavson Drilling (1964) Ltd. v. M.N.R.*, [1977] 1 S.C.R. 271 [*Gustavson*]. See also *Dikranian v. Quebec (Attorney General)*, [2005] 3 S.C.R. 530 at paras. 29–31 [*Dikranian*].

6   E.A. Driedger, "Statutes: Retroactive, Retrospective Reflections" (1978) 56 Can. Bar Rev. 264 at 268–69.

While this distinction is insightful, it has caused considerable confusion. This is because Driedger used the term "retroactive" for legislation that changes the past effects of a past event and reserved "retrospective" for legislation that changes the future effects of a past event. Prior to 1978, although most judges used the terms interchangeably to describe legislation that changes the past effects of a past event, they tended to prefer "retrospective"—as Buckley J. does in the excerpt from *West v. Gwynne* above. And that is often still the case. The upshot is that on encountering the term "retroactive" in a modern judgment, one can be fairly certain that the reference is to changing the past effects of a past event. However, when one encounters the term "retrospective," it is necessary to determine whether the court is using the term in Driedger's special sense or as Buckley J. does, as a synonym for "retroactive." There is hope that this particular confusion will soon be clarified, as the Supreme Court of Canada has accepted Driedger's terminology, at least in the *Charter* context.[7]

The Court has also adopted terminology from civil law, notably the contrast between the "immediate application" of new legislation and the "survival" of previous law. The distinction can be illustrated using the facts in *Bellechasse Hospital Corp v. Pilotte*.[8] In that case, the relations between the appellant hospital and the respondent physician were governed by a series of one-year contracts, the last of which was to come to an end on 31 July 1969. On 1 April 1969, legislation came into force that imposed specific duties on hospitals wishing to terminate the services of a physician. In early July, the hospital wrote to the physician indicating that his contract would not be renewed when it expired at the end of the month. However, the hospital did not follow the procedures for termination laid down in the new legislation.

The question for the court was which law to apply. Did the new legislation that came into force on April 1st apply "immediately" to contracts in existence on that day, in effect changing their terms for the remainder of the contract? Or were existing contracts governed by the law in force when those contracts were made? If so, despite its replacement by new legislation, the former law would continue to apply. This is what is meant by "survival": the former law is applied to facts that are still in existence after it has been repealed or displaced by new legislation. When former law survives, the application of the new legislation

---

7   See *Benner v. Canada (Secretary of State)*, [1997] 1 S.C.R. 358 at para. 39 [*Benner*]. See also *Épiciers Unis Métro-Richelieu Inc. v. Collin*, [2004] 3 S.C.R. 257 at para. 46, applying the distinction to the *Civil Code*.

8   [1975] 2 S.C.R. 454.

is "postponed"; it is limited to facts, all of which have begun after the new legislation comes into force.

Notice that "retrospective" and "immediate" are mutually exclusive terms. If legislation attaches future legal effects to *a past event*, it is "retrospective" not "immediate"; the term "immediate" is reserved for legislation that attaches future legal effects to *an ongoing situation*, such as a status or condition or an incomplete series of events.[9]

A final point on terminology is the distinction between retroactive, retrospective, or immediate *legislation* and retroactive, retrospective, or immediate *application*.

- "Retroactive legislation," "retrospective legislation," and "legislation having an immediate effect" make statements about the *intention of legislature*. Retroactive legislation is legislation that is *intended* to apply retroactively so as to produce a retroactive effect; retrospective legislation is *intended* to apply retrospectively, and so on.
- "Retroactive application," "retrospective application," and "immediate application" make statements about the *effect* of applying legislation to particular facts whether or not that effect is intended. The *effect* is retroactive, retrospective, or immediate, depending on how the facts are situated in time: an application is retroactive or retrospective if the facts are already past, but immediate if the facts are ongoing.

d) Summary

Legislation may be applied to:

i)   change the past legal effect of a past situation (a "retroactive" application);

ii) change the future legal effect of a past situation (a "retrospective" application);

iii) change the future legal effect of an ongoing situation (an "immediate" application); and

iv) take away or diminish a legally protected expectation or interest (interference with "vested, accrued or accruing rights").

3) Underlying Values

The rules governing the temporal application of legislation are rooted in common-law values, primarily rule of law, fairness, and the protection of private property. The most important concern is rule of law,

---

9   This is the approach taken by the Supreme Court of Canada in dealing with the temporal application of the *Charter*. The cases are reviewed in *Benner*, above note 5.

which requires that law be certain, predictable, stable, rational, and formally equal.[10] Law that violates these values undermines the public's sense of security and individual autonomy, its ability to plan and carry out constructive activities, and its respect for law. It is impossible to comply with law that changes retroactively. It is difficult to trust law that changes retrospectively.

Fairness is also important and overlaps with rule of law. It is unfair to change a law after people have relied on it in planning their affairs. Those who have relied on law to their detriment are justifiably aggrieved. Those who have not relied on the law, but observed its unfairness to others, are justifiably alarmed.

A final concern is protecting interests and expectations that the law thinks worthy of protection—property rights most obviously, including rights of action.

4) Methodology

Most legislative provisions contain two elements: 1) "the situation": a statement of the facts that must be proven, the conditions that must be met, in order to trigger the legal consequence; and 2) "the legal effect": a statement of the legal consequences that follow when the situation in fact occurs. Consider the following provisions:

a) A person who enters onto private property without the consent of the occupier of that property is guilty of an offence and is liable to a fine.
b) A person is eligible to be called to the Bar of Nova Scotia if he or she has obtained a degree in law at an accredited Canadian law school, has successfully completed Nova Scotia's bar admission course and has paid a fee of $500.

In the first example, the situation consists of failure to obtain consent and entry onto private property. The legal effect is liability to conviction and punishment. In the second example, the situation consists of obtaining the degree, completing the course, and paying the fee. The legal effect is entitlement to be called to the Bar.

To resolve an issue involving the temporal application of legislation both law and facts must be situated in time. The following methodology is recommended.

Step 1: Establish the coming into force date of the provision to be applied.

---

10 Formal equality requires that like cases be treated alike and different cases differently.

Step 2: Identify the facts and conditions that comprise the "situation." This step involves analyzing the legislative provision to determine what facts must be established to trigger the legal effect.

Step 3: Establish what actually happened and situate those facts in time. This step involves establishing the facts that have occurred or not occurred, picking out the acts and omissions that are relevant to the situation, and then noting when those acts or omissions occurred, that is, when they began and when they ended.

Step 4: Determine whether the relevant facts

- were complete,
- were ongoing, or
- had not yet commenced,

when the provision came into force.

If the relevant facts were complete, the application of the provision is either retroactive or retrospective and therefore problematic. The provision will not apply unless the presumption against such an application is rebutted.

If the relevant facts were ongoing, the application of the provision is immediate and therefore not problematic unless its application interferes with vested rights.

Step 5: Determine whether applying the provision to the relevant facts would interfere with vested rights.

This step involves determining first whether the litigant has an interest or expectation which the law considers to be a right, second whether that right has vested or accrued, and finally whether applying the provision to the facts in question would diminish or destroy the right.

Notice that an application may interfere with vested rights not only if it is retroactive or retrospective but also if it is immediate. In fact, many immediate applications have that effect. In *Bellechasse Hospital Corp v. Pilotte*,[11] for example, the new legislation was applied to a contract that had not been fully executed when the legislation came into force. This was an immediate application, and it clearly interfered with the contractual right of the hospital to end its relation with Dr. Pilotte by giving him timely notice. The hospital was now obliged to follow the more onerous statutory procedure.

Step 6: If the application is retroactive or retrospective or interferes with vested rights, determine whether the presumption against such application is rebutted.

---

11 Above note 8.

This step involves relying on the usual techniques of statutory interpretation to determine the intention of the legislature, with special emphasis on the values underlying the presumptions. The interpreter should ask questions such as: Whether there is a good reason why the legislature might have wanted to enact retroactive or retrospective legislation or to disregard vested rights—or whether the immediate application of the legislation would be unfair or violate the rule of law.

Retroactive applications are the most objectionable because they deem the past consequences of past actions to be different from what they were. Retrospective applications do not purport to change the past, but they are still objectionable because they attach new consequences to past actions when it is too late for those to whom the new legislation applies to do anything to avoid the new consequences. Immediate applications are not objectionable because (often) at the time the new legislation is applied it is still possible for those subject to it to adjust their affairs. Each of these three categories of application may, in a given case, turn out to interfere with vested rights. Such interference is considered objectionable because it takes people by surprise and in some cases amounts to expropriating a person's property without compensation.

5) Examples

Example 1: On 1 January 2000, a provision came into force making it an offence for a person to discharge a firearm within a municipality.

This provision creates no temporal application challenges because the situation is clear: it refers to a single short-lived event—discharge of a firearm. Such an event is easily situated in time. To apply the new provision to a discharge that occurred before 1 January 2000 would clearly be retroactive. To apply it to a discharge that occurred on or after that day would be prospective. Finally, a court would be very unlikely to recognize a person's interest in discharging a gun as a vested right. There is little to argue about here.

Example 2: On 1 January 2000, a provision came into force making it an offence for a person to park a vehicle on municipal streets for more than forty-eight consecutive hours.

Once again the situation is easily identified—forty-eight hours of continuous parking—but this time it is a continuing state of affairs, not an event. To apply this provision in respect of parking that ended at noon on 31 December 1999 would be retroactive since by that time all the facts comprising the situation would already have come to an end. Such an application would effectively change the past legal effect of a completed set of facts.

To apply this provision in respect of parking that began at noon on 31 December 1999 and ended fifty hours later would be immediate rather than retroactive or retrospective. It would be immediate because the parking was still in progress when the provision came into force. It was still possible to avoid the legal effect at that point by moving the car.

Example 3: On 1 January 2000, a provision came into force requiring every contract of automobile insurance to include certain stipulated no-fault benefits.

Ms. X was issued a policy of insurance in December of 1999 that did not provide for no-fault benefits. In June 2000 she was injured in an accident for which she alone was responsible. She claimed the stipulated no-fault benefits.

Here the situation is not self-evident. Is the trigger fact an event (the signing of the contract) or a state of affairs (the subsisting contractual relation)? In practice, the answer must be determined largely by policy considerations. For example, in these circumstances it would be unfair to the insurer to impose onerous new obligations that were not reflected in the price of the contract. A court would probably conclude that applying the new provision to these facts would attach new consequences to a past event and would therefore be retrospective rather than immediate. Alternatively to protect the insurer the court could rely on the presumption against interference with vested rights.

Example 4: On 1 January 2000 a provision came into force prohibiting insurers to include any discriminatory clauses in a contract of insurance.

Ms. X was issued a policy of insurance in December of 1999 that contained a clause permitting the insured to end the contract on any grounds it considered appropriate. In June 2000 the insurer attempted to end the contract on a discriminatory ground. Ms. X objected, relying on the new provision.

The situation once again consists of a past event (signing the contract) and a state of affairs (a subsisting contractual relation). But here the policy considerations would likely produce a different result. Applying the new provision immediately would not produce significant costs for the insurer. And even if it did, arguably it would not be unfair to make an insurer bear the costs of its own discriminatory practices. Nor could an insurer claim to be taken by surprise by the new legislation. Human rights legislation of this sort has been around for a long time. In all likelihood, a court would conclude that applying the new provision to these facts would be immediate rather than retrospective.

The court would then have to consider interference with vested rights. It is clear that when the new provision came into force, the insurer had an existing contractual right to end the contract on whatever grounds it thought fit. The burden would therefore be on Ms. X to rebut the presumption against interference with the right. She could rely on the quasi-constitutional character of human rights legislation and the need to give it a liberal, purposive interpretation. She could also point out that the new provision produces at most a modest burden on the insurer, whereas postponing the application of the new provision imposes a heavy burden on her. She not only loses the benefit of the insurance, but she also suffers the humiliation of discrimination.

Example 5: On 1 January 2000, a provision came into force providing that a person who is convicted of three designated sexual offences under the *Criminal Code* must be declared a dangerous offender.

Suppose that Mr. Jones was convicted of an offence in 1998 and another in 1999, both of which came to be listed as designated offences in the new legislation. Then, in 2001 he was convicted of a third designated offence. Would it be retrospective or immediate if the new provision were applied to him in these circumstances?

Here the situation is neither a single discreet event nor an ongoing state of affairs, but a series of events, namely, convictions under the *Criminal Code* that fall into the class of "designated sexual offences." Since the situation was incomplete when the legislation came into force in 2000, applying it to Mr. Jones' third conviction would produce an immediate rather than a retrospective effect. When the new provision came into force, Mr. Jones would be able to avoid its effect by altering his conduct.

6) Presumption against Retroactive Application

a) The Drawbacks and Advantages of Retroactivity

It is strongly presumed that legislation is not meant to be applied to facts that were already past when the legislation came into force. This presumption is grounded in rule of law principles. In order to comply with the law or rely on it in a useful way, a person must know what the law is prior to acting. As noted above, the retroactive application of legislation makes it impossible for the law to be known in advance of acting: the content of the law becomes known only when it is too late to do anything about it. In effect, the law is deemed to have been different from what it actually was. This sort of tampering with reality is inherently arbitrary, and it undermines social security and stability. It is also unfair in so far as it inflicts loss or hardship on particular persons in ways that could not have been anticipated or prevented.

Of course, in certain circumstances the benefits of retroactive legislation are significant and may outweigh the disadvantages outlined above.

There are a number of situations in which the legislature commonly resorts to retroactivity and this is considered acceptable. For example, amendments to fiscal legislation are often made retroactive to prevent taxpayers who have notice of the impending change to arrange their affairs so as to avoid the impact of the amendments. Declaratory legislation is another example. It sets out the correct understanding of existing legislation not only for the future but also for the past. It is thus inherently retroactive. But in so far as it offers a clear and plausible solution to a genuine ambiguity in existing legislation, it assists rather than offends the rule of law.

Generally speaking, however, retroactive legislation is considered offensive and the presumption against the retroactive application is heavily weighted and difficult to rebut. Ideally there will be a provision in the legislation that deems it to have come into force prior to enactment or one that makes it expressly applicable to past facts. For example, For example, a Consumer Protection Act, enacted on 4 November 2002 and commencing on 1 January 2003, might contain a provision making Part IV of the Act (governing credit transactions) applicable to any credit transaction entered after 15 July 2002. The presumption can also be rebutted by necessary implication.

b) How the Presumption Is Applied

Judicial reliance on the presumption against retroactive application is illustrated in the British Columbia Court of Appeal's judgment in *MacKenzie v. British Columbia (Commissioner of Teachers' Pensions)*.[12] Under British Columbia's *Pension (Teachers) Act* as first enacted, teachers upon retirement were obliged to choose one of four pension plans. When the applicant's husband retired in 1978 he chose the "single life" plan, which maximized the benefits to which he was entitled during his lifetime but ended upon his death. In 1988 a new section was added to the Act providing that "[w]here an employee is married on the date he elects a plan ... he shall be deemed to have elected that 60% of his superannuation allowance be paid on the joint life and last survivor plan." The amendment did not state that it applied to elections made prior to 1988. For the next year, until his death in 1989, the husband continued to receive 100 percent of his allowance under the single life plan. After he died, the applicant claimed to be entitled to 60 percent of his allowance pursuant to the 1988 amendment.

The court concluded that to apply the amendment to past elections would give it a retroactive application and, in these circumstances, the presumption against such application was not rebutted. Woods J.A. wrote:

---

12   (1992), 94 D.L.R. (4th) 532 (B.C.C.A.).

To intercede in this scheme, by retroactively changing the election of individual retirees after payments have been made to them, would leave the plan underfunded and thus destroy its actuarial integrity, something which the whole scheme of the present Act, and its predecessors, has sought to maintain .... I must conclude that there is nothing about the overall purpose or scheme of the statute, or the amendment, which would overcome the presumption that the 1988 amendment to the *Pension (Teachers) Act* should be confined to a prospective application.[13]

The court's analysis in *MacKenzie* is interesting because it shows the important role that policy plays in deciding whether an application should be classified as retroactive or immediate. Given the circumstances and the wording of the new section, it was open to the court to say that the relevant fact was not election, a fact already past, but the joint lives of the retired employee and his or her spouse, a fact in progress. On this analysis, the provision would have applied immediately. However, applying the provision to this applicant would give her a windfall at the expense of other contributors to the fund. Because of the timing of her husband's election, and the choice he made, she would garner the advantages of both the single and the joint plans while avoiding their associated disadvantages. Clearly, the court did not think that this was an appropriate outcome, and it therefore analyzed the problem as a retroactive application of a provision to a past event, the election of a pension plan, rather than an immediate application of a provision to ongoing lives.

7) Presumption against Retrospective Application

a) Overview
Driedger took it for granted that there was a presumption against the retrospective application of legislation, and perhaps he is correct. However, outside the *Charter* context, there are few examples in the case law of the presumption being applied. Legislation that is purely procedural or beneficial or designed to protect the public does not attract the presumption and retrospective legislation that interferes with a person's interests or expectations is generally dealt with under the presumption against interference with vested rights. However, with the coming into force of the *Charter*, the courts were faced with some novel problems. One significant way in which *Charter* analysis differs from the analysis of ordinary statutes is that subjects cannot claim to have a vested right

---

13   *Ibid.* at 540.

in *Charter* rights or freedoms. This limitation has thrown a spotlight on the issue of retrospective application.

From the beginning, the courts have held that the *Charter* cannot be applied either retroactively or retrospectively. The *Benner* case offers an excellent overview of judicial thinking in this area.[14] In that case, Iacobucci J. wrote:

> The terms, "retroactivity" and "retrospectivity", while frequently used in relation to statutory construction, can be confusing. E.A. Driedger, in "Statutes: Retroactive Retrospective Reflections" (1978), 56 Can. Bar Rev. 264, at pp. 268–69, has offered these concise definitions which I find helpful:
>
> > A retroactive statute is one that operates as of a time prior to its enactment. A retrospective statute is one that operates for the future only. It is prospective, but it imposes new results in respect of a past event. A retroactive statute *operates backwards*. A retrospective statute *operates forwards*, but it looks backwards in that it attaches new consequences *for the future* to an event that took place before the statute was enacted. A retroactive statute changes the law from what it was; a retrospective statute changes the law from what it otherwise would be with respect to a prior event. [Emphasis in original.]
>
> The *Charter* does not apply retroactively and this Court has stated on numerous occasions that it cannot apply retrospectively.[15]

Iacobucci J. points out that in the *Charter* context the presumption against retrospective application is a flexible tool:

> the Court has also rejected a rigid test for determining when a particular application of the *Charter* would be retrospective, preferring to weigh each case in its own factual and legal context, with attention to the nature of the particular *Charter* right at issue. Not every situation involving events which took place before the *Charter* came into force will necessarily involve a retrospective application of the *Charter*. In Gamble[16]..., Wilson J. wrote at pp. 625–27 for the majority that:

---

14   *Benner*, above note 7.

15   *Ibid.* at paras. 39–40. Iacobucci J. cites the following authorities: *R. v. Stevens*, [1988] 1 S.C.R. 1153 at 1157; *R. v. Stewart*, [1991] 3 S.C.R. 324 at 325; *Reference re Workers' Compensation Act, 1983 (Nfld.)*, [1989] 1 S.C.R. 922, *Dubois v. The Queen*, [1985] 2 S.C.R. 350.

16   *R. v. Gamble*, [1988] 2 S.C.R. 595.

In approaching this crucial question it seems to me preferable … to avoid an all or nothing approach which artificially
divides the chronology of events into the mutually exclusive
categories of pre and post-*Charter*. Frequently an alleged
current violation will have to be placed in the context of its
pre-*Charter* history in order to be fully appreciated.

Another crucial consideration will be the nature of the
particular constitutional right alleged to be violated…. Such
an approach seems to me to be consistent with our general
purposive approach to the interpretation of constitutional
rights. Different rights and freedoms, depending on their
purpose and the interests they are meant to protect, will
crystallize and protect the individual at different times.

…

Some rights and freedoms in the *Charter* seem to me to be
particularly susceptible of current application even although
such application will of necessity take cognizance of pre-
Charter events. Those *Charter* rights the purpose of which is
to prohibit certain conditions or states of affairs would appear to fall into this category. Such rights are not designed to
protect against discrete events but rather to protect against
an ongoing condition state of affairs…. Section 15 may …
fall into this category.[17]

Iacobucci J.'s gloss on these passages from *Gamble* is found in the following paragraph.

Section 15 cannot be used to attack a discrete act which took place
before the *Charter* came into effect. It cannot, for example, be invoked to challenge a pre-*Charter* conviction…. Where the effect of
a law is simply to impose an on-going discriminatory status or disability on an individual, however, then it will not be insulated from
Charter review simply because it happened to be passed before April
17, 1985. If it continues to impose its effects on new applicants today,
then it is susceptible to *Charter* scrutiny today.[18]

As Iacobucci J. suggests, it is not permissible to rely on new legislation
to change the legal consequences of a past action. However, the *Charter*
does apply immediately to continuing or ongoing situations.

---

17   *Benner*, above note 7 at paras. 41–43.
18   *Ibid.* at para. 44.

b) Exceptions

In his 1978 article, in summarizing the law governing the presumption against retrospective application of legislation, Driedger writes:

> 3. The presumption does not apply unless the consequences attaching to the prior event are prejudicial ones, namely, a new penalty, disability or duty.
>
> 4. The presumption does not apply if the new prejudicial consequences are intended as protections for the public rather than as punishment for a prior event.[19]

The presumption also does not apply if the consequences are purely procedural in character, even though the new law might be less advantageous to an accused or a litigant than the former law.

i) Beneficial Legislation

The reasoning behind the first exception is easy to understand. If legislation confers a benefit on persons, with no corresponding prejudice to others, there is little for anyone to object to. It is true that beneficial legislation may impose costs on government. However, by enacting such legislation, the legislature makes it clear that it intends government to absorb those costs. Giving an immediate application to beneficial legislation is consistent with the general principle that such legislation is to be given a liberal, purposive interpretation.

ii) Legislation Designed to Protect the Public

While this exception is formulated broadly, the case law applying it typically deals with disqualifications attaching to persons who have run afoul of the law. For example, legislation is enacted prohibiting a person who has been convicted of fraud from becoming a certified public accountant. If this legislation were applied to persons convicted before it came into force, it would not be considered retrospective under the exception because it is designed to protect the public.[20] The exception has also been applied to disqualifications attaching to bankrupts.

iii) Legislation That Is Purely Procedural

Procedural law is law that does not affect substantive rights in any way; it merely sets out modalities for the enforcement of existing rights,

---

19   Driedger, above note 6 at 276.

20   The leading Canadian case is *Brosseau v. Alberta Securities Commission*, [1989] 1 S.C.R. 301.

obligations, or prohibitions. It is well established that procedural law applies immediately to pending cases, that is, to cases that have not been definitively dealt with by the legal system.[21] This includes not only cases at first instance, but also cases on appeal.

The distinction between procedure and substance is often hard to draw. In drawing the distinction, the courts appropriately look to the real impact of the provision on the position of the parties.[22]

8) Immediate Application

An application of legislation is immediate if the effect is to attach new legal consequences to facts that have not yet fully occurred when the legislation comes into force. There is no presumption against the immediate application of legislation; such applications are considered to be prospective rather than retroactive or retrospective.

The importance of distinguishing between completed facts and facts in progress is well illustrated by the *Benner* case. In *Benner,* the appellant was a man born outside Canada before 15 February 1977, to a Canadian mother and a non-Canadian father. Under the *Citizenship Act,* a person in the appellant's position born to a Canadian father was entitled to claim Canadian citizenship simply by registering. However, because the appellant's connection to Canada was through his mother, he was required to apply for citizenship, a process that involved passing criminal clearance and security checks. When the appellant's application was refused, he invoked section 15 of the *Charter* to challenge the validity of this differential treatment. The first issue dealt with by the Court was whether applying section 15 to these facts would be a retroactive or retrospective application of the *Charter.* Here is the Court's conclusion:

> In my view, this case does not involve either a retroactive or a retrospective application of the *Charter.*
>
> The respondent urged us to find that the key point in the chronology of events was the appellant's birth in 1962.... Whatever discrimination took place in the appellant's case, therefore, took place when he was born, since that is when his rights were determined under the impugned legislation. To revisit these rights in light of s. 15, according to the respondent, is therefore inescapably to go back

---

21   For a recent case affirming and applying this proposition, see *Re Application under s. 83.28 of the Criminal Code,* [2004] S.C.R. 248.

22   For an excellent account of the temporal application of procedural law, see P.-A. Côté, *The Interpretation of Legislation in Canada,* 3d ed. (Scarborough, ON: Carswell: 2000) 176*ff.*

and alter a distribution of rights which took place years before the creation of the *Charter*.

I am uncomfortable with the idea of rights or entitlements crystallizing at birth, particularly in the context of s. 15. This suggests that whenever a person born before April 17, 1985, suffers the discriminatory effects of a piece of legislation, these effects may be immunized from *Charter* review. Our skin colour is determined at birth—rights or entitlements assigned on the basis of skin colour by a particular law would, by this logic, "crystallize" then. Under the approach proposed by the respondent, individuals born before s. 15 came into effect would therefore be unable to invoke the *Charter* to challenge even a recent application of such a law. In fact, Parliament or a legislature could insulate discriminatory laws from review by providing that they applied only to persons born before 1985.

The preferable way, in my opinion, to characterize the appellant's position is in terms of status or on-going condition. From the time of his birth, he has been a child, born outside Canada prior to February 15, 1977, of a Canadian mother and a non-Canadian father. This is no less a "status" than being of a particular skin colour or ethnic or religious background: it is an ongoing state of affairs.[23]

By characterizing the relevant fact situation as an ongoing status rather than an event, the court could conclude that applying the *Charter* was immediate rather than retroactive or retrospective.

9) Presumption against Interference with Vested Rights

a) Overview

It is presumed that new legislation is not intended to be applied so as to interfere with vested common law rights, or with "acquired, accrued or accruing" statutory rights. If rights have vested or accrued at the moment new legislation comes into force, it is presumed that the former law under which those rights were acquired survives and application of the new legislation is postponed.

To avoid confusion, it is important to distinguish between interfering with rights and interfering with vested rights. It is presumed that the legislature does not wish to do either, but these are distinct presumptions. A right is an interest or an expectation that is recognized

---

23   Above note 7 at paras. 49–52. For examples of the immediate application of ordinary legislation, see *Venne v. Québec (Commission de protection du territoire agricole)*, [1989] 1 S.C.R. 880 at 907–15; *Quebec (Attorney General) v. Quebec (Expropriation Tribunal)*, [1986] 1 S.C.R. 732 at 741 and 744.

and protected by law, either by common law or statute. By providing a means for persons to acquire and preserve defined interests or expectations and to maintain them in relation to others, the law transforms them into rights. Once recognized by law, rights exist in two ways—first as abstractions, as potentialities that any qualifying individual may have or acquire, and second in concrete form, as interests or expectations actually held by particular persons in particular circumstances. The presumption against interfering with rights is concerned with rights in the abstract: it is presumed that the legislature wishes to preserve or enlarge, but not contract, the class of interests or expectations that the law protects as rights. By contrast, the presumption against interfering with vested rights is concerned with the concrete rights of particular persons: it is presumed that legislation that interferes with rights in the abstract is not meant to apply to concrete rights definitively acquired by persons before the legislation came into force.

Suppose, for example, that a provision was enacted lowering the age to which parents are required to provide financial support for their children from eighteen to fifteen: "Every parent of a child shall provide financial support for that child until he or she attains the age of fifteen." This provision clearly takes away rights formerly enjoyed by children as a class, some of which would have vested or accrued in individual children. In applying the presumption against interfering with rights, a court might construe the provision strictly (and somewhat implausibly) by defining "parent" to mean "divorced parent" or "support" to mean "support for things other than the necessities of life." But regardless of how the language of the provision is understood, its effect will be to limit children's rights. If the provision is applied immediately, it will affect the rights of all children under the age of eighteen, including those who have already reached fifteen. However, children over fifteen could argue that they had a vested and not just a potential right to be supported to the age of eighteen. If a court agreed with this analysis, the rights of children in this class would be protected by the presumption against vested rights. In the absence of something to rebut the presumption, the provision would not apply to them. Of course, there is nothing to prevent children under fifteen from also claiming a vested right, but their claim would be less compelling. Children not yet born when the legislation came into force could have no such claim.

As this example shows, to benefit from the presumption against interfering with vested rights a person must show that the right for which protection is sought has vested (or accrued or is accruing). The courts decide which personal interests or expectations are important enough to be labelled "rights" and whether, given the circumstances, they should be considered "vested" or "accrued." The standard common law rights are well defined, and there are rules indicating when they vest or accrue. Outside the traditional categories, however, it is often difficult to predict when a given interest or expectation will be protected as a right.

A vast array of benefits, entitlements, exemptions, and remedies may be sought under legislation, and a wide range of procedures exist for claiming these statutory advantages. In each case the court must decide at what point in the procedure a claimant's hope of receiving the advantage sought is sufficiently crystallized to be recognized as a vested right. The question of what makes an interest or expectation a vested right was recently addressed by the Supreme Court of Canada in *Dikranian v. Quebec (Attorney General)*.[24] Speaking for the majority, Bastarache J. wrote:

> [Professor] Côté maintains that an individual must meet two criteria to have a vested right: (1) the individual's legal (juridical) situation must be tangible and concrete rather than general and abstract; and (2) this legal situation must have been sufficiently constituted at the time of the new statute's commencement (Côté,[25] at pp. 160–61).
>
> I am satisfied from a review of the case law of this Court and the courts of the other provinces that [this] analytical framework ... is the correct one.
>
> A court cannot therefore find that a vested right exists if the juridical situation under consideration is not tangible, concrete and distinctive. The mere possibility of availing oneself of a specific statute is not a basis for arguing that a vested right exists: Côté, at p. 161. As Dickson J. (as he then was) clearly stated in *Gustavson Drilling*,[26] at p. 283, the mere right existing in the members of the community or any class of them at the date of the repeal of a statute to take advantage of the repealed statute is not a right accrued.
>
> But there is more. The situation must also have materialized (Côté, at p. 163). When does a right become sufficiently concrete? This will vary depending on the juridical situation in question.... [J]ust as the hopes or expectations of a person's heirs become rights the instant the person dies ..., and just as a tort or delict instantaneously gives rise to the right to compensation..., rights and obligations resulting from a contract are usually created at the same time as the contract itself (see Côté, at p. 163).[27]

---

24   Above note 5.
25   Côté, *Interpretation of Legislation*, above note 22.
26   *Gustavson*, above note 5.
27   *Dikranian*, above note 5 at paras. 37–40.

The examples of vesting given by Bastarache J. in the final paragraph are easy cases, because both the common law and the *Civil Code* address and resolve the issue of when these expectations ripen into vested rights. However, when it comes to statutory rights the "juridical situation" is generally not governed by existing rules and the court must come up with a new solution. In such cases, the governing considerations are degree of surprise and degree of unfairness: the more unexpected the change and the more unfair it would be to diminish or abolish the claimant's expectation or interest, the more likely the court is to recognize and protect that expectation or interest as a vested right. The most common form of unfairness is detrimental reliance.

b) Rebuttal

The presumption against interference with vested rights is rooted in the same considerations as the presumption against retroactivity. However, while the presumption against retroactivity is heavily weighted and difficult to rebut, the presumption against interfering with vested rights is more fluid. As the courts frequently point out, many legislative initiatives interfere to some extent with existing rights and are obviously meant to do so; such interference is a normal by-product of change. To determine whether the presumption is rebutted, the courts balance several factors: the degree of unfairness the interference would create, the importance of the policies implemented by the new legislation, and the impact that limiting or delaying its application would have, as well as any textual or other evidence of the legislature's intent.

The presumption against interference with vested rights was applied by the British Columbia Court of Appeal in *Canada (Attorney-General) v. Lavery*.[28] In 1987 the federal government began an action *per quod servitium amisit* to recover damages suffered by one of its servants. In 1988, while this action was pending, the British Columbia legislature enacted a provision abolishing this cause of action. Although the government's *per quod* action was squarely within the provision, the court refused to apply the provision to these facts because to do so would destroy the government's vested right. Taylor J.A. wrote:

> The simple statement that "the action per quod servitium amisit is abolished", without more, is, in my view, clearly inadequate to overcome the presumption ....
>
> The purpose of rules of restrictive interpretation of this sort is ... to guard against the danger of giving to words of the legislature wider

---

28   (1991), 76 D.L.R. (4th) 97 (B.C.C.A.).

effect than the legislators may in fact have intended... . [T]he court must be satisfied that the legislators did indeed intend to take away rights already "vested".[29]

In the *Lavery* case there was no evidence that the newly enacted provision was meant to apply immediately to pending as well as future actions. In the absence of any evidence to rebut the presumption, the provision did not apply to the government's vested right of action.

To rebut the presumption against interfering with vested rights, express words are not necessary. The court looks at all relevant evidence of legislative intent. The judgment of Cameron J.A. in *National Trust Co. v. Larsen*[30] is exemplary in this respect. The parties in this case had agreed to a mortgage in which the mortgagee National Trust was protected by the mortgagor Larsen's personal promise to pay as well as its rights in the mortgaged property. A short while later the Saskatchewan legislature enacted a provision abolishing the mortgagee's personal right of action and limiting mortgagees to their real property rights. When Larsen defaulted, the trust company tried to sue on his promise to pay. It argued that since its right to enforce the promise arose before the new provision came into force, it was a vested right protected by the presumption. Although the court agreed with this analysis, it went on to conclude that in this case the presumption was rebutted.

In reaching this conclusion, the court relied on a number of factors. First of all, the new provision could not have upset the expectations of National Trust to any great extent. Legislation abolishing the mortgagee's personal action was common in Canada and already existed in Saskatchewan in other contexts. Moreover, the prior legislation on which the mortgagee relied was unclear, and, in the view of some, did not allow for personal actions in any event. Thirdly, the provision was not a shockingly unfair expropriation of property. In the event of a default, the mortgagee retained the right to be paid from the proceeds of sale of the secured property. A commercial mortgagee was well placed to bear the risk of falling property values. Finally, remedial legislation of this sort should be given a liberal interpretation. Cameron J.A. wrote:

> [I]t is manifestly clear that the change in the law was remedial ... in the beneficial sense of correcting an imperfection in the prior law. Of course, one person's benefit is another's burden. But ... the legislature was setting the interests of the one, the mortgagor, ahead of the other, the mortgagee. And that being so, I think it fair to say the amendment

29   *Ibid.* at 99.
30   (1989), 61 D.L.R. (4th) 270 (Sask. C.A.).

might more readily be construed as having been intended to encroach upon the right in issue than would otherwise be the case.[31]

While none of these factors alone is likely to have been sufficient, their cumulative impact was enough to rebut the presumption.

10) Transitional Provisions

There are few constitutional constraints on the jurisdiction of legislatures to enact retroactive or retrospective legislation. Paragraph 11(g) of the *Charter* provides that a person is not to be found guilty of an offence for an act or omission that did not constitute an offence at the time it occurred. Paragraph 11(i) provides that a person found guilty of an offence is entitled to the benefit of the least oppressive punishment imposed for that offence between the time of commission and the time of sentencing. Section 7 of the *Charter* may also provide grounds for resisting the retroactive or retrospective application of legislation that threatens the life, liberty or security of persons.

Subject to these limited constraints, a legislature may enact whatever transitional provisions it thinks appropriate, expressing its intention to make new legislation retroactive, retrospective, or immediate, as well as its intention to interfere with or preserve vested rights. In *Medovarski v. Canada (Minister of Citizenship and Immigration)*, the relevant transitional provision was interpreted using the entire range of interpretive rules and techniques, with an emphasis on purposive analysis, to conclude that Parliament indeed intended to take away the appellants' vested rights to appeal their deportation orders.[32]

However, at about the same time, the Supreme Court of Canada offered an extremely narrow interpretation of a transitional provision in the *Dikranian* case. Under Quebec's *Act respecting financial assistance to students*, students borrowed money from private financial institutions while the government guaranteed the loans and paid any interest owing during a stipulated grace period. The issue there was whether newly enacted legislation that shortened this grace period applied to students whose loan contracts were entered before the new legislation came into force. The amending legislation contained transitional provisions. The applicable one was in the following terms:

---

31 *Ibid.* at 279. For similar reasoning, see *Ell v. Alberta*, [2003] 1 S.C.R. 857 at paras. 49–51.

32 [2005] 2 S.C.R. 539 at para. 14*ff.*

13. The other provisions introduced by this Act and the first regulations made thereunder are applicable to the juridical situations in progress at the time of their coming into force.

It would be plausible to interpret this provision as expressing the legislature's intention to have the new grace period apply to subsisting loan contracts, that is, contracts entered but not yet fully executed when the new legislation came into force.[33] However, a majority of the Supreme Court of Canada did not see it that way. It concluded that the words "juridical situations in progress" applied not to signed and subsisting contracts but rather to situations where students had received authorization from the government to borrow money from a private financial institution but had not yet done so.[34]

C. PRESUMPTION AGAINST EXTRATERRITORIAL APPLICATION

The presumption that legislation does not apply to persons or things outside the territory of the enacting jurisdiction is grounded in the international law doctrine of territorial sovereignty. This doctrine says that each state has sovereign power over its own territory but must not intrude on the territory of its equally sovereign neighbours. Nor must it intrude on territory that is outside the boundaries of all sovereign states, and to which each may claim access. The territorial reach of provincial legislatures is also limited constitutionally by the words "in the Province" that appear in section 92 of the *Constitution Act, 1867*.[35] As a practical matter, where different jurisdictions can claim to have the same powers, the only way to avoid conflict is to impose territorial limits on the reach of those powers. As Binnie J. writes in *Society of Composers, Authors and Music Publishers of Canada v. Canadian Association of Internet Providers*:

> While the Parliament of Canada, unlike the legislatures of the Provinces, has the legislative competence to enact laws having extraterri-

---

33   This is how the provision was interpreted in the strong dissenting judgment of Deschamps J. See *Dikranian*, above note 5 at para. 59*ff.*

34   *Ibid.* at para. 45*ff.*

35   See *British Columbia v. Imperial Tobacco Canada Ltd.*, [2005] 2 S.C.R. 473 at para. 26; *Unifund Assurance Co. v. Insurance Corp. of British Columbia*, [2003] 2 S.C.R. 63 at paras. 50–51. The *Unifund Assurance* case offers a comprehensive review of the rules and case law governing the territorial limitation on provincial jurisdiction.

torial effect, it is presumed not to intend to do so, in the absence of clear words or necessary implication to the contrary. This is because "[i]n our modern world of easy travel and with the emergence of a global economic order, chaotic situations would often result if the principle of territorial jurisdiction were not, at least generally, respected".[36]

The idea that legislation is limited in its territorial application is easy to grasp but hard to apply in practice. Because of the complex and highly mobile character of modern life, the matters dealt with in legislation often are not confined to a single jurisdiction. Obviously, some extraterritorial application must be tolerated; otherwise, transborder and multijurisdictional facts would effectively be outside the law. The test to determine whether an application of legislation to transborder or multijurisdictional facts is consistent with territorial limitations has two parts: first, the court determines whether there is a sufficient connection between the facts and the enacting jurisdiction, and second, it determines whether applying the legislation to these facts would interfere unduly with the interests or affairs of any other jurisdictions involved.

This test was applied in *R. v. Libman*[37] to make the offence of fraud as defined in the *Criminal Code* applicable to a Canadian-based, multinational telephone scam. The accused ran a telephone solicitation operation in which persons in Ontario phoned residents of the United States and, under false pretences, induced them to send money to addresses in Panama and Costa Rica. The accused defended on the grounds that Parliament could not have intended the *Criminal Code* to apply to activity that occurred primarily outside Canada. The Supreme Court of Canada rejected this defence. La Forest J. wrote:

> [I]n considering whether a transaction falls outside Canadian territory … we must, in my view, take into account all relevant facts that take place in Canada that may legitimately give this country an interest in prosecuting the offence. One must then consider whether there is anything in those facts that offends international comity.[38]

Comity, whether international or interprovincial, refers to the conventions of mutual respect and cooperation practised among sovereign jurisdictions to ensure good relations.

---

36   *Society of Composers, Authors and Music Publishers of Canada v. Canadian Assn. of Internet Providers*, [2004] 2 S.C.R. 427 at para. 54 [*SOCAN*], citing *Tolofson v. Jensen*, [1994] 3 S.C.R. 1022 at 1051, La Forest J.

37   [1985] 2 S.C.R. 178.

38   *Ibid.* at 211.

Not surprisingly, the issue of extraterritoriality has frequently arisen in cases dealing with Internet use. A good review is found in the *SOCAN* case, where the issue was the applicability of Canada's *Copyright Act* to Internet service providers who facilitate the downloading in Canada of musical works originating outside Canada. After reviewing the case law, Binnie J. concluded as follows.

> A real and substantial connection to Canada is sufficient to support the application of our *Copyright Act* to international Internet transmissions in a way that will accord with international comity and be consistent with the objectives of order and fairness.
>
> In terms of the Internet, relevant connecting factors would include the *situs* of the content provider, the host server, the intermediaries and the end user. The weight to be given to any particular factor will vary with the circumstances and the nature of the dispute.
>
> Canada clearly has a significant interest in the flow of information in and out of the country. Canada regulates the reception of broadcasting signals in Canada wherever originated.... Our courts and tribunals regularly take jurisdiction in matters of civil liability arising out of foreign transmissions which are received and have their impact here.
>
> ...
>
> Generally speaking, this Court has recognized, as a sufficient "connection" for taking jurisdiction, situations where Canada is the country of transmission or the country of reception.... This jurisdictional posture is consistent with international copyright practice.[39]

In *Libman* and *SOCAN*, the application of Canadian legislation to multijurisdictional facts was found to be consistent with the presumption of limited territorial application. In *Goodman v. Manitoba (Criminal Injuries Compensation Board)*,[40] the presumption was relied on to preclude the application of the legislation to multijurisdictional facts. Manitoba's *Criminal Injuries Compensation Act* provided compensation for injuries sustained

a)   by victims of a criminal offence in Manitoba,
b)   by persons while assisting a police officer "in carrying out his duties ... in Manitoba," and
c)   by persons while attempting to "arrest any person or preserve the peace" or "prevent lawfully the commission of a criminal offence."

---

39   *SOCAN*, above note 36 at paras. 60–63. [Citations omitted.]
40   (1980), 120 D.L.R. (3d) 235 (Man. C.A.).

The claimant, a resident of Manitoba, was injured trying to protect his wife from a criminal assault that occurred while the couple was in Nevada. The claimant argued that because his injuries were sustained while trying to prevent a crime and because the words "in Manitoba" did not appear in paragraph (c), he was entitled to compensation under the Act. This argument failed before the Manitoba Court of Appeal. O'Sullivan J.A. wrote:

> Standing alone, without the implication of any qualification ... [paragraph (c)] would give a right to apply for compensation to anyone in the world for acts or omissions anywhere in the world. This would be absurd. It is unthinkable that the legislature of Manitoba intended to give a right of compensation to all citizens of Russia, China, Jamaica, Uganda, etc., who are injured in those countries as a result of endeavouring to preserve the peace .... [I]t is necessary to imply some qualification: either they are limited by the residence of the applicant or they are limited by the place of occurrence.[41]

The court concluded that the feature chosen by the legislature to ensure a sufficient territorial connection between Manitoba and the facts was the place of the occurrence rather than the residence of the injured person: "[T]he statute read as a whole creates a scheme whereby victims of crime and related acts can be compensated, regardless of their residence, if the acts or omissions giving rise to their injuries occur in Manitoba."[42] Thus, despite the legislature's failure to include the words "in Manitoba" in paragraph (c) (contrary to sound drafting practice), the provision was interpreted to apply only to events giving rise to injury within Manitoba.

D. PRESUMPTION AGAINST APPLICATION TO THE CROWN

1) Overview

It is presumed at common law that legislation is not intended to apply to the Crown if its application would prejudice the Crown in any way. This presumption is codified in Canadian Interpretation Acts. The federal *Interpretation Act* provides:

---

41   *Ibid.* at 238.
42   *Ibid.*

17. No enactment is binding on Her Majesty or affects Her Majesty's rights or prerogatives in any manner, except as mentioned or referred to in the enactment.[43]

In two provinces, British Columbia and Prince Edward Island, the presumption of immunity has been replaced by a presumption of non-immunity. The Prince Edward Island provision provides:

14.(1) Unless an Act otherwise specifically provides, every Act and every regulation made thereunder, is binding on her Majesty.[44]

The references to "Her Majesty" (or to the Crown, the State, or the government) in the various Interpretation Act provisions dealing with Crown immunity have been interpreted to include Her Majesty in right of both Canada and the provinces.[45]

Most Interpretation Acts say that in order to bind Her Majesty, an enactment must expressly refer to Her Majesty or expressly declare that she is bound. However, despite this statutory language, the courts have developed a number of common law exceptions that permit them to conclude that the legislature intended to bind the Crown and its agents even though it did not say so expressly.[46] These exceptions are rooted in the leading case on Crown immunity, *Bombay Province v. Bombay Municipal Corporation*. In that case, Lord du Parcq wrote:

The maxim of the law in early times was that no statute bound the Crown unless the Crown was expressly named therein... . But the rule so laid down is subject to at least one exception. The Crown may be bound ... "by necessary implication." If, that is to say, it is manifest from the very terms of the statute, that it was the intention of the legislature that the Crown should be bound, then the result is the same as if the Crown had been expressly named.[47]

This has become known as the "logical or necessary implication" test. Lord du Parcq also wrote:

If it can be affirmed that, at the time when the statute was passed and received the royal sanction, it was apparent from its terms that its benefi-

---

43   R.S.C. 1985, c. I-21, s. 17.
44   *Interpretation Act*, R.S.P.E.I. 1988, c. I-8, s. 14(1).
45   See *CNCP Telecommunications v. Alberta Government Telephones*, [1989] 2 S.C.R. 225 at 274; *Canada v. Murray*, [1967] S.C.R. 262.
46   Most Interpretation Acts say that they apply unless a contrary intention appears. The common law exceptions can be understood as indicators of the legislature's contrary intention.
47   [1947] A.C. 58 at 61 (P.C.).

cent purpose must be wholly frustrated unless the Crown were bound, then it may be inferred that the Crown has agreed to be bound.[48]

This has become known as the "wholly frustrated purpose" test.

There is also a "benefit/burden" exception. This exception was originally based on the idea of waiver: when the Crown invokes a statute to secure the benefit of provisions that work to its advantage, it is taken to voluntarily submit to any corresponding burdens. More recent analyses suggest that the Crown has no choice: since it can claim only as much benefit as the statute allows, it must accept whatever conditions or qualifications the statute may impose. In other words, the Crown must take the law as it finds it. If it seeks to rely on an Act for one purpose, it is effectively bound by that Act for all purposes.[49]

Several aspects of the presumption of Crown immunity were explored by the Supreme Court of Canada in *Friends of the Oldman River Society v. Canada (Minister of Transport).*[50] In this case the court had to determine whether the federal *Navigable Waters Protection Act* applied to the Crown in right of Alberta. Since the Crown was not mentioned in the statute, under section 17 of the federal *Interpretation Act*, "unless a contrary intention appeared," neither the federal nor the provincial Crowns were bound. This meant that the Crown and its agents at both levels of government were entitled to introduce obstructions into navigable rivers free of the restraints and conditions imposed by the *Navigable Waters Protection Act*. Before accepting this result, the court considered whether the Act came within any of the common law exceptions outlined above.

In applying the "logical or necessary implication" test, La Forest J. emphasized the importance of looking at the whole of the statute in context, including the legal and external context existing when the statute was first enacted. He noted that provinces frequently initiate projects like dams and bridges that interfere with navigation, that under the Constitution only Parliament could authorize such interference, and that the *Navigable Waters Protection Act* was the only legal mechanism by which such authorization could be granted. Given these premises, it followed that Parliament must have intended the provinces to be bound.

La Forest J. also applied the "wholly frustrated purpose" test and found that excluding the provinces from the ambit of the Act would completely undermine its effective operation:

---

48   *Ibid.* at 63.
49   The leading modern case on the benefit/burden exception is *Sparling v. Quebec*, [1988] 2 S.C.R. 1015.
50   [1992] 1 S.C.R. 3.

> The regulation of navigable waters must be viewed functionally as an integrated whole, and when so viewed it would result in an absurdity if the Crown in right of a province was left to obstruct navigation with impunity at one point along a navigational system, while Parliament assiduously worked to preserve its navigability at another point.[51]

On the basis of this evidence, the court inferred that Parliament must have intended its legislation to apply to the provincial Crowns and their agents despite its failure to say so expressly in the Act itself.

2) Crown Agents

The immunity enjoyed by the Crown extends to the Crown's agents. Persons or bodies are agents of the Crown if they are declared by statute to act for the Crown or if they meet the common law test of ministerial control. At common law, when the Crown through its ministers has the legal right to control the activities of a person or body, the latter is an agent of the Crown. However, the immunity enjoyed by Crown agents is subject to an important qualification. As Dickson J. explained in *R. v. Eldorado Nuclear Ltd.*:

> When a Crown agent acts within the scope of the public purposes it is statutorily empowered to pursue, it is entitled to Crown immunity from the operation of statutes, because it is acting on behalf of the Crown. When the agent steps outside the ambit of Crown purposes, however, it acts personally, and not on behalf of the state, and cannot claim to be immune as an agent of the Crown.[52]

Agents step outside the ambit of Crown purposes, and therefore lose immunity, if they do something that they are not authorized by their statute to do or if they do something authorized for an unauthorized purpose.

---

51 *Ibid.* at 60–61.
52 [1983] 2 S.C.R. 551 at 565–566. See also *Nova Scotia Power Inc. v. Canada*, [2004] 3 S.C.R. 53.

CHAPTER 14

EXTRINSIC AIDS

A. INTRODUCTION

Courts sometimes rely on materials called "extrinsic aids" when interpreting legislation. There is no exact definition of this expression. Historically, it referred to anything outside the legislative text of which judicial notice could not be taken. Some extrinsic aids were considered inadmissible; others could be looked at only if the text itself was ambiguous. Over the past century, the courts have moved from a reluctance to look at extrinsic aids to ever-increasing acceptance of these materials. However, the rules governing their admissibility and use are not as clear as one might wish. Not all extrinsic aids are treated the same way, and it is not always clear whether a given aid may be relied on in the absence of ambiguity.

Most lists of extrinsic aids would include the following:

1. **Legislative history—materials generated in the course of enacting bills or making regulations:** Anything that is prepared to facilitate the passage of legislation forms part of its legislative history. This includes any material brought to the attention of the legislature during the enactment of a bill, regardless of source, as well as materials prepared by the government for public consumption. In the case of regulations, legislative history consists of materials considered by the executive branch or prepared by it to justify and explain proposed regulations.

2. **Model legislation:** In preparing new enactments, a legislature some-times relies on model legislation created by bodies like the Uniform Law Conference of Canada or Law Reform Commissions. Often the legislature draws on statutes from other jurisdictions facing similar problems. These legislative models may be adopted in whole or in part, with minor or major changes. Formerly, Canadian drafters tended to model bills on British statute law. More recently, particu-larly in the commercial area, Canadian legislation is more likely to follow American examples. Occasionally, legislation is based on European or Commonwealh law or international law instruments. Both the model legislation itself and case law interpreting it may be relied on in interpretation.

3. **Legislative evolution—the previous and subsequent versions of the provision to be interpreted:** The previous and subsequent ver-sions of a provision form its legislative evolution, beginning with the first enactment followed by subsequent re-enactments and amendments to final repeal. Each version is compared with the one that preceded it, noting any changes and classifying them as either stylistic or substantive.

4. **International agreements:** International treaties and conventions that have been signed and ratified by Canada may or may not have been implemented by the relevant jurisdiction, federal or provin-cial, so as to make them part of domestic law. When legislation is enacted to give domestic effect to an international agreement, the agreement to be implemented is considered an extrinsic aid that may be relied on in interpretation.

5. **The opinion of other interpreters:** The opinion of other courts and tribunals concerning the meaning or purpose of a legislative text has always been an important aid to statutory interpretion. Al-though case law is not normally labelled "extrinsic," it is obviously external to the text to be interpreted. This category also includes the opinion of legal scholars and of government departments and agen-cies, along with the practice of officials who administer the law.

B. LEGISLATIVE HISTORY

1) Legislative History Defined

The materials that may be included in the legislative history of an en-actment have not been identified with precision. The concept appears to embrace everything connected to the preparation and passage of legislation, from preliminary research through the legislative process to royal assent. It includes anything brought to the attention of the legislature or generated by the legislature during the enactment process. It may even include government materials prepared for stakeholders or the general public. Typical examples of legislative history material are government white papers, commission reports, background materials tabled in the legislature, briefs and testimony submitted to legislative committees, committee reports and the records of legislative debate. The courts have also taken into account explanatory notes prepared by the Department of Justice and background papers prepared by the Library of Parliament, Parliamentary Research Branch.[1] A new and most interesting type of legislative history consists of the bijural terminology records prepared by the Department of Justice in the course of its revision of federal statute law to harmonize it with Quebec's new *Civil Code*.[2] The one form of legislative history that has not been accepted is the testimony of bureaucrats involved in the legislative process.[3]

When interpreting regulations, it is well established that materials such as policy papers and cost-benefit assessments or impact analyses prepared by or relied on by the government in the course of the regulation-making process are admissible extrinsic aids.[4] Courts have also looked to the submissions of stakeholders about proposed regulations, pre-enactment publications, ministerial correspondence, and the like.[5]

As reliance on the legislative history of enactments becomes more common, the courts may wish to explore the justification for admitting these materials and define their scope with greater care. In principle, use of these materials should be tied to a rationale for admitting them.

Most courts use the term "legislative history" to include what in this text is called "legislative evolution." Although this judicial usage is well established, it is confusing and to some extent misleading. The

---

1 See, for example, *Société des alcools du Québec v. Canada*, [2001] 1 F.C. 386 at paras. 45–46 (T.D.); *St-Hilaire v. Canada (Attorney General)*, [2001] 4 F.C. 289 at para. 66 (C.A.).

2 See, for example, *Schreiber v. Canada (Attorney General)*, [2002] 3 S.C.R. 269 at para. 66*ff* [*Schreiber*].

3 But see *Animal Alliance of Canada v. Canada (Attorney General)*, [1999] 4 F.C. 72 at para. 25*ff* (T.D.). The affidavit material admitted by the judge seems to have been allowed in for general background.

4 See, for example, *Bristol-Myers Squibb Co. v. Canada (Attorney General)*, [2005] 1 S.C.R. 533 at para. 156.

5 See, for example, *Apotex Inc. v. Canada (Attorney General)*, [2000] F.C.J. No. 634 at paras. 55 and 73–74 (C.A.).

considerations affecting the admissibility and use of legislative history differ significantly from those affecting legislative evolution.[6]

2) The Exclusionary Rule and Its Demise

In the seventeenth century, British courts determined that the legislative history of an enactment should not be admissible to assist in interpretation. The justification usually given for this exclusion was that the materials forming legislative history are irrelevant to its interpretation. Although they tell us something of the views and understanding of certain participants in the legislative process, they tell us nothing of the views and understandings of Parliament itself. As a corporate entity, a legislature expresses itself through the text it enacts. The only access to its intentions is through inference based on that text.

Apart from this theoretical justification, there are practical reasons for the exclusionary rule. Until recently, much of the material that formed legislative history was not readily accessible to interpreters. The material that was available often turned out to be inaccurate or unreliable as well as irrelevant to the issue before the court. In most cases, the cost of acquiring such material outweighed any benefit that could be derived from it. With new technologies in place, the force of these objections is blunted, but there is still cause to wonder if, generally speaking, the insight gained from looking at the legislative history of an enactment is worth the time and cost.

The exclusionary rule is no longer good law in Canada.[7] The exceptions created by courts have hollowed out the rule to such an extent that there is little left of it. However, there are still some materials, such as the testimony of persons recalling their role in the legislative process, that the courts refuse to look at. And it remains unclear whether legislative history may be relied on as direct evidence of the intended meaning of a word or expression used in a legislative text.

a) Ways to Use Legislative History to Determine Legislative Intent

Historically, the courts distinguished three ways to use legislative history materials. First, they might be used as *indirect evidence of purpose or meaning*. On this approach the court looks for evidence of circumstances and conditions existing at the time of enactment to which the legislation is a plausible response. The legislature's intention is then inferred from

---

6   See Section D, below in this chapter.
7   See Stephane Beaulac, "Recent Developments at the Supreme Court of Canada on the Use of Parliamentary Debates" (2000), 63 Sask. L. Rev. 581–616.

reading the legislative text in light of those background facts. Second, legislative history materials might be used as *direct evidence of purpose*. On this approach, the court looks for explicit explanations or descriptions of purpose offered by an authoritative source—such as the minister responsible for a bill. Finally, these materials might be used as *direct evidence of meaning*. Here the court looks for indications of how the legislature understood the meaning of its text—how it imagined it would apply to particular facts, which sense of a word was intended, how provisions were supposed to work together. Direct evidence of meaning gives "the answer" to particular interpretation questions, based on the legislature's own explanation or description of the meaning of a provision.

b)   Direct versus Indirect Evidence of Legislative Intent

As the exclusionary rule was relaxed, the courts became willing to look at legislative history as indirect but not direct evidence of legislative purpose or meaning. The rationale underlying this distinction was explained by Lord Denning in *Letang v. Cooper*.[8] The issue there was whether section 2 of Britain's *Limitation Act, 1939*, applied to the plaintiff's action for trespass to the person. As amended in 1954, section 2 imposed a shortened three-year limitation period on actions in damages for personal injury caused by "negligence, nuisance or breach of duty." If this language extended to actions in trespass, the plaintiff was out of time. She argued that "breach of duty" meant breach of statutory duty, not trespass, and her interpretation was supported by a commission report preceding the 1954 amendment. In this report the commission had urged the adoption of a two-year period for personal injury cases subject to certain exceptions: "We wish, however, to make it clear that we do not include in that category actions for trespass to the person, false imprisonment, malicious prosecution or defamation of character, but we do include such actions as claims for negligence against doctors."[9] Because it addressed the very issue before the court, this statement was direct evidence of meaning. Yet the court refused to look at it. This outcome is explained by Lord Denning in the following passage:

> It is legitimate to look at the report of such a committee, so as to see what was the mischief at which the Act was directed. You can get the facts and surrounding circumstances from the report, so as to see the background against which the legislation was enacted.... But you cannot look at what the committee recommended ... for the simple

---

8   [1964] 2 All E.R. 929 (C.A.).
9   Quoted by Denning M.R., *ibid.* at 933.

reason that Parliament may, and often does, decide to do something different to cure the mischief.[10]

This reasoning has been adopted by Canadian courts in refusing to rely on direct evidence of the legislature's intended meaning.

c)   Constitutional Case Law

Judicial reluctance to look at direct evidence of legislative purpose was first relaxed in the context of constitutional challenges. When the validity of legislation is challenged, whether under the *Constitution Act, 1867*, or the *Charter*, legislative history is admissible both as indirect evidence of meaning or purpose and as direct evidence of purpose. The only restriction is that these materials must not be used as direct evidence of meaning and they must not be "inherently unreliable" or offend against public policy.[11] This exception was relied on by the Supreme Court of Canada in *Churchill Falls (Labrador) Corp. v. Newfoundland (Attorney General)*[12] The court there had to determine whether the main purpose of Newfoundland's legislation was to abolish the contractual rights of persons outside the province, something Newfoundland lacked the authority to do under its territorially limited grant of power. The court looked at speeches by government officials and members of the legislature, press interviews, correspondence, and information pamphlets produced by the government. McIntyre J. wrote:

> [S]uch evidence is *not* receivable as an aid to construction of the statute. However ... in constitutional cases, particularly where there are allegations of colourability, extrinsic evidence may be considered to ascertain not only the operation and effect of the impugned legislation but its true object and purpose as well.[13]

McIntyre J. relied in particular on an information pamphlet issued by the government:

> The purpose of this pamphlet, explained in the pamphlet itself, is to inform the financial community of the Government's reasons for enacting the *Reversion Act*. It was published by the Government less than one month before the *Reversion Act* was given Royal Assent, and actually includes a copy of the Act. It is my opinion that this pamph-

---

10   *Ibid.*
11   This language comes from *Reference Re Residential Tenancies Act of Ontario*, [1981] 1 S.C.R. 714 at 723.
12   [1984] 1 S.C.R. 297.
13   *Ibid.* at 318. [Emphasis in original.]

let comes within the categorization of materials which are "not inherently unreliable or offending against public policy" ... and are receivable as evidence of the intent and purpose of the Legislature of Newfoundland in enacting the *Reversion Act*.[14]

This pamphlet offered a direct description of the legislature's purpose and, since that purpose included the destruction of extraterritorial rights, the Act was declared unconstitutional.

d)   Current Position

In the *Rizzo Shoes* case,[15] which adopted Driedger's modern principle as the governing approach to statutory interpretation, the court concluded that employees laid off as a result of their employer's bankruptcy were entitled to benefits under sections 40 and 40(a) of Ontario's *Employment Standards Act* (ESA). This conclusion put a somewhat strained interpretation on the wording of the sections, but was well justified by a range of factors including comments made by the minister of labour when introducing the amendment that added section 40(a) to the Act. Iacobucci J. wrote:

> This interpretation is also consistent with statements made by the Minister of Labour at the time he introduced the 1981 amendments to the ESA....
>
> Although the frailties of Hansard evidence are many, this Court has recognized that it can play a limited role in the interpretation of legislation. Writing for the Court in *R. v. Morgentaler*, [1993] 3 S.C.R. 463, at p. 484, Sopinka J. stated:
>
> > until recently the courts have balked at admitting evidence of legislative debates and speeches.... The main criticism of such evidence has been that it cannot represent the "intent" of the legislature, an incorporeal body, but that is equally true of other forms of legislative history. Provided that the court remains mindful of the limited reliability and weight of Hansard evidence, it should be admitted as relevant to both the background and the purpose of legislation.[16]

The notion that legislative history is admissible to fill out the background and establish the purpose of legislation is frequently repeated by the Supreme Court of Canada. In *H.L. v. Canada (Attorney General)*,

---

14   *Ibid.* at 319.
15   *Rizzo & Rizzo Shoes Ltd. (Re)*, [1998] 1 S.C.R. 27.
16   *Ibid.* at para. 34.

for example, Fish J. wrote: "Though of limited weight, Hansard evidence can assist in determining the background and purpose of legislation."[17] Binnie J. made the same remark in *Re Canada 3000 Inc.*[18] A review of the case law suggests that in practice legislative history is most often used to establish purpose, whether directly or indirectly.[19] However, there are other, broader formulations of the rule that appear to reject any limitation on the use of legislative history other than reliability and relevance. In *Bristol-Myers Squibb Co. v. Canada (Attorney General)*, for example, Bastarache J. wrote:

> It has long been established that the usage of admissible extrinsic sources regarding a provision's legislative history and its context of enactment could be examined. I held in *Francis v. Baker...* that "[p]roper statutory interpretation principles therefore require that all evidence of legislative intent be considered, provided that it is relevant and reliable".[20] Consequently, *in order to confirm the purpose of the impugned regulation, the intended application of an amendment to the regulation or the meaning of the legislative language*, it is useful to examine the RIAS,[21] prepared as part of the regulatory process.[22] [Emphasis added.]

In fact, the RIAS was used by Bastarache J. for the limited purpose of establishing the purpose of the regulations the court was called on to interpret.

A more expansive use of legislative history is found in the judgments of Abella J. and Deschamps J. in *Hilewitz v. Canada (Minister of Citizenship and Immigration)*.[23] In that case, the Supreme Court of Canada was called on to interpret section 19(1)(a)(ii) of the *Immigration Act*, which denied admission to Canada to anyone belonging to a class of persons suffering from a disability such that their admission, in the opinion of a medical officer, "would cause or might reasonably be expected to cause excessive demands on health or social services."

---

17 [2005] 1 S.C.R. 401 at para. 106 [*H.L.*].
18 [2006] 1 S.C.R. 865 at para. 57.
19 See, for example, *Re Application under s. 83.28 of the Criminal Code*, [2004] 2 S.C.R. 248 at para. 37*ff*; *Canada Trustco Mortgage Co. v. Canada*, [2005] 2 S.C.R. 601 at paras. 15–16.
20 [1999] 3 S.C.R. 250 at para. 35.
21 Regulatory Impact Analysis Statement, prepared by a sponsoring department to justify proposed regulations and published in the *Canada Gazette*.
22 Above note 4 at para. 156. In this case, Bastarache J. wrote a dissenting judgment, but the dispute between the majority and dissent did not concern the proper use of legislative history materials.
23 [2005] 2 S.C.R. 706.

In forming their opinions under this provision, the department's medical officers considered the nature, severity, and duration of applicants' disabilities but disregarded their individual circumstances, such as the wealth of their family and their family's willingness to assume the burden of care. The issue was whether a given applicant's access to private financial support was a factor to be taken into account in assessing whether the applicant would or might cause excessive demands on Canadian services.

A majority of the court answered yes, the availability of private support in an individual case was indeed a relevant factor. Three of nine judges dissented. An interesting feature of both judgments is their reliance on legislative history, consisting of:

- a document submitted to the Standing Committee on Labour, Manpower and Immigration by the minister of labour, manpower, and immigration outlining the purpose and content of possible regulations under the Act; and
- the answer to a question put by a committee member to the deputy minister of labour, manpower, and immigration at a subsequent meeting of the same committee.

The document indicated that the purpose of the regulations would be to ensure that medical officers, in judging excessive demands on Canadian services, looked at all relevant factors and ignored irrelevant ones. It continued: "Such non-medical factors as the availability of private support ... can enter realistically into the assessment of risk, so that each decision will apply to the particular individual and not to a particular disease, disability or other medical condition."[24] The question put to the deputy minister was whether a disabled applicant who could prove that he or she would place no demands on Canadian services would be admitted. The DM responded: "If the family can provide assurances that the immigrant will not cause excessive demands on health or social serices, then the individual will be admitted as a landed immigrant."[25]

Speaking for the majority, Abella J. concluded that the legislative history reviewed above "indicates a legislative intention to shift from an approach based on categorical exclusion to one calling for individualized assessments" taking into account all relevant personal circumstances,

24   Canada, House of Commons, "Factors to be Considered by Medical Officers" in *Minutes of Proceedings and Evidence of the Standing Committee on Labour, Manpower and Immigration*, No. 11 (5 April 1977) at 11A:42–11A:43.
25   Canada, House of Commons, *Minutes of Proceedings and Evidence of the Standing Committee on Labour, Manpower and Immigration*, No. 42 (28 June 1977) at 42:76.

including the availability of private support.[26] Looking at the same material, Deschamps J. reached a very different conclusion. She wrote:

> Also instructive is the fact that Parliament considered whether family support was relevant to an "excessive demands" opinion and chose not to include it in either the *IA* [*Interpretation Act*] or the regulations. In a document entitled "Factors to be considered by medical officers" ... reference was made to the "availability of private support" as a factor that could be considered by medical officers. Excerpts from a discussion [between the Deputy Minister and a committee member] ... provide additional evidence that Parliament considered the impact of family support on the "excessive demands" assessment. In my view, the fact that Parliament expressly considered family support but chose not to include it in either the provision or the accompanying regulations strongly suggests that Parliament did not intend wealth to be a relevant factor.[27]

There are two things to notice about the majority opinion. First, it uses legislative history as direct evidence of the meaning of the provision in question. Second, it attaches considerable weight to the views of the sponsoring department as revealed in committee proceedings. Abella J. takes the subsequent enactment of the bill by Parliament to be an acceptance, in effect a confirmation of departmental intentions, implicitly acknowledging that in so far as "parliamentary intent" refers to real mental events, it refers to the intentions of government bureaucrats and ministers. The dissent is interesting in its identification of a House of Commons committee with Parliament as a whole. The rationale here, it appears, is that since the minutes of committee proceedings and its reports are carried out on behalf of one House or the other, and are available to all parliamentarians, it can fairly be assumed that Parliament enacts its legislation with this material in mind.

In conclusion, the exclusionary rule no longer governs the use of legislative history in Canada. Currently most courts seem willing to look at just about anything, provided the legislation is ambiguous and the legislative history is relevant and reliable.[28] Further, it seems they

---

26   Above note 23 at paras. 53 and 56.

27   *Ibid.* at para. 97. For other examples in which legislative history was relied on as evidence of a text's meaning, see *H.L.*, above note 17 at paras. 10, 82, 103*ff.*; *Schreiber*, above note 2 at para. 34*ff* and para. 47*ff*; *Therrien (Re)*, [2001] 2 S.C.R. 3 at para. 117.

28   To date, the Supreme Court of Canada has had little to say about reliability. The remarks of a responsible minister introducing a bill at second reading are considered reliable, and so apparently are submissions by ministers and deputy ministers to legislative committees. The court does not explain *why* these materials are reliable.

are willing to look at it for any useful purpose. In *Diamond Estate v. Robbins*, for example, the Newfoundland and Labrador Court of Appeal had to determine the reference of certain words in Newfoundland's *Limitations Act*. Mercer J.A. wrote:

> As observed by this Court in [several earlier judgments] …, the *Limitations Act* is based on the extensively researched work of the Newfoundland Law Reform Commission (Commission) and gives effect to substantially all of the recommendations of the Commission thereof. Accordingly it is appropriate to refer to the Commission's reports as evidence of context, legislative purpose and textual meaning.[29]

The one sure limit on the use of such materials is that they may not be relied on to contradict a legislative text whose meaning is clear.[30]

While the trend toward greater admissibility and reliance is clear, a number of questions have not been fully addressed by the Supreme Court of Canada. The most important is the issue of reliability, and how reliability is to be determined. This issue arose in an interesting way in *R. v. Lavigne*. The Court there had to decide whether a judge could take account of an offender's ability to pay when ordering him or her to pay a fine under section 462.37 of the *Criminal Code*. Deschamps J. wrote:

> Comments made during the debate on a bill must of course be treated with caution. Sometimes, they represent no more than the opinion of the person who made them, and that opinion was not necessarily determinative of how members voted. The final text is the one that is submitted for consideration by the courts, which attempt to give it meaning by applying the rules of interpretation. Statements made during a debate are therefore merely one interpretative tool among many others. The weakness of such evidence is illustrated by the fact that one witness who testified before the legislative committee considering the proceeds of crime bill expressed the opinion that it was not necessary to make certain requested amendments because the courts were armed with a broad discretion. He then said that in his opinion a court could take the offender's ability to pay into consideration.[31]

The court was here referring to the testimony before a legislative committee by a Senior General Counsel from the Department of Justice. In the court's

---

29 [2006] N.J. No. 3 at para. 62 (C.A.).

30 In *Contino v. Leonelli-Contino*, for example, the legislative history relied on by the appellant was dismissed as unhelpful because in the opinion of the court it was inconsistent with the statute: [2005] S.C.C. 63 at para. 36.

31 [2006] 1 S.C.R. 392 at para 41.

view, the opinion expressed by the witness was weak primarily because it was wrong. But without more, this is circular reasoning. The court could conclude the witness' opinion was wrong only by disregarding it in reaching its own opinion. What is required is a set of articulated principles that would enable courts to judge how much weight may legitimately attach to various forms of legislative history in various circumstances.

C. MODEL LEGISLATION

Courts sometimes find it helpful to compare the legislation they are interpreting with other legislation on which it appears to have been modelled. To the extent the legislation resembles the model, the meaning is assumed to be the same. Departures from the model are presumed to indicate an intention to express a different meaning.

Some model legislation is prepared by non-legislative bodies like the Uniform Law Conference of Canada or the various law reform commissions. In using this type of model, the court relies not only on the proposed draft legislation but also on the commentary accompanying the draft. Such commentary usually explains the thinking of the commissioners, what they were trying to achieve, and why they made the choices they did. This material is relied on for external context and purpose and often for the meaning of particular terms.

In *844903 Ontario Ltd. v. Vander Pluijm*,[32] for example, the New Brunswick Court of Queen's Bench had to interpret section 2 of New Brunswick's *Foreign Judgments Act*. This section provided that foreign judgments would be recognized "in the following cases only." The rest of the section listed all the circumstances in which foreign judgments were recognized at common law at the time of enactment. Subsequently the common law evolved to permit recognition in a new circumstance, where the foreign court making the judgment had a "real and substantial connection" to the dispute. The issue was whether this new common law test could be applied in New Brunswick. In concluding that it could not, Deschênes J. pointed out that New Brunswick's legislation was an adoption of the *Uniform Foreign Judgments Act* proposed by the Uniform Law Conference in 1933. As it happened, prior to approving its model Act, the conference debated the very point before the court and decided that the list of circumstances set out in the Act should be exhaustive and should preclude further common law development. In light of this, Deschênes J. concluded:

32   (1992), 130 N.B.R. (2d) 361 (Q.B.).

[A]ssuming that the intent of the legislator corresponds with what the Commissioners intended when they recommended the adoption of what is our s. 2 ... there is no question in my mind that s. 2 is an obstacle to the application in New Brunswick of the "real and substantial connection" test.[33]

By making this assumption, Deschênes J. relied on the extrinsic materials as direct evidence of legislative meaning.

D. LEGISLATIVE EVOLUTION

The legislative history of an enactment is its pre-enactment history. Legislative evolution, on the other hand, refers to the post-enactment history of an enactment. Specifically, it consists of each enacted formulation of the provision from the first one, through subsequent amendments and revisions, to the formulation in force when the relevant facts occurred. It is well established that the evolution of a provision may be looked at by courts to help determine its meaning or purpose, to resolve conflict among competing provisions, or to detect drafting errors. It is less well established whether a provision must be ambiguous before reliance may be placed on legislative evolution.

In *Merk v. International Association of Bridge, Structural, Ornamental and Reinforcing Iron Workers, Local 771*, Binnie J. stated that legislative evolution is part of Driedger's "entire context."[34] If this is so, then ambiguity is not a prerequisite. More importantly, perhaps, legislative evolution differs quite significantly from legislative history and the concerns motivating the exclusionary rule do not apply to legislative evolution. Legislative evolution consists of provisions that have been duly enacted and published to the public at large. Those who apply and interpret legislation are generally familiar in practice with its previous versions and members of the public are deemed to know the law. It is hard to see how such material could ever be considered inadmissible by a court.

1) Steps to Follow in Tracing Evolution

To trace the evolution of a provision from initial enactment to final repeal, these are the steps to follow.

---

33   *Ibid.* at 375–76.
34   [2005] 3 S.C.R. 425 at para. 28.

Step 1: Determine the purpose and meaning of the provision as originally enacted.

The original enactment may codify a common law rule, or it may introduce something new into the law. To determine the purpose and meaning of the original, the interpreter relies on the usual methods: textual, purposive, and consequential analysis, policy analysis, and the scrutiny of admissible extrinsic aids.

Step 2: Examine each subsequent change to the wording of the provision to determine whether it is substantive or formal.

Changes made to legislation in the course of a general statute revision are presumed to be purely formal; the wording of legislation may be different, but the substance of the law remains the same. Changes made to legislation by way of amendment may be either substantive or formal.[35] There is a weak presumption in favour of substantive amendment. However, in Canada purely formal amendment is not unusual. Formal amendments are made to correct drafting errors, to clarify doubtful provisions, or to improve drafting style.[36]

When the change is purely formal, the interpreter may look to the previous formulation of the provision for clarification of its meaning. Errors in the revision process are sometimes exposed in this way. And because legislation was formerly drafted in a more prolix style, the additional detail and precision of earlier formulations can sometimes shed light on the scope or denotation of a provision.

Step 3: If the change is substantive, determine the purpose and meaning of the new provision.

Generally it is helpful to identify the "evil" or concern that prompted the amendment—a change in economic climate or technology, the evolution of new social attitudes, or an unacceptable judicial decision perhaps. The legislative history of an amendment is often useful in suggesting its purpose or meaning. Because attention is focused on a few provisions to be changed rather than on the Act as a whole, the relevant materials (Hansard, RIAS, backround papers) are likely to offer precise descriptions of purpose, or address concrete interpretive concerns.

Step 4: Draw relevant inferences from the pattern of formal and substantive change.

If the changes have all been formal, the interpreter must conclude that the purpose and meaning of the legislation have not changed since

---

35   For discussion of purely formal changes to legislation, see Chapter 1, Section D(5) on re-enactment and Section D(9) on statute revision.

36   See Chapter 1, Section D(6).

initial enactment. If the changes have been substantive, the interpreter must try to discover the reasons for the change. It is sometimes possible to detect trends or patterns in successive amendments. For example, an interpreter may note a recurring concern or a persistent movement away from a particular policy. Or there may be a correlation between a shift in policy and a particular external event. Once documented, such patterns and correlations can be strong evidence of legislative intent.

It is not always necessary to trace the evolution of a provision back to its origins. What the interpreter requires is a starting point, a version of the provision that is clear in meaning and in purpose. The interpreter can then work forward, identifying the formal changes and explaining the substantive ones.

2) Example of Formal Change

In *R. v. Skoke-Graham*,[37] the Supreme Court of Canada was concerned with the scope of a *Criminal Code* provision that made it an offence to wilfully do "anything that disturbs the order or solemnity" of a religious assembly. In a concurring judgment, Wilson J. pointed out that the ordinary meaning of "anything" was all-encompassing and potentially made the section too inclusive. A basis had to be found for confining it to conduct that Parliament might plausibly have intended to criminalize. For this purpose Wilson J. looked to its legislative evolution. When first introduced in 1869, the provision read:

> 37. Whosoever wilfully disturbs ... any assemblage of persons met for religious worship ... *by profane discourse, by rude, or indecent behaviour, or by making a noise,* either within the place of such meeting or so near it as to disturb the order or solemnity of the meeting [is guilty of an offence]. [Emphasis added.]

This language became part of the *Criminal Code* in 1892 and continued unamended until 1954. At that time, the wording was changed so that the provision henceforth read:

> 161.(3) Every one who, at or near a meeting ... [for religious worship] wilfully *does anything* that disturbs the order or solemnity of the meeting is guilty of an offence. [Emphasis added.]

The Crown argued that this change in wording signalled Parliament's intention to enlarge the scope of the section so as to capture any sort of conduct capable of disturbing a meeting. However, this change in wording

---

37   [1985] 1 S.C.R. 106.

was part of a major revision of the *Criminal Code* carried out in 1953–54,[38] and in the view of Wilson J. the change was purely formal. She wrote:

> It seems to me that all Parliament intended to do in enacting s. 161(3) of the 1953–54 *Code* was to use general rather than specific words to cover the types of things which were considered capable of disturbing the order or solemnity of a meeting. I do not believe they were seeking to expand the scope of the provision to cover peaceful acts of defiance of religious authority.... I believe, therefore, that the word "anything" must be read down so as to extend only to things in the nature of profane discourse, rude or indecent behaviour or making a noise.[39]

Here, the scope of the criminalized conduct was clear in the original provision, but had become obscured with subsequent change. By identifying that subsequent change as formal only, a re-enactment in a more modern drafting style rather than a substantive amendment, Wilson J. was able to clarify the meaning of the provision.

3) Example of Substantive Change

In *Crupi v. Canada (Employment & Immigration Commission)*,[40] the Federal Court of Appeal had to determine whether a psychiatric hospital that had a maximum security section and that was part of a penitentiary complex was a "prison, penitentiary or other similar institution" within the meaning of section 45 of the *Unemployment Insurance Act*. Prior to amendment, the provision read:

> 45. A claimant is not entitled to receive benefit while he is an inmate of any prison or penitentiary or an institution supported wholly or partly out of public funds or, while he is resident, whether temporarily or permanently, out of Canada, except as may otherwise be provided by the regulations.

After amendment in 1976 it read:

> 45. Except under s. 31, a claimant is not entitled to receive benefit for any period during which
> (a) he is an inmate of any prison or similar institution; or
> (b) he is not in Canada,
>
> except as may otherwise be prescribed.

---

38 The 1953–54 *Code* was primarily a revision but included amendments as well.
39 *Ibid.* at 130–31.
40 [1986] 3 F.C. 3 (C.A.).

Heald J. wrote:

> In determining the proper construction to be given the words "an inmate of any prison or similar institution", as used in section 45, I find it instructive to compare the present section 45 with the previous section....
>
> Clearly the former section 45 had much wider parameters than the present section 45. It seems certain that if the case at bar were being adjudicated under the previous section 45, the applicant would have been disqualified since it can be assumed, in my view, that the Penetanguishene Mental Health Centre is supported by public funds. ... [B]y this amendment, hospitals and other publicly funded institutions have been removed from the reach of section 45 which is now restricted to prisons and institutions similar to prisons. The change in the language used in section 45 is clearly purposive and must be presumed to have some significance.[41]

Heald J. went on to identify the purpose, which was to make "a clear distinction between inmates of penal institutions on the one hand, and, individuals suffering from illness, on the other hand."[42] Although both inmates and ill persons fail to meet the requirement of being available for work, there were sound policy reasons for treating them differently: hence the 1976 amendment.[43]

4) Combining Legislative Evolution and Legislative History

The courts sometimes rely on legislative history in tracing the evolution of legislation, a technique that often proves highly instructive. In the *Hilewitz* case,[44] for example, as mentioned above, the issue was whether the availability of private financial support was relevant in assessing whether a person with a disability, if allowed to immigrate to Canada, "would cause or might reasonably be expected to cause excessive demands on health or social services" within the meaning of subsection 19(1)(a)(ii) of the *Immigration Act*. Abella J. traced the evolution of this provision from legislation first enacted in 1869, through the *Immigra-*

---

41   *Ibid.* at 10.
42   *Ibid.* at 13.
43   For an example of legislative evolution that reveals a trend in legislative thinking, see *Zeitel v. Ellscheid*, [1994] 2 S.C.R. 142, discussed in Chapter 10, Section C(4).
44   Above note 22.

tion Acts of 1886, 1906, 1910, 1927, 1952, 1976, and 1985.[45] She noted that the initial legislation was designed to attract immigrants, and applicants with disabilities were welcomed if they were not likely to become a permanent public charge. In 1906, only applicants with mental disabilities were required to meet this standard. In 1910, however, the trend shifted. Parliament adopted a "prohibited class approach" and persons with mental disabilities were excluded regardless of their circumstances, while those with physical disabilities could be admitted only with evidence of earning capacity or family support. In 1927, this prohibited class was redefined to include persons with any type of disability affecting their ability to earn a living.

In the 1960s, however, the tide turned once again. At this point in recounting the evolution of the legislation, Abella J. turned to legislative history, relying on a *White Paper on Immigration* released by the minister of manpower and immigration in 1966. She wrote:

> [T]he 1966 *White Paper on Immigration* … emphasized that it was "neither practical nor realistic" to block all those who fell within a prohibited class of the *Immigration Act*, since many posed no real risk to the country (p.24).… It recommended a return to the original policy of permitting entry to persons with mental or physical disabilities if they had family assistance.
>
> In line with the views expressed in the 1966 White Paper, Parliament enacted the *Immigration Act*, 1976, S.C. 1976, c. 52. In it, an "excessive demands" standard replaced the wholesale rejection of "prohibited classes" for those who were mentally and physically disabled. Section 19(1) in the 1985 Act under which these appeals were argued is identical to the "excessive demands" provision in the 1976 legislation.[46]

Here the legislative history makes it clear that the 1976 amendment was designed to change the law in a significant way, not re-enact it or make a modest incremental change.

E. INTERNATIONAL AGREEMENTS

There are two ways in which an international agreement can be given the force of domestic law: through the enactment of implementing legislation or through incorporation by reference.

---

45   *Ibid.* at para. 41*ff.*
46   *Ibid.* at paras. 49–50.

1) Implementing Legislation

The purpose of implementing legislation is to carry out, more or less fully and more or less exactly, Canada's part under an international agreement. Sometimes the legislation closely mirrors the agreement; at other times there may be significant differences between the two. Since domestic law is paramount over international law, in the event of a conflict between Canadian legislation and the terms of an international agreement, the Canadian legislation prevails.

Even though Canadian legislatures are not bound by international law, there is a presumption that the legislature intends to comply with Canada's international law obligations. Thus, in interpreting implementing legislation it is normal for courts to look at and, where appropriate, rely on the underlying international agreement. The agreement may be relied on both to suggest the purpose of the legislation and to clarify the meaning of particular terms. It is not necessary that the legislation expressly refer to the agreement.

In *Canada (Attorney General) v. Ward*,[47] for example, the Supreme Court of Canada relied on the 1951 *International Convention Relating to the Status of Refugees* to interpret the definition of "Convention refugee" in section 2 of Canada's *Immigration Act*. According to this definition, a "Convention refugee" is a person who is "outside the country of his nationality" and unable or unwilling to return to that country. The issue for the court was how to apply this definition to a person with dual citizenship. Although the *Immigration Act* was silent on this point, the Convention addressed the point expressly. It provided that "in the case of a person who has more than one nationality, the term 'the country of his nationality' shall mean each of the countries of which he is a national." In adopting this interpretation, La Forest J. wrote:

> Although never incorporated into the *Immigration Act* and thus not strictly binding, … the 1951 Convention infuses suitable content into the meaning of "Convention refugee" …. The fact that this Convention provision was not specifically copied into the Act does not render it irrelevant.[48]

La Forest J. also studied the preamble to the *Convention* to reveal its purpose, which was in turn relied on to help establish the scope of the statutory definition.

---

47   [1993] 2 S.C.R. 689 [*Ward*]. See also *National Corn Growers Association v. Canada (Import Tribunal)*, [1990] 2 S.C.R. 1324.

48   *Ward, ibid.* at 751–52.

2) Incorporation by Reference

The other technique used to give effect to international agreements is incorporation by reference. In this technique, legislation is drafted that simply refers to the international agreement, in whole or in part, and declares that it is enacted into law. The text of the incorporated agreement is usually set out in a schedule to the legislation.

To interpret international agreements that have been incorporated into Canadian law, the courts apply international law principles.[49] The first principle governing the interpretation of treaties and other conventions is to give effect to the purpose. As the Ontario Court of Appeal explained in *R. v. Palacios*:

> The basic rule of international law governing the interpretation of treaties is stated by O'Connell, *International Law* ... as follows: "The primary end of treaty implementation is to give effect to the intentions of the parties, and not frustrate them." This is sometimes called the effectiveness principle which requires courts to read a treaty as a whole to ascertain its purpose and intent and to give effect thereto rather than to rely on literal interpretation.[50]

International interpretation law used to differ from domestic law in its emphasis on purpose and in permitting freer access to and greater reliance on extrinsic materials, especially *travaux préparatoires*. However, these differences have all but disappeared.

In *Crown Forest Industries Ltd. v. Canada*,[51] for example, the Supreme Court of Canada had to determine the meaning of "resident of a Contracting State" in Article IV of the *Convention between Canada and the United States of America with respect to Taxes on Income and on Capital*, enacted into law in Canada by the *Canada–United States Tax Convention Act, 1984*. Iacobucci J. adopted a somewhat strained interpretation, restricting the application of "resident of a state" to residents who paid tax in the state on their worldwide income. This outcome was justified because it was consistent with the purpose of the convention and with the extrinsic materials consulted by the court, including the OECD *Model Double Taxation Convention on Income and on Capital*, the

---

49   These principles, which are part of customary international law, are partially codified in Articles 31 and 32 of the *Vienna Convention on the Law of Treaties*, 23 May 1969, 63 A.J.I.L. 875 (1969).

50   (1984), 45 O.R. (2d) 269 at 277–78 (C.A.), Blair J.A., quoting D.P. O'Connell, *International Law*, vol. 1, 2d ed. (London: Stevens, 1970) at 251.

51   [1995] 2 S.C.R. 802.

Official Commentaries to the Model Convention, as well as debate in the American Senate on the U.S. implementing legislation.

F. AUTHORITATIVE OPINION

1) Judicial Interpretation

In interpreting legislation, the courts sometimes rely on case law as part of the legal context.[52] Cases are also relied on as precedents establishing the meaning of particular texts. Because legislative meaning is always established in relation to particular facts, the force of a precedent can often be avoided through distinctions based on fact. However, the rule of law requires that courts maintain a degree of consistency in their reading of legislation. When an interpretation issue has been authoritatively resolved, subsequent courts will be slow to depart from the established understanding.

In *R. v. McIntosh*,[53] for example, the Ontario Court of Appeal was asked to adopt a new and arguably a more plausible interpretation of section 34 of the *Criminal Code* governing the defence of self-defence. Austin J.A. wrote:

> The main issue is whether the words "without having provoked the assault" should be read into s. 34(2). This court has already decided in *Stubbs* that they should not. That conclusion was followed in *Nelson*. No binding authority or persuasive reason has been suggested why those cases should not now be followed. I therefore conclude that the words "without having provoked the assault" are not to be implied or read into s. 34(2).[54]

Case law dealing with the very words to be interpreted but used in a different context may also be relied on by courts as persuasive authority. The persuasive value of these cases depends on how closely related the contexts are, linguistically and legally. The words may appear in a different provision in the same Act, or a different Act, or an Act of a different jurisdiction. In *Flieger v. New Brunswick*,[55] for example, the Supreme Court of Canada had to interpret the phrase "discontinuance of a function" in New Brunswick's *Civil Service Act*. Cory J. wrote:

---

52   This use of case law is examined in Chapter 8.
53   (1993), 15 O.R. (3d) 450 (C.A.), aff'd [1995] 1 S.C.R. 686.
54   *Ibid.* at 461 (C.A.).
55   [1993] 2 S.C.R. 651.

Neither the New Brunswick *Civil Service Act* nor its regulations define this term. As a result it may be helpful to see if any satisfactory definition of this term has evolved in the case law. The same phrase "discontinuance of a function" appears in the [federal] *Public Service Employment Act* ... and the *Canada Labour Code* ... and the courts have considered the meaning of the phrase as it is used in those Acts.[56]

The court examined this case law and devised a definition of the phrase in the New Brunswick Act based on a synthesis of judicial interpretations of this phrase in the federal Acts.

2) Interpretation by Tribunals

Although tribunals like labour relations boards or human rights adjudicators occupy a low rank in the judicial hierarchy and their decisions are not binding, these decisions are sometimes given significant weight. It is well established that inferior tribunals have no special expertise on issues of statutory interpretation. Their decisions may nonetheless derive authority from the force of their analysis or from widespread acceptance of their reasoning. In *Janzen v. Platy Enterprises Ltd.*,[57] for example, the Supreme Court of Canada relied on the reasoning of an adjudicator under Ontario's *Human Rights Code* to decide whether sexual harassment was sex discrimination within the meaning of Manitoba's *Human Rights Act*. Dickson C.J. wrote:

> In ... [the Ontario decision], in the course of determining whether sexual harassment was included in the concept of sex discrimination in s. 4 of the Ontario *Human Rights Code*, Adjudicator Shime, in *obiter*, made the following oft-quoted remarks.
>
> ...
>
> Adjudicator Shime's view that certain forms of sexual harassment fall within the statutory prohibition on sex discrimination has been adopted by human rights adjudication boards and tribunals across the country.[58]

3) Administrative Interpretation

While the primary interpreters in the legal system are judges, they are only a small minority of the persons—fishery officers, building in-

---

56   *Ibid.* at 659.
57   [1989] 1 S.C.R. 1252.
58   *Ibid.* at 1276–78.

spectors, customs officials, police and parole officers, and government bureaucrats of all descriptions—who interpret legislation as part of their job. Officials who administer legislation are often well placed to interpret it. They may develop extensive knowledge of the matters dealt with in the legislation. They usually have a clear grasp of its purpose and scheme, and they see how it operates in practice on a day-to-day basis. Because of their familiarity with this context, they can readily imagine the consequences of possible interpretations.

On the other hand, most administrative officials are not trained in the law or in legal interpretation. Their interpretations may be inappropriately influenced by departmental or agency interests or by their professional culture. Another drawback to administrative interpretation is that it is often private and inaccessible. While some administrative agencies issue official interpretation documents addressed to the public at large, most administrative interpretation is set out in internal memoranda or individual case files. Much of it is never systematically recorded. Judicial reluctance to rely on administrative interpretation is due in part at least to its lack of accessibility.

The basic rule governing judicial use of administrative materials was stated by Dickson J. in *R. v. Nowegijick*: "Administrative policy and interpretation are not determinative but are entitled to weight and can be an 'important factor' in case of doubt about the meaning of legislation."[59] In other words, these materials are admissible to resolve interpretative doubt, but their weight is dependent on the circumstances. Most of the cases in which administrative interpretation has been relied on have involved interpretation bulletins published by the Department of Revenue and widely circulated among taxpayers. A taxpayer who relies in good faith on the department's understanding of a provision and arranges his or her affairs accordingly often receives a sympathetic reception from the court. However, as LeBel J. points out in *Imperial Oil Ltd. v. Canada*, "If an [administrative] interpretation is wrong, it does not make law. Estoppel by interpretation has not yet become a recognized doctrine of statutory construction."[60]

4) Scholarly Interpretation

The opinion of legal scholars has become a significant aid to interpretation not only in *Charter* cases but also in ordinary cases. The courts

---

59   [1983] 1 S.C.R. 29 at 37.
60   [2006] 2 S.C.R. 447 at para. 59. See also *Placer Dome Canada Ltd. v. Ontario (Minister of Finance)*, [2006] 1 S.C.R. 715 at para. 39*ff*.

look to textbooks, monographs, reports and studies, and law review articles. These materials may form part of the legislative history of an enactment, but more often they are brought in as part of counsel's argument or the judge's private research in dealing with a case.

Scholarly material may explore the purpose of an enactment, or analyze its scheme, or examine the case law interpreting a particular provision, or suggest relevant policy concerns. It may also propose solutions to particular interpretation issues. The courts make whatever use of this material seems appropriate. In *Guerin v. Canada*,[61] the Supreme Court of Canada adopted Professor Weinrib's test for determining when a fiduciary duty is owed. In a number of cases, it has relied on articles by feminist legal scholars to help them understand the impact of rape and rape trials on women.[62] In *Central Alberta Dairy Pool v. Alberta (Human Rights Commission)*,[63] it relied on scholarly criticism of its own interpretation in a previous case to justify adopting a new approach. The weight accorded to such scholarly opinion depends to some extent perhaps on the reputation of the scholar, but the key consideration is the apparent quality of the research and the persuasive force of the argument.

---

61   [1984] 2 S.C.R. 335.
62   See, for example, *R. v. McCraw*, [1991] 3 S.C.R. 72.
63   [1990] 2 S.C.R. 489 at 516.

OVERLAP AND CONFLICT

Because of the pervasiveness of law in modern life, it is normal for a single event or set of facts to be governed by more than one legislative provision or by both legislation and the common law. Such overlaps are governed by complex rules, derived partly from constitutional law principles such as the sovereignty of Parliament and partly from common law presumptions about drafting and legislative intent.

A. OVERLAP WITH OTHER LEGISLATION

When two (or more) legislative provisions apply to the same facts, there are four possibilities:

1) The overlapping provisions do not conflict, and since both apply, the court gives effect to both.
2) The overlapping provisions might conflict, but the conflict is avoided through legislative fiat or judicial interpretation.
3) The overlapping provisions do not conflict, but the court concludes that one of the provisions was meant to be exhaustive and therefore applies to the exclusion of the other.
4) The overlapping provisions conflict and, in order to resolve the conflict, the court applies a paramountcy rule.

1) Overlap without Conflict

The courts rarely comment on harmonious overlap among provisions because normally it is not a problem. The overlapping provisions are simply applied in accordance with their terms. For example, the use of rented premises for operating a daycare centre might simultaneously be subject to provisions in the *Landlord and Tenants Act*, the *Occupier's Liability Act*, the *Professional Child Care Act*, various municipal by-laws, and more. Although these provisions would impose disparate and overlapping obligations on the operator, this in itself would not amount to conflict. The courts have repeatedly held that provisions do not conflict simply because they deal differently with the same facts. A conflict arises only if it would be impossible, contradictory, or contrary to legislative intent to apply them all together. In the absence of conflict, the presumption is that they all apply.

This presumption is illustrated in the judgment of the Federal Court of Appeal in *Canada (Attorney General) v. Michael*.[1] The court was asked to review a ruling by the Unemployment Insurance Commission concerning a claim for benefit under the *Unemployment Insurance Act*. The commission found that the claimant had frivolously rejected two job offers. This meant, under section 14 of the Act, that she lost her entitlement to benefits for the relevant period and, under section 27(1), that she was subject to a six-week disqualification for each refusal. The claimant argued that these provisions were mutually exclusive and that the commission erred in applying both. The court upheld the commission. It affirmed that where the facts of a case come within two or more provisions, and the provisions do not conflict, the presumption is that they all apply. There is nothing problematic, inappropriate, or even unusual in attaching more than one legal consequence to a fact or a set of facts. While the presumption may be rebutted, usually by evidence that one of the overlapping provisions was meant to be exhaustive, there was nothing in the scheme or wording of the legislation or its underlying policies to rebut the presumption here.

2) Conflict Avoidance

a) Legislative Fiat
In the complete statute book of a jurisdiction, whether federal, provincial, or municipal, there is inevitably a significant potential for conflict between provisions. Part of the job of a legislative drafter, when draft-

---

1   (1994), 175 N.R. 325 (Fed. C.A.).

ing new legislation, is to search out such conflicts and seek instruction on how to deal with them—by repeal perhaps or by designating one of them to be paramount. The latter is conventionally rendered by introducing the paramount provision with words like "notwithstanding (or despite) section xx" or introducing the subordinate provision with words like "subject to section yy." Sometimes general notwithstanding clauses are included that make certain provisions or an entire Act paramount over anything else that might conflict with it.[2]

b) Judicial Interpretation

To minimize the incidence of conflict among overlapping provisions, the courts have developed two strategies. The first is to work with a narrow definition of conflict: overlapping provisions do not conflict unless they contradict each other or both cannot be applied to the same set of facts, at least not without defeating the purpose of one of them. The second is a rule of interpretation. It is presumed that the legislature intends to produce coherent, internally consistent legislation; therefore, an interpretation that avoids conflict is preferred over one that does not. To achieve harmony, the scope of one or both overlapping provisions may be narrowed to make room for the other.

The first of these strategies was used by the Supreme Court of Canada in *Friends of the Oldman River Society v. Canada (Minister of Transport)*.[3] The issue in this case was whether the minister of transport was required by regulations made under the *Department of the Environment Act* to conduct an environmental assessment before approving plans to build a dam across the Oldman River. Section 5 of the *Navigable Waters Protection Act* provided that no dam could be built across a navigable river unless the plans were approved by the minister "on such terms and conditions as the Minister deems fit." Section 3 of the *Environmental Assessment and Review Process Guidelines Order* provided that a minister must carry out an environmental assessment before granting any approval that might have an environmental impact on an area of federal responsibility. Counsel argued that because the *Guidelines Order* narrowed the scope of the discretion conferred on the minister by the *Navigable Waters Protection Act* and because it significantly altered the mix of considerations on which the minister might lawfully base his decision, the order was in conflict with the Act. This argument did

---

2   It may not be safe to rely on a general clause of this sort. Sometimes the provisions in conflict are *both* covered by a general notwithstanding clause, in which case the problem of paramountcy must be resolved through interpretation.

3   [1992] 1 S.C.R. 3 [*Friends of the Oldman River*].

not succeed. La Forest J. first drew attention to the stringent test for conflict and the presumption of internal harmony:

> [A]s a matter of construction a court will, where possible, prefer an interpretation that permits reconciliation of the two [conflicting provisions]. "Inconsistency" in this context refers to a situation where two legislative enactments cannot stand together.[4]

To avoid potential conflict, the Court may adopt a strained or even an implausible interpretation. But no such strategy was necessary in this case. As La Forest J. explained:

> It is likely that the Minister of Transport in exercising his functions under s. 5 always did take into account the environmental impact of a work.... However that may be, the *Guidelines Order* now formally mandates him to do so, and I see nothing in this that is inconsistent with his duties under s. 5. As Stone J.A. put it in the Court of Appeal, it created a duty which is "superadded" to any other statutory power residing in him which can stand with that power. In my view the Minister's duty under the *Guidelines Order* is indeed supplemental to his responsibility under the *Navigable Waters Protection Act*, and he cannot resort to an excessively narrow interpretation of his existing statutory powers to avoid compliance with the *Guidelines Order.*[5]

The Court further supported this interpretation with purposive analysis. The legislature must have intended that the order would narrow and control the discretion conferred on decision makers under other legislation; otherwise, the protectionist goals of the *Department of the Environment Act* would be defeated. To avoid defeating the purpose, the broader interpretation, consistent with the ordinary meaning, was preferred.

The second strategy is well illustrated by the majority judgment of the Supreme Court of Canada in *Charlebois v. Saint John (City).*[6] The issue in that case was whether the term "institution" in New Brunswick's *Official Languages Act* applied to municipalities. "Institution" was defined in section 2 and on its face this definition was certainly broad enough to include municipalities. However, adopting that interpretation gave rise to certain anomalies. As Charron J. points out, if the obligations imposed on institutions under various provisions of the

---

4   *Ibid.* at 38. For an excellent, comprehensive account of the evolving concept of conflict in the context of federal paramountcy, see *Rothmans, Benson & Hedges Inc. v. Saskatchewan*, [2003] S.J. No. 606 at para. 54*ff* (C.A.).

5   *Friends of the Oldman River, ibid.* at 39–40.

6   [2005] 3 S.C.R. 563.

Act (sections 27–30) extended to municipalities, then a number of the provisions set out under the heading "Municipalities" (sections 35–38) would make no sense. She wrote:

> If all municipalities, as institutions, are obliged to print and publish their by-laws in both official languages under s. 29, why would it matter what percentage was represented by the official language minority population in any given municipality? Likewise, what would be the sense of prescribing by regulation those services and communications required to be offered in both official languages if all municipalities, as institutions, were required under ss. 27 to 30 to provide them all? What is left for a municipality to declare itself bound under s. 37 if it is already bound by the general obligations imposed on institutions? Those are the "incoherent and illogical consequences" that Daigle J.A. [in the court below] found determinative in the search for the Legislature's intent. I agree, particularly because, if the opposite interpretation is adopted and "institution" is read as not including municipalities, the internal coherence is restored.[7]

Even though *Official Languages Acts* are quasi-constitutional legislation and therefore attract a broad, goal-promoting interpretation, the presumption of coherence in these circumstances justified the majority preference for the more restrictive interpretation.

3) One of the Provisions Is Meant to Be Exhaustive

The legislature sometimes enacts a provision, a series of provisions or a statute that is meant to be an exhaustive regulation of a matter. Once it is established that given legislation is meant to be exhaustive, it is applied to the exclusion of any other provisions that would otherwise apply. The absence of conflict between the exhaustive provision and other provisions is irrelevant; what matters here is the intention of the legislature. Legislation that is meant to provide an exhaustive exposition of the law on a matter is often labelled a code.

In considering whether legislation is meant to be exhaustive, the courts rely on the full range of interpretive rules and techniques. However, their analysis tends to focus on three things. The first is whether the legislation is sufficiently complete and comprehensive to stand alone. Legislation that establishes a complete scheme or expressly addresses all aspects of a matter is readily found to be exhaustive; legislation that is vague or that leaves regulatory gaps is not. A second, related

---

7   *Ibid.* at para. 19.

consideration is whether the particular policy or goal that the legislation is meant to attain might be undermined by the application of other provisions. To avoid defeating the purpose, a court may conclude that the legislation was meant to be exhaustive.

A third consideration is whether the legislation would do any useful work if it were not treated as exhaustive. Suppose a provision in the *Fisheries Act* empowered the minister of fisheries to issue licences to fish on whatever terms she thinks fit; suppose another provision empowered the minister to grant two-week licences to fish for cod. Most courts would conclude that the second provision was exhaustive of the minister's power to license cod fishing. This conclusion does not follow from the fact that the provision is more specific, but rather from the fact that it would have no point if it were not considered exhaustive. Under the general licensing power conferred by the first provision, the minister may grant licences to fish for cod for two-week terms or for any other term that seems appropriate. The second provision thus adds nothing to the first and does no work at all, contrary to the presumption against tautology, unless it is interpreted to be exhaustive of the minister's powers to confer cod-fishing licences.

The reasoning used to determine whether legislation is meant to be exhaustive is well illustrated by the British Columbia Court of Appeal in *British Columbia Teachers' Federation v. British Columbia (Attorney-General)*.[8] Under British Columbia's *Financial Administration Act*, the Treasury Board was empowered by section 4 to issue directives respecting government expenditures and by section 24 to set limits or fix conditions for any kind of government expenditure. Acting pursuant to these sections, the Treasury Board issued a directive that cut back government funding to any local school board that voted to lay some teachers off while increasing the salaries of those who remained. Despite the broad wording of sections 4 and 24, the court concluded that the directive was beyond the Treasury Board's powers. In its opinion, Part 7 of British Columbia's *School Act* set out an exhaustive code dealing with the hiring, firing, and remuneration of teachers. Since the provisions in the *School Act* were meant to be exhaustive, sections 4 and 24 of the *Financial Administration Act* had to be "read down" to exclude applications to the matters dealt with in Part 7.

---

8   (1985), 23 D.L.R. (4th) 161 (B.C.C.A.). For other examples of legislation that was held to be exhaustive and therefore precluded the application of other provisions that might otherwise apply, see *G.(C.) v. Catholic Children's Aid Society of Hamilton-Wentworth* (1998), 40 O.R. (3d) 334 (C.A.); *Carpenter v. Vancouver (City) Police Board* (1985), 63 B.C.L.R. 310 (C.A.).

In reaching this conclusion the court emphasized the elaborate and detailed regulatory scheme found in Part 7 of the *School Act*. This scheme covered every aspect of teacher employment, including hiring, firing, and suspensions. It provided a detailed process for negotiating salaries, which was meant to be comprehensive and self-contained. Furthermore, the purpose of the scheme was to ensure that the matters covered by Part 7 were dealt with not centrally but at the local level. This policy would be undermined if Treasury Board could exercise its powers under the *Financial Administration Act* to influence layoffs and teachers' salaries. In the view of the court, the legislature would not have gone to the trouble of establishing a comprehensive regulatory scheme designed to implement a specific policy unless it intended its scheme to occupy the field and to displace other ways of dealing with the same matter.

The court also noted that certain sections of the *School Act* and other BC enactments expressly conferred powers on the executive branch of government to encroach on the powers of local school boards and to influence or second-guess their decisions. Based on its examination of these provisions, the court concluded that when the BC legislature wanted to create an exception to the policy of having teachers' employment issues dealt with locally under Part 7, it drafted a special provision setting out in explicit and precise language the conditions and scope of the exception. These provisions would serve no purpose unless Part 7 was meant to be exhaustive. The court therefore concluded that unless the Treasury Board directive came within one of these specific exceptions, it was beyond the power of the Board.

4) Conflict Resolution

As mentioned above, when two provisions are in conflict, the legislature sometimes provides an express solution.[9] Or it may be apparent from the scheme and purpose of the legislation that one provision was intended to have priority over the other. In the absence of an express or implicit legislative solution, the conflict must be dealt with under common law paramountcy rules. These are essentially ranking rules. They assign a relative status to each of the provisions in conflict, with the higher ranked or paramount provision prevailing over the lower ranked or subordinate one. The paramount provision is applied in accordance with its terms, while the subordinate provision is rendered inoperative to the extent it is in conflict with the paramount law. When legislation is rendered inoperative, it remains a valid part of the law, but in so far as

---

9   See Section A(2), above in this chapter.

it is inoperative it cannot be applied. It remains in this suspended state until the conflict disappears, usually through repeal or amendment of one or both of the conflicting laws. There are five paramountcy rules.

a)   Federal Legislation

There is considerable overlap in the division of powers between Parliament and the provincial legislatures under sections 91 and 92 of the *Constitution Act, 1867*. As a result, some matters may validly be dealt with at both the federal and the provincial levels. This overlap creates the possibility of conflict and the need for a paramountcy rule. In the event of conflict, legislation enacted by Parliament or under the authority of Parliament is paramount over provincial law. The federal law is paramount even if the provincial law was enacted to protect human rights, or was subsequently enacted, or is more specific. In other words, the rule of federal paramountcy is applied first and outranks other paramountcy rules.

b)   Human Rights Legislation

Federal and provincial human rights Acts do not form part of the entrenched constitution, but because they express fundamental political values they are considered constitutional or "quasi-constitutional" law. As such, they warrant special treatment. Under the liberal construction doctrine, human rights legislation is interpreted broadly and purposefully.[10] It also benefits from a flexible application of the original meaning rule.[11] And finally, in the event of a conflict between human rights legislation and other legislation, the human rights legislation is paramount. It prevails even if the other legislation was subsequently enacted or is more specific.[12]

c)   Implied Exception (*Specialia Generalibus Non Derogant*)

This paramountcy rule is generally stated in the form of the Latin maxim *specialia generalibus non derogant*—the general does not derogate from the specific. In the event of a conflict between a specific provision dealing with a particular matter and a more general provision dealing not only with that matter but with others as well, the specific provision prevails. It prevails even if the general legislation was subsequently en-

---

10   This application of the liberal construction doctrine is discussed in Chapter 12, Section B.

11   This exception to the original meaning rule is less well established. However, given the general language in which such Acts are typically drafted, the are likely. to attract a dynamic interpretation in any case. See Chapter 6, Section D(3).

12   *Insurance Corp. of British Columbia v. Heerspink*, [1982] 2 S.C.R. 145 at 154.

acted. The specific provision is treated as an exception to the rule embodied in the more general provision.

d) Implied Repeal

Since a legislature cannot bind its successors, in the event of a conflict between two provisions, the more recent expression of the legislature's will prevails over the earlier one. Implied repeal is sometimes considered a method of actual repeal rather than a rule of paramountcy. It is certainly possible to analyze it this way: by enacting a provision that is inconsistent with existing legislation, a legislature impliedly expresses an intention to repeal the existing law and replace it with something else.

In the United Kingdom, where Parliament does not produce general statute revisions and legislation sometimes remained on the books for centuries, this way of analyzing implied repeal makes sense. In Canada, however, we have a well-established convention of explicit formal repeal. When a legislature wants to introduce new law, it actively reviews the existing statute book and prepares an express repeal of each provision that is judged to be inconsistent with the new law. If anything is overlooked by the legislature at this point, it is likely to be noticed and corrected in the next statute revision. Given these practices, it is better to treat implied repeal as a rule of paramountcy rather than a method of repeal. On this approach, a subsequently enacted provision renders a previously enacted provision inoperative to the extent of any conflict. However, the inoperative provision remains valid law and will become applicable again if for any reason the conflict disappears.

e) Delegated Legislation

Statutes are considered paramount over delegated legislation because legislatures are sovereign law makers, whereas the persons or bodies that exercise delegated law-making authority are not. Their authority is derived from the legislature and can be modified or taken back at will. However, it is possible for a sovereign legislature to authorize the making of subordinate or delegated legislation that is intended to prevail over the enabling statute or over other designated statutes in the event of conflict. In *Friends of the Oldman River Society v. Canada (Minister of Transport)*, La Forest J. wrote:

> Just as subordinate legislation cannot conflict with its parent legislation
> … so too it cannot conflict with other Acts of Parliament … *unless a statute
> so authorizes.*… Ordinarily, then, an Act of Parliament must prevail over
> inconsistent or conflicting subordinate legislation.[13] [Emphasis added.]

---

13   Above note 3 at 38.

As this passage indicates, the paramountcy of statutes over delegated legislation operates as a presumption. In the event of conflict, the statute is presumed to prevail, but this presumption is rebuttable by clear evidence of a contrary intent.

The relation between this rule and the other paramountcy rules is complex and depends on the circumstances. Although statutes generally are paramount over regulations, a federal regulation would prevail over a provincial Act and a regulation made under a human rights code might prevail over an ordinary Act.

f) How the Rules Are Applied

The application of conflict resolution rules is illustrated in the following examples. In *Insurance Corp. of British Columbia v. Heerspink*,[14] the Supreme Court of Canada had to deal with overlapping provisions from British Columbia's *Insurance Act* and its *Human Rights Code*. The *Insurance Act* provided that insurers were entitled to terminate contracts of insurance upon fifteen days' notice. The *Human Rights Code* provided that a service customarily available to the public could not be withdrawn without reasonable cause. Under the *Insurance Act* an insurer was free to terminate a contract for any cause, so long as the requisite notice was given. Under the *Human Rights Code*, cancellation for discriminatory reasons was prohibited. To the extent these provisions were in conflict, the *Human Rights Code* prevailed.

Had the *Insurance Act* been federal legislation, it would have prevailed over the provincial *Human Rights Code* to the extent of any conflict. But since both enactments were enacted by British Columbia, the federal paramountcy rule did not apply.

Counsel for the insurers argued that a provision dealing specifically with the cancellation of insurance coverage should prevail over a provision dealing with the cancellation of services in general, even though the general provision was enacted after the more specific one. He invoked the implied exception rule: a law of general application does not derogate from a law that makes specific provision for a particular thing. This argument did not succeed. Lamer J. wrote:

> [S]hort of that legislature speaking to the contrary in express and unequivocal language ... it is intended that the [Human Rights] Code supersede all other laws when conflict arises.
>
> As a result, the legal proposition *generalia specialibus non derogant* cannot be applied to such a code. Indeed the *Human Rights Code*,

---

14   Above note 12.

when in conflict with "particular and specific legislation", is not to be treated as another ordinary law of general application. It should be recognized for what it is, a fundamental law.[15]

In *Dunn v. Dunn Estate*,[16] an Ontario court was faced with overlapping provisions from two provincial statutes. Section 196 of Ontario's *Insurance Act* provided that where the beneficiary of an insurance policy has been designated by the purchaser of the policy, the proceeds do not form part of the purchaser's estate. Section 72(1)(f) of the *Succession Law Reform Act* provided that proceeds payable under an insurance policy on the life of a deceased person are deemed to form part of the deceased's estate for certain purposes.

In this case, both enactments were provincial and neither could be classified as human rights legislation. The conflict was resolved by applying the implied exception rule: the specific provision was treated as an exception to the more general one. Haley J. wrote:

> The *Insurance Act* section is a general provision dealing with the effect of a designation of a beneficiary in all contracts.... The *Succession Law Reform Act* section is a provision affecting only proceeds of an insurance policy owned by the deceased and effected on his life in circumstances where dependency considerations rise. In my opinion, the *Succession Law Reform Act* provision is a special provision which can be interpreted as creating an exception to the general provision of the *Insurance Act*.[17]

Since the *Succession Law Reform Act* provision was enacted after the *Insurance Act* provision, the same result could have been reached by applying the implied repeal rule.

B. OVERLAP WITH COMMON LAW

In a parliamentary democracy, the legislature is the primary and paramount source of law, and judges — like everyone else — must take direction from the legislature. This basic principle has several implications. First, it means that judge-made law is subordinate to valid legislation, whether federal or provincial, Act or regulation. In the event of a conflict between legislation and the common law, the legislation

---

15 *Ibid.* at 158.
16 (1992), 9 O.R. (3d) 95 (Gen. Div.), aff'd (1993), 12 O.R. (3d) 601 (Div. Ct.) [*Dunn*]. See also *Diamond Estate v. Robbins*, [2006] N.J. No. 3 at para. 69*ff* (C.A.).
17 *Dunn, ibid.* at 103.

always prevails. Second, by enacting an exhaustive set of rules dealing with a matter, the legislature may occupy the field and preclude further recourse to the common law. Third, the power of judges to create new common law is limited to incremental change; in most areas, significant policy initiatives must be left to the legislature.

Despite the constitutional primacy of the legislature, the common law is sometimes difficult to displace. Most rules of statutory interpretation are judicial inventions, and a number of them are designed to preserve the common law from legislative encroachment. For example, it is presumed that the legislature does not intend to change the common law, to introduce exceptions to general principles (which often originate in common law), to interfere with common law rights and freedoms, or to take away the jurisdiction of common law courts. Apart from these presumptions, the common law supplies the intellectual framework within which much legislation is read. Many of the legal concepts and categories referred to in legislation are derived from the common law. Finally, the common law is a major source of the assumptions, policies, and principles that make up our legal culture. Even in an area like criminal law, which has been codified for more than a century in Canada, common law conceptions of *mens rea* and the claims of natural justice continue to dominate our thinking.

In cases of overlap between legislation and the common law, there are four possibilities:

1) The legislation incorporates or codifies the common law, giving statutory force to common law rules or understandings.
2) The legislation supplements the common law without creating conflict; in cases of overlap, both apply.
3) The legislation supplements the common law without creating conflict, but the legislation is meant to be exhaustive and therefore displaces the common law.
4) The legislation conflicts with the common law and displaces it to the extent of the conflict.

1) Legislation Incorporates or Codifies the Common Law

Legislatures in common law jurisdictions often incorporate common law concepts or terms into legislation and they sometimes codify common law principles and rules. A provision that uses an expression or concept that has a fixed common law meaning may be said to "incorporate" the expression or concept. When a concept or expression is thus incorporated, the court is expected to go to common law sources for its meaning and legal significance.

A provision that reproduces a common law principle or rule without changing it in any way is said to "codify" the common law. In such a case, the statute and the common law are identical, so the problem of conflict does not arise. Insofar as the codified rule incorporates common law concepts, the court appropriately relies on the common law meaning. However, as a result of codification, the statute displaces the common law. This means that all subsequent applications of the rule must invoke the statute rather than the common law, and also that subsequent evolution of the codified law must be based on the statute and managed through the techniques of interpretation rather than ordinary common law development. Although this does not mean that the law is now ossified, its future evolution is controlled by the statutory context and purpose, and by the primacy of the legislature in effecting legislative change.

A good example of incorporation is found in *Positive Action Against Pornography v. Minister of National Revenue*,[18] a judgment of the Federal Court of Appeal. The court there had to determine whether the appellant was a "charitable organization" within the meaning of the *Income Tax Act*. Stone J. wrote:

> In order to properly assess the relative merits of … [the appellant's arguments], they must be viewed in the light of applicable common law principles, the definition of the word "charity" found in the Act furnishing little or no assistance.… Paragraph 149.1(1)(*d*) merely defines that word as meaning "a charitable organization or charitable foundation", both of which terms are in turn defined in paragraphs [149.1(1)](*a*) and [149.1(1)](*b*) respectively of that same subsection but not in any helpful way. Instead, the Act appears clearly to envisage a resort to the common law for a definition of "charity" in its legal sense as well as for the principles that should guide us in applying that definition.[19]

The court found the help it was looking for in the case law establishing the common law of charity, which it treated as an extensive gloss on the meaning of the statutory language. In effect, the entire law of charitable gifts was incorporated into the Act through the word "charitable."

In the *Positive Action* case, the court's suggestion that the legislature intended to incorporate the common law definition of charity into the *Income Tax Act* is highly plausible. The distinction between charitable and non-charitable was crucial to the operation of the statutory scheme, yet the Act gave no hint of how that distinction was to be

---

18   [1988] 2 F.C. 340 (C.A.) [*Positive Action*].
19   *Ibid.* at para. 8.

drawn. However, there was a rich line of common law cases reaching back to the seventeenth century addressing the issue of what is charitable in the eyes of the law. In these circumstances, incorporation was an obvious solution. It would be very difficult to codify case law of such complexity, and it would be undesirable to detach the concept of charity under the *Income Tax Act* from its understanding in other legal contexts. By relying on incorporation rather than codification, the legislature achieved a better solution.

An interesting example of codification is found in *R. v. Di Pietro*.[20] In this case the Supreme Court of Canada had to determine whether operating premises in which customers paid by the hour to play billiards constituted keeping a common gaming house within the meaning of section 179(1) of the *Criminal Code*. In creating this offence, the *Code* offered elaborate and apparently comprehensive definitions of "gaming" and "common gaming house." Lamer J. wrote:

> According to the definition of a common gaming house found in s. 179(1), the constituent elements of the offence, are:
> 1. keeping a place;
> 2. for gain;
> 3. resorted to by persons for the purpose of playing games;
> 4. which games are games of chance or mixed chance and skill.
> ...
>
> Although the *Criminal Code* is silent as to the necessity of wagering on the outcome of the game by the players thereof in order to establish that gaming did take place, it has long been recognized by the common law that this is an essential element of gaming.... [T]he courts defined "gaming" as "playing a game for stakes hazarded by the players".[21]

In effect, the court concluded that section 179(1) of the *Code* was meant to be a codification of the common law offence. And since wagering was the essence of the offence at common law, it must be part of the statutory offence as well.

By adding the element of wagering to the *Code's* definition of "gaming," the court significantly narrows the scope of the offence. Its reason for doing this is evident: otherwise any number of perfectly "innocent" operations, like chess clubs or bridge clubs, would be criminalized. This cannot have been Parliament's intention. By concluding that section 179 codified the common law offence and therefore included the

---

20   [1986] 1 S.C.R. 250.
21   *Ibid.* at 258–59.

element of wagering (despite the absence of any reference to this element in the definition of "gaming house"), the absurdity was avoided.

2) Legislation Supplements the Common Law

In keeping with the presumptions aimed at preserving the common law, the courts presume that legislation is meant to supplement rather than displace common law rules or remedies. So long as the legislation does not entirely duplicate or subsume the common law, so long as the common law rules or remedies have some distinct purpose of their own, the courts are loath to get rid of them. On the whole, it is better for subjects to have a greater rather than a lesser choice of rules, remedies, and fora. Also, where courts believe that a legislative scheme is flawed, that the remedy offered by the legislature is inadequate, or that the common law offers some benefit or advantage not available under the legislation, they are likely to conclude that the legislature intended to supplement rather than displace the common law.

In *Rawluk v. Rawluk*,[22] for example, the issue was whether Ontario's *Family Law Act* precluded recourse to the common law remedy of constructive trust. Even though the Act provided a detailed and comprehensive scheme for the equalization of property upon marriage breakdown, including a range of remedies, a majority of the Supreme Court of Canada held that it did not displace the common law approach. Cory J. wrote: "The constructive trust is used in the matrimonial property context to allocate proprietary interests, a function that is totally distinct from the … equalization process."[23] Also, as Cory J. noted, the constructive trust gives a successful claimant a share in the ownership of property and not just a personal entitlement as offered under the Act. The courts are reluctant to see the elimination of what they take to be a common law advantage. In the circumstances, a majority of the court concluded that the legislation was meant to supplement rather than displace the common law constructive trust.

The *Rawluk* case can be used to illustrate one of the problems with the court's tendency to preserve perceived common law advantages. Where the law is used to resolve disputes between parties, generally speaking the advantages conferred on one party are had at the expense of the other. To the extent the constructive trust is a better remedy for the plaintiff, it represents a loss to the defendant. In failing to incorporate the constructive trust mechanism into its Act, the Ontario legisla-

---

22   [1990] 1 S.C.R. 70.
23   *Ibid.* at 93.

ture may have deliberately chosen to favour defendants over plaintiffs in matrimonial property disputes. If so, this choice was undermined by the majority decision to treat the Act as supplementing rather than displacing the common law.

3) Legislation Is Meant to Be Exhaustive

When it appears that legislation is meant to provide an exhaustive regulation of a matter, the legislation prevails over and displaces the common law. In considering whether legislation is meant to be exhaustive, the courts rely on the considerations discussed above in connection with overlapping legislation.[24] They focus on whether the legislation is complete and comprehensive, whether it provides adequate remedies, whether it implements a policy or scheme that might be undermined by resort to the common law, and whether it would be superfluous if it were not meant to be exhaustive.

In *Gendron v. P.S.A.C., Supply & Services Union, Local 50057*,[25] for example, an employee whose relations with his union and employer were governed by the *Canada Labour Code* sought to bring an action against his union on the basis of the common law duty of fair representation. The Supreme Court of Canada ruled that the matter of fair representation was adequately dealt with in the *Code* and that resort to the common law was therefore precluded. L'Heureux-Dubé J. wrote:

> In reviewing the legislation it becomes clear that, at least as regards the duty of fair representation, Parliament has enacted a comprehensive, exclusive code. An overview of the *Code* puts the statutory duty of fair representation in its proper context, that of a complete and comprehensive scheme that both supplies the duty and provides the necessary adjudicative machinery such that resort to the common law is duplicative in any situation where the statute applies.[26]

Since resort to the common law would add nothing to the statute, the employee was limited to his statutory remedy.

A statute that is complete and comprehensive, provides adequate remedies, and would be undermined by resort to the common law is likely to be labelled a code, and codes displace the common law. However, the tests for exhaustiveness outlined above need not be applied to entire statutes. Often the focus is on one or more provisions at issue

---

24   Section A(3), above in this chapter.
25   [1990] 1 S.C.R. 1298.
26   *Ibid.* at 1317.

in the case. Even though a statute may not be a complete code, one or more of its provisions may deal exhaustively with a particular matter so as to displace the common law. In *Buschau v. Rogers Communications Inc.*,[27] for example, the issue was whether the employees for whom a pension trust was established by an employer could collapse the trust under rule in *Saunders v. Vautier.*[28] Writing for the majority, Deschamps J. concluded that the rule in *Saunders v. Vautier* had been displaced by the *Pension Benefits Standards Act, 1985.* She wrote:

> First, pension plans are heavily regulated. The *PBSA* regulates the termination of a plan and the distribution of the fund and the trust assets.... The *PBSA* deals extensively with the termination of plans and the distribution of assets. It is clear from this explicit legislation that Parliament intended its provisions to displace the common law rule. To the extent that it provides a means to reach the distribution stage, the *PBSA* prevails over the traditional rule in *Saunders v. Vautier.*[29]
>
> ...
>
> The *PBSA* is not a complete code. However, when recourse is available to plan members, they should use it. Termination is dealt with explicitly in the *PBSA.*[30]

Because the statute provided an adequate remedy, one that took into account the complex mix of policies involved in the regulation of pension plans, there was no room left for the operation of the common law rule.[31]

4) Legislation Conflicts with Common Law

If there is an outright conflict between legislation and the common law, the matter is easily resolved: the legislation prevails. The application of this rule is illustrated in the judgment of the Supreme Court of Canada in *Québec (Attorney General) v. Carrières Ste-Thérèse Ltée.*[32] The issue in the case was whether a power conferred on the minister of social affairs by section 55 of Quebec's *Public Health Act* could be delegated to a deputy

---

27   [2006] 1 S.C.R. 973.
28   This equitable rule permits the beneficiaries of a trust to join together to bring a trust to an end in advance of the time stipulated by the settlor.
29   *Ibid.* at para. 28.
30   *Ibid.* at para. 35.
31   Although in some contexts common law (that is, law made by judges of the common law courts) contrasts with equity (law made by the King's Chancellor), in other contexts common law includes equity because both are made by judges rather than legislators.
32   [1985] 1 S.C.R. 831.

minister. Under the common law, ministers can delegate their powers to deputy ministers. However, section 55 of the *Public Health Act* provided that the minister of social affairs "may himself exercise directly" certain powers set out in the Act. In the view of the court, this provision meant that the minister had to exercise the powers himself and could not delegate to the deputy. Since the statutory provision was in direct contradiction of the common law rule, both could not apply, and the statutory rule prevailed. Although the common law would continue to apply to other ministers and to the minister of social affairs with respect to other powers, this particular power could not be legally delegated.[33]

Similarly, in *Prebushewski v. Dodge City Auto (1984) Ltd.*,[34] the Supreme Court of Canada ruled that section 65 of Saskatchewan's *Consumer Protection Act* did not codify the common law rules respecting exemplary damages, but rather changed them and therefore displaced them. Section 65 provided that "a consumer ... may recover exemplary damages from any manufacturer ... who has committed a wilful violation of this Part." Speaking for the court, Abella J. explained:

> At common law, exemplary or punitive damages are awarded only in exceptional cases to meet the goals of retribution, deterrence and denunciation in cases of "malicious, oppressive and high-handed" conduct that "offends the court's sense of decency".
>
> ...
>
> The language of s. 65(1) is clear and unambiguous: once a wilful—or deliberate—violation has been found, the trial judge has a discretion to award exemplary damages. Had the legislature intended that the common law—and more exacting—test apply, it could easily have used words affiliated with the traditional approach to exemplary damages, such as "malicious" or "oppressive". By designating instead that "wilful" violations of the Act are sufficient to trigger a judge's discretion, the legislature has signalled an intention to lower the threshold and grant easier access to the remedy of exemplary damages.[35]

Abella J. supported this conclusion with reference to a number of other interpretive techniques, including textual analysis, scheme analysis, and legislative history and evolution.[36]

---

33   *Ibid.* at 838–39.
34   [2005] 1 S.C.R. 649.
35   *Ibid.* at paras. 23–24.
36   *Ibid.* at para. 26*ff.*

TABLE OF CASES

INDEX

ABOUT THE AUTHOR

Ruth Sullivan is a Professor of Law at the University of Ottawa, Common Law Section. She holds degrees in Common Law and Civil Law as well as Master's degrees in English and Legislation. She has worked as legislative counsel for the Department of Justice and has offered training in legislative drafting and statutory interpretation to many audiences in Canada and abroad. She has been publishing books and articles on statutory interpretation for the past 15 years.